D0873965



A book of Irish quotations.

*A Book of Irish Quotations*

For Christa, Mark and Ruairi

# A Book of Irish Quotations

COMPILED BY
SEAN McMAHON

TEMPLEGATE PUBLISHERS
SPRINGFIELD, ILLINOIS

First published 1984 by The O'Brien Press
20 Victoria Road, Rathgar, Dublin 6

First published in the United States by
TEMPLEGATE PUBLISHERS
302 E. Adams St., P. O. Box 5152
Springfield, Illinois 62705



ISBN 0-87243-127-4

Book design: Jacques Teljeur
Cover photograph: interior Marsh's Library, Dublin,
photographed by Pieterse Davison.
Reproduced by kind permission
of the National Heritage Trust.

# *Contents*

Introduction 7

Quotations 9

Index by subject 167

Bibliography 225

Acknowledgements 227

# *Introduction*

Dr Sam. Johnson, that prince of dictionary makers, once defined the word lexicographer as 'a harmless drudge'. He was entitled to that whimsy after nine years of unremitting toil. Even in his time compilation was not work for one person and nowadays any dictionary worth its name needs a panel of well-paid, full-time researchers who will work for as long as it takes. This book, as the part-time work of another harmless drudge, is no dictionary; its title, *A Book of Irish Quotations*, stresses this limitation. That a dictionary is required, modelled on the excellent *Oxford Dictionary of Quotations*, is beyond doubt. This book came into existence because for years I had been reaching for such and it was not there. This may be regarded as a first step, a general clearing of the ground, the catch of a large-mesh net.

It is certain that in the nature of things many quotations, *your* favourites for example, are not included. Wer hat die Wahl hat die Qual! The selection is limited by space, bias and ignorance. I have tried to make as general a compilation as I could but I must admit to a greater fondness for literary sources and a distaste for the political, born of a continuing despair of Irish history. In general, poets and rhetoricians find their places more easily than novelists or philosophers. The memorable phrase or line is perfectly appropriate in poem or pulpit but may be singularly out of place in a novel or treatise. I hope that in spite of such limitations this collection will prove a useful tool for journalist and debater and a pleasant Irish bedside book for the pleasantly tired layman.

The editing of such a collection with its splendid opportunities for bibliographical error was daunting. This task was undertaken and executed with patience and flair by Antony Farrell, who also researched some of the modern political material and unearthed many valuable quotations from literary sources. My further thanks are due to Frank D'Arcy, P. J. Doherty, Hugh McGeown, Paul Wilkins and Art Byrne of Derry; the staff of the National Library, Dublin; John Killen and Ronnie Adams of the Linenhall Library, Belfast; Alan Roberts of the Library of Magee College, Derry; Peter Fallon, whose suggestions on contemporary poetry were invaluable and Michael O'Brien, my publisher.

*Sean McMahon*

## HOW TO USE THIS BOOK

The quotations are arranged in alphabetical order by author and are numbered. To find your quotation go to the relevant section according to alphabetical order. There is an index by subject on page 167. Subjects are arranged in alphabetical order. Find the subject you require. Under each subject heading quotations are listed by page number then by quotation number.

# A

**Adamnan, St** 679-704

1 Hic anno secondo post Culdrebinae bellum, aetatis vero suae xlii de Scotia ad Britanniam pro Christo perigrinari volens, enavigavit.

*Vita Sancti Columbae*, Praef. 2

*In that year [563] the second after the battle of Culdrevny when in fact he was 42 years of age he embarked from Ireland for Britain wishing to become an exile for Christ.*

*The Life of St Columba*, 2nd Preface

2 Ille in nocte qua sanctus Columba de terra ad caelos felici et beato fine transiit, ego et alii mecum laborantes in captura piscium in valle piscosi fluminis Fendae; subito totum aerei illustratum caeli spatium vidimus cuius miraculi subitatione permoti, oculos ad orientem elevatos convertimus, et ecce, quasi quaedam pergrandis ignea apparuit columna, quae in illa nocte media sursum ascendens ita nobis videbatur mundum illustrare totum, sicuti aesteus et meridianus sol, et postquam illa penetravit columna caelum quasi post occasum solis, tenebrae succedunt. Ib., Lib. iii

*On that night in which Saint Columba passed from earth to heaven by a happy and holy death I and other men who were fishing in the rich valley of the Finn suddenly noticed that the whole of the broad heaven was brightened. Disturbed by this wonder we turned our eyes to the East and behold there had appeared in the sky the likeness of a massively tall pillar of fire which rising as it did in the middle of the night seemed to us to illuminate the whole earth like the noonday summer sun. When this pillar had pierced the heavens darkness as after a sunset returned.*

Ib., Bk 3

**Alexander, Mrs Cecil Frances** 1818-1895

3 All things bright and beautiful, / All creatures great and small, / All things wise and wonderful, / The Lord God made them all.

'All Things Bright and Beautiful'

4 The rich man in his castle, / The poor man at his gate, / God made them, high or lowly, / And ordered their estate.

Ib.

5 Once in Royal David's city /Stood a lowly cattle shed, / Where a Mother laid her Baby / In a manger for His bed: / Mary was that Mother mild, / Jesus Christ her little child.

'Once in Royal David's City'

6 There is a green hill far away, / Without a city wall, / Where the dear Lord was crucified, / Who died to save us all.

'There is a Green Hill Far Away'

1 'Twas the Lord who gave the word when his people drew the sword / For the freedom of the present, for the future that awaits. / O Child! thou must remember that bleak day in December / When the 'Prentice-boys of Derry rose up and shut the gates.

'The Siege of Derry'

**Alexander, Rev. William, Primate of Armagh,** 1824-1911

2 Home Rule morally is a great betrayal; / Logically it is a great fallacy. / Religiously a great sectarianism / Financially a great swindle / Socially a great break up / And imperially a great breakdown. 'Home Rule in a Nutshell', Unionist broadsheet from sermon

**Allingham, William** 1824-1889

3 Yet dearer still that Irish hill than all the world beside; / It's home, sweet home, where'er I roam, through lands and waters wide. / And if the Lord allows me, I surely will return / To my native Belashanny and the winding banks of Erne. 'Adieu to Belashanny'

4 The Poet launched a stately fleet; it sank. / His fame was rescued by a single plank. 'Blackberries'

5 *History of Ireland* - lawlessness and turbulency, robbery and oppression, hatred and revenge, blind selfishness everywhere - no principle, no heroism. What can be done with it?

*Diary*, 11 November 1866

6 Up the airy mountain, / Down the rushy glen, / We daren't go a-hunting, / For fear of little men; / Wee folk, good folk, / Trooping all together; / Green jacket, red cap, / And white owl's feather! 'The Fairies'

7 Ireland, forsooth, a nation once again! / If Ireland was a nation, tell me when? / For since the civil modern world began / What's Irish history? Walks the child a man?

*Lawrence Bloomfield in Ireland*

8 What Ireland might have been, if wisely school'd / I know not: far too briefly Cromwell ruled. Ib.

9 Four ducks on a pond, / A grass-bank beyond, / A blue sky of spring, / White birds on the wing: / What a little thing / To remember for years - / To remember with tears. 'A Memory'

**Andrews, John M.** 1871-1951

10 Another allegation made against the government, which is untrue, is that of 31 porters at Stormont 28 are Roman Catholics. I have investigated the matter and I have found that there are 30 Protestants and only one Roman Catholic, there only temporarily.

12 July 1933, quoted in Farrell, *Northern Ireland: The Orange State*

**Anonymous** undated

11 Mé tuc in n-uball an-úas / do-chúaid tar cumang mo chraís; / in céin marat sain re lá, / de ní scarat mná re baís. 'Eve'

*It was I who plucked the apple; it went past the narrow of my gullet; as long as they live in daylight women will not cease from folly on account of that.*

12 Hibernicis ipsis Hibernior.

*More Irish than the Irish.*

**Anonymous** 7th Century

13 Colum Cille, caindel, Néill / ní fríth i curp cumma dó.

'Hymn to St Colum Cille

*Colum Cille, candle of Ireland, none like him was ever found in human body.*

1 'Is é a bés,' ól Ísu, / 'nach indéuin benar / for-cain in cách noda ben / nach sí for-canar.' 'Jesus at School'

*'It is the custom,' said Jesus, 'any anvil that is struck teaches the one who strikes it; it is not itself that is taught.'*

2 Fuiniud i mmedón laa, / ní hord baa a rían rom; / matan i n-aidchi, in dedól / réna medón, cia mó col? 'Prayer for a Long Life'

*Sunset at midday - its premature course is no good order; morning in the night-time, daybreak before midnight, what greater sin?*

3 Benchuir bona regula, / recta atque divina, / stricta, sancta, sedula, / summa, iusta ac mira. 'Versiculi Familiae Benchuir'

*The little rule of Bangor is correct and godlike, strict, holy and active, high, just and admirable.*
'Verselets about the Bangor Community'

**Anonymous** 8th Century

4 Críst limm, Críst reum, Críst im degaid / Críst indium, Críst íssum, Críst úassum / Críst dessum, Críst túathum / Críst i llius, Críst i ssius, Críst i n-érus / Críst i cridiú cach duini rodom scrútadar / Críst i ngiun cach oín rodom labrathar / Críst i cach rusc nom dercadar / Críst i cach clúais rodom-chloathar. 'St Patrick's Breastplate'

*Christ with me, Christ before me, Christ behind me, Christ in me, Christ under me, Christ over me, Christ to the right of me, Christ where I lie down, Christ where I sit, Christ where I rise, Christ in the heart of everyone who scrutinizes me, Christ in the mouth of everyone who speaks to me, Christ in every eye that sees me, Christ in every ear that hears me.*

5 Ní báitter mo shechtchaindel. / Am dún díthogail / am ail anscuichthe / am lia lógmar / am sén sechtmaínech. 'A Second Breastplate'

*May my seven candles not be quenched. I am an invincible fortress, I am an unshakable cliff, I am a precious stone, I am the symbol of seven riches.*

6 Cluiche n-aímin, indel áig, / aigtit fri findimmarbáig / fir is mná míni, fo doss, / cen pheccad, cen immorbus. 'The Two Worlds'

*A noble arrangement, they play pleasant games in innocent conflict, men and gentle women, under the boughs, without blame, without original sin.*

**Anonymous** 9th Century

7 Cride hé / daire cnó / ócán é / pócán dó. 'Cride Hé'

*Tender lad, a darling this, grove of nuts, worth a kiss.*

8 Síabra mo chobra, mo gné, / a ben, nacham aicille. 'The Dead Lover'

*My speech, my face are ghostly. Woman, do not speak to me.*

9 Int én bec / ro léic feit / do rinn guip / glanbuidi: / fo-ceird faíd / ós Loch Laíg, / lon do chraíb / charnbuidi.

*The little bird which has whistled from the end of a bright-yellow bill: it utters a note above Belfast Lough - a blackbird from a yellow-heaped branch.*

10 Ísucán / alar lemm im dísiurtán / cía beth cléirech co lín sét / is bréc uile acht Ísucán. 'Ísucán'

*Isucan, I nurse him in my lonely place; though a priest have stores of wealth, all is vain save Isucan.* 'St Ite's Song'

1 Mé Líadan / ro carussa Cuirithir; / is fírithir ad-fíadar. 'Liadan'

*I am Liadan; I have loved Cuirithir: it is true as they say.*

2 Meisse ocus Pangur Bán / cechtar nathar fria shaindán; / bíth a menmasam fri seilgg / mo menma céin im shaincheird.

Caraim-se foss, ferr cach clú / oc mo lebrán léir ingnu; / ní foirmtech frimm Pangur Bán, / caraid cesin a maccdán.
'The Scholar and His Cat'

*Myself and White Pangur are each at his own trade; he has his mind on hunting, my mind is on my own task.*

*Better than any fame I prefer peace with my book, pursuing knowledge; White Pangur does not envy me, he loves his own childish trade.*

3 Acht chena is álainn cech nderg, / is gel cach nua, / is caín cech n-ard, is serb cech ngnáth / cáid cech n-écmais, is faill cech n-aichnid / co festar cech n-éolas.
'The Sick-bed of Cú Chulainn'

*But indeed everything red is beautiful, everything new is bright, everything unattainable is lovely, everything familiar is bitter, everything absent is perfect, everything known is neglected, until all knowledge is known.*

4 Trí gena ata messa brón: / gen snechtai oc legad, / gen mná fritt iar feis la fer n-aile, / gen con foilmnich.

*Three smiles that are worse than grief: the smile of snow melting, the smile of your wife after sleeping with another man, the smile of a leaping dog.*

5 Téora seithir góa: / bés, dóig, toimte!

*Three sisters of lying: perhaps, maybe, guess!*

6 Trí aithgin in domuin: / brú mná, úth bó, ness gobann.

*Three renewals of the world: a woman's belly, a cow's udder, a smith's furnace.*

7 Is aicher in gaeth in-nocht, / fo-fúasna fairrge findfholt / ní águr réimm mora mind / dond laechraid lainn ó Lothlind.
'Viking Times'

*Bitter is the wind tonight, it tosses the sea's white hair; I do not fear the wild warriors from Norway, who course on a quiet sea.*

8 Gáeth ard úar / ísel grían / gair a rrith / ruirthech rían. 'Winter'

*The wind is high and cold, the sun is low; its course is brief, the tide runs high.*

9 Dé bráth nom Coimmdiu coíma! / Caín scríbaimm fo roída ross.
'Writing Out-of-doors'

*The Lord be good to me on Judgement Day! I write well under the woodland trees.*

**Anonymous** 10th Century

10 Ní fetar / cía lassa fífea Etan; / acht ro-fetar Etan Bán / nícon fhífea a hoenurán. 'Etan'

*I do not know who Etan will sleep with, but I do know that Blonde Etan will not sleep alone.*

11 A-tá ben as-tír / ní eprimm a hainm; / maidid essi a deilm / amal chloich a tailm. 'A Flatulent Woman'

*There's a woman in the country - I do not mention her name - who breaks wind like a stone from a sling.*

1 Dúthracar, a Maic Dé bí, / a Rí suthain sen, / bothán deirrit díthreba / commad sí mo threb. 'The Hermitage'

*O Son of the living God, old eternal King, I desire a hidden hut in the wilderness, that it may be my home.*

2 Canaid cóir, a ingena, / d'fhuir dliges bar císucán; / atá 'na phurt túas-acán / cia beth im ucht Ísucán.
'Ita and the Infant Jesus'

*Sing a chorus, girls, to the man you owe your little rent to - Jesuseen, who is in his home above although he is at my breast.*

3 Techt do Róim / mór saítho, becc torbai; / in Rí con-daigi i foss, / manim bera latt ní fhogbai.
'The Pilgrim to Rome'

*To go to Rome is much labour, little profit; the King you seek there, unless you bring Him with you, you will not find Him.*

4 Maidid glass for cach lus, / bilech doss daire glais; / tánic sam, ro fáith gam, / goinit dam cuilinn chais. 'Summer'

*Green bursts out from every plant; leafy is the shoot of the green oakwood. Summer has come, winter gone, twisted hollies hurt the stag.*

5 Siúbhladh ar iasc Inse Fáil / ní fhuil tráigh nach tiobrann tonn; / a mbrógaibh nocha tá broc / ní léir cloch, ní labhair corr. 'Winter'

*The fish of Ireland are in motion. There is no strand the waves do not pound. There is no badger in the lands; no stony path is clear, no crane talks.*

**Anonymous** 11th Century

6 Fil súil nglais / fégbas Éirinn dar a hais; / nocho n-aicceba íarmo-thá / firu Érenn nách a mná. 'Fil Súil nGlais'

*Grey eye there is that backward looks and gazes; never will it see again - Ireland's women, Ireland's men.*
'The Backward Look'

7 Is scíth mo chrob ón scríbainn; / ní dígainn mo glés géroll; / sceithid penn - gulban caelda - / dig ndaelda do dub glégorm. 'The Scribe'

*My hand is tired from writing; my sharp pen is not steady; the pen, a slender beak, spouts a dark stream of blue ink.*

8 Ráite fó foiss fogamar.
'The Four Seasons'

*Autumn is an excellent season for staying at home.*

9 Gaim dub dorcha dethaite. Ib.

*Winter: black, dark and smoky.*

10 Glass úar errach aigide; / úacht ina gaíth gignither. Ib.

*Bitter-cold is icy spring; cold will be born in its wind.*

11 Fó sín samrad síthaister. Ib.

*Summer is a fine season for long journeys.*

12 Is mé Caillech Bérri Buí, / no meilinn léini mbithnuí / in-diu táthum dom shéimi / ná melainn cid aithléini.
'The Nun of Beare'

*I am the Nun of Bearra Baoi. I used to*

*wear a shift that was always new. Today I have become so thin that I would not wear out even an old shift.*

**Anonymous** 12th Century

1 [Oisin] / Do bádussa úair / fa folt buide chas, / is nách fuil trem chenn / acht finnfad gerr glas.

*[Oisin speaks] Once I was yellow-haired, ringleted; now my head puts forth only a short grey crop.*

2 Tréide as dile lem for-ácbas / ar bith buidnech - / Durmag, Doire, dinn ard ainglech, / is Tír Luigdech.

'Colum Cille in Exile'

*I have left the three things I love best in the populated world - Durrow, Derry, the high, angelic homestead, and Tír Luigdech.*

3 Codail beagán beagán beag, / uair ní heagail duit a bheag, / a giolla dá dtardas seirc, / a mhic Uí Dhuibhne, a Dhiarmaid.

'Lullaby of Adventurous Love'

*Sleep a little, a little little, for you have little to fear, lad I gave love to, Diarmait son of O Duibne.*

4 Gel cech nua - sásad nglé! / utmall álcha ócduine, / áilli bretha bíte im sheirc, / millsi bríathra fir thochmairc.

'A Girl's Song'

*Everything new is neat - cheers! A young man is changeable in his desire, lovely are decisions about love and sweet are the words of a man who comes a-wooing.*

5 Úar ind adaig i Móin Móir / feraid dertan ní deróil; / dordán fris tib in gaeth glan / géissid ós caille clithar.

'The Great Bog'

*Cold is the night in the Great Bog, a terrible rainstorm beats down; a deep song at which the clear wind laughs screams over the shelter of the wood.*

**Anonymous** 14th Century

6 Icham of Irlaunde / Ant of the holy londe of irlande / Gode sir pray ich ye / for of saynte charite, / come ant daunce wyt me, / in irlaunde.

7 . . . now many English of the said land, forsaking the English language, fashion, manner of riding, laws and customs, live and govern themselves by the manners, fashion, and language of the Irish enemies. Statutes of Kilkenny 1366(Language modernised)

8 Dá mba liom Alba uile, / Ótha a broine go a bile / Rob fhearr liomsa áit toighe / Agam ar lar caomh Doire / Is air a charaim Doire / Ar a réidhe ar a ghloine; / 'S ar iomad a haingeal bhfionn / Ón cionn go soich aroile.

'Aoibhinn Bheith ar Binn Éadair'

*If I owned the whole of Scotland from one side to the other, I would rather have my house in Derry's gentle centre. This is my reason for loving Derry - it is with all its width and strength filled with a shining peace, for it is peopled by God's angels only.*

'Tis Pleasant to be on Howth Head'

**Anonymous** 16th Century

9 And further they [the English] are the greatest murderers and the proudest people in all Europe and I am surprised that God tolerates them so long in power - except that He is long-suffering and that His avenging hand is slow but sure. 1578, quoted in Quinn, *The Elizabethans and the Irish*

**Anonymous** 17th Century

1 Jew, Turk or atheist / May enter here, but not a papist.

Inscription by townsmen on walls of Bandon

2 Whoever wrote this wrote it well / For the same is written on the gates of hell.

Reply by local Irish

3 Ná thrácht ar an mhinistéir Gallda, / Ná ar a chreideamh gan bheann, gan bhrí, / Mar níl mar bhuan-chloch dá theampuill, / Ach magairle Annraoi, Rí.

Quoted and translated in Brendan Behan, *Borstal Boy*

*Don't speak of the alien minister, / Nor of his church without meaning or faith, / For the foundation stone of his temple / Is the ballocks of Henry the Eighth.*

4 Ní bhfuighe mise bás duit, / a bhean úd an chuirp mar ghéis / daoine leamha ar mharbhais riamh, / ní hionnann iad is mé féin.

'Ní Bhfuighe Mise Bás Duit'

*I will not die for you, / lady with swanlike body. / Meagre men you have killed so far, / and not the likes of me.*

5 Aoibhinn beatha an scoláire / bhíos ag déanamh a léighinn / is follas díbh, a dhaoine, / gurab dó is aoibhne in Éirinn.

'Beatha an Scoláire'

*Sweet is the scholar's life, / busy about his studies, / the sweetest lot in Ireland / as all of you know well.*

'The Scholar's Life'

6 Truagh mo thuras go Loch Dearg / a Rí na gceall is na gclog, / ag caoineadh Do chneadh is Do chréacht, / 's nach bhfaghaim déar as mo rosc.

'Truagh mo Thuras go Loch Dearg'

*Vain was my visit to Loch Dearg, / King of the bells and cells. / I mourn Your cuts and stabs / but can find no tear in my eye.*

7 Triúr atá ag brath ar mo bhás, / gé atáid de ghnáth im bhun - / truagh gan a gcrochadh le crann! - / an diabhal, 's an chlann, 's an chnumh.

'Triúr atá ag Brath ar mo Bhás'

*There are three who await my death / and are always close at hand / (I wish them hung on a gibbet!) / - devil, family, maggot.*

8 Binn sin, a luin Doire an Chairn! / Ní chuala mé in aird sa bhith / ceol ba binne ná do cheol / agus tú fá bhun do nid.

'Binn Sin, a Luin Doire an Chairn!'

*Beautiful - black bird of Doire an Chairn! / Nowhere on earth have I heard / a lovelier music than yours / there as you guard your nest.*

**Anonymous** 18th Century

9 Is go nglaofad ar mo chrúiscín lán, lán, lán! / Is go nglaofad ar mo chrúiscín lán! / Ólfaimid an crúiscín, / Sláinte geal mo mhuirnín / An bhfuil ag taisteal chugainn thar taoide, slán, slán, slán.

'An Crúiscín Lán'

*May I call for my jar to be full, full, full. May I call for my jar to be full! We will drink the jar, the best of health, my dear, and safety to all who are travelling across the sea.*

'The Full Jar'

10 Tá mo mháthair 'na codladh / is mise im dhúiseacht, / tá m'fhorthún im dhorn / is mé ullamh chun siúil leat.

'An Cuimhin Leat an Oíche Úd?'

*My mother is asleep, but I am wide awake, my fortune in my hand, I am ready to go with you.*

'Do You Remember That Night?'

1 Go réidh, a bhean na dtrí mbó! / As do bhólacht ná bí teann / Do chonaic mise gan gó, / Bean is ba dhá mhó a beann.

'Bean na dTrí mBó

*Right, woman with the three cows, do not be too proud of your herd. I truly saw a woman, and she had twice as many cattle.*

*'The woman of the Three Cows'*

2 Chuaigh mé chun aonaigh is dhíol mé mo bhó / Ar chúig phunta airgid is ar ghiní bhuí óir; / Má ólaim an t-airgead is má phronnaim an t-ór / Ó, caidé sin don té sin nach mbaineann sin dó?

'Caidé Sin don Té Sin'

*I went to the fair and I sold my cow, for five pounds of silver and a yellow golden guinea; if I drink the silver and give the gold as a present, what business is that of anyone's?* 'Whose Business Is It?'

3 Phósfainn thú gan bha gan phunt gan áireamh spré. 'Caiseal Mumhan'

*I'd wed you without herds, without money, or rich array.*

'Cashel of Munster', version by Samuel Ferguson

4 Is cuir do cheann dílis, dílis, dílis, / cuir do cheann dílis tharam anall.

'Ceann Dubh Dílis'

*Then put your head, darling, darling, darling, your darling black head my heart above.* 'Dear Dark Head', trans. Samuel Ferguson

5 Cad a dhéanfaimid feasta gan adhmad? / Tá deireadh na gcoillte ar lár; / Níl trácht ar Chill Chais ná a teaghlach / Is ní cluinfear a cling go bráth. 'Cill Chais'

*What will we do for timber now the last of the woods is gone? No one speaks of Kilcash or its household and its bell will be rung no more.* 'Kilcash'

6 Do threascair an saol is shéid an ghaoth mar smál / Alastrann, Caesar, 's an méid sin a bhí 'na bpáirt; / tá an Teamair 'na féar, is féach an Traoi mar tá, / is na Sasanaigh féin do b'féidir go bhfaighidís bás!

*The world laid low, and the wind blew - like a dust - / Alexander, Caesar, and all their followers. / Tara is grass; and look how it stands with Troy. / And even the English - maybe they might die.*

7 Má phósann tú an sistealóir, is tú bheas ag caoineadh, / A mhuirnín dílis is a fhaoileann óg; / Uch! beidh tú dod thachtadh le barrach na tíre / A mhuirnín dílis is a fhaoileann óg.

'Ceol An Phíobaire'

*If you marry the cistern maker you will weep, my dear true young maiden. Ugh! you will be choked by country tow, my dear true young maiden.*

'Pipe-Music'

8 's go bhfuil mo ghrá-sa mar bhláth na n-airní atá ar an droighneán donn.

'An Droighneán Donn'

*O my beloved is like sloe-blossom on the dark thorn tree!* 'The Dark Thorn Tree'

9 A dhroimeann donn dílis 's a fhíorscoth na mbó / cá ngabhann tú san oíche 's cá mbíonn tú sa ló? 'Droimeann Donn Dílis'

*My dear Droimeann Donn, o choicest of cows, / where go you at night, and where are you by day?*

'Beloved Brown White-backed Cow' [Apostrophe for Ireland]

10 Mo bhrón ar an bhfarraige / is í atá mór, / 's í ag gabháil idir mé / is mo mhíle stór. 'Mo Bhrón ar an bhFarraige'

*My grief on the sea, / How the waves of it roll! / For they heave between me / And the love of my soul.*

Version by Douglas Hyde

1 Crádh ort a Dhoiminic Uí Domhnaill / Nach mairg ariamh a chonnaic thú; / Bhí tú 'do shagart Dia Dómhnaigh, / 's ar maidin Dia Luain do mhinistir.

Pill, pill, a rúin ó, / Pill a rúin ó, is ná h-imthigh uaim; / Pill ort, a chuid den tsaol mhór, / No chan fheiceann tú'n ghlóir mur'bpill tú.

'Pill, pill, a Rúin Ó'

*Sorrow is your portion, and pitiful the lot of your friends; you a priest on Sunday, by Monday morning were a minister.*

*Come back, come back, my dear one! Come back my dear and do not abandon me. May all your worldly goods recoil on you, for you will never see heaven unless you return.*

2 Maidin mhoch do ghabhas amach / Ar bhruach Locha Léin; / An Samhradh ag teacht san chraoibh len ais, / Agus lonradh te ón ngréin; / Ar taisteal dom tré bhailte poirt / Agus bánta míne, réidhe; / Cé gheobhainn lem ais ach cúileann deas / Le fáinne geal an lae.

'Fáinne Geal an Lae'

*Early one morning I went out, on the shores of Loch Léin. Summer was coming back in the branches and the sun's rays were warm. As I travelled through the fortified towns and the rich level lands, who should I find beside me but a beautiful woman, at the bright breaking of the day.*

'The Bright Dawn of Day'

3 A Róisín ná bíodh brón ort fár éirigh duit - tá na bráithre ag teacht ar sáile is iad ag triall ar muir / tiocfaidh do phardún ón bPápa is ón Róimh anoir / is ní spáráilfear fíon Spáinneach ar mo Róisín Dubh.

'Róisín Dubh'

*O, my dark Rosaleen, / do not sigh, do not weep! / The priests are on the ocean green, / they march along the deep; / there's wine from the royal Pope / upon the ocean green; / And Spanish ale shall give you hope, / My Dark Rosaleen.*

'Dark Rosaleen', version by James Clarence Mangan

4 Tá blas gan ceart ag an Muimhneach; / Tá ceart gan blas ag an Ultach; / Níl ceart ná blas ag an Laighneach; / Tá ceart agus blas ag an gConnachtach.

*The Munsterman's speech is tuneful but inaccurate; The Ulsterman is accurate but tuneless; The Leinsterman's speech has neither flavour nor accuracy; The Connachtman has both accuracy and tunefulness.*

5 A wet winter, a dry spring, / A bloody summer, and no king.

Irish prophecy for 1798

6 Brian O'Linn and his wife and wife's mother, / They all crossed over the bridge together, / The bridge broke down and they all tumbled in - / 'We'll go home by water,' says Brian O'Linn!

'Brian O'Linn'

7 In Dublin's fair city / Where the girls are so pretty, / I first set my eyes on sweet Mollie Malone. / She wheeled her wheel-barrow / Through streets broad and narrow, / Crying, 'Cockles and mussels, alive, alive, oh!'

'Cockles and Mussels'

8 I am a ramblin' hayro, and by love I am betrayed, / Near to the town of Baltinglass, there dwells a lovely maid,

/ She's fairer than Hypatia bright, and she's free from earthly pride. / She's a darlin' maid, her dwellin' place is - down by the tanyard side.

'Down by the Tanyard Side'

1 You haven't an arm and you haven't a leg, / You're an eyeless, noseless, chickenless egg; / You'll have to be put with a bowl to beg: / Och, Johnny, I hardly knew ye!

'Johnny, I Hardly Knew Ye'

2 Oh, Donnybrook, jewel! full of mirth is your quiver, / Where all flock from Dublin to gape and to stare / At two elegant bridges, without e'er a river: / So, success to the humours of Donnybrook Fair!

'The Humours of Donnybrook Fair'

3 Oh, Donnybrook capers, to sweet catgut-scrapers, / They bother the vapours, and drive away care; / And what is more glorious - there's naught more uproarious - / Huzza for the humours of Donnybrook Fair! Ib.

4 I would I were on yonder hill, / 'Tis there I'd sit and cry my fill, / And every tear would turn a mill, / Is go dtéidh tú, a mhúirnín, slán! 'Shule Aroon'

5 Siúil, siúil, siúil, a rúin / Siúil, go socair, agus siúil go ciuin, / Siúil go dtí an doras agus éalaí liom / Is go dtéidh tú, a mhúirnín, slán! Ib.

*Hurry, hurry, hurry my love, hasten but quietly; come to the door and we'll fly together and may you be safe, my darling, for ever.*

6 O Paddy dear, an' did ye hear the news that's goin' round? / The shamrock is by law forbid to grow on Irish ground! / No more St Patrick's Day we'll keep, his colour can't be seen, / For there's a cruel law agin the wearin' o' the Green! / I met wid Napper Tandy and he took me by the hand, / And he said, 'How's poor ould Ireland, and how does she stand?' / She's the most disthressful country that iver yet was seen, / For they're hangin' men and women there for the wearin' o' the Green.

'The Wearin' o' the Green'
Boucicault used a version of this in *Arrah-na-Pogue.*

**Anonymous** 19th Century

7 'Sé Dónall binn Ó Conaill caoin / An planda fíor den Ghael-fhuil; / Gur le foghlaim dlí is meabhair a chinn / Do scól sé síos an craos-sclíocht.

*It was noble Daniel O'Connell, true scion of the Gael, who, with wit and knowledge of the law, scourged the race of grabbers.*

8 Ag Críost an síol / Ag Críost an fómhar: / In iothlainn Dé / Go dtugtar sinn. 'Ag Críost an Síol'

*Christ owns the seed, Christ owns the harvest; may we be brought into the granary of God.*

'Christ Owns the Seed'

9 For she's a big stout lump of an agricultural Irish girl / She neither paints nor powders and her figure is all her own.

'The Agricultural Irish Girl'

10 The hare she led on with a wonderful view, / And swift as the wind o'er the green field she flew. / But he jumped on her back and he held up his paw / 'Three cheers for old Ireland,' says Master McGrath.

'A Ballad of Master McGrath'

11 'Tis pretty to be in Ballinderry / 'Tis pretty to be in Aghalee / 'Tis prettier to be in bonny Ram's Island / Sitting

under an ivy tree. / Och hone! Och hone! Och hone! Och hone!

'Ballinderry'

1 And when sergeant death in his cold arms shall embrace me, / O lull me to sleep with sweet Erin go bragh, / By the side of my Kathleen, my young wife, O place me, / Then forget Phelim Brady, the Bard of Armagh.

'The Bard of Armagh'

2 In the tents play the pipers, the fiddlers, the fifers, / Those rollicking lilts such as Ireland best knows; / While Paddy is prancing, his colleen is dancing, / Demure, with her eyes quite intent on his toes. / More power to you Micky! faith, your foot isn't sticky, / But bounds from the board like a pea from a quill. / Oh, 'twould a rheumatic — he'd jump up ecstatic, / At 'Tatter Jack Welsh' upon Bellewstown Hill.

'Bellewstown Hill'

3 The trees are growing tall my love, / The grass is growing green / And many's the cruel and bitter day / That I must lie alone, / Oh the bonny boy was young / But was growing.

'The Bonny Boy'

4 For ramblin', for rovin', for football or sportin' / For emptin' a bowl sure as fast as you'd fill / In all your days scovin', you'd find none so jovial / As the Muskerry sportsman, the bould Thady Quill. 'The Bould Thady Quill'

5 Brennan on the Moor, Brennan on the Moor, / A brave undaunted robber was bold Brennan on the Moor.

'Brennan on the Moor'

6 Oh, come listen to my story, Molly Bawn, / For I'm bound for death or glory, Molly Bawn, / For I've listed in the army where no more those eyes can harm me, / Faith, they'd kill me tho' they charm me, Molly Bawn.

'Brian Óg and Molly Bawn'

7 Her voice it was chanting melodious / She left me scarce able to go / My heart it is soothed in solace / My cailín deas crúite na mbó.

'Cailín Deas Crúite na mBó'
('Pretty Milkmaid')

8 There are fine walks in these pleasant gardens, / And seats most charming in shady bowers. / The gladiators both bold and daring / Each night and morning do watch the flowers, / There's a church for service in this fine arbour / Where nobles often do coaches ride / To view the groves and meadows charming, / The pleasant gardens of Castle Hyde. 'Castle Hyde'

9 Will you come to the bow'r o'er the free boundless ocean / Where the stupendous waves roll in thunderin' motion / Where the mermaids are seen and the fierce tempest gathers / To lov'd Erin the Green, the dear land of our fathers, / Will you come, will you, will you, will you come to the bower?

'Come to the Bower'

10 I said she did invite me, but she gave a flat denial, / For assault she did indict me, and I was sent for trial. / She swore I robbed the house in spite of all her screechin' / So I six months went round the rack for courtin' in the kitchen.

'Courtin' in the Kitchen'

11 Come all ye dry-land sailors bold and listen to my song, / There are only forty verses, so I won't detain you long. / 'Tis all about the history of a bold young Irish tar, / Who sailed as man before the mast on board of the *Calabar*. 'The Cruise of the *Calabar*'

1 Let the farmer praise his grounds, / Let the huntsman praise his hounds, / The shepherd his dew-scented lawn; / But I, more blest than they, / Spend each happy night and day / With my charming little cruiskeen lawn, lawn, lawn, / My charming little cruiskeen lawn. / Grá ma chree ma cruiskeen / Sláinte geal mavourneen, / Grá machree a coolin bawn.

'The Cruiskeen Lawn'

2 Och, Dublin City, there is no doubtin', / Bates every city upon the say; / 'Tis there you'll see O'Connell spoutin', / An' Lady Morgan makin' tay; / For 'tis the capital of the finest nation, / wid charmin' pisintry on a fruitful sod, / Fightin' like divils for conciliation, / An' hatin' each other for the love of God.

'Dublin City', sometimes attributed to Charles Lever. In her *Memoirs* Lady Morgan mentions this compliment paid to her by a street ballad singer on 23 October 1826.

3 Oh, it's true I do love her and now she won't have me, / For her sake I'll wander through valley and dell, / And for her sake I'll wander where no one shall find me, / And I'll die for the sake of my factory girl. 'The Factory Girl'

4 Remember '98, says the gay old hag, / When our Boys you did defeat, says the gay old hag, / Then our Boys you did defeat, but we'll beat you out compleat, / Now you're nearly out of date, says the fine old hag. 'The Gay Old Hag'

5 It's there you'll see confectioners with sugar sticks and dainties / The lozenges and oranges, lemonade and the raisins; / The gingerbread and spices to accommodate the ladies, / And a big crubeen for threepence to be picking while you're able. 'The Galway Races'

6 Last night I had a happy dream, / Tho' restless where I be. / I thought again brave Irishmen / Had set old Ireland free, / And how I got excited / When the canons loud did roar. / It's grá-mo-chroí / I'd like to see old Ireland free once more.

'Grá-mo-chroí'

7 The gown she wore was stained with gore all by a ruffian band, / Her lips so sweet that monarchs kissed are now grown pale and wan, / The tears of grief fell from her eyes; each tear was large as hail, / None could express the deep distress of poor old Granuaile.

'Granuaile'

8 Let lads and lasses all be true and listen to these couple of lines, / If you take a glass along with a lass, you're sure to miss your hiring time.

'The Hiring Fair'

9 When I went to bed at night upon it I would roll, / The fleas they made a strong attack my kidneys for to hole, / I shouted holy murder as my skin they tried to tan, / And I'd pray, 'What made me hire with this man called Tom McCann?'

'The Hiring Fair at Hamilton's Bawn'

10 Adieu my fair young maiden, ten thousand times adieu, / We must bid good-bye to the Holy Ground, and the girls that we love true.

'The Holy Ground'

11 I know where I'm going, she said, / And I know who's going with me; / I know who I love — / But the dear knows who I'll marry / Feather beds are soft, / And painted rooms are bonny, / But I'll forsake them all / To go with my love Johnny.

'I Know Where I'm Going'

1 'Oh, Dan, me dear, you're welcome here,' / 'I thank you Ma'am,' says Dan.

'I Thank You, Ma'am,' says Dan'

2 'Twas very early in the month of June, / As I was sitting in my room, / I heard a thrush sing in a bush / And the song he sang was a jug of punch.

'The Jug of Punch'

3 Now I've been a divil the most of me life, / Right fol, right fol, titty fol lay. / Now I've been a divil the most of me life, / But I ne'er was in hell till I met with yer wife, / With a right fol da dol, titty fol lol, / Fol da-da dol, da dol da-da day.

'Killyburn Brae'

4 So it's true that the women are worse than the men / For they went down to Hell and were threw out again.

Ib.

5 They were starting all sorts of nonsensical dances, / Turning around in a nate whirligig; / But Julia soon scattered their fancies, / And tipped them the twist of a rale Irish jig. / Och mavrone! 'twas then she got glad o' me: / We danced till we thought the old ceiling would fall, / (For I spent a whole fortnight in Doolan's Academy / Learning a step for Lanigan's ball.)

'Lanigan's Ball'

6 Where the high walls of Derry look dismal and grey, / And so does lovely Johnny, he is now goin' away, / He is going to bonny England, some sweetheart to see, / May the high powers above send him safe back to me.

'Lovely Johnny'

7 If I rap and I call and I pay for all, my money is all my own, / I've never spent aught o' your fortune, for I hear that you've got none. / You thought you had my poor heart broke in talking to me now, / But I'll leave you where I found you, at the foot of the Sweet Brown Knowe.

'The Maid of the Sweet Brown Knowe'

8 And I wished I was in Sweet Dungloe and seated on the grass / And by my side a bottle of wine and on my knee a lass, / I'd call for liquor of the best and I'd pay before I would go / And I'd roll my Mary in my arms in the town of Sweet Dungloe.

'Mary from Dungloe'

9 'Oh Mrs McGrath,' the sergeant said, / 'Would you like to make a soldier out of your son, Ted, / With a scarlet coat and a big cocked hat, / Now, Mrs McGrath wouldn't you like that?'

'Mrs McGrath'

10 There was an elopement down in Mullingar, / But sad to relate the pair didn't get far, / 'Oh fly,' said he, 'Darling, and see how it feels.' / But the Mullingar heifer was beef to the heels.

'The Mullingar Heifer'

11 The ladies from Carrick I oft times have seen, / Bringing down their wee washing to the Muttonburn Stream, / No powder nor soap used, a wee dunt makes them clean, / It has great cleansing power, the Muttonburn Stream.

'The Muttonburn Stream'

12 Now to conclude and finish all you fair maids that's true, / 'Tis never place your mind on gold as lovers sometimes do, / If I possessed all the wealth that's in St Patrick's Isle, / I would part it all and ten times more for one glimpse of Edward Boyle.

'My Charming Edward Boyle'

13 The night before Larry was stretched, / The boys they all paid him a visit; / A bait in their sacks, too, they fetched; / They sweated their duds till they riz it.

'The Night before Larry was Stretched'

1 When he came to the nubbling chit, / He was tucked up so neat and pretty, / The rumbler jogged off from his feet, / And he died with his face to the city.

Ib.

2 Oh, well do I remember the bleak December day / The landlord and the sheriff came to drive us all away; / They set my roof on fire with their cursed English spleen, / And that's another reason why I left old Skibbereen.

'Old Skibbereen'

3 'Now it's love since you'll have me, I'll pray you remember, / You must use me genteel, for you know I'm but tender, / She was three-score and ten on the nineteenth of November, / On Patrick's Day in the morning.

'On Patrick's Day in the Morning'

4 Beauing, belle-ing, dancing, drinking, / Breaking windows, damning, sinking, / ever raking, never thinking, / Live the rakes of Mallow.

'The Rakes of Mallow'

5 Living short but merry lives; / Going where the devil drives; / Having sweethearts but no wives, / Live the rakes of Mallow.

Ib.

6 Then to end this raking life / They get sober, take a wife, / Ever after live in strife, / And wish again for Mallow.

Ib.

7 Let grasses grow and waters flow / In a free and easy way, / But give me enough of the rare old stuff / That's made near Galway Bay. / The gangers all from Donegal, / Sligo and Leitrim too, / Oh we'll give them the slip and we'll take a sip / of the real old Mountain Dew.

'The Real Old Mountain Dew'

8 I cut a stout blackthorn to banish ghost and goblin, / In a bran new pair of brogues I rattled o'er the bogs / And frightened all the dogs on the rocky road to Dublin.

'The Rocky Road to Dublin'

9 This ould man was feeble and his bones were cold as clay, / And like a frozen ice-berg he there beside me lay. / I often laid in bed and prayed that the Lord would on him call, / And I'd have for mine, a youth so fine, to roll me from the wall.

'Roll Me from the Wall'

10 'Oh! the French are in the bay, / They'll be here by break of day, / And the Orange will decay,' / Says the Shan Van Vocht.

'The Shan Van Vocht'
(lit. 'the poor old woman', i.e. Ireland)

11 As I went a-walking one morning in May / To view yon fair valleys and mountains so gay, / I was thinking on those flowers, all doomed to decay / That bloom around ye, bonny, bonny Sliabh Gallion braes.

'Sliabh Gallion Braes'

12 Out of her pocket she drew a cross / And she laid it on his breast / Saying, 'Here is back your plighted troth / And in heaven your soul find rest — rest.'

'Sweet William's Ghost'

13 As I roved out one evening fair / By the verdant banks of Skreen, / I set my back to a hawthorn tree / To view the sun in the west country / The dew on the forest green.

'The Verdant Banks of Skreen'

14 Here's a nice bit of advice / I got from an old fishmonger: / When food is scarce and you see the hearse / You'll know you died of hunger.

'The Waxies' Dargle'

1 Kind friends and companions come join me in rhyme, / Come lift up your voices in chorus with mine, / Let's drink and be merry all griefs to refrain / For we may and might never all meet here again. 'We May and Might Never All Meet Here Again'

2 Oh! It's six miles from Bangor to Donaghadee. 'The Widow of Donaghadee'

3 It was the tyrant Gladstone and he said unto himself, / 'I nivir will be aisy till Parnell is on the shelf, / So make the warrant out in haste and take it by the mail, / And we'll clap the pride of Erin's isle into cold Kilmainham Jail.' October 1881

4 The want of cleanliness, for which the lower orders of the Irish are in general distinguished, together with the inflammatory state of body created by the quantity of ardent spirits which they swallow, must make those diseases which are the scourge of such crimes, more violent in their symptoms than in other places. Ireland, in 1804

5 To Crichton of Fermanagh, thus 'twas Buckshot Forster spoke: / 'I find, my lord, upon my word, this business is no joke: / To gather in your agent's crops bring Orange Ulster down, / And we'll defend the diggers with the army of the Crown.' 'Bycut's Volunteers' or Relief of Lough Mask', *The Nation*, 20 November 1880

6 But 'tis said that his purtectors have put Bycut to great cost; / With trampled lawns and trees cut down and much good substance lost: / The throopers of her Majesty made free with his young lambs, / And ate his mutton and his ducks, and thanked him with G-d d-s. Ib.

7 I, A B, in the presence of Almighty God, do solemnly swear allegiance to the Irish republic now virtually established, and that I will do my utmost, at every risk, while life lasts, to defend its independence and integrity, and finally, that I will yield implicit obedience in all things not contrary to the laws of God, to the commands of my superior officers. So help me God! Amen. The Fenian Oath, 1859

**Anonymous** 20th Century

8 The Bells of Shandon / Sound so grand on / The lovely waters of the Lee / But the Bells of St Nicholas / Sound so ridiculous / On the dirty waters / Of Sullivan's Quay. Rhyme chanted by actors on visit to Cork

9 We defeated Conscription in spite of their threats, / And we're going to defeat old Lloyd-George and his pets; / For Ireland and Freedom we're here to a man, / And we'll humble the pride of the bold Black and Tan. 'The Bold Black and Tan'

10 I went to see David, to London to David, / I went to see David and what did he do? / He gave me a Free State, a nice little Free State, / A Free State that's tied up with Red, White and Blue. 'The Irish Free State'

11 In Mountjoy jail one Monday morning, / High upon the gallows tree, / Kevin Barry gave his young life / For the cause of liberty. 'Kevin Barry'

12 Another martyr for old Ireland / Another murder for the crown / Whose brutal laws may kill the Irish / But can't keep their spirit down. Ib.

13 If I was a blackbird, I'd whistle and sing / And I'd follow the ship that my true love sails in, / And on the top riggings

I'd there build my nest, / And I'd pillow my head on his lily white breast.

'If I was a Blackbird'

1 Being convinced in our consciences that Home Rule would be disastrous to the material well-being of Ulster as well as of the whole of Ireland, subversive of our civil and religious freedom, destructive of our citizenship and perilous to the unity of the Empire, we, whose names are undersigned, men of Ulster, loyal subjects of His Gracious Majesty King George V, humbly relying on the God whom our fathers in days of stress and trial confidently trusted, do hereby pledge ourselves in solemn Covenant throughout this our time of threatened calamity to stand by one another in defending for ourselves and our children our cherished position of equal citizenship in the United Kingdom and in using all means which may be found necessary to defeat the present conspiracy to set up a Home Rule parliament in Ireland.

Ulster's Solemn League and Covenant, 28 September 1912

2 Irishmen and Irishwomen: in the name of God and of the dead generations from which she receives her old tradition of nationhood, Ireland, through us, summons her children to her flag and strikes for her freedom.

Proclamation of the Republic, 24 April 1916

3 PUT HIM IN TO GET HIM OUT!

Election slogan for Joe MacGuiness, republican prisoner, Longford by-election, May 1917

## Anonymous, Seanfhocla (Proverbs)

4 Ceó i ndeireadh gealaí, / Fearthainn i ndeireadh an lae, / Galar súl seanduine — / Trí ní nach dtig a leigheas.
*Mist at the end of a moon; rain at the end of the day; disease in the eyes of an old person — three things that cannot be cured.*

5 Is deise cabhair Dé nó an doras.
*The help of God is nearer than the door.*

6 Ná bí mór nó beag leis a'chléir.
*Be neither intimate nor distant with the clergy.*

7 Níl áit a'chait sa luaith aige.
*He is not allowed even the cat's place by the fire.*

8 An áit a mbíonn toit bíonn tine, / An áit a mbíonn tine bíonn teas, / An áit a mbíonn teas bíonn mná, / An áit a mbíonn mná bíonn gab.
*Where there is smoke there is fire; where there is fire there is heat; where there is heat the women are; and where the women are there is gossip.*

9 Pós bean sléibhe is pósfaidh tú an sliabh uilig.
*Marry a mountain woman and you will marry the whole mountain.*

10 Cailín Domhnaigh.
*Sunday girl, i.e. lazy, well-dressed woman.*

11 Is treise dúchas ná an oiliúint.
*Nature is stronger than rearing.*

12 Briseann an dúchas tré shúile a'chait.
*Nature cannot be hidden (lit. nature breaks through the eyes of the cat).*

13 Nuair a bhéas an t-úll apaigh, tuitfidh sé.
*When the apple is ripe it will fall. (To everything there is a season.)*

14 Is binn béal 'na thost.
*A silent mouth is melodious.*

1 Níl meas ar an uisce go triomaítear an tobar.
*The water is not thought much of till the well goes dry.*

2 Nuair chaith tú an choinneal, caith an t-órlach.
*Since you've burnt the candle, burn the inch.*

3 Bíonn súil le muir, ach ní bhíonn súil le cill.
*There is hope from the sea but none from the grave.*

4 Fiche bliain 'do leinbh / Fiche bliain ar mire / Fiche bliain 'do dhuine, / Agus 'na dhiaidh sin 'thairiscint do urnaí.
*Twenty years a child; twenty years running wild; twenty years a mature man — and after that, praying.*

5 Casacht reilige.
*A graveyard cough. (A very bad cough.)*

6 Is maith an t-anlann an t-ocras.
*Hunger is good sauce.*

7 Marbh le tae is marbh gan é.
*Dead with tea and dead without it.*

8 Is fearr dreóilín sa dorn ná corr ar cairde.
*Better a wren in your fist than a heron on loan.*

9 Cómhairle Cholmchille — / 'Sé sin an chómhairle chóir — Rud nach mbaineann duit / Na bain dó.
*Colmcille's advice – and wise advice too – don't concern yourself with what doesn't concern you.*

10 Tá adharca fada ar bhuaibh i gConnacht.
*Cows in Connacht have long horns. (Far away hills are green.)*

11 Nollag ghlas, reilig mhéith.
*Green December fills the graveyard (lit. a green Christmas, a fat graveyard.)*

12 Sgread mhaidne ort.
*The morning screech on you. (Imprecation recalling the factory whistle which was alien to the Irish worker.)*

13 Ní bhfuair sé ó'n ghaoith é.
*He did not get it from the wind (said of some hereditary quality).*

14 Aithníonn ciaróg ciaróg eile.
*One beetle will find out another.*

15 Nuair a críonas an tslat ní bhíonn uirri trácht.
*When the wood hardens there is no give in it.*

**Antonin, Duc de Lauzun** 1633-1723

16 It is unnecessary for the English to bring cannon to such a place as this. What you call ramparts might be battered down with roasted apples.

Before Limerick, 20 July 1690

**Armour, James Brown ('Armour of Ballymoney')** 1841-1928

17 [Belfast] . . . a New Jerusalem created largely by jerry-builders. Attrib.

**Ashe, Thomas** 1884-1917

18 Let me carry your Cross for Ireland, Lord! / The hour of her trial drawn near, / And the pangs and the pains of the sacrifice / May be borne by comrades dear.

'Let Me Carry Your Cross'

19 I die in a good cause.

Remark to Laurence O'Neill, Lord Mayor of Dublin when asked to give up his hunger-strike.

**Auden, W[ystan] H[ugh]** 1907-1973

1 . . . mad Ireland hurt you into poetry. / Now Ireland has her madness and her weather still, / For poetry makes nothing happen.

'In Memory of W. B. Yeats'

2 Earth receive an honoured guest: / William Yeats is laid to rest. / Let the Irish vessel lie / Emptied of its poetry.

Ib.

# B

**Bairéad, Riocard** 1792-1819

1 Is iomaí slí sin do bhíos ag daoine, / Ag cruinniú píosaí is ag déanamh stóir. / Is a laighead a chuimhníos do réir an tsaoil seo, / Go mbeidh siad sínte fé leic go fóill. / Más tiarna tíre, Duke nó Rí thú, / Ní rachaidh pingin leat faoin bhfód, / Mar sin, dá bhrí sin, níl beart níos críonna / Ná bheith go síoraí ag cur preab san ól. 'Preab San Ól'

*People have discovered many ways of gathering money and amassing wealth, little thinking that their life will end and that they will soon be laid in the grave. Whether you're a landlord, a duke or a king, not a penny will accompany you under the sod, and so, therefore, there's no better employment than the enjoyment of life with plenty to drink.*
'Drink Dabbling'

**'Ballyhooley' (Robert J. Martin)** late 19th Century

2 Anyone acquainted with Ireland knows that the morning of St Patrick's Day consists of the night of the 17th of March, flavoured strongly with the morning of the 18th.
'St Patrick's Day in the Morning'

3 What is the reason of all our ills? / (A question the Saxon shirks) — / It is either the English Government / Or the Irish Board of Works. 'An Alternative'

**Banim, John** 1798-1842

4 Who on the winter's night, / Soggarth Aroon, / When the cawld blast did bite, / Soggarth Aroon, / Came to my cabin door / And on my earthen-flure / Knelt by me rich and poor, / Soggarth Aroon?
'Soggarth Aroon'

**Banville, John** *b.* 1945

5 When I opened the shutters in the summerhouse by the lake a trembling disc of sunlight settled on the charred circle on the floor where Granny Godkin exploded. *Birchwood*

6 I distrust such acts of kindness, they shake my lack of faith in human nature.
Ib.

7 In the city of the flesh I travel without maps, a worried tourist: and Ottolie was a very Venice. I stumbled lost in the blue shade of her pavements. Here was a dreamy stillness, a swaying, the splash of an oar. Then, when I least expected it, suddenly I stepped out into the great square, the sunlight, and she was a flock of birds scattering with soft cries in my arms. *The Newton Letter*

**Barlow, Jane** 1857-1917

8 . . . the lads do be tired of starvin' — the crathurs. *Irish Idylls*

1 To put a private quarrel or injury into the hands of the peelers was a disloyal making of terms with the public foe; a condoning of great permanent wrongs for the sake of a trivial temporary convenience. Lisconnell has never been skilled in the profitable and ignoble art of utilizing its enemies.

*Strangers at Lisconnell*

2 The *United Irishman* is wildly seditious and therefore as delightful to me as a British disaster.

Letter, December 1900

3 That old yahoo George Moore . . . His stories impressed me as being on the whole like gruel spooned up off a dirty floor. Letter, November 1914

**Barrington, Sir Jonah** 1760-1834

4 At the great house all disputes among the tenants were then settled — quarrels reconciled — old debts arbitrated: a kind Irish landlord reigned despotic in the ardent affections of the tenantry, their pride and pleasure being to obey and support him. *Personal Sketches*

5 In those days the common people ideally separated the gentry of the country into three classes, and treated each class according to the relative degree of respect to which they considered it was entitled. They generally divided them thus: 1 Half-mounted gentlemen; 2 Gentlemen every inch of them; 3 Gentlemen to the backbone.

Ib.

6 I stood well with all parties. Ib.

7 The glorious, pious and immortal memory of the great and good King William: — not forgetting Oliver Cromwell, who assisted in redeeming us from popery, slavery, arbitrary power, and wooden shoes. May we never want a Williamite to kick the **** of a Jacobite! and a **** for the *Bishop of Cork*! And that he won't drink this, whether he be priest, bishop, deacon, bellows-blower, grave-digger, or any other of the fraternity of *the clergy*; may a north wind blow him to the south, and a west wind blow him to the east! May he have a dark night — a lee shore — a rank storm — and a leaky vessel, to carry him over the river Styx! May the dog Cerberus make a meal of his rump, and Pluto a snuff-box of his skull; and may the devil jump down his throat with a red-hot harrow, with every pin to tear a gut, and blow him with a *clean* carcass to hell! *Amen*!

Orange toast, quoted in Barrington

**Barry, Kevin** 1902-1920

8 Among the many crimes put down to this dangerous man is that he did put pepper in the cat's milk and steal a penny from a blind man, besides wilfully, feloniously and of his malice aforethought of smiling derisively at a policeman. Written on eve of execution, 31 October 1920

**Beaumont, Gustave-Auguste de la Bonninière de la** 1802-1866

9 L'Irlande est une petite contrée sur laquelle se debattent les plus grandes questions de la politique, de la morale et de l'humanité.

*Ireland is a small country where the great issues of politics, morals and humanity are fought out.*

Preface, *L'Irlande Sociale, Politique et Réligieuse*, 1839

10 Violent and vindictive, the Irishman displays the most ferocious cruelty in his acts of vengeance . . . The evicted tenant takes terrible reprisals . . . and the punishment he invents in his savage fury cannot be contemplated without

horror. Often in his anger he is as unjust as he is cruel and he takes revenge on persons quite innocent of the misfortunes he has experienced.

*L'Irlande Sociale, Politique et Réligieuse,* quoted in Mansergh, *The Irish Question* 1840-1921

**Beckett, Mary** *b.* 1926

1 There is hope for all of us. Well, anyway, if you don't die you live through it, day in, day out.

'A Belfast Woman'

**Beckett, Samuel** *b.* 1906

2 The memory came faint and cold of the story I might have told, a story in the like of my life I mean without the courage to end or the strength to go on.

'The End'

3 Personally I have no bone to pick with graveyards, I take the air there willingly, perhaps more willingly than elsewhere, when take the air I must.

'First Love'

4 Yes, I believe all their blather about the life to come, it cheers me up, and unhappiness like mine, there's no annihilating that.

'From an Abandoned Work'

5 Perhaps my best years are gone . . . but I wouldn't want them back. Not with the fire in me now. *Krapp's Last Tape*

6 The sun shone, having no alternative, on the nothing new. *Murphy*

7 Murphy's mind pictured itself as a large hollow sphere, hermetically closed to the universe without. This was not an impoverishment, for it excluded nothing that it did not itself contain. Ib.

8 'With regard to the disposal of these my body, mind and soul, I desire that they be burnt and placed in a paper bag and brought to the Abbey Theatre, Lr. Abbey Street, Dublin, and without pause into what the great and good Lord Chesterfield calls the necessary house, where their happiest hours have been spent, on the right as one goes down into the pit, and I desire that the chain be there pulled upon them, if possible during the performance of a piece, the whole to be executed without ceremony or show of grief.' Ib.

9 You must go on, I can't go on, I'll go on. *The Unnamable*

10 ESTRAGON: . . . Let's go.
VLADIMIR: We can't.
ESTRAGON: Why not?
VLADIMIR: We're waiting for Godot.

*Waiting for Godot*

11 VLADIMIR: That passed the time.
ESTRAGON: It would have passed in any case.
VLADIMIR: Yes but not so rapidly. Ib.

12 One of the thieves was saved. It's a reasonable percentage. Ib.

13 They give birth astride of a grave, the light gleams an instant, then it's night once more. Ib.

14 No symbols where none intended.

*Watt*

**Behan, Brendan Francis** 1923-1964

15 Compliments pass when the quality meet. *Borstal Boy*

16 So many belonging to me lay buried in Kilbarrack, the healthiest graveyard in Ireland, they said, because it was so near the sea. Ib.

17 If I'm anything at all, I am a man of letters. I'm a writer, a word that doesn't

mean anything in either the English, Irish or American language.
*Confessions of an Irish Rebel*

1 A hungry feeling came o'er me stealing / And the mice were squealing in my prison cell, / And that old triangle / Went jingle jangle, / Along the banks of the Royal Canal. *The Quare Fellow*

2 HEALEY: Well, we have one consolation, Regan, the condemned man gets the priest and the sacraments, more than his victim got maybe. I venture to suggest that some of them die holier deaths than if they had finished their natural span.
WARDER REGAN: We can't advertise 'Commit a murder and die a happy death', sir. We'd have them all at it. They take their religion very seriously in this country. Ib.

3 By the moon that shines above us, / In the misty morn and night, / Let us cease to run ourselves down, / But praise God that we are white, / And better still are English, / Tea and toast and muffin rings, / Old ladies with stern faces, / And the captains and the kings.
*The Hostage*

**Bell, Sam Hanna** *b.*1909

4 Ravara meeting-house mouldered among its gravestones like a mother surrounded by her spinster children.
*December Bride*

5 Then followed those days when the memory closes over and subsides like a new grave. Ib.

6 Armagh: where two cathedrals sit upon opposing hills like the horns of a dilemma. 'In Praise of Ulster', radio feature

7 Ulster: where every hill has its hero and every bog its bones. Ib.

8 Kilrea for drinking tay, / Garvagh for asses, / Limavady for Irish lace, / And Coleraine for lasses. Local rhyme in *Within Our Province*

**Berkeley, Bishop George** 1685-1753

9 Westward the course of empire takes its way; / The first four acts already past, / A fifth shall close the drama with the day; / Time's noble offspring is the last.
'On the Prospect of Planting Arts and Learning in America'

10 Some queries proposed to the consideration of the public: Whether there be upon earth any Christian or civilised people so beggarly wretched and destitute as the common Irish? *The Querist*

11 Whether, if there was a wall of brass a thousand cubits high round their kingdom, our natives might not nevertheless live cleanly and comfortably, till the land, and reap the fruits of it? Ib.

12 Whether there be not every year more cash circulated at the card-tables of Dublin than at all the fairs of Ireland?
Ib.

**Berryman, John** 1914-1972

13 The Irish have the thickest ankles in the world / & the best complexions.
*The Dream Songs* 275

14 Your first day in Dublin is always your worst. Ib.299

15 Land of ruined abbeys, / discredited Saints — brainless senators, / roofless castles, enemies of Joyce and Swift, / enemies of Synge. Ib.321

**Betjeman, Sir John** 1906-1984

16 Bells are booming down the bohreens, / White the mist along the grass. / Now the Julias, Maeves and Maureens / Move between the fields to Mass.
'Ireland with Emily'

1 No! the lough and the mountains, the ruins and rain / And purple-blue distances bound your demesne, / For the tunes to the elegant measures you trod / Have chords of deep longing for Ireland and God. 'Ireland's Own' or 'The Burial of Thomas Moore

2 Through the midlands of Ireland I journeyed by diesel / And bright in the sun shone the emerald plain. 'A Lament for Moira McCavendish'

3 O my small town of Ireland, the raindrops caress you, / The sun sparkles bright on your field and your Square / As here on your bridge I salute you and bless you, / Your murmuring waters and turf-scented air. 'The Small Towns of Ireland'

**Bickerstaff, Isaac** 1735-1812

4 How happy is the sailor's life, / From coast to coast to roam; / In every port he finds a wife, / In every land a home. 'Thomas and Sally'

**Birmingham, George A. (Canon James Owen Hannay)** 1865-1950

5 The Irish police barrack is invariably clean, occasionally picturesque, but it is never comfortable. *General John Regan*

6 To any friend I have left in Ireland after the publication of this book. Dedication in *Up the Rebels!*

7 A poet, writing, as some of them will, a parody on the work of another poet, has these words — 'To every Irishman on earth / Arrest comes soon or late.' Patsy Devlin did not read much poetry, and had never come across the lines. If he had met them, he would have recognized at once that they express a great truth. *The Search Party*

**Blacker, Col. William** 1777-1855

8 He comes, the open rebel fierce — he comes, the Jesuit sly; / But put your trust in God, my boys, and keep your powder dry. 'Oliver [Cromwell]'s Advice'

**Blathmacc** *fl.* 750-770

9 Soer a ngein ro génair úait; / rot rath, a Maire, mórbúaid, / Críst macc Dé Athar di nim / é ron-ucais i mBeithil.

*You gave birth to a noble child; Mary, a great gift was given to you; Christ the Son of God the Father from heaven, it was He whom you bore in Bethlehem.* 'The Nativity'

10 Ba dorchae uile in bith / talam for-rabai rochrith; / oc Ísu úasail aidid / ro memdatar márailig.

*The whole world became dark, great trembling came on the earth; at the death of noble Jesus great rocks burst open.* 'The Crucifixion'

**Blount, Charles, 8th Lord Mountjoy** 1563-1606

11 That it may please her excellent majesty to conceive of this her kingdom of Ireland, that it is one of the goodliest provinces of the world, being in itself either in quantity or quality little inferior to her realm of England. Address to Elizabeth I, 1601, (modernised)

**Boland, Eavan Aisling** *b.* 1945

12 I think of what great art removes: / Hazard and death, the future and the past. 'From the painting *Back from Market* by Chardin'

13 The captain's Spanish tears / Falling like doubloons in the headstrong light. 'New Territory'

**Boucicault, Dion Lardner** 1820-1890

1 ANNE: No its that marauder there that leant me his top-coat in the thunderstorm.
MYLES: Bedad ma'am, your beauty left a lining in it that has kept me warm ever since! *The Colleen Bawn*

2 Oh, Limerick is beautiful, as everyone knows, / The river Shannon's full of fish, beside that city flows; / But it is not the river, nor the fish that preys upon my mind, / Nor with the town of Limerick have I any fault to find. / The girl I love is beautiful, she's fairer than the dawn: / She lives in Garryowen, and she's called the Colleen Bawn. Ib.

3 'Come home now,' ses I, 'asy' and threw my leg across her. Be gabers! no sooner was I on her bare back than whoo! holy rocket! she was over the gate, an' tearin' like mad afther the hounds. 'Yoicks!' ses I, 'come back the thief of the world, where are you takin' me to?' as she went through the huntin' field an' laid me beside the masther of the hounds, Squire Foley himself. He turned the colour of his leather breeches. 'Mother of Moses!' ses he, 'is that Conn the Shaughraun on my brown mare?' 'Bad luck to me!' ses I. 'It's no one else!' 'You shtole my horse,' says the Squire. 'That's a lie!' ses I, 'for it was your horse shtole me!' *The Shaughraun*

4 The fire and energy that consist of dancing around the stage in an expletive manner, and indulging in ridiculous capers and extravagancies of language and gesture, form the materials of a clowning character, known as 'the stage Irishman', which it has been my vocation, as an artist and as a dramatist, to abolish. Letter to a Christchurch newspaper, 1885

5 Nature did me that honour. When asked if he were an Irishman

**Bovet, Marie-Anne de** *fl.* 1880

6 Mais si vous offencez l'amour propre professionel des domestiques irlandais en dédaignant des services d'ont vous n'avez nil besoin, par contre n'attendez pas d'eux qu'ile vous rendent avec ponctualité ceux que vous leur demandez. *Trois Mois en Irlande*

*But if you hurt the professional feelings of Irish servants by refusing services of which you have no need, you must not expect from them the punctual performance of those you ask for.* *Three Months in Ireland*

7 La 'difficulté irlandaise' présente tant de faces et de facettes que demeurer impartial est un travail d'equilibriste. Ib.

*The Irish Question has so many sides and points that it is an impossible task to stay neutral.* Ib.

**Bowen, Elizabeth Dorothea Cole** 1899-1973

8 The road was in Ireland. The light, the air from the distance, the air of evening rushed traversely through the open sides of the car. 'Summer Night'

9 Herbert's feet, from dangling so long in the tram, had died of cold in his boots; he stamped the couple of coffins on blue-and-buff mosaic. 'The Tommy Crans'

10 Along Dublin Bay, on a sunny July morning, the public gardens along the Dalkey tramline look bright as a series of parasols. 'Unwelcome Idea'

**Boyd, Thomas** 1867-1927

11 His voice is of the deep. His path / With the fair deed is strewn; / Awful

upon his brow he hath / The great horns of the moon. 'The Brown Bull'

**Boyle, Patrick** 1905-1982

1 Never get old, child, I tell you. Never get old. There's a poor way on you when you do. *Age, I Do Abhor Thee*

**Boyle, William** 1853-1922

2 You're like Lanna Macree's dog — a piece of the road with everybody. *The Eloquent Dempsey*

3 You'll go anywhere and subscribe to anything if they'll only let you make a speech about it. Jerry, you're a rag on every bush, fluttering to every wind that blows; and if you weren't the best husband and the best father that ever broke the bread of life, I'd say you were the biggest rascal in the whole of Ireland. Ib.

**Bradford, Roy** *b.* 1921

4 When it comes to asserting the integrity of this province [Northern Ireland] against attack, moderation must go hand in hand with the mailed fist. *The Irish Times*, 'This Week They Said', 17 October 1970

5 Northern Ireland cannot remain static and suspended like Mahomet's coffin between heaven and earth. Ib., 17 March 1973

**Breen, Dan** 1894-1969

6 I went out to kill French, and, if it were possible, to kill the last link of British supremacy in this country. . . . I ask the men who stood with us in the dark days of 1921 to examine their consciences now and to come over and help us to remove the last vestige of British interests from this country. On Constitution (Removal of Oath) Bill, Dáil Éireann, 28 April 1932

7 My Fight for Irish Freedom Title of book

**Broderick, John** *b.* 1927

8 What I mean is that some people live through adapting themselves to others . . . I often wonder if they disappear when they go into a room alone. They coil around others, knowing exactly the weak spots where eventually they will tighten their hold and strangle their prey. Because in the end they always destroy. That's the sort of people they are. *The Fugitives*

9 The city dweller who passes through a country town, and imagines it sleepy and apathetic is very far from the truth: it is watchful as the jungle. *The Pilgrimage*

10 'Priests are human, Willie.' 'Yes, very.' *The Waking of Willie Ryan*

**Brooke, Charlotte** 1740-1793

11 It is really astonishing of what various and comprehensive powers this neglected language [Irish] is possessed. In the pathetic it breathes the most beautiful and affecting simplicity; and in the bolder species of composition it is distinguished by a freedom of expression, a sublime dignity, and rapid energy, which it is scarcely possible for any translation fully to convey. Preface, *Reliques of Irish Poetry*

**Brook, Sir Basil,**
**1st Viscount Brookeborough** 1888-1973

12 Many in the audience employ Catholics, but I have not one about my place. Catholics are out to destroy Ulster with all their might and power. They want to nullify the Protestant vote, take all they can out of Ulster and then see it go to hell. Speech at Mulladuff, Newtownbutler, 12 July 1933

13 We are carrying on a Protestant Par-

liament for a Protestant people.
Speech at Stormont, 21 November 1934

**Browne, Dr Noel** *b.* 1915

1 No one can seriously doubt but that the Catholic Church has behaved to all our political parties in an identical way as the Orange Order in its control of the Unionist Party in the North — a sectarian and bigoted politically conservative pressure group.
*The Irish Times*, 'This Week They Said', 1 May 1971

2 The courts are open to anyone — like the Ritz. Ib., 17 July 1971

3 Yeats's *Terrible Beauty* truly has become a sick and sectarian, angry and repressive old crone.
Ib., 23 December 1972

**Bulfin, William** 1864-1910

4 The high councils of fanatics and schemers, who direct the No-Popery campaigns, may be said to be in permanent session [in Belfast].
*Rambles in Eirinn*

5 Come back again — Come back to us, sometime — won't you? Oh the heart-cry of the Gael! It is heard so often in Eirinn that the very echoes of the land have learned it. Ib.

**Bullock, Shan F.** 1865-1935

6 In our Colony the Protestant was top dog always, and both dogs alike could but snap at the conquering Saxon's feet.
*By Thrasna River*

7 Hannah Lunny gave Jane a straight look that expressed the desolation it was to be the mother of a fool.
*The Loughsiders*

8 For five minutes, perhaps, they sat, silent, without a move, joined happily hand in hand, some gentle fires of passion, let us hope, burning in their mature breasts. Ib.

**Burke, Edmund** 1729-1797

9 It is the nature of all greatness not to be exact. *American Taxation*

10 The march of the human mind is slow. Ib.

11 . . . to tax and to please, no more than to love and be wise, is not given to men. Ib.

12 Magnanimity in politics is not seldom the truest wisdom; and a great empire and little minds go ill together. Ib.

13 It is now sixteen or seventeen years since I saw the Queen of France, then the Dauphiness, at Versailles; and surely never lighted on this orb, which she hardly seemed to touch, a more delightful vision.
*Reflections on the Revolution in France*

14 But the age of chivalry is gone. That of the sophisters, economists and calculators has succeeded; and the glory of Europe is extinguished for ever. Ib.

15 We must not always judge of the generality of the opinion by the noise of the acclamation. *Letters on a Regicide Peace*

16 As to their old friends, the transition is easy: from friendship to civility, from civility to enmity: few are the steps from dereliction to persecution.
*The State of the Nation*

17 How often has public calamity been arrested on the very brink of ruin by the seasonable energy of one man.
*Letter to William Eliot*

1 The great must submit to the dominion of prudence and of virtue; or none will submit long to the dominion of the great. Ib.

2 As long as men hold charity and justice to be essential, integral parts of religion, there can be little danger from a strong attachment to particular tenets of faith.
*Letter to William Smith*

3 Too nice an inquisition ought not to be made into opinions that are dying away by themselves. Ib.

4 England and Ireland may flourish together. The world is large enough for us both. Let it be our care not to make ourselves too little for it.
*Letter to Samuel Span*

5 The most favourable laws can do very little towards the happiness of people when the disposition of the ruling power is adverse to them. *Letters*

6 There is nothing which will not yield to perseverance and method. Ib.

**Burke, Helen Lucy**

7 Two choices lay at her disposal. She could choose religion and be his tyrant until the day one or other of them died. Or she could choose sex and meet him unarmed, with the virtual certainty of becoming his victim.

Was it to be peace or the sword — sex or sanctity — austerity or generosity?
*Close Connections*

8 Spring brought to Rome the first of the wild asparagus and the baby new potatoes from the South of Italy. It also brought the first and heaviest crop of mothers. 'A Season for Mothers'

**Bushe, Charles Kendal** 1767-1843

9 I strip this formidable measure of all its pretences and all its aggravations. I look at it nakedly and abstractedly. I see nothing in it but one question — 'Will you give up your country?'
Speech against Act of Union, January 1800

**Butt, Isaac** 1813-1879

10 There was one trait of Mrs Jephson's character which it required no great penetration to discover. She had an overwhelming and ill-concealed desire to make for her daughters what she called good matches.
*Chapters of a College Romance*

11 I have been accustomed to understand by Ireland, not merely a country possessing certain geographical features but a country inhabited by a certain people whom I know.
*The Irish People and the Irish Land*

12 I meant to have got sixpence apiece all round.
At Madame Tussaud's Waxworks, objecting in mock anger to a friend's revelation that he was not a guide

13 I see good for Ireland. An orator shall yet arise whose voice shall teach her people wisdom, and whose efforts shall procure for him the epithet of father of his country.
Speech as President of Historical Society, Trinity College, 1833

14 'You are idle' is the cry of the English press and ministry to our people. 'Ye are idle, ye are idle' said Pharaoh's taskmasters to the Israelites because they could not make bricks without straw. The people of this country are not idle. Let no man tell me this, when I see a peasant from Connaught going over to reap the harvest in England and carefully abstaining from spending a penny beyond the bare necessaries of

life, that he might be able to bring back his hard-won earnings to his wretched wife and children.

Speech in defence of Thomas Francis Meagher, 1848

**Byrne, Donn**
**(Brian Oswald Donn-Byrne)** 1889-1928

1 The most important week in Ireland is the week of the Dublin Horse Show. The best hunters, the best draught horses, and the nippiest harness ponies in the world are on show. Grafton Street becomes a garden of girls.

*Destiny Bay*

**Byron, George Gordon Noel,**
**Lord Byron,** 1788-1824

2 What is England without Ireland, what is Ireland without Catholics? It is on the basis of your tyranny Napoleon hopes to build his own. So grateful must the oppression of Catholics be to his mind, that doubtless . . . the next cartel will convey to this country cargoes of Sèvres china and blue ribands.

On Catholic emancipation, House of Lords, 21 April 1812

3 But he comes! the Messiah of royalty comes! / Like a goodly Leviathan roll'd from the waves; / Then receive him as best such an advent becomes, / With a legion of cooks, and an army of slaves.

'The Irish Avatar', September 1821, on George IV's visit to Ireland

4 Yesterday, I dined out with a largeish party, where were Sheridan and Colman . . . and others, of note and notoriety. Like other parties of the kind, it was first silent, then talky, then argumentative, then disputatious, then unintelligible, then altogethery, then inarticulate, and then drunk. When we had reached the last step of this glorious ladder, it was difficult to get down again without stumbling.

Letter to Thomas Moore, London, 31 October 1815

5 My boat is on the shore, / And my bark is on the sea; / But, before I go, Tom Moore, / Here's a double health to thee! . . . This should have been written fifteen moons ago — the first stanza was. I am just come out from an hour's swim in the Adriatic; and I write to you with a black-eyed Venetian girl before me, reading Boccac[c]io.

Ib., Venice, 10 July 1817

**Callanan, Jeremiah Joseph** 1795-1829

1 How hard is my fortune / And vain my repining; / The strong rope of fate / For this young neck is twining!
'The Convict of Clonmel'

2 There is a green island in lone Gougane Barra, / Where Allua of songs rushes forth as an arrow; / In deep-valley'd Desmond—a thousand wild fountains / Come down to that lake from their home in the mountains.
'Gougane Barra'

3 O many a day have I made good ale in the glen, / That came not of stream, or malt, like the brewing of men. / My bed was the ground, my roof, the greenwood above, / And the wealth that I sought—one far kind glance from my love.
'The Outlaw of Loch Lene'

4 Awake thee, my Bessy, the morning is fair, / The breath of young roses is fresh on the air. 'Song'

5 'Tis the rose o' the desert, / So lovely so wild, / In the lap of the desert / Its infancy smiled.
'Written to a Young Lady on Entering a Convent'

**Cambrensis, Giraldus** *c.* 1147 - *c.*1223

6 This [the Irish] is a filthy people, wallowing in vice. Of all peoples it is the least instructed in the rudiments of the Faith. *Topographica Hiberniae*, trans. J. J. O'Meara

7 It is in the cultivation of instrumental music I consider the proficiency of this people to be worthy of commendation; and in this their skill is, beyond all comparison, beyond that of any nation I have ever seen. Ib.

**Campbell, James Henry Mussen, 1st Baron Glenavy** 1851-1931

8 Personally I always feel very lonely when I know in the morning as I get up that there is going to be no meeting of the Seanad. On Future Business, Seanad Éireann, 21 May 1924

**Campbell, Joseph** 1879-1944

9 But he dances there / As if his kin were dead: / Clay in his thoughts, / And lightning in his head. 'The Dancer'

10 I am the gilly of Christ, / The mate of Mary's son; / I run the roads at seeding time / And then the harvest's done.
'I am the Gilly of Christ'

11 My father and mother were Irish, / And I am Irish too: / I bought a wee fidil for ninepence, / And it is Irish too.
'The Ninepenny Fidil'

1 As a white candle / In a holy place, / So is the beauty / Of an aged face.

'The Old Woman'

2 As I walked down through Dublin City / At the hour of twelve in the night / Who should I spy but a Spanish Lady / Washing her feet by candlelight, / First she dipped them, then she dried them / Over a fire of ambery coal / Never in all my life did I see / A maid so neat about the sole. 'The Spanish Lady'

**Campbell, Patrick,**
**3rd Baron Glenavy** 1913-1980

3 Shortly after my return to Dublin, Mr Mac Entee asked me what Lord Beaverbrook thought about Ireland. I struggled with my recollections for some minutes in almost complete silence. I remember a light beading of perspiration even appeared upon my forehead. But in the end I had to admit that I could not recall Lord Beaverbrook ever actually referring to the subject in my presence.

'London Lions',
*The Bell*, March 1942

4 From my earliest days I have enjoyed an attractive impediment in my speech. I have never permitted the use of the word 'stammer'. I can't say it myself.

'Unaccustomed As I Am',
*The P-P-Penguin Patrick Campbell*

5 Bit by bit I learned that *greed-aid foo-ib* was called 'Gradig-voove', and that *dear-caid romhaib,* almost surprisingly, came out as 'Darkigrove' until eventually my grasp of the Irish language became so firm that I often greeted my fellow-marines with a fluent *Céad Míle Fáilte* when meeting them off duty in the mess.

'By the Right — Go Mear Máirseáil', ib.

6 What Alice and I did was to start screaming, steadily, into one another's faces. Alice, I think, believed that the Young Master had come for her at last.

'Tooking for a Lowel', ib.

7 When a fellow is faced by armed men it's my honest opinion that he should have his mother around, if the situation is not to descend into flurry and confusion. 'A Boy's Best Bodyguard',
*Thirty-five Years on the Job*

8 Short Trots with a Cultured Mind

Title of book

**Carbery, Ethna (Anna MacManus)**
1866-1902

9 The brown wind of Connacht — / Across the bogland blown, / The brown wind of Connacht / Turns my heart to a stone.

'The Brown Wind of Connacht'

10 I met the Love-Talker one eve in the glen, / He was handsomer than any of our handsome young men, / His eyes were blacker than the sloe, his voice sweeter far / Than the crooning of old Kevin's pipes beyond in Coolnagar.

'The Love-Talker'

11 They come with vengeance in their eyes — / Too late, too late are they — / For Rody McCorley goes to die / On the Bridge of Toome today.

'Rody McCorley'

12 Oh, Kathaleen Ni Houlihan, your road's a thorny way, / And 'tis a faithful soul would walk the flints with you for aye, / Would walk the sharp and cruel flints until his locks grew grey. 'The Passing of the Gael'

**Carleton, William** 1794-1869

13 Mr Matthew Kavanagh, Philomath and Professor of the Learned Languages, begs to inform the Inhabitants of

Findramore and its vicinity, that he Lectures on the following branches of Education, in his Seminary at the above recited place. *The Hedge Schoolmaster*

1 ... together with various other branches of learning and scholastic profundity – *quos enumerare longum est* – along with Irish radically, and a small taste of Hebrew upon the Masoretic text. Ib.

2 As for the Captain O'Cutters, O'Blunders and Dennis Bulgrudderies of the English stage, they never had any existence except in the imagination of those who were as ignorant of the Irish people as they were of their language and feelings.

Introduction, *Traits and Stories of the Irish Peasantry*

3 During some of the years of Irish famine, such were the unhappy circumstances of the country, that she was exporting provisions of every description in the most prodigal abundance, which the generosity of England was sending back again for our support. So it was with literature. Our men and women of genius uniformly carried their talents to the English market, whilst we laboured at home under all the dark privations of literary famine.

Ib.

4 I remember on one occasion, when she [his mother] was asked to sing the English version of that touching melody 'The Red-haired Man's Wife', she replied, 'I will sing it for you; but the English words and the air are like a quarrelling man and wife; *the Irish melts into the tune,* but the English doesn't.' Ib.

**Carroll, Paul Vincent** 1900-1968

5 CANON SKERRITT: O my child, this wilderness . . . knaves, fools, spirit-grocers and their women . . . clerical football-kickers . . . palavering CCs and one only scoundrel.

*Shadow and Substance*

6 O'FLINGSLEY: And now O'Connor, you're an Irish schoolmaster! In other words, a clerical handyman, a piece of furniture in a chapel house, a brusher-out of barn schools, a Canon's yesman.

Ib.

7 SYLVESTER TIFFNEY: We have been given our freedom but none of us have ever accepted the responsibilities of that freedom. It has given us not greater sanctity, and greater understanding of each other. It has given us instead swarms of unnecessary state-paid humbugs, a new class of unsufferable Gaelic snobs, and a young priesthood who run motor-cars and the GAA for the greater glory of God. *The Wise Have Not Spoken*

8 Returning 300 years later in search of Finn he [Oisin] finds all the great heroes dead and the land swarming with priests and little black men.

Programme note to *The White Steed*

9 CANON LAVELLE: Ten thousand sages of the Church have refused to write certain laws on paper, but you rushing in with a Gaelic tag in your mouth, scrawl them across the page with a schoolboy's pen. *The White Steed*

**Carson, Edward Henry** 1854-1935

10 You are going to pass Home Rule . . . by a pure act of force. . . . Your act of force will be resisted by force.

Speech in House of Commons, 8 August 1911

11 If they were to be my last and latest words I should still say to you, 'Arm yourselves. . . . Arm and prepare to

acquit yourselves like men, for the day of your ordeal is at hand.'

Anti-Home Rule speech at Manchester, 25 October 1912

1 My one affection left me is my love for Ireland. Quoted in Kee, *The Green Flag*

2 We do not want sentence of death with stay of execution for six years.

Quoted in Colvin, *Life of Lord Carson*

3 Of course it [the Ulster Provincial Government] was illegal: so were the Volunteers; but they dared not interfere. September 1913

4 If these men [Ulster Unionists] are not morally justified when they are attempted to be driven out of one government with which they are satisfied and put under another which they loathe, I do not see how resistance ever can be justified in history at all.

February 1914

## Casement, Sir Roger 1864-1916

5 The Empire that has grown from an island and spread with the winds and the waves to the uttermost shores will fight and be fought for on water and will be ended where it began.

That island, I believe, will be Ireland and not Great Britain.

*The Crime Against Ireland*, pamphlet, August 1911

6 I want help. I am here alone. I want officers. I want men. I want a fighting fund . . . I came here for one thing only, to try to help national Ireland — and if there is no such thing in existence then the sooner I pay for my illusions the better. Letter to Joe McGarrity, 29 April 1915

7 If today when all Europe is dying for national ends, whole peoples marching down with songs of joy to the valley of eternal night, we alone stand by idle or moved only to words, then we are in truth the most contemptible of all the peoples of Europe. Ib.

8 I was always an Irish separatist in heart and thought. Memorandum to close friends, Brixton Prison, 1916

9 It is a strange, strange fate, and now, as I stand face to face with death, I feel just as if they were going to kill a boy. For I feel like a boy — and my hands are so free from blood and my heart always so compassionate and pitiful that I cannot comprehend that anyone wants to hang me. MS found in Casement's condemned cell

## Casey, John Keegan 1846-1870

10 Out from many a mud-wall cabin / Eyes were watching thro' that night, / Many a manly chest was throbbing / For the blessed warning light. / Murmurs passed along the valley / Like the banshee's lonely croon, / And a thousand blades were flashing / At the risin' of the moon.

'The Rising of the Moon A.D. 1798'

11 Over the dim blue hills / Strays a wild river, / Over the dim blue hills / Rests my heart ever. 'Maire, My Girl'

## Caulfeild, James, 1st Earl of Charlemont 1728-1799

12 O Belfast, Belfast, dear object of my love and my pride, how art thou changed! Shall the prop of Ireland become its battering-ram?

Quoted in Craig, *The Volunteer Earl*

13 The dragon's teeth were sown, and the fertile soil everywhere produced a plenteous crop of soldiers.

On the origin of the Irish Volunteers. Attrib.

**Céitinn, Seathrún (Geoffrey Keating)** 1580-*c.*1644

1 A bhean lán de stuaim / coingibh uaim do lámh: / ní fear gníomha sinn, / cé taoi tinn dár ngrádh.
'A Bhean Lán De Stuaim'

*O woman full of wile, / Forbid your hand to rove: / Your hurt I cannot heal, / I may not seal our love.*

**Cherry, Andrew** 1762-1812

2 Loud roared the dreadful thunder, / The rain a deluge showers, / The clouds were rent asunder / By lightning's vivid powers. 'The Bay of Biscay'

3 There's a dear little plant that grows in our isle, / 'Twas St Patrick himself sure that set it. 'The Green Little Shamrock'

4 It thrives through the bog, through the brake, and the mireland; / And he called it the dear little shamrock of Ireland. Ib.

5 Sir: I am not so great a fool as you take me for. I have been bitten once by you, and I will never give you an opportunity of making two bites of A. Cherry
Letter to manager of a Dublin theatre. Attrib.

**Chesson, Nora Hopper** 1871-1906

6 The fern uncurled to look at her, so very fair was she, / With her hair as bright as seaweed new-drawn from out the sea. 'The Short Cut to the Rosses'

**Chesterton, G[ilbert] K[eith]** 1874-1936

7 For the great Gaels of Ireland / Are the men that God made mad, / For all their wars are merry / And all their songs are sad. 'Ballad of the White Horse'

**Childers, Robert Erskine** 1870-1922

8 I was bound by honour, conscience and principle to oppose the Treaty by speech, writing, and action, when it came to the disastrous point, in war. For we hold that a nation has no right to surrender its declared and established Independence, and that even a minority has a right to resist that surrender in arms. Speech at court-martial, 18 November 1922

9 It seems perfectly simple and inevitable, like lying down after a long day's work.
Letter to wife from prison, November 1922

**Churchill, Lord Randolph Spencer** 1849-1894

10 . . . foul Ulster Tories who have always ruined our party. 16 November 1885, quoted in Kee, *The Green Flag*

11 I decided some time ago that if the GOM [Gladstone] went for Home Rule, the Orange Card would be the one to play. Please God it may turn out the ace of trumps and not the two.
Letter to Lord Justice Fitzgibbon, 16 February 1886

12 Ulster at the proper moment will resort to its supreme arbitrament of force. Ulster will fight, and Ulster will be right. On landing at Larne, 22 February 1886

13 [Gladstone] reserved for his closing days a conspiracy against the honour of Britain and the welfare of Ireland more startlingly base and nefarious than any of those other numerous designs and plots which, during the last quarter of a century, have occupied his imagination. . . . [His] design for the separation of Ireland from Britain, this insane recurrence to heptarchical arrangements, this trafficking with treason, this condonation of crime, this exaltation of the disloyal, this abasement of the legal, this desertion of our Protes-

tant co-religionists, this monstrous mixture of imbecility, extravagance and hysterics . . . this farrago of superlative nonsense . . . [were such as] the combined genius of Bedlam and Colney Hatch would strive in vain to produce. . . . [And why?] For this reason and no other: to gratify the ambition of an old man in a hurry! To the electors of Paddington, 20 June 1886, quoted in W. S. Churchill, *Lord Randolph Churchill*

**Churchill, Sir Winston Leonard Spencer** 1874-1964

1 Then came the great war. Every institution, almost, in the world was strained. Great Empires have been overturned. The whole map of Europe has been changed. . . . The modes of thought of men, the whole outlook on affairs, the grouping of parties, all have encountered violent and tremendous changes in the deluge of the world. But as the deluge subsides and the waters fall short, we see the dreary steeples of Fermanagh and Tyrone emerging once again. The integrity of their quarrel is one of the few institutions that has been unaltered in the cataclysm which has swept the world.

House of Commons, 1922, quoted in Rose, *Governing Without Consensus*

2 NOW IS YOUR CHANCE. NOW OR NEVER. 'A NATION ONCE AGAIN'. AM VERY READY TO MEET YOU AT ANY TIME. Secret telegram to de Valera, 8 December 1941, after Japanese bombing of Pearl Harbor, quoted in Carroll, *Ireland in the War Years*

3 Owing to the action of the Dublin government . . . the approaches which the southern Irish ports and airfields could so easily have guarded were closed by hostile aircraft and U-boats. This was indeed a deadly moment in our life, and if it had not been for the loyalty and friendship of Northern Ireland, we should have been forced to come to close quarters with Mr de Valera, or perish forever from the earth.

Victory broadcast, 13 May 1945

**Clarke, Austin** 1896-1974

4 Yeats had not dreamed an unstubbed butt, / Ill match, would bring his curtain down. 'The Abbey Theatre Fire'

5 Pity poor lovers who may not do what they please / With their kisses under a hedge, before a raindrop / unhouses it.

'The Envy of Poor Lovers'

6 . . . our Gaelic satirist [description of Flann O'Brien]

'More Extracts from a Diary of Dreams'

7 Burn Ovid with the rest. Lovers will find / A hedge-school for themselves and learn by heart / All that the clergy banish from the mind, / When hands are joined and head bows in the dark.

'Penal Law'

8 They say that her beauty / Was music in mouth. 'The Planter's Daughter'

9 . . . the house of the planter / Is known by the trees. Ib.

10 And O she was the Sunday / In every week. Ib.

11 And yet I tremble lest she may deceive me / And leave me in this land, where every woman's son / Must carry his own coffin and believe, / In dread, all that the clergy teach their young.

'The Straying Student'

12 KING: But I will say my prayers / *(Raising his eyes, in pious tones)* | O . . . *(The* DEMON *tempts him)*

cabbage, boiled / With bacon, thy butter green as peasoup
KING: *(Bewildered):* Thoughts / Have tripped my words and I must say an act / Of nutrition. *The Son of Learning*

1 As children, we were told that anyone who ran round the church [St Mary's Chapel-of-Ease] three times after dark would meet the Devil on the third time round. *Twice Round the Black Church*

**Clarke, Joseph Ignatius Constantine** 1846-1925

2 'There were blossoms of blood on our sprigs of green — / Kelly and Burke and Shea. / And the dead didn't brag.' 'Well here's to the flag!' / Said Kelly and Burke and Shea.

'The Fighting Race'

**Clarke, Thomas James** 1857-1916

3 Clinch your teeth hard and never say die. / Keep your thoughts off yourself all you can. / Guard your self-respect (if you lost that you'd lose the backbone of your manhood). / Get your eyes open and don't bang your head against the wall. / These and a few others, which the deferential regard my prison pen / has for The Rules prevent me from mentioning, are *The Golden Rules of Life for a Long Sentence Prisoner.*

*Glimpses of an Irish Felon's Prison Life*

4 Wait till they [Irish Volunteers] get their fist clutching the steel barrel of a business rifle and then Irish instinctive manhood can be relied on.

Letter to Joe McGarrity, Clan na Gael, November 1913

5 I am to be shot at dawn. I am glad I am getting a soldier's death. I feared it might be hanging or imprisonment. I have had enough of jail.

Letter to wife, 2 May 1916

**Clifford, Sigerson** *b.* 1913

6 These things were long before my day, / I only speak with borrowed words. / But that is how the story goes / In Iveragh of the singing birds.

'The Ballad of the Tinker's Daughter'

**Coghill, Rhoda** *b.* 1903

7 I had warning, last night, in a dream without reason or rhyme; / But the words may not be true ones: '*Obedience is ice to the wine.*'

'The Young Bride's Dream'

**Collins, Michael** 1890-1922

8 I found that those fellows we put on the spot were going to put a lot of us on the spot, so I got there first.

About Bloody Sunday, 21 November 1920, quoted in Lyons, *Ireland Since the Famine*

9 There is no crime in detecting and destroying in war-time, the spy and the informer. They have destroyed without trial. I have paid them back in their own coin.

Private document on Bloody Sunday, quoted in Taylor, *Michael Collins*

10 When will it all end? When can a man get down to a book in peace?

November 1920, quoted in Taylor *op. cit.*

11 This is a real nest of singing birds. They chirrup mightily one to the other — and there's the falseness of it all, because not one trusts the other.

Letter to John O'Kane, 23 October 1921, on early moves in Treaty negotiations, quoted in Taylor, *op. cit.*

12 Think what I have got for Ireland? Something which she has wanted these past seven hundred years. Will anyone

be satisfied with the bargain? Will anyone? I tell you this — early this morning I signed my death warrant. I thought at the time how odd, how ridiculous — a bullet may just as well have done the job five years ago.

Letter, 6 December 1921

1 [The Treaty Settlement] offers freedom to achieve freedom.

Dáil Éireann, 19 December 1921

2 With equitable taxation and flourishing trade our North-East countrymen will need no persuasion to come and share in the healthy economic life of the country. *The Path to Freedom*

3 The Long Hoor [soubriquet for de Valera). Ib., *Passim*

**Collisson, W. A. Houston** *fl.* 1880-1920

4 When Percy French sends me a new manuscript on a postcard or part of a bandbox, to set music to a song, it usually means I have to sit down and rock with laughter at the real fun contained in it before I dare think of setting it to music.

*Dr Collisson in and on Ireland*

**Colmcille, St** 521-597

5 Altus prosator, vetustus / dierum et ingenitus / erat absque origine primordii et crepidine, / est et erit in saecula / saeculorum infinitus.

'Altus Prosator'

*Great progenitor, ancient / of days and unbegotten, / before time began or / space was Thou wert, / Infinite Thou art and wilt be, / world without end.*

6 Manet in meo corde Dei amoris flamma, / ut in argenti vase auri ponitur gemma. 'Noli, Pater'

*The fire of God's love stays in my heart / As a jewel set in gold in a silver vessel.*

*'Do not, Father'*

**Colum, Mary** 1884-1957

7 The thought of seeing a real play by living writers who were Irish and one of whom used to be referred to by my elders as 'old Parson Yeats' grandson' brought a thrill of rapturous excitement. *Life and the Dream*

**Colum, Padraic** 1881-1972

8 . . . an ink whose lustre will keep fresh / For fifty generations of our flesh.

'The Book of Kells'

9 O, men from the fields! / Come gently within. / Tread softly, softly, / O! men coming in. 'A Cradle Song'

10 Then the wet, winding roads, / Brown bogs with black water, / And my thoughts on white ships / And the King o' Spain's daughter. 'A Drover'

11 And soldiers, red soldiers! / You've seen many lands, / But you walk two by two, / And by captain's commands!

Ib.

12 Och! but I'm weary of mist and dark, / And roads where there's never a house or bush!

'An Old Woman of the Roads'

13 She stepped away from me and she moved through the fair, / And fondly I watched her go here and go there, / Then she went her way homeward with one star awake, / As the swan in the evening moves over the lake.

'She Moved Through the Fair'

**Columbanus, St** 543?-615

14 Caveto, filole, / Feminarum species / Per quas mors ingreditur / Non parva pernicies. 'De Mundi Transitu', attrib.

*Beware, my son, / Womankind / By whom death enters; / A grevious danger!*
'On the Passing of Earthly Things'

1 En silvis caesa fluctu meat acta carina / Bicornis Hreni et pelagus perlabitur uncta / Heia viri! nostrum reboans echo sonet heia! 'Carmen Navale'

*Lo, little bark on the twin-horned Rhine / From forests hewn to skim the brine, / Heave, lads, and let the echoes ring.* 'Boat Song'

2 Nos enim sanctorum Petri et Pauli et omnium discipulorum divinum canonem spiritu sancto scribentium discipuli sumus, toti Iberi, ultimi habitatores mundi, nihil extra evangelicam et apostolicam recipientes.
Epistula ad Bonifatium Papam

*For all of us Irish, inhabitants of the world's edge, are receivers of the divine rule of Ss Peter and Paul and all the disciples, written on the inspiration of the Holy Spirit, and do not admit any teaching not according to the gospel and the apostles.* Letter to Pope Boniface IV

**Concanen, Matthew** ? - 1749

3 First Paddy struck the ball. John stop't its course / And sent it backward with redoubled force. / Dick met, and meeting, smote the light machine / Reptile it ran, and skimmed along the green. 'A Mock-Heroic Poem on a Game of Football'

**Congreve, William** 1670-1729

4 She lays it on with a trowel.
*The Double Dealer*

5 Invention flags, his brain grows muddy, / And black despair succeeds brown study. *An Impossible Thing*

6 Thou liar of the first magnitude.
*Love for Love*

7 Oh fie Miss, you must not kiss and tell.
Ib.

8 A branch of one of your antediluvian families, fellows that the flood could not wash away. Ib.

9 Music hath charms to soothe a savage breast, / To soften rocks, or bend a knotted oak. *The Mourning Bride*

10 You were about to tell me something, child — but you left off before you began. *The Old Bachelor*

11 Thus grief still treads upon the heels of pleasure: / Marry'd in haste, we may repent at leisure. Ib.

12 Alack he's gone the way of all flesh.
*'Squire Bickerstaff Detected'*
Attrib. to Congreve

13 Here she comes i'faith full sail, with her fan spread and streamers out, and a shoal of fools for tenders.
*The Way of the World*

**Connell, James** 1852-1929

14 Oh, we hate the cruel tiger / And hyena and jackal / But the false and dirty blackleg / Is the vilest beast of all.
Broadsheet, Dublin transport strike, 1913

15 The people's flag is deepest red; / It shrouded oft our martyred dead.
'The Red Flag'

16 Though cowards flinch and traitors sneer / We'll keep the red flag flying here. Ib.

**Connolly, James** 1868-1916

1 Apostles of Freedom are ever idolised when dead, but crucified when alive.
*Workers Republic*, 13 August 1898

2 The struggle for Irish freedom has two aspects; it is national and it is social . . . It is social and economic because no matter what the form of the government may be, as long as one class owns as private property the land and instruments of labour from which mankind derive their substance, that class will always have it in their power to plunder and enslave the remainder of their fellow creatures.
Quoted in Lyons, *Ireland Since the Famine*

3 Successful revolutions are not the product of our brains, but of ripe material conditions.
*Labour in Irish History*, 1910

4 The time has long since gone when Irishmen and Irish women could be kept from thinking, by hurling priestly thunder at their heads.
*Labour, Nationality and Religion*, 18 April, 1914

5 Governments in a capitalist society are but committees of the rich to manage the affairs of the capitalist class.
*Irish Worker*, 29 August, 1914

6 Boys are always a great problem to parents, and parents are a never failing source of disappointment to boys.
*Nodlaig na bFianna*, December 1914

7 A revolutionist who surrenders the initiative to the enemy is already defeated before a blow is struck.
*Workers Republic*, 4 December 1914

8 The worker is the slave of the capitalist society, the female worker is the slave of that slave.
*The Reconquest of Ireland*, 1915

**Cooper, Major Bryan Ricco** 1884-1930

9 Whenever I see a hen sitting for two years on an egg I know that the egg is addled, and whenever I see a Minister sitting for two years on a Bill, I have a very strong suspicion that the same will be the case. Army Pensions (No. 2) Bill 1926, Dáil Éireann, 25 January 1927

**Corkery, Daniel** 1878-1964

10 One turns to it [Lecky's *History of England in the Eighteenth Century*] for what it contains — for information on the material conditions of the country or for the story of the Dublin Parliament, that noisy side-show, so bizarre in its lineaments and so tragic-comic in its fate. Introduction, *The Hidden Ireland*

11 An opera company, like any other company, must pay its way.
'The Breath of Life', *A Munster Twilight*

12 Midnight had come and gone. The stillness of the small hours began to creep into the revel.
'The Lady of the Glassy Palace', ib.

13 And so they leaped from their pit of sorrow, as the spancelled will until time be over; in no other way is it possible for them - this is their sorry philosophy - to revenge themselves on fortune, to give scorn for scorn.
'The Spancelled', ib.

14 It was a rich night in Autumn; the earth was fruiting. 'Joy', ib.

15 More than once he told himself that he didn't ever remember the sky to have been so full of stars. Somehow he felt like raising his hand towards them.
'The Awakening', *The Stormy Hills*

1 Unless a writer sink himself into the heart of his own people, he will never, let his own gifts be what they may, accomplish work of such a nature as permanently satisfies the human spirit.

*Synge and Anglo-Irish Literature*

**Cosgrave, Liam** *b.* 1920

2 Not for the first time has this party stood between the people of this country and anarchy. And remember . . . those people who comment so freely and write so freely . . . some of them aren't even Irish . . . Some of these are blow-ins. Now as far as we're concerned they can blow out, or blow up.

Fine Gael Ard Fheis address, *The Irish Times*, 23 May 1977

**Cosgrave, William Thomas** 1880-1965

3 No nation has had war made upon its vital interests with such bitter disregard of every principle of morality or good government as this country of ours has had to suffer during the last twelve months.

On Dublin Housing Grant, Seanad Éireann, 7 February 1923

4 There was a reference made here to Southern Ireland. I do not know what particular part of Southern Ireland Donegal is, but it certainly is not in Southern Ireland.

On Revenue Commissioners Order, Seanad Éireann, 21 February 1923

5 . . . The Oireachtas has laid the foundation of the State. . . . We have lived from a time fraught with the consciousness of danger to the period in which we have enjoyed the consciousness of peace.

Review of the Work of the Dáil, 20 May 1927

**Costello, John Aloysius** 1891-1976

6 I, as a Catholic, obey my Church authorities and will continue to do so, in spite of *The Irish Times* or anything else.

Dáil Éireann, April 1951, following Dr Browne's resignation on withdrawal of Mother and Child scheme

**Cousins, James Henry Sproull** 1873-1955

7 I have winged thro' the mists of the ages, / Where sages drone and drowse.

'Behind the Plough'

**Craig, James, 1st Viscount Craigavon** 1871-1940

8 We must be prepared . . . the morning Home Rule passes, ourselves to become responsible for the government of the Protestant province of Ulster.

Quoted in Lyons, *Ireland since the Famine*

9 Ours is a Protestant Government and I am an Orangeman.

Speech at Poyntzpass, 12 July 1932

10 We are King's men and we shall be with you to the end.

Broadcast to Britain, 1939

**Craig, Maurice James** *b.* 1919

11 Red brick in the suburbs, white horse on the wall, / Eyetalian marbles in the City Hall: / O stranger from England, why stand so aghast? / May the Lord in His mercy be kind to Belfast.

'Ballad to a Traditional Refrain'

12 . . . at Stormont we're nailing the flag to the mast. Ib.

13 It's to hell with the future and live on the past. Ib.

**Crawford, Julia** *fl.* 1835

14 Kathleen Mavourneen! the grey dawn is breaking, / The horn of the hunter is heard on the hill. 'Kathleen Mavourneen'

1 Oh! hast thou forgotten this day we must part? / It may be for years and it may be for ever. Ib.

**Croke, Archbishop Thomas William** 1824-1902

2 And what have we got in their [Irish games and pastimes] stead? We have got such foreign and fantastic field sports as lawn tennis, polo, croquet, cricket and the like — very excellent, I believe, and health-giving exercises in their way, still not racy of the soil but rather alien.

Letter accepting patronage of GAA, November 1884

**Cromwell, Oliver** 1599-1658

3 It has pleased God to bless our endeavours at Drogheda . . . I believe we put to the sword the whole number of the defendants. I do not think thirty of the whole number escaped with their lives. Those that did, are in safe custody for the Barbadoes . . . I wish that all honest hearts may give the glory of this to God alone, to whom indeed the praise of this mercy belongs.

Letter to the Hon. John Bradshaw, President of the Council of State, September 1649

4 I had rather be overrun with a cavalierish interest than a Scotch interest; I had rather be overrun by a Scotch interest than an Irish interest, and I think of all this is the most dangerous. Speech to Council of State, 15 March 1649

**Cronin, Anthony** *b.* 1925

5 Forgive us that we have not lived through a virtuous day, / That we ask to be judged in the end by our own compassion, / Thief calling to thief from his cross with no Christ in between. 'Apology'

6 Dublin in the late nineteen-forties was an odd and, in many respects, unhappy place . . . Neutrality had left a wound, set up complexes in many, including myself, which the post-war did little to cure. *Dead As Doornails*

7 She herself lived in a sort of hostel with fifty or sixty of her fellows, a kind of virginal beehive, full of song, and gossip and rinsing noises.

*The Life of Riley*

8 It was indeed hard to muster up enthusiasm for the extension of the carageen moss industry, in the possible utilisation of the various parts of the herring's anatomy, down to the tail and the fin, in portable, prefabricated factories themselves made of herring-bone cement along the west coast. Ib.

9 Turf smoke is talked upon the darker blue / And leaves a sweet, rich, poor man's smell in cloth. 'RMS Titanic'

10 Down underneath the Irish poor are singing / Their songs of Philadelphia in the morning. Ib.

11 And they will bless the Pope this time in building / It in a Belfast of exorbitant virtue. Ib.

**Cross, Eric** 1905-1980

12 In the town land of Garrynapeaka, in the district of Inchigeela, in the parish of Iveleary, in the barony of West Muskerry, in the county of Cork, in the province of Munster . . .

Tim Buckley the Tailor's address, *The Tailor and Ansty*

13 General De Wet's father was from Laune, west of Killarney . . . He had no English, but only the Irish, and to each man he met he said, 'Dia Dhuit'. That was his salute . . . They called him De

Wet, which was as near as they could get to the Irish, thinking it was his name. Ib.

1 Take the world fine and aisy and the world will take you fine and aisy. Ib.

2 The world is only a blue bag. Knock a squeeze out of it when you can. Ib.

3 Now the Ratschilds were the richest people in the whole world, and the head of them lived in Tipperary. (I'll tell you afterwards how they came to get the money and the name.) Ib.

**Cullen, Paul Cardinal** 1803-1878

4 If I were asked am I an Ultramontane, I would say I am in this sense — that I respect the decision of the Head of the Church, and that I am always an obedient subject in religious matters to the Pope. Letters

5 As to what is called Fenianism, you are aware that looking on it as a compound of folly and wickedness wearing a mask of patriotism to make dupes of the unwary, and as the work of a few fanatics and knaves, wicked enough to jeopardize others in order to promote their own sordid views, I have repeatedly raised my voice against it since it first became known at M'Manus's funeral.

Pastoral letter, 10 October 1865

**Curran, John Philpot** 1750-1817

6 Dear Erin, how sweetly thy green bosom rises! / An emerald set in the ring of the sea. / Each blade of thy meadows my faithful heart prizes, / Thou queen of the west! the world's cushla ma chree! 'Cushla Ma Chree'

7 No more a rover, or hapless lover, / My griefs are over — my glass runs low; / Then for that reason, and for a season, / Let us be merry before we go.

'Let Us Be Merry Before We Go'

8 I have never yet heard of a murderer who was not afraid of a ghost.

To an Irish peer who said he hated the sight of the late Parliament building at College Green. Attrib.

9 My brethren, be chaste — till you're tempted; / While sober, be grave and discreet; / And humble your bodies with fasting, / As oft as you've nothing to eat. 'The Monks of the Screw'

10 Riding alone, my lord!

When asked by the judge, Lord Norbury, where he would be if a gallows they were passing were to have its due. Attrib.

11 The condition upon which God has given liberty to man is eternal vigilance; which condition if he break, servitude is at once the consequence of his crime, and the punishment of his guilt.

Speech on night of election of Lord Mayor of Dublin, 10 July 1790

**Curran, Sarah** 1782-1808

12 The only regret of your unworthy representative is that he did not put him to some easy death upon the spot, and try perhaps how the body of a spy would answer your cherry-trees.

Letter found on Robert Emmet at his arrest, August 1803

**Daiken, Leslie** *b.* 1912

1 The passion of bigotry is a fine fashioner of riposte. *Out Goes She,* 'a compilation of Dublin street rhymes'

2 Auld Jo he is a bo / He goes to Church each Sunday / He prays to God to give him strength / To bash the kids on Monday. Ib.

3 A tinker an' / A tailor an' / An IRA; / An Auxie man / A Black-and-Tan / A thief. Ib.

4 Now when the buildings of all Europe don their sackcloth / And the places and the plazas prepare for raiders, all lamps hidden, / Night spreads her spangled quilt of silk on Galway City. 'Nightfall in Galway'

**D'Alton, John** 1792-1867

5 Oh! Erin! in thine hour of need / Thy warriors wander o'er the earth; / For others' liberties they bleed, / Nor guard the land that gave them birth. 'Oh! Erin!'

**Daly, Ita** *b.* 1944

6 For a short time, she had been mistress of her flesh. For a short time, she had come into her own. Once when she was nineteen and a virgin in Rome. With a brother and no money and tight blue jeans. 'Virginibus Puerisque', *The Lady with the Red Shoes*

**Darley, George** 1795-1846

7 O blest unfabled Incense Tree, / That burns in glorious Araby, / With red scent chalicing the air, / Till earth-life grow Elysian there! 'Nepenthe'

8 In the wormless sand shall he / Feast for no foul glutton be: / Dingle-dong, the dead-bells chime! / Mermen keep the tone and time! 'The Sea Ritual'

**Davis, Francis ('The Belfast Man')** 1810-1855

9 We've been riven, / We've been driven, / The crafty spoilers' prey; / But your Ulstermen / And Orangemen / Are Irishmen today. 'The Ulstermen'

**Davis, Thomas** 1814-1845

10 And Ireland long a province be / A Nation once again! 'A Nation Once Again'

11 . . . in far foreign fields from Dunkirk to Belgrade, / Lie the soldiers and chiefs of The Irish Brigade. 'The Battle Eve of the Brigade'

12 *Viva la,* the New Brigade! / *Viva la,* the Old One, too! / *Viva la,* the rose shall

fade, / And the Shamrock shine for ever new! 'Clare's Dragoons'

1 'Did they dare, did they dare, to slay Eoghan Ruadh O'Neill?' / 'Yes, they slew with poison him they feared to meet with steel.' / 'May God wither up their hearts! May their blood cease to flow! / May they walk in living death, who poisoned Eoghan Ruadh!'
'Lament for the Death of Owen Roe O'Neill'

2 Be my epitaph writ on my country's mind, / *'He served his country and loved his kind.'* 'My Grave'

3 The summer sun is falling soft on Carbery's hundred isles.
'The Sack of Baltimore'

4 In Bodenstown Churchyard there is a green grave, / And freely around it let winter winds rave — / Far better they suit him – the ruin and the gloom – / Till Ireland, a nation, can build him a tomb. 'Tone's Grave'

5 Be sure the great God never planned / For slumbering slaves, a home so grand. 'The West's Asleep'

6 But – hark! – some voice like thunder spake, / *'The West's awake, the West's awake'* — / 'Sing oh! hurrah! let England quake, / We'll watch till death for Erin's sake!' Ib.

7 We have no hope from English justice. The English call themselves just and in their private dealings they have, or had, some claim to the title. But if said of their public polity it is an idle boast.
'English Justice', *Essays*

8 To lose your native tongue, and learn that of an alien, is the worst badge of conquest — it is the chain on the soul. To have lost entirely the national language is death; the fetter has worn through. 'The National Language'

9 Almost all the Irish political songs are too desponding or weak to content a people marching to independence as proudly as if they never had been slaves.
'Our Music and Poetry', ib.

10 Your country will, I fear, need all your devotion. She has no foreign friends. Beyond the limits of green Erin there is none to aid her. She may gain by the feuds of the stranger; she cannot hope for his peaceful help, be he distant, be he near; her trust is in her sons.
Auditor's address to Historical Association, Trinity College, 1840

**Deane, Seamus Francis** *b.* 1940

11 This is the honeymoon / Of the cockroach, the small / Spiderless eternity of the fly.
'After Derry, 30 January 1972'

12 The unemployment in our bones / Erupting on our hands in stones; / The thought of violence a relief, / The act of violence a grief; / Our bitterness and love / Hand in glove. 'Derry'

13 God hungers for situations / That only the devil could invent. 'Bonfire'

**De Courcy, John** *d.* 1219

14 In burgo Duno tumulo; tumulantur in uno / Brigida, Patricius, atque Columba Pius.

*In Down three saints one grave do fill, / Brigid, Patrick and Colmcille.* Attrib.

**De hÓra, Seán** *c.* 1710-1780

15 Ár nAthair atá ins na flaithis go hard, / Go naomhaítear tráth d'ainmse, / Go

dtige do ríocht, do thoil ar an saol, / Mar déantar i gcrích Pharrthais.
'Aithrí Sheáin de hÓra'

*Our Father who reigns in heavenly fame, / Thy hallowed name be past all price; / May thy kingdom come, thy will be done / And earth be one with Paradise.* *'Penance of Seán de hÓra'*

**Denham, Sir John** 1615-1669

1 Such is our pride, our folly, or our fate / That few but such as cannot write, translate. 'To Sir Richard Fanshawe'

**De Valera, Eamon** 1882-1975

2 It [partition] is after all only an old fortress of crumbled masonry — held together with the plaster of fiction.
Draft speech for South Armagh By-election, January 1818

3 No offer will be accepted by the nation if that offer deprives us of the essentials of freedom. Now, it is a hard thing to know what are the essentials of freedom. Freedom is a thing that you cannot cut in two — you are either all free or you are not free. It is, therefore, for complete freedom that we are struggling, and we tell everybody that this nation will continue to struggle for its freedom until it has got the whole of it. Limerick, 5 October 1921

4 I am against this treaty, not because I am a man of war, but a man of peace. I am against this treaty because it will not end the centuries of conflict between the two nations of Great Britain and Ireland. 19 December 1921

5 I stand as a symbol for the Republic. Neither publicly nor privately have I lowered that position. It would be a matter for impeachment if I did. I didn't go to London because I wished to keep that symbol of the Republic pure even from insinuation, or even a word across the table that would give away the Republic. Dáil Éireann, 4 January 1922

6 Whenever I wanted to know what the Irish people wanted, I had only to examine my own heart and it told me straight off what the Irish people wanted. Dáil Éireann, 6 January 1922, in reply to a jibe at his 'foreignness' in the *Freeman's Journal*

7 Soldiers of the Republic, Legion of the Rearguard: The Republic can no longer be defended successfully by your arms. Further sacrifice of life would now be vain and continuance of the struggle in arms unwise in the national interest and prejudicial to the future of our cause. Military victory must be allowed to rest for the moment with those who have destroyed the Republic.
Cease-fire order at end of Civil War, 24 May 1923

8 No longer shall our children, like our cattle, be brought up for export.
Dáil Éireann, 19 December 1934

9 I am not prepared to take an oath. I am not going to take an oath. I am prepared to put my name down in this book in order to get into the Dáil, but it has no other significance. July 1927

10 . . . a land whose countryside would be bright with cozy homesteads, whose fields and villages would be joyous with the sounds of industry, with the rompings of sturdy children, the contests of athletic youths and the laughter of comely maidens, whose firesides would be forums for the wisdom of serene old age. It would, in a word, be the home of a people living the life that God desires that man should live.
Address, St Patrick's Day, 1943

1 Mr Churchill is proud of Britain's stand alone after France had fallen and before America entered the war. Could he not find in his heart the generosity to acknowledge that there is a small nation that stood alone, not for one year or two, but for several hundred years against aggression; that endured spoliations, famines, massacres, in endless succession; that was clubbed many times into insensibility but each time on regaining consciousness, took up the fight anew; a small nation that could never be got to accept defeat and has never surrendered her soul?

Radio broadcast, 16 May 1945

**De Vere, Aubrey** 1814-1902

2 The little Black Rose shall be red at last! / What made it black but the East wind dry, / And the tear of the widow that fell on it fast? / It shall redden the hills when June is nigh.

'The Little Black Rose'

**Devlin, Anne** 1780-1851

3 Horror came over me when I perceived the blood of Mr Emmet on the scaffold where his head had been cut off. Dogs and pigs were lapping up his blood from between the paving stones. Journal

**Devlin, Bernadette** *b.* 1947

4 Among the best traitors Ireland has ever had, Mother Church ranks at the very top, a massive obstacle in the path to equality and freedom.

*The Price of my Soul*

5 For half a century, it [Unionist Party Government] has misgoverned us. Now we are witnessing its dying convulsions; and with traditional Irish mercy, when we've got it down, we will kick it into the ground. Ib.

6 There are no illegitimate children, only illegitimate parents — if the term is to be used at all.

*The Irish Times*, 'This Week They Said', 31 July 1971

7 I have a right, as the only representative who was a witness, to ask a question of that murdering hypocrite.

Spoken preparatory to assault on British Home Secretary Reginald Maudling in House of Commons, 31 January 1972, after 13 shot dead at Bogside rally in Derry the previous day.

8 I am just sorry I did not go for his throat. To reporters, after assault above

**Devoy, John** 1842-1928

9 I think the only true solution of the land question is the abolition of landlordism. The land of Ireland belongs to the people of Ireland. October 1878

10 His [Davitt's] impetuous temperament and lack of tact, to say nothing of his social standing, made him impossible.

*Gaelic-American*, 1906

**Dillon, James** *b.* 1902

11 As so often happens in this unhappy country, the provocative insolence of British politicians gets the colour of vindication by things we in our folly do. On Constitution (Removal of Oath) Bill, Dáil Éireann, 27 April 1932

**Dillon, John** 1851-1927

12 I say without fear that if tomorrow, in asserting the freedom of Ireland, we were to exchange for servitude to Westminster servitude to . . . any body of cardinals in Rome, then I would say goodbye for ever to the struggle for Irish freedom. Speech at Drogheda, 1888, quoted in Lyons *Ireland Since the Famine*

1 It is the first rebellion that ever took place in Ireland where you had the majority on your side. It is the fruit of our [the Irish Parliamentary Party's] life work . . . now you are washing out our whole life work in a sea of blood. . . . it is not murderers who are being executed; it is insurgents who have fought a clean fight, a brave fight, however misguided, and it would be a damned good thing for you if your soldiers were able to put as good a fight as these men in Dublin — three thousand men against twenty thousand with machine-guns and artillery.

On Ireland: Continuance of Martial Law, House of Commons, 11 May 1916

**Disraeli, Benjamin** 1804-1881

2 Thus you have a starving population, an absentee aristocracy, and an alien Church, and in addition the weakest executive in the world. That is the Irish Question. Speech in House of Commons, 16 February 1844

**Doherty, John** 1798-1854

3 If machines could be so constructed as to convey us to any part of the globe with utmost dispatch, no one could question their advantage.

*Voice of the People*

**Donegan, Patrick Sarsfield** *b.* 1923

4 She'll get a boot up the transom and be told to get out of our waters fast.

Commenting, as Minister of Defence, on Cypriot gun-running coaster *Claudia*, 29 March 1973, *(The Irish Times)*

5 It was amazing when the President [of Ireland, Cearbhall Ó Dálaigh] sent the Emergency Powers Bill to the Supreme Court. . . . In my opinion he is a thundering * disgrace.

Speech at Columb Barracks, Mullingar, 18 October 1976 *(The Irish Times)*
**Some reports substitute another word.*

**Donleavy, James Patrick** *b.* 1926

6 To marry the Irish is to look for poverty. *The Ginger Man*

7 When I die I want to decompose in a barrel of porter and have it served in all the pubs in Dublin. Ib.

**Donnelly, Charles** 1914-1937

8 Body awaits the tolerance of crows.

'The Tolerance of Crows'

**Dowland, John** 1562-1626

9 Weep no more, sad fountains; / What need you flow so fast? / Look how the snowy mountains / Heaven's sun doth gently waste. 'Weep No More'

**Doyle, Lynn – alias Lynn C. Doyle (Leslie A. Montgomery)** 1873-1961

10 The country folk of Ulster are not much given to literature.

*An Ulster Childhood*

11 An' if it falls within the scope / O'God's almighty plan / To save a single Papish sowl / I hope it's Michael Dan. 'An Ulsterman'

**Doyle, Sir Arthur Conan** 1859-1930

12 Said the King to the Colonel / 'The complaints are eternal / That you Irish give more trouble / Than any other corps.' 'The Irish Colonel'

13 Said the Colonel to the King: / 'This complaint is no new thing, / For your foemen, Sire, have made it / A hundred times before.' Ib.

**Drennan, William** 1754-1820

14 Men of Eire! awake, and make haste to be blest, / Rise — Arch of the Ocean, and Queen of the West! 'Eire'

15 Here our murdered brother lies — / Wake him not with women's cries; /

Mourn the way that manhood ought; / Sit in silent trance of thought.

'The Wake of William Orr'

**Drummond, Thomas** 1797-1840

1 Property has its duties as well as its rights. Letter to Earl of Donoughmore, 22 May 1838

**Dufferin, Lady Helen Selina Sheridan Blackwood** 1807-1867

2 I'm sittin' on the stile, Mary, / Where we sat side by side.

'Lament of the Irish Emigrant'

3 I'm very lonely now, Mary, / For the poor make no new friends. Ib.

4 And when you come back to me, Kathleen, / None the better will I be off then — / You'll be spaking such beautiful English, / Sure, I won't know my Kathleen again? 'Terence's Farewell'

**Duffy, George Gavan** 1882-1951

5 Let me remind the House of the Council of Constance in 1415, when the King of England applied for admission and was told that he did not represent one of the ancient nations of Christendom, and could not be admitted. When he found himself in that position he said, 'but I have another string to my bow, I am also King of Ireland, and in that capacity I claim the right of admission', and in that capacity they let him in.

On Proposal to join League of Nations, Dáil Éireann, 18 September 1922

**Duffy, Sir Charles Gavan** 1816-1903

6 God bless the gray mountains of dark Donegal / God bless royal Aileach, the pride of them all; / For she sits evermore like a queen on her throne, / And smiles on the valleys of Green Innishowen. 'Innishowen'

7 He left Ireland believing there was no more hope for the Irish cause than for the corpse on the dissecting table.

Quoted in *Devoy's Post Bag 1871-1928*

**Durcan, Paul** *b.* 1944

8 The answer to your question is that I am not your mother; / Your mother was another mother and she died in Russia.

'Trauma Junction'

# E

**Edgeworth, Maria** 1767-1849

1 . . . born to little or no fortune of his own, he [Sir Condy Rackrent] was bred to the bar, at which having many friends to push him, and no mean abilities of his own, he doubtless would in process of time, if he could have borne the drudgery of that study, have been rapidly made king's counsel at the least. *Castle Rackrent*

2 Our Irish blunders are never blunders of the heart. *Essay on Irish Bulls*

**Eglinton, John**
**(William Kirkpatrick Magee)** 1868-1961

3 Carleton was the man sent by God in response to the general clamour for an Irish Walter Scott. *Anglo-Irish Essays*

4 [On the modern Irishman] . . . it is easy to see that, however picturesque his mother may be as she sits crooning songs of hatred against her betrayer, a young nationality, with a world of new enterprise and purpose in his soul, new thought and invention in his brain, passion as yet unexpended in his heart, must find something lacking in a mental and spiritual attitude so uncompromisingly negative. *United Irishman*, 22 March 1902

5 I should like to live to see the day of what might be called, without any disrespect to Davis, the de-Davisisation of Irish national literature, that is to say the getting rid of the notion that in Ireland a writer is to think first and foremost of interpreting the nationality of his country, and not simply of the burden which he has to deliver.

Ib., 31 March 1902

**Emmet, Robert** 1778-1803

6 No rising column marks this spot, / Where many a victim lies, / But oh! the blood which here has streamed, / To heaven for justice cries.

'Lines on Arbour Hill'

7 My lords, you are impatient for the sacrifice. Speech from the dock

8 I have but a few more words to say . . . I am going to my cold and silent grave — my lamp of life is nearly extinguished — my race is run — the grave opens to receive me, and I sink into its bosom. I have but one request to make at my departure from this world, it is — the charity of its silence. Let no man write my epitaph; for as no man who knows my motives dare now vindicate them, let not prejudice or ignorance asperse them. Let them rest in obscurity and peace! Let my memory be left in oblivion, my tomb remain uninscribed, until other times and other men can do justice to my character. When my

country takes her place among the nations of the earth, *then*, and *not till then*, let my epitaph be written. Ib.

**Engels, Friedrich** 1820-1896

1 By consistent oppression they [the Irish] have been artificially converted into an utterly demoralized nation and now fulfil the notorious function of supplying England, America, Australia, etc., with prostitutes, casual labourers, pimps, thieves, swindlers, beggars and other rabble. This demoralized character persists in the aristocracy too. . . . These fellows ought to be shot. Of mixed blood, mostly tall, strong, handsome chaps, they all wear enormous moustaches under colossal Roman noses, give themselves the sham military airs of retired colonels, travel around the country after all sorts of pleasures, and if one makes an inquiry, they haven't a penny, are laden with debts, and live in dread of the Encumbered Estates Court. Letter to Karl Marx, 23 May 1856

2 Ireland still remains the Holy Isle whose aspirations must on no account be mixed with the profane class-struggles of the rest of the sinful world . . . the Irish peasant must not on any account know that the Socialist workers are his sole allies in Europe.

Ib., 9 December 1869

**Eriugena, Johannes Scotus** *c.* 810-877

3 Tabula tantum!
*The width of a table.*

Riposte to Charles the Bald's jibe, 'Quid distat inter Scottum et sotum? *(What is the difference between an Irishman and a drunkard?)*

**Ervine, St John Greer** 1883-1971

4 . . . it appears that in addition to being a dromedary I'm a whited sepulchre.

*Boyd's Shop*

5 The Right Honourable Sir Edward Henry Carson, Privy Councillor, Master of Arts of Trinity College, Dublin, LLD (Hon Causa), Member of Parliament and Kings Counsellor, the leader of the Ulster Unionist movement and the starry hero of all the politest young ladies of Belfast has not done anything to promote the well-being of Ireland, never has done anything, and never will. *Sir Edward Carson*

6 Sir Edward is a stage Irishman . . . the last of the Broths of a Boy. Ib.

7 . . . with less complaint than a Sinn Feiner makes about his obsolete language which he cannot speak, will not write, and does not wish to learn.

*Some Impressions of My Elders*

**Fahy, Francis Arthur** 1854-1935

1 Oh, I'd rather live in poverty with little Mary Cassidy / Than Emperor without her be o'er Germany or Spain.
'Little Mary Cassidy'

2 Not far from old Kinvara, in the merry month of May, / When birds were singing cheerily, there came across my way, / As if from out the sky above an angel chanced to fall, / A little Irish cailin in an ould plaid shawl.
'The Ould Plaid Shawl'

3 When she's loaded down with fish till the water lips the gunwhale, / Not a drop she'll take on board her that would wash a fly away.
'The Queen of Connemara'

**Fallon, Padraic** 1905-1974

4 A man must go naked to an island, / Let the weather lend / A skin till he grows one.
'An Island'

5 They were the eagles in the morning sun; / A country rising from its knees / To upset all the histories.
'The Young Fenians'

6 Somewhere a man will touch his image and burn / Like a candle before it.
'Yeats's Tower at Ballylee'

**Fallon, Peter** *b.* 1951

7 We were masters of reserve. / 'Why?' 'That's the why.' 'Ah why?' 'Because . . .' / When all fruit fails we welcome haws.
'Home'

8 All I approve persists, / is here, at home. I think it exquisite / to stand in the yard, my feet on the ground, / in cowshit and horseshit and sheepshit.
'Winter Work'

**Farquhar, George** 1677-1707

9 I have fed purely upon ale; I have eat my ale, drank my ale, and I always sleep upon ale.
*The Beaux Stratagem*

10 My Lady Bountiful
Ib.

11 Says little, thinks less, and does — nothing at all, faith.
Ib.

12 There's no scandal like rags, nor any crime as shameful as poverty.
Ib.

13 Spare all I have and take my life.
Ib.

14 Grant me some wild expressions, Heavens, or I shall burst. . . . Words, words, or I shall burst.
*The Constant Couple*

15 Poetry's a mere drug, Sir.
*Love and a Bottle*

1 He answered the description the page gave to a T, Sir. Ib.

2 Hanging and marriage, you know, go by Destiny. *The Recruiting Officer*

3 SUBTLEMAN: And how do you intend to live?
TEAGUE: By eating, dear joy, fen I can get it; and by sleeping when I can get none: 'tish the fashion of Ireland. *The Twin-Rivals*

4 Attach! no dear joy, I cannot attach you — but I can catch you by the troat, after the fashion of Ireland. Ib.

**Farrar, Dean Frederick William** 1831-1903

5 Russell . . . acted invariably from the highest principles. *Eric, or Little By Little*

6 Russell, let me always call you Edwin, and call me Eric. Ib.

**Farren, Robert (Roibeárd Ó Faracháin)** *b.* 1909

7 Whisper: Old Cahal Bwee Mac Gilla Gunne / turns lovely mourning for your drouthy throat / Ledwidge renames you, keening for Tom MacDonagh / who keyed the mourning to another note. 'Rime, Gentlemen, Please'

8 Brimstone on evil / A grey eye weeping. 'Colmcille on the Battle of Cooldrevny'

**Faulkner, Arthur Brian** 1921-1977

9 You can do three things in Irish politics, the right thing, the wrong thing, or nothing at all. I have always thought it better to do the wrong thing than to do nothing at all. Speech, July 1974

**Fay, Frank J.** *fl.* 1890-1920

10 Histrionic ability is not lacking in Ireland; but it is very difficult to get Irish people to understand that acting cannot be played at: that it must be taken seriously if it is to be of the smallest use. 'Samhain', *United Irishman*, 26 October 1901

**Fay, William George** 1872-1947

11 He [Synge] came to Dublin for the rehearsals — a tawny, thick-set fellow with the head of a lion and a terrifying moustache, and looking at least forty though he actually was just turned thirty-two. *The Fays of the Abbey Theatre*

12 Once I found the proper 'tune' I never had any difficulty with the dialect in any of his plays. Ib.

**Feiritéar, Piaras** *c.* 1600-1635

13 Léig dhíot th'airm, a mhacaoimh mná, / muna fearr leat cách do lot; / muna léige th'airmse dhíot, / cuirfead bannaidhe ón rígh ort. 'Léig Díot Th'airm, A Mhacaoimh Mná'

*Lay your weapons down, young lady. / Do you want to ruin us all? / Lay your weapons down, or else / I'll have you under royal restraint.*

**Ferguson, Sir Samuel** 1810-1886

14 Then put your head, darling, darling, darling, / Your darling black head my heart above; / Oh, mouth of honey, with the thyme for fragrance, / Who, with heart in breast, could deny you love? 'Cean Dubh Deelish'

15 . . . I grieve not, eagle of the empty eyrie, / That thy wrathful cry is still. 'Lament for the death of Thomas Davis'

16 O brave young men, my love, my pride, my promise, / 'Tis on you my hopes are set, / In manliness, in kindliness, in justice, / To make Erin a nation yet; / Self respecting, self-relying, self-advancing, / In union or in

severance, free and strong, / And if God grant this, then, under God, to Thomas Davis / Let the greater praise belong! Ib.

1 Dear thoughts are in my mind / And my soul soars enchanted, / As I hear the sweet lark sing / In the clear air of the day. 'The Lark in the Clear Air'

**Figaro, Le**

2 Les gais irlandais ont inventé un nouveau mot, ils disent à présent 'boycotter', quelqu'un, cela signifie le mettre interdit.

*The lively Irish have invented a new word; they are saying now to 'boycott' someone, meaning to ostracise him.*

24 November 1880

**Figgis, Darrell Edmund** 1882-1925

3 There are people in this country of the devoutest faith who would be reluctant to thieve or lie, but who will go in with the utmost cheerfulness to thieve or lie when they get inside a polling booth.

On Prevention of Corrupt Practices at Elections, Dáil Éireann, 20 October 1922

**Fitzgibbon, John, 1st Earl of Clare** 1749-1802

4 . . . if it is to remain at the discretion of every adventurer of feeble and ostentatious talents, ungoverned by a particle of judgement or discretion, to dress up fictitious grievances for popular delusion and let loose a savage and barbarous people upon the property and respect of the Irish nation, what gentleman who has the means of living out of this country will be induced to remain in it? Speech favouring Act of Union, 10 February 1800

**Fitzmaurice, George** 1878-1963

5 Pats will buy me an arm-chair, he said, and I can sit at the fire and do my knitting and sewing at my ease — that's when we are all living together in the slate house. The fear of the Workhouse will never again come before my old eyes. The Country Dressmaker

6 . . . and following the light didn't I see Roger being carried away by the Hag and the Son of the Hag. Riding on two Spanish asses they were, holding him between them by a whisker each, and his whiskers were the length of six feet you'd think, and his nose was the length of six feet you'd think, and his eyes were the size of turnips bulging outside his head. *The Dandy Dolls*

7 Down on your knees now, you haunted thing. Keep looking at me or I'll send this red-hot tongs fizzling down into your baistly guts. Sacramento, Dominus vobiscum, mea culpa, mea maxima culpa, kyrie eleison, excelsior! I abjure thee by these words, tell me what you are and what you aren't. Are you Catholic? *The Magic Glasses*

8 . . . if it isn't time from God I'll get, maybe the devil will give me time! Let the devil himself give me time, then, let him give me time to finish my pie-dish, and it's his I'll be for ever more body and soul! *The Pie-Dish*

9 It's a good stroke is in that long bony arm by you still, Shuwawn Daly, and take this stick and smash this skull and knock what's in it out of it, for the brains that are in that head have no right to be in the head of Michael Clancy.

*Twixt the Giltinans and the Carmodys*

**Flanagan, Oliver John** *b.* 1920

10 Let us hope and trust that there are sufficient proud and ignorant people left in this country to stand up to the intellectuals who are out to destroy

faith and fatherland. *The Irish Times*, 'This Week They Said', 10 April 1971

**Flood, Henry** 1732-1791

1 A voice from America shouted to liberty, the echo of it caught your people as it passed along the Atlantic, and they renewed the voice till it reverberated here. Renunciation at establishment of Grattan's Parliament, 1783

2 The right honourable gentleman [Attorney-General Yelverton] cannot bear to hear of Volunteers; but I will ask him, and I will have a starling taught to halloo in his ear — Who gave you the Free Trade? Who gave you the Free Constitution? Who made you a nation? The Volunteers! Speech vindicating Irish Volunteers, 1783

**Forster, William Edward** 1819-1886.

3 It is more humane that buckshot be used [in riot dispersal by the RIC]. Speech in House of Commons, 23 August 1880

**Frazer, John de Jean** 1809-1852

4 Behold how green the gallant stem / On which the flower is blowing; / How is one heavenly breeze and beam / Both flower and stem are glowing. / The same good soil, sustaining both, / Make both united flourish / But cannot give the Orange growth, / And cease the Green to flourish. 'Song for July 12, 1843'

5 Till then the Orange lily be / Thy badge my patriot brother — / The everlasting Green for me; / And — we for one another. Ib.

**French, William Percy** 1854-1920

6 There's a grave where the waves of the blue Danube roll / And on it in characters clear / Is: 'Stranger, remember to pray for the soul / Of Abdulla Bulbul Ameer.' / A Muscovite maiden her vigil doth keep / By the light of the true lover's star / And the name that she whispers so sadly in sleep / Is Ivan Potschjinski Skidar. 'Abdulla Bulbul Ameer'

7 I'm simply surrounded by lovers, / Since Da made his fortune in land; / They're coming in clouds like the plovers / To ax for me hand. / There's clerks and policemen and teachers, / Some sandy, some black as the crow; / Ma says ye get used to the creatures / But, ach I dunno! 'Ach I Dunno'

8 The Garden of Eden has vanished, they say, / But I know the lie of it still; / Just turn to the left at the bridge of Finea / And stop when half-way to Cootehill. / 'Tis there I will find it; I know sure enough / When fortune has come to me call. / Oh, the grass it is green around Ballyjamesduff / And the blue sky is over it all; / And tones that are tender and tones that are gruff / Are whispering over the sea, / 'Come back, Paddy Reilly, to Ballyjamesduff, / Come home, Paddy Reilly, to me.' 'Come Back, Paddy Reilly'

9 There's not one girl in the wide, wide world / like the girl from the County Clare. 'The Darlin' Girl from Clare'

10 Eileen Oge, and that the darlin's name is, / Through the Barony her features they were famous, / If we loved her who was there to blame us, / For wasn't she the Pride of Petravore. 'Eileen Oge'

11 Dear Danny: I'm takin' the pen in me hand / To tell you we're just out of sight of the land; / In the grand Allen liner we're sailin' in style / But we're sailin' away from the Emerald Isle; /

And a long sort of sigh seemed to rise from us all / As the waves hid the last bit of ould Donegal. / Och! it's well to be you to be takin' yer tay / Where they're cutting the corn down in Creeshlough the day.

'The Emigrant's Letter'

1 I've a shelter for the hens and a stable for the ass, / And what can a man want more? / I dunno, maybe so, / And a bachelor is happy and he's free.

'Little Brigid Flynn'

2 The schoolmaster said with a great deal of sense / 'We'll reduce the two girls to shillings and pence.'

'MacBreen's Heifer'

3 But if at those roses you ventured to sip, / The colour might all come away on your lip / So I'll wait for the wild rose that's waitin' for me — / Where the Mountains of Mourne sweep down to the sea. 'The Mountains of Mourne'

4 You've heard o' Julius Caesar, an' the great Napoleon too, / An' how the Cork Militia bate the Turks at Waterloo, / But there's a page of glory that, as yet, remains uncut, / An' that's the Martial story o' the Shlathery's Mounted Fut. 'Slattery's Mounted Fut'

5 Have you heard of Phil the Fluther, of the town of Ballymuck? / The times were going hard with him, in fact the man was broke; / So he just sent out a notice to his neighbours one and all / As to how he'd like their company that evening at a ball. / And when writin' out he was careful to suggest to them, / That if they found a hat of his convanient to the dure, / The more they put in, whenever he requested them, / The better would the music be for batterin' the flure.

'Phil the Fluther's Ball'

6 With a toot of the flute / And the twiddle of the fiddle, O; / Hoppin' in the middle / Like a herrin' on the griddle, O. / Up down, hands aroun' / Crossin' to the wall / Oh! hadn't we the gaiety at / Phil the Fluther's Ball. Ib.

7 'An' I think there's a slate,' sez she, / 'Off Willie Yeats,' sez she, / 'He should be at home,' sez she, / 'French polishin' a pome,' sez she, / 'An' not writin' letters,' sez she, / 'About his betters,' sez she, / 'Paradin' me crimes,' sez she, / 'in *The Irish Times*,' sez she.

'The Queen's After-Dinner Speech'

**Friel, Brian** *b.* 1929

8 FOX: Not sick so much as desperate; desperate for something that . . . has nothing to do with all this. Restless, Gabby boy, restless. And a man with a restlessness is a savage bugger.

*Crystal and Fox*

9 FOX: Once, maybe twice in your life, the fog lifts, and you get a glimpse, an intuition; and you know that this can't be all there is to it — there has to be something better than this. Ib.

10 FOX: . . . because the whole thing's fixed, my love, fixed — fixed — fixed . . . But who am I to cloud your bright eyes or kill your belief that love is all. A penny a time and you think you'll be happy for life. Ib.

11 COLUMBA: What more do you demand of me, damned Ireland? My soul? My immortal soul? Damned, damned, damned Ireland! — Soft, green Ireland – my lovely green Ireland. O my Ireland. *The Enemy Within*

1 DODDS: The result is that people with a culture of poverty suffer much less repression than we of the middle-class suffer and indeed, if I may make the suggestion with due qualification, they often have a hell of a lot more fun than we have. *The Freedom of the City*

2 SIR: It is here on May 24 some years ago that our story is set, as they say — as if it were a feast laid out for consumption or a trap waiting to spring. *Living Quarters*

3 CASS: The story begins where I say it begins, and I say it begins with me stuck in the gawddam workhouse! *The Loves of Cass Maguire*

4 ANDY: I mean to say, people think that when you're... well, when you're over the forty mark, that you're passified. But aul Hanna, by God, I'll say that for her, she was keen as a terrier in those days. If that couch could write a book — Shakespeare, how are you? 'Losers', *Lovers*

5 May We Write Your Epitaph Now, Mr Emmet? *The Mundy Scheme*, subtitle

6 No one will understand the fun there was; for there *was* fun and there *was* laughing — foolish, silly fun and foolish silly laughing but what it was all about you can't remember can you? Just the memory of – that's all you have now – just the memory; and even now, even so soon, it is being distilled of all its coarseness, and what is left is going to be precious, precious gold. *Philadelphia, Here I Come!*

7 Keep the camera whirrin; for this is a film you'll run over and over again — Madge Going To Bed On My Last Night At Home. Ib.

8 YOLLAND: Poteen – poteen – poteen. Even if I did speak Irish I'd always be an outsider here, wouldn't I? I may learn the password but the language of the tribe will always elude me, won't it. The private core will always be . . . hermetic, won't it? *Translations*

9 HUGH: Wordsworth? . . . no I'm afraid we're not familiar with your literature, Lieutenant. We feel closer to the warm Mediterranean. We tend to overlook your island. Ib.

10 HUGH: Yes, it is a rich language, Lieutenant, full of the mythologies of fantasy and hope and self-deception — a syntax opulent with tomorrows. It is our response to mud cabins and a diet of potatoes; our only method of replying to . . . inevitabilities. Ib.

11 HUGH: . . . it can happen that a civilisation can be imprisoned in a linguistic contour which no longer matches the landscape of . . . fact. Ib.

12 HUGH: . . . it is not the literal past, the 'facts' of history, that shape us, but images of the past embodied in language. Ib.

13 The past did have meaning. It was neither reality nor dreams, neither today's patchy oaks nor the great woods of his boyhood. It was simply continuance, life repeating itself and surviving. 'Among the Ruins'

14 The Sergeant turned and waddled towards the building. For a man of his years and shape, he carried himself with considerable dignity. 'The Saucer of Larks'

**Furlong, Alice** *c.* 1875-?

15 Ah my poor lips freeze / Kissing your gravestone. 'All Souls Night'

**Gallagher, Patrick ('Paddy the Cope')** 1873-1964

1 Wright asked me about all we had done. He found it hard to say co-op and could only say co-co-co until in the end he gave it a name he could say — 'The Cope'. That was the christening. *My Story*

2 The women had hardly a stitch on them from the waists up except a little strap on each shoulder like a pair of braces, to keep a wee bit of cloth half-way up their breasts, I thought I was in a bad house and the sooner I was out the better. Ib.

**Galvin, Patrick** *b.* 1927

3 To-night / With London's ghost / I walk the streets / As easy as November fog / Among the reeds. 'Christ in London'

4 With my little red knife / I raised her up / With my little red knife / I ripped her / And there in the gloom and rolling night / I cut her throat by candlelight / And hurried home to my waiting wife / Who damned my little red knife. 'Little Red Knife'

**Gerson, Justice Luke** *fl.* 1620

5 Ireland is at all poynts like a young wench that hath a greensickness. She is very fayre of visage, and hath a smooth skinn of tender grasse. *Ireland Delineated*

6 She is of a gentle nature. If the anger of heaven be against her she will not bluster or storme, but she will weep many days together. Ib.

**Gibbon, William Monk** *b.* 1896

7 That wrong-headed old man, / Whose phrase was always right. 'On Re-reading Yeats'

8 The world pulls itself up, not with the help of its own bootstraps, but with the help of its enthusiasts. *The Pupil*

9 Love is the discovery of an unsuspected and exceptional value in a particular individual. Ib.

10 Any lyrical element in our lives is red-lettered in memory as though we really belonged to a different, and in one sense, a more real world, like a foreigner in a great city who hears his tongue spoken for the first time for many months by a passing stranger, so all such occasions are endowed with powers of survival for us. Ib.

**Given, Thomas** 1850-1917

11 I ne'er was blessed wae gift o'gab, / Like some great learned men, / Instead o' school, I wove my wab, / Before that I was ten. 'The Weaver Question'

**Gladstone, William Ewart** 1809-1898

1 I cannot trace the line of my own future life, but I hope and pray it may not always be where it is . . . Ireland, Ireland! that cloud in the west, that coming storm, the minister of God's retribution upon cruel and inveterate and but half-atoned injustice.

To Mrs Gladstone, 1845, quoted in Morely, *Life of Gladstone*

2 My mission is to pacify Ireland.

On being asked to form a government, 1 December 1868

3 Only now by a long, slow, and painful process have we arrived at the conclusion that Ireland is to be dealt with in all respects as a free country, and is to be governed like every other free country according to the sentiments of its majority and not of its minority.

To Queen Victoria, explaining the Disestablishment of the Irish Church, January 1869

4 To apply, in all their unmitigated authority, the principles of abstract political economy to the people and circumstances of Ireland, exactly as if he had been proposing to legislate for the inhabitants of Saturn or Jupiter.

On the Land Law (Ireland) Bill, House of Commons, 7 April 1881

5 Ireland stands at your bar expectant, hopeful, almost suppliant. Her words are the words of truth and soberness. She asks a blessed oblivion of the past, and in that oblivion our interest is deeper than even hers. My right Hon. Friend, the Member for East Edinburgh [Mr Goschen] asks us tonight to abide by the traditions of which we are the heirs. What traditions? By the Irish traditions? Go into the length and breadth of the world, ransack the literature of all countries, find, if you can, a single voice, a single book, . . . in which the conduct of England towards Ireland is anywhere treated except with profound and bitter condemnation. Are these the traditions by which we are exhorted to stand? No; they are a sad exception to the glory of our country. They are a broad and black blot upon the pages of its history; and what we want to do is stand by the traditions of which we are the heirs in all matters except our relations with Ireland.

On the first Home Rule Bill, House of Commons, 7 June 1886

**Goethe, Johann Wolfgang von** 1749-1832

6 The Irish seem to me like a pack of hounds, always dragging down some noble stag.

Quoted about Parnell in Yeats, *Autobiographies.* First recorded in *Conversations with Eckermann,* in praise of Wellington's stand against Catholic Emancipation.

**Gogarty, Oliver St John** 1878-1957

7 Golden stockings you had on / In the meadow where you ran; / And your little knees together / Bobbed like pippins in the weather.

'Golden Stockings'

8 Our friends go with us as we go / Down the long path where Beauty wends / Where all we love foregathers, so / Why should we fear to join our friends?

'Non Dolet'

9 Keep you these calm and lovely things, / And float them on your clearest water.

'To the Liffey with the Swans'

10 Next to me I noticed a tall man seated. He wore a suit of navy blue serge. I knew from the way his Adam's apple went up and down that he was tall. His moustache was golden and his blue eyes were looking straight ahead, fixed like

all Irish eyes on futurity. In my best social accent I addressed him. I said, 'It is most extraordinary weather for this time of year.' He replied, 'Ah, it isn't this time of year at all.'

*It Isn't This Time of Year at All*

1 Belfast owes us a mighty grudge for not supporting in Dublin that sink of acidity — Lord Carson. He used the enemies of Ireland as a springboard, and is now safely deposited on the English Woolsack. . . . His spiritual life has been exaggerated by a chronic attack of mental gall-stones.

On Election of Chairman, Seanad Éireann, 12 December 1922

2 I conceive that the Liffey is to the Shannon as a halfpenny dip is to an arc lamp. Shannon Scheme Bill, Seanad Éireann, 31 March 1925

3 Dunlop tyres are made by darkies in Calcutta and Japan. As a matter of fact, we lost that industry here as a penalty for the highly developed aestheticism of Dublin, which objected to the smell when it was proposed to start that industry in Dublin.

Tariff Commission Bill, Seanad Éireann, 14 July 1926

4 As long as there is English spoken in the home, whatever is taught in the morning will be undone in the evening by the parents, and the greatest enthusiast has not suggested the shooting of mothers of English-speaking children. On The Gaeltacht Commission Report, Senate, 10 March 1927

5 I do not know of any greater monstrosity than the Wellington monument. There is no shelter on it for a sparrow.

The Merrion Square (Dublin) Bill, Senate, 9 March 1927

**Goldsmith, Oliver** 1730-1774

6 Sweet Auburn, loveliest village of the plain, / Where health and plenty cheered the labouring swain.

'The Deserted Village'

7 The loud laugh that spoke the vacant mind Ib.

8 A man he was to all the country dear, / And passing rich with forty pounds a year; / Remote from towns he ran his godly race, / Nor e'er had chang'd nor wished to change his place; / Unpractis'd he to fawn, or seek for power, / By doctrines fashion'd to the varying hour. Ib.

9 Truth from his lips prevail'd with double sway, / And fools, who came to scoff, remained to pray. Ib.

10 Amazed the gazing rustics rang'd around, / And still they gaz'd and still the wonder grew, / That one small head could carry all he knew. Ib.

11 Man wants but little here below, / Nor wants that little long.

'Edwin and Angelina' or 'The Hermit'

12 The man recover'd of the bite / The dog it was that died.

'Elegy on the Death of a Mad Dog'

13 On the stage he [Garrick] was natural, simple, affecting. 'Twas only that when he was off he was acting. 'Retaliation'

14 This is Liberty-Hall, gentlemen.

*She Stoops to Conquer*

15 The first blow is half the battle. Ib.

16 The very pink of perfection. Ib.

17 Ye brave Irish lads, hark away to the crack, / Assist me, I pray, in this

woeful attack; / For sure I don't wrong you, you seldom are slack, / When the ladies are calling, to blush and hang back. Epilogue, *She Stoops to Conquer*

1 When lovely woman stoops to folly / And finds too late that men betray, / What charm can soothe her melancholy, / What art can wash her guilt away?

Song, *The Vicar of Wakefield*

2 To begin with Ireland, the most western part of the continent, the natives are peculiarly remarkable for the gaiety and levity of their dispositions; the English, transplanted there, in time lose their serious melancholy air, and become gay and thoughtless, more fond of pleasure and less addicted to reasoning. 'A Comparative View of Races and Nations'

3 Almost every fountain in this country is under the patronage of some saint, where the people once a year meet to show their strength and best clothes, drink muddy ale, dance with their mistresses, get drunk, beat each other with cudgels most unmercifully. These religious meetings are never known to pass without bloodshed and battery, and their priests often put themselves at the head of opposite parties, and gain more renown in cudgel-playing than in piety. 'A Decription of the Manners and Customs of the Native Irish'

4 The manner by which children are brought up in that country [Ireland] is certainly very commendable; for, some time after birth the infant is plunged every day in cold water, which at once gives an elasticity to the solids, and fits perhaps the mind not less than the body for vigour and dispatch.

Life of the Hon. Robert Boyle

**Goold, Thomas** 1766-1846

5 The God of nature never intended that Ireland should be a province, and by God she never will.

Meeting of Irish Bar against Act of Union, 9 December 1799

**Gore-Booth, Eva** 1870-1926

6 The grand road from the mountain goes shining to the sea, / And there is traffic in it and many a horse and cart, / But the little roads of Cloonagh are dearer far to me, / And the little roads of Cloonagh go rambling through my heart. 'The Little Waves of Breffny'

7 But the little waves of Breffny have drenched my heart in spray. Ib.

**Grattan, Henry** 1746-1820

8 I wish for nothing but to breathe, in this our island, in common with our fellow subjects, the air of liberty . . . I never will be satisfied as long as the meanest cottager in Ireland has a link of the British chain clanking to his rags; he may be naked he shall not be in irons . . . I shall move you, 'That the King's most excellent Majesty and the Lords and Commons of Ireland, are the only power competent to make laws to bind Ireland.' Speech in Irish House of Commons, 19 April 1780

9 I found Ireland on her knees, I watched over her with a paternal solicitude; I have traced her progress from injuries to arms, and from arms to liberty.

Speech demanding repeal of laws giving English Parliament power over Ireland, 16 April 1782

10 The curse of Swift is upon him — to have been born an Irishman; to have possessed a genius, and to have used his talents for the good of his country.

On Dr Kirwan, 1792

1 Yet I do not give up the country; I see her in a swoon, but she is not dead. Though in her tomb she lies helpless and motionless, still there is on her lips a spirit of life, and on her cheek a glow of beauty. Speech against Act of Union, 26 May 1800

2 While a plank of the vessel sticks together, I will not leave her. Let the courtier present his flimsy sail, and carry the light bark of his faith with every new breath of wind: I will remain anchored here with fidelity to the fortunes of my country, faithful to her freedom, faithful to her fall. Ib.

**Graves, Arthur Perceval**
1846-1931

3 Of priests we can offer a charmin' variety, / Far renowned for larnin' and piety; / Still, I'd advance ye widout impropriety, / Father O'Flynn as the flower of them all. 'Father O'Flynn'

4 O swan of slenderness, / Dove of tenderness / Jewel of joy arise! / The little red lark / Like a rosy spark / Of song to his sunburst flies.
'The Little Red Lark'

5 Trottin' to the fair, / Me and Moll Maloney, / Sated, I declare / On a single pony, / How am I to know that / Molly's safe behind, / Wid our heads in oh! that / Awk'ard way inclined.
'Riding Double'

**Greacen, Robert** *b.* 1920

6 He got no hero's inch of radio breath / For his was merely — accidental death.
'Death Was Accidental'

7 The Irish faults are not so very new. / We're still that vainly violent, lawless crew. 'Written on the Sense of Isolation in War-time Ireland'

8 Life has long ago taken on a new and satisfying rhythm, even without Irene.
*Even Without Irene*

**Gregory, Lady Isabella Augusta Persse** 1852-1932

9 SERGEANT: The Department of Agriculture is sending round a lecturer in furtherance of the moral development of the rural classes. *(Reads)* 'A lecture will be given this evening in Cloon courthouse, illustrated by magic lantern slides —' Those will not be in it; I am informed they were all broken in the first journey, the railway company taking them to be eggs. The subject of the lecture is 'The Building of Character.' *Hyacinth Halvey*

10 MARY CUSHIN: It is certain it could be no other place. There was surely never in the world such a terrible height of a wall. *The Gaol Gate*

11 MARY CUSHIN: What way will I be in the night time, and none but the dog calling after you? Two women to be mixing a cake, and not a man in the house to break it! Ib.

12 SERGEANT: There's many a thing a man might know and might not have any wish for. *The Rising of the Moon*

13 MAN: . . . You did me a good turn tonight, and I'm obliged to you. Maybe I'll be able to do as much for you when the small rise up and the big fall down . . . when we all change places at the Rising of the Moon. Ib.

14 MAGISTRATE: The smoke from that man's pipe has a greenish look; he may be growing unlicensed tobacco at home. I wish I had brought my telescope to this district. Come to the post-office, I will telegraph for it. I

found it very useful in the Andaman Islands. *Spreading the News*

1 MICHAEL MISKELL: I did well taking out a summons against you that time. It is a great wonder you not to have been bound over through your lifetime, but the laws of England is queer.
*The Workhouse Ward*

2 MIKE MCINERNEY: I'd sooner than ten pound in my hand, I to know that my shadow and my ghost will not be knocking about with your shadow and your ghost, and the both of us waiting our time. I'd sooner be delayed in Purgatory. Ib.

**Gregory, Padraic** 1886-1949?

3 Padric sits in the garden / Inundher the bright new moon / An' from his fidil coaxes / A lovely dreamy tune.
'Padric the Fidiler'

**Griffin, Gerald** 1803-1849

4 Youth must with time decay, / Aileen aroon! / Beauty must fade away, / Aileen aroon! / Castles are sacked in war, / Chieftains are scattered far, / Truth is a fixed star, / Aileen aroon!
'Aileen Aroon!'

5 Men thought it a region of sunshine and rest, / And they called it Hy-Brasail, the isle of the blest. 'Hy-Brasail'

6 I love my love in the morning, / For she like the morning is fair.
'I Love My Love in the Morning'

**Griffith, Arthur** 1871-1922

7 Fly the city, brothers tried, / Join us on the mountain side / Where we've England's power defied, / Twenty men from Dublin town.
'Twenty Men from Dublin Town'

8 All of us know that Irish women are the most virtuous in the world . . . in no country so faithful to the marriage bond.
Review of Synge's *In the Shadow of the Glen*, *United Irishman*, 17 October 1903

9 If the Irish theatre ceases to reflect Irish life and embody Irish aspiration the world will wag its head away from it.
Ib., 31 October 1903

10 We believe that when Swift wrote to the whole people of Ireland 170 years ago that by the law of God, of nature and of nations they had a right to be as free a people as the people of England he wrote commonsense. *United Irishman*, No. 1, 4 March 1899

11 We call upon our countrymen abroad to withdraw all assistance from the promoters of a useless, degrading and demoralising policy until such times as the members of the Irish parliamentary party substitute for it the policy of the Hungarian deputies of 1861, and refusing to attend the British parliament or to recognise its right to legislate for Ireland remain at home to help in promoting Ireland's interests and to aid in guarding its national rights.
Motion at Cumann na nGaedhal convention, 26 October 1902

12 What I have signed I will stand by, in the belief that the end of the conflict of centuries is at hand.
Statement before Dáil debate on Treaty, December 1921

13 It [the Treaty Settlement] has no more finality than we are the final generation on the face of the earth.
Dáil Éireann, 7 January 1922

14 We were sent to make some compromise, bargain or arrangement; we made an arrangement; the arrangement

is not satisfactory to many people. Let them criticise on that point, but do not let them say that we were sent to get one thing and that we got something else.

Ib.

**Guernsey, Wellington** 1817-1885

1 There is a tavern in the town, / And there my true love sits him down, / And drinks his wine 'mid laughter free / And never, never thinks of me. / Fare thee well for I must leave thee / Do not let this parting grieve thee, / And remember that the best of friends must part. / Adieu, adieu, kind friends, adieu, adieu adieu, / I can no longer stay with you. / I'll hang my harp on a weeping willow-tree, / And may the world go well with thee.

'There is a Tavern in the Town'

**Gwynn, Stephen Lucius** 1864-1950

2 They fall, they pass; the nation still moves on with purpose set; / For them that never knew despair, no womanish regret! / But 'tis my grief that Parnell should be lying cold and low / And Michael Davitt underneath the sod in far Mayo.

'Davitt's Grave'

**Hall, Joseph, Bishop of Exeter and Norwich** 1574-1656

1 I have heard of an Irish traitor that when he lay pining on the wheel with his bones broke, asked his friend if he changed his countenance at all, caring less for the pain than the show of fear.

Quoted in Quinn, *The Elizabethans and the Irish*

**Halpine, Charles Graham** 1829-1868

2 You'll see O'Ryan any night / Amid the constellations. *Irish Astronomy*

**Harbinson, Robert** *b.* 1928

3 The mountain was inaccessible because to reach it we had to cross territory held by the Mickeys. Being children of a staunch Protestant quarter, to go near the Catholic idolators was more than we dared for fear of having one of our members cut off. *No Surrender*

4 For one particular crime we could forgive the Mickeys: their hatred of the Bible. All Catholics were under orders, we were told, to burn any scripture they found especially New Testaments.

Ib.

**Hartnett, Michael** *b.* 1941

5 . . . finding English a necessary sin / the perfect language to sell pigs in.

'A Farewell to English'

**Haughey, Charles** *b.* 1925

6 Every T.D., from the youngest or newest in the House, dreams of being Taoiseach. *The Irish Times*, 'This Week They Said', 23 May 1970

**Hazlitt, William** 1778-1830

7 We cannot except the *Irish Melodies* from . . . censure. If these national airs do express the impassioned feeling in his countrymen, the case of Ireland is hopeless. If these prettinesses pass for patriotism, if a country can heave from its heart's core only these vapid, varnished sentiments, lip-deep, and let its tears of blood evaporate in an empty conceit, let it be governed as it has been. There are here no tones to awaken Liberty, to console Humanity. Mr Moore converts the wild harp of Erin into a musical snuff-box.

'The Spirit of the Age'

**Heaney, Seamus** *b.* 1939

8 I push back / through dictions, / Elizabeth canopies, / Norman devices, / the erotic mayflowers / of Provence / and the ivied Latins of churchmen // to the scope's / twang, the iron / flash of consonants / cleaving the line.

'Bone Dreams'

9 Between my finger and my thumb / The squat pen rests. / I'll dig with it.

'Digging'

1 An adept at banter, IUU crossed the lines with carefully enunciated passwords, manned every speech with checkpoints and reported back to nobody. 'England's Difficulty'

2 I am neither internee nor informer; / An inner emigré, grown long-haired / And thoughtful; a wood-kerne // Escaped from the massacre.
'Exposure'

3 But today / It is my father who keeps stumbling / Behind me, and will not go away. 'Follower'

4 All I know is a door into the dark.
'The Forge'

5 I come from scraggy farm and moss, / Old patchworks that the pitch and toss / Of history has left dishevelled.
'A Peacock's Feather'

6 I rhyme / To see myself, to set the darkness echoing. 'Personal Helicon'

7 Until, on Vinegar Hill, the fatal conclave. / Terraced thousands died, shaking scythes at cannon. / The hillside blushed, soaked in our broken wave. / They buried us without shroud or coffin / And in August the barley grew up out of the grave.
'Requiem for the Croppies'

8 And here is love / like a tinsmith's scoop / sunk past its gleam / in the meal-bin. 'Sunlight'

9 Out there in Jutland / In the old man-killing parishes / I will feel lost, / Unhappy and at home.
'The Tollund Man'

10 Is there a life before death? That's chalked up / In Ballymurphy. Competence with pain, / Coherent miseries, a bite and sup, / We hug our little destiny again.
'Whatever You Say, Say Nothing'

11 I began as a poet when my roots were crossed with my reading. I think of the personal and Irish pieties as vowels, and the literary awareness nourished on English as consonants.
*The Irish Times*, 'This Week They Said', 27 May 1972

**Henry VII** 1457-1509

12 Then he [Garret More, Earl of Kildare] is fit to rule all Ireland seeing that all Ireland cannot rule him.
In answer to Bishop of Meath's complaint, 'All Ireland cannot rule yonder gentleman.'
*Book of Howth*

**Hervey, Frederick Augustus, 4th Earl of Bristol** 1730-1803

13 I will jump no more. I have beaten you all, for I have jumped from Cloyne to Derry. On his appointment to diocese of Derry, January 1768. Attrib.

14 Oh Emma, who'd ever be wise, / If madness be loving of thee?
To Lady Hamilton, Naples, 1794

**Hewitt, John** *b.* 1907

15 There was great slaughter then, men, woman, child, / with fire and pillage of our timbered houses; / we had to build in stone for ever after. / That terror dogs us. 'The Colony'

16 We took the kindlier soils. It had been theirs, / this patient, temperate, slow, indifferent, / crop-yielding, crop-denying, in-neglect — / quickly-returning-to-the-nettle-and-bracken, / sodden and friendly land. We took it from them. Ib.

17 This is our fate: eight hundred years' disaster, / crazily tangled like the Book

of Kells: / the dream's distortion and the land's division, / the midnight raiders and the prison cells. / Yet like Lir's children banished to the waters / our hearts still listen for the landward bells. 'An Irishman in Coventry'

1 Once alien here my fathers built their house. 'Once Alien Here'

2 I'll take my stand by the Ulster names, / each clean hard name like a weathered stone; / Tyrella, Rostrevor, are flickering flames: / The names I mean are The Moy, Malone, / Strabane, Slieve Gullion and Portglenone.
'Ulster Names'

**Higgins, Frederick Robert** 1896-1941

3 If I go by many a sloe bush / Or crab tree from Renvyle, / In Kylemore or Clifden / I'll lay my bones a while.
'Dotage'

4 Only last week, walking the hushed fields / Of our most lovely Meath, now thinned by November, / I came to where the road from Laracor leads / To the Boyne river. 'Father and Son'

5 . . . some fine fish-women / In the best shawls of the Coombe.
'The Old Jockey'

6 They've paid the last respects in sad tobacco / And silent is this wakehouse in its haze.
'Padraic O'Conaire, Gaelic Storyteller'

**Hinkson, Katherine Tynan** 1861-1931

7 All in the April evening, / April airs were abroad, / I saw the sheep with their lambs / And thought on the Lamb of God. 'Sheep and Lambs'

**Hobson, Bulmer** 1883-1969

8 He [Pearse] had evolved a strange theory that it was necessary that there should be a blood sacrifice in every generation. He had visions of himself as the scapegoat for the people.
*Ireland, Yesterday, Today and Tomorrow*

9 Let England fight her own battles — we have done so long enough.
Anti-Enlistment leaflet, 1905

**Hogan, Michael** 1832-1899

10 At half-past one the town was silent, / Except a row raised in the Island, / Where Thady, foe to sober thinking, / With comrade lads, sat gaily drinking. / A table and a pack of cards / Stood in the midst of four blackguards.
'Drunken Thady'
*Lays and Legends of Lomond*

**Holloway, Joseph** 1861-1944

11 On coming out, Lady Gregory asked me, 'What was the cause of the disturbances' [The Playboy Riot]. And my monosyllabic answer was, 'Blackguardism!' To which she queried, 'On which side?' 'The stage!' came from me pat, and then I passed on and the incident was closed.
*Impressions of a Dublin Playgoer*, 26 January 1907

12 John Burke remarked, 'Last year it was all Sean O'Casey: now it is all shun O'Casey.' Ib. 30 August 1926

**Hope, James (Jemmy)** 1746-1846

13 I was not qualified for public speaking. My mind was like Swift's church: the more that was inside the slower the mass came out. Attrib.

14 The organisation of the north being thus deranged, the colonels flinched and the chief of the Antrim men Robert Simms not appearing, the duty fell on Henry J. McCracken. Attrib.

**Hopkins, Gerard Manley** 1844-1889

1 Tomorrow I shall have been three years in Ireland, three hard wearying years . . .' In those I have done God's will (in the main) and many many examination papers. Letter to Robert Bridges, 1887

**Howard-Jones, Stuart** 1904-1974

2 Then hear sung, MARVELL, by a wiser Muse, / This land of Popes and Pigs and Booze, / For *Lycidas* (and MILTON makes it plain) / Preferred to drown than visit it again. 'Hibernia'

**Humbert, General Jean Joseph** 1755-1823

3 Union! Liberty! the Irish Republic! — such is your shout. Let us march. Our hearts are devoted to you; our glory is in your happiness.

Proclamation at Ballina, 23 August 1798

**Hume, John** *b.* 1937

4 The truth is that Ulster Unionists are not loyal to the crown, but the half-crown. *The Irish Times*, 'This Week They Said', 23 August 1969

**Hutchinson, Pearse** *b.* 1927

5 Under the conical menace of a Gothic mountain, / in these green fields I pray against barbed wire / and never forget to take my pills. 'Connemara'

**Hyde, Douglas**
**(An Craoibhín Aoibhinn)** 1860-1949

6 Tamall beag roimh 1880 do cuireadh an Bord Oideachais ar a dtugadh an Bord Idirmheánach, ar bun. Ní bhéadh aon áit do'n Ghaeilge ar an mBord san acht gur bhain mo chara agus mo chomharsa féin, Ó Conchubhair Donn, áit amach dí, nuair bhí an bille ag dul tríd an bParlaiméid i Sacsana. Tugadh cead do'n Bhord scrúdú do bheith aca do mhacaibh léinn, i Laidin i nGréigis agus i bhFrainncis, 'agus i gCeiltis' arsa Ó Conchubhair Donn do bhí 'na fheisire an uair sin. 'Sea!' ar siad, agus iad go léir tuirseach de'n obair, 'sea! i gCeiltis, leis.' Focal deas séimh é 'Ceiltis', focal nach scannróchadh duine ar bith. Dá n-abradh sé Gaeilge, ní dóigh go n-éireóchadh leis. Acht níl aon Cheiltis eile i nÉirinn acht Gaeilge, ar an ábhar sin b'ionann Ceiltis agus Gaeilge, rud nár léir do'n Pharlaiméid is dóigh, i láthair na huaire sin!

*Mise agus an Connradh*

*Shortly before 1880 a Board of Education, which was called the Intermediate Board, was set up. That Board would have had no place for Irish if my friend and neighbour, the O Conor Don, had not obtained a place for the language when the bill was going through the English Parliament. The Board was permitted to examine students in Latin, Greek, and French, 'and in Celtic', said the O Conor Don, who was an MP at the time. 'All right,' they said, fed up with the whole business, 'all right, in Celtic too.' 'Celtic' was a nice respectable word that wouldn't have frightened any one. If he had said 'Irish', I doubt if he would have succeeded. But the only form of Celtic in Ireland is Irish, so Celtic and Irish were identical, a fact of which the Parliament was presumably unaware at that time.*

*The League and I*

7 It has always been very curious to me how Irish sentiment sticks in this half-way house — how it continues to apparently hate the English and at the same time continues to imitate them.

'On the necessity for de-Anglicising the Irish People'. Lecture in Leinster Hall, Molesworth Street, Dublin, 25 November 1892

8 I appeal to every one whatever his politics – for this is no political matter – to do his best to help the Irish race to

develop in future upon Irish lines, even at the risk of encouraging national aspirations, because upon Irish lines alone can the Irish race once more become what it was of yore — one of the most original, artistic, literary, and charming people of Europe. Ib.

1 My ambition had always been to use the language as a neutral field upon which all Irishmen could meet . . . So long as we remained non-political, there was no end to what we could do.

Address at Árd-Fheis, Dundalk, 1915

2 Ó áit go háit ba bhreá mo shiúl / Is dob ard mo léim ar bharr an tsléibh'; / I loing is i mbád ba mhór mo dhúil / Is ba bheo mo chroí i lár mo chléibh. / Mar chois an ghiorria, do bhí mo chos, / Mar iarann gach alt is féith, / Bhí an sonas romham thall is abhus / Ins an ngleann nar tógadh mé.

'An Gleann Nar Tógadh Mé'

*My walk was fine from place to place, / My jump was high on the top of the hill. / I had a great fondness for ships and boats / My heart was lively in my breast, / My feet as fleet as those of the hare, / Every muscle and joint like iron, / Good fortune confronted me everywhere / In the glen where I was reared.*

*'My Native Glen'*

# I

**Ingram, John Kells** 1823-1907

1 Who fears to speak of Ninety-Eight? / Who blushes at the name? / When cowards mock the patriot's fate / Who hangs his head for shame? / He's all a knave or half a slave / Who slights his country thus: / But a true man, like you, man, / Will fill your glass with us.
'The Memory of the Dead'

**Ireland, Denis** 1894-1980

2 The Irish Treaty is in the air. The real struggle is not between England and Ireland, but between two ways of looking at life, and what secretly enrages the Englishman is that he knows in his heart that our philosophy will prove indestructible, for the excellent reason that it takes little account of externals.
*From the Irish Shore*

3 It was a typical 'Ulster' conversation, with gaps and deliberate omissions reaching right back to the Boyne and the Penal Laws. Better keep your mouth shut and no harm done.
*From the Jungle of Belfast*

**Iremonger, Valentin** *b.* 1918

4 But star-chaser, big-time-going, chancer Icarus / Like a dog on the sea lay and the girls forgot him / And Daedalus, too busy hammering another job, / Remembered him only in pubs. 'Icarus'

5 Elizabeth frigidly stretched, / On a spring day surprised us / With her starched dignity and the quietness / Of her hands, clasping a black cross.
'This Houre Her Vigill'

**Irvine, Alexander** 1863-1941

6 Religion in our town had arrayed the inhabitants into two hostile camps. She never had any sympathy with the fight . . . She pointed out to the fanatics around her that the basis of religion was love and that religion that expressed itself in faction fights must have hate at the bottom of it.
*My Lady of the Chimney Corner*

7 'See them ants.' 'Aye.' 'Now if Withero thought thim ants hated aych other like the men o' Antrim d'ye know what I'd do?' 'What?' 'I'd pour a kittle of boilin' wather on thim an' roast th' hides off ivery mother's son ov thim. Aye, that's what I'd do, shure as a gun's iron!' Ib.

8 'Me an' Jamie wor pirta sack people, purty d - d rough, too, but yer Ma was a piece ov fine linen from th' day she walked down this road wi' yer Dah.'
Ib.

9 Nobody but an Ulsterman can understand the Ulster mind and an Ulsterman is never more than half convinced that he knows himself. *The Souls of Poor Folk*

**James, Henry** 1843-1916

1 I was deeply moved by the tragic shabbiness of this sinister country.

On visiting Dublin, March 1895, quoted in Leon Edel *The Life of Henry James*

**Johnson, Dr* Samuel** 1709-1784

(*Conferred by Trinity College, Dublin)

2 Dublin, though a place much worse than London, is not as bad as Iceland.

Letter to Mrs Christopher Smart, 1791

3 The Irish are a fair people;—they never speak well of one another.

Boswell, *Life of Johnson*, 1775

4 Boswell: Is not the Giant's Causeway worth seeing? Johnson: Worth seeing? yes; but not worth going to see.

Ib., 12 October 1779

**Johnson, Thomas** 1872-1963

5 I am not a lawyer, and the ways of lawyers are like the ways of the Heathen Chinese, peculiar and dark.

On Current Postal Strike, Dáil Éireann, 13 September 1922

**Johnston, Jennifer Prudence** *b.* 1930

6 The angel of death would be unlikely to arrive with socks to darn.

*The Captains and the Kings*

7 Cathleen wept her thousand welcomes and farewells. Her cold tears splattered the airport runways, and the quaysides of Dublin, Galway and Belfast.

*The Gates*

8 About a hundred and fifty years earlier, a MacMahon had tipped his hat to the King of England, turned his back on Rome and his fellow countrymen, and had been granted gracious permission to build himself a mansion house in the grand style, on what had been for many hundreds of years, his own land. Ib.

9 'The Irish breed like rabbits,' Mrs MacMahon had said once to some London friends. 'I'm told, indeed, when there's no food in the house they boil the baby.' Ib.

10 Our first casualty was some poor fool who cut his wrists before we even landed in England.

*How Many Miles to Babylon?*

11 We were ordered not to eat pork when we got up near the front, as the pigs that remained alive, not many I may say, fed and grew temptingly fat on human flesh. Ib.

12 Because I'm an officer and a gentleman they have not taken away my bootlaces or my pen, so I sit and wait and write. Ib.

**Johnston, William Denis** 1901-1984

1 It means that Good is not worth while — that Evil is our only means of self-preservation, that like the Vampire, Dracula, he has bitten me upon the throat, and I must die or be a monster too! 'Buchenwald', *The Bell,* March 1951

2 Strumpet City in the Sunset . . . / Wilful city of savage dreamers / So old, so rich with memories! *The Old Lady Says 'No!'*

**Joyce, James Augustine** 1882-1941

3 Yes, the newspapers were right; snow was general all over Ireland. It was falling on every part of the dark central plain, on the treeless hills, falling softly upon the Bog of Allen and, farther westward, softly falling into the dark mutinous Shannon waves. It was falling, too, upon every part of the lonely churchyard on the hill where Michael Furey lay buried. It lay thickly drifted on the crooked crosses and headstones, on the spears of the little gate, on the barren thorns. His soul swooned slowly as he heard the snow falling faintly through the universe and faintly falling, like the descent of their last end, upon all the living and the dead.

'The Dead', *Dubliners*

4 The grey warm evening of August had descended upon the city, and a mild warm air, a memory of summer, circulated in the streets. The streets, shuttered for the repose of Sunday, swarmed with a gaily coloured crowd. Like illumined pearls the lamps shone from the summits of their tall poles upon the living texture below, which, changing shape and hue increasingly, sent up into the warm grey evening air an unchanging, unceasing murmur.

'Two Gallants', Ib.

5 riverrun, past Eve and Adam's, from swerve of shore to bend of bay, brings us by a commodious vicus of recirculation back to Howth Castle and Environs. *Finnegans Wake*

6 O
tell me all about
Anna Livia! I want to hear all
about Anna Livia. Well, you know
Anna Livia? Yes, of course, we all know
Anna Livia. Tell me all. Tell me now.
You'll die when you hear. Ib.

7 ROBERT *(rapidly):* Those are moments of sheer madness when we feel an intense passion for a woman. We see nothing. We think of nothing. Only to possess her. Call it brutal, bestial, what you will.

RICHARD *(a little timidly):* I am afraid that that longing to possess a woman is not love.

ROBERT *(impatiently):* No man ever yet lived on this earth who did not long to possess – I mean possess in the flesh – the woman whom he loves. It is nature's law.

RICHARD *(contemptuously):* What is that to me? Did I vote it? *Exiles*

8 This lovely land that always sent / Her writers and artists to banishment / And in the spirit of Irish fun / Betrayed her own leaders, one by one.

'Gas from a Burner'

9 O Ireland my first and only love / Where Christ and Caesar are hand in glove! Ib.

10 But all these men of whom I speak / Make me the sewer of their clique. / That they may dream their dreamy dreams / I carry off their filthy streams. For I can do those things for them / Through which I lost my diadem, / Those things for which Grandmother Church / Left me severely in the lurch.

/ Thus I relieve their timid arses, / Perform my office of Katharsis.
'The Holy Office'

1 Stephen Dedalus is my name, / Ireland is my nation. / Clongowes is my dwellingplace / And heaven my expectation. *A Portrait of the Artist as a Young Man*

2 He turned over the flyleaf and looked wearily at the green round earth in the middle of the maroon clouds. He wondered which was right, to be for the green or for the maroon, because Dante had ripped the green velvet back off the brush that was for Parnell one day with her scissors and told him that Parnell was a bad man. He wondered if they were arguing at home about that. That was called politics. Ib.

3 Do you know what Ireland is? asked Stephen with cold violence. Ireland is the old sow that eats her farrow. Ib.

4 I will not serve that in which I no longer believe, whether it call itself my home, my fatherland, or my church: and I will try to express myself in some mode of life or art as freely as I can and as wholly as I can, using for my defence the only arms I allow myself to use — silence, exile, and cunning. Ib.

5 I go to encounter for the millionth time the reality of experience and to forge in the smithy of my soul the uncreated conscience of my race. Old father, old artificer, stand me now and ever in good stead. Ib.

6 Rain on Rahoon falls softly, softly falling, / Where my dark lover lies. / Sad is his voice that calls me, sadly calling, / At grey moonrise.
'She Weeps Over Rahoon'

7 It seems to me you do not care what banality a man expresses so long as he expresses it in Irish. *Stephen Hero*

8 —Hell today. —And what kind of sermon was it? —Usual kind of thing. Stink in the morning and pain of loss in the evening. Ib.

9 Stately, plump Buck Mulligan came from the stairhead, bearing a bowl of lather on which a mirror and a razor lay crossed. A yellow dressing-gown, ungirdled, was sustained gently behind him by the mild morning air. He held the bowl aloft and intoned:
*—Introibo ad altare Dei.* *Ulysses*

10 —It is a symbol of Irish art. The cracked lookingglass of a servant. Ib.

11 Ineluctable modality of the visible: at least that if no more, thought through my eyes. Ib.

12 Mr Leopold Bloom ate with relish the inner organs of beasts and fowls. He liked thick giblet soup, nutty gizzards, a stuffed roast heart, liver slices fried with crustcrumbs, fried hencod's roes. Most of all he liked grilled mutton kidneys which gave to his palate a fine tang of finely scented urine. Ib.

13 Agenbite of inwit. Ib.

14 Buck Mulligan thought, puzzled: — Shakespeare? he said. I seem to know the name. A flying sunny smile rayed in his loose features. —To be sure, he said, remembering brightly. The chap that writes like Synge. Ib.

15 He crossed under Tommy Moore's roguish finger. They did right to put him over a urinal: meeting of the waters. Ought to be places for women. Running into cakeshops. Settle my hat

straight. *There is not in this wide world a vallee.* Great song of Julia Morkan's. Kept her voice up to the very last. Pupil of Michael Balfe's wasn't she? Ib.

1 . . . and how he kissed me under the Moorish wall and I thought well as well him as another and then I asked him with my eyes to ask again yes and then he asked me would I yes to say yes my mountain flower and first I put my arms around him yes and drew him down to me so he could feel my breasts all perfume yes and his heart was going like mad and yes I said yes I will yes. Ib.

**Joyce, Robert Dwyer** 1830-1883

2 We are the boys of Wexford / Who fought with heart and hand / To break in twain the galling chain / And free our native land. 'The Boys of Wexford'

3 He hammered and sang with tiny voice, / And sipped his mountain dew; / Oh! I laughed to think he was caught at last, / But the fairy was laughing, too. 'The Leprechaun'

4 And round her grave I wander drear / Noon, night, and morning early, / With breaking heart whene'er I hear / 'The wind that shakes the barley.' 'The Wind that shakes the Barley'

# K

**Kavanagh, Patrick** 1904-1967

1 Cassiopeia was over / Cassidy's hanging hill. 'A Christmas Childhood'

2 . . . I made the Iliad from such / A local row. Gods make their own importance. 'Epic'

3 . . . the undying difference in the corner of a field. 'Father Mat'

4 Clay is the word and clay is the flesh. 'The Great Hunger'

5 And he is not so sure now if his mother was right / When she praised the man who made a field for his bride. Ib.

6 Sitting on a wooden gate / Sitting on a wooden gate / Sitting on a wooden gate / He didn't care a damn. Ib.

7 He stands in the doorway of his house / A ragged sculpture of the wind, / October creaks the rotted mattress, / The bedposts fall. No hope. No lust. / The hungry fiend / Screams the apocalypse of clay / In every corner of this land. Ib.

8 O commemorate me where there is water. 'Lines Written on a Seat . . .'

9 My soul was an old horse / Offered for sale in twenty fairs. 'Pegasus'

10 My black hills have never seen the sun rising / Eternally they look north towards Armagh. 'Shancoduff'

11 My hills hoard the bright shillings of March. Ib.

12 O stony grey soil of Monaghan / The laugh from my love you thieved. 'Stony Grey Soil'

13 The barrels of blue potato-spray / Stood on a headland of July / Beside an orchard wall where roses / Were young girls hanging from the sky. 'Spraying the Potatoes'

14 I mistook Gogarty's white-robed maid for his wife — or his mistress. I expected every poet to have a spare wife. *The Green Fool*

15 I returned to Ireland. Ireland green and chaste and foolish. And when I wandered over my own hills and talked again to my own people I looked into the heart of this life and saw that it was good. Ib.

16 It wasn't the men from Shercock / Or the men from Ballybay, / But the dalin' men from Crossmaglen / Put whiskey in me tay. Quoted in *The Green Fool*

1 He [Tarry] loved virtuous girls, and that was one of the things he admired the Catholic religion for — because it kept girls virtuous until such time as he'd meet them. *Tarry Flynn*

2 He sat very still not wishing to annoy his mother, for he knew that she would be annoyed at his going upstairs to what she called 'the curse-o'-God rhyming'. Ib.

**Kavanagh, Seamus**

3 Flow on lovely river, flow gently along, / By your waters so clear sounds the lark's merry song, / On your green banks I'll wander where first I did join / With you, lovely Molly, the Rose of Mooncoin. 'The Rose of Mooncoin'

4 I'm a buxom fine widow, I live in a spot, / In Dublin they call it the Coombe; / My shops and my stalls are laid out on the streets, / And my palace consists of one room. / I sell apples and oranges, nuts and split peas, / Bananas and sugar-stick sweet, / On a Saturday night I sell second-hand clothes / From the floor of my stall on the street. 'Biddy Mulligan'

5 At Patrick Street corner for sixty-four years, / I've stood and no one can deny, / That while I stood there, no person could dare / To say black was the white of my eye. Ib.

**Kearney, Peadar** 1883-1942

6 Soldiers are we, whose lives are pledged to Ireland. 'A Soldier's Song'

7 The South Down Militia / Is the terrors of the land! 'The South Down Militia'

8 So all around my hat I wear a three-coloured ribbon, / All around my hat until death comes to me, / And if anybody's asking why I'm wearing that ribbon, / It's all for my true love I ne'er more shall see. 'The Three-Coloured Ribbon'

9 I sing you a song of peace and love, / Whack fol the diddle lol the di do day / To the land that reigns all lands above, / Whack . . . / May peace and plenty be her share / Who kept our homes from want and care, / Oh God bless England is our prayer / Whack . . . 'Whack Fol the Diddle'

10 Oh Irishmen forget the past / Whack . . . / And think of the day that is coming fast, / Whack . . . / When we shall all be civilized / Neat and clean and well advised / Oh won't Mother England be surprised! / Whack . . . Ib.

**Keegan, John** 1809-1849

11 I start in my sleep, and I weep when I'm waking. / Oh, I long for the blush of eternity's dawn, / When again I shall meet my own Bouchaleen bawn! 'Bouchaleen Bawn'

**Kelly, John Maurice** *b.* 1931

12 If tomorrow we found ourselves in the charge of a junta of colonels up from the Curragh, how many people would take to the barricades in defence of the Dáil? *The Irish Times*, 'This Week They Said', 12 June 1971

**Kelly, Maeve** *b.* 1930

13 There was no place more fitting for a false god than the brassy temples of American eating houses. He would go back where he belonged. 'A False God', *A Life of Her Own*

**Kelly, Michael** 1764-1826

14 It certainly was not in nature that I should stutter all through the part and when I came to the *sestetto*, speak plain,

and after that piece of music was over return to stuttering.

Riposte to Mozart's instructions for First Night of *La Nozze de Figaro*, 1 May 1786, in *Reminiscences*

**Keneally, William** 19th Century

1 I watched last night the rising moon, / Upon a foreign strand, / Till mem'ries came like flowers of June, / Of home and fatherland; / I dreamt I was a child once more / Beside the rippling rill, / When first I saw, in days of yore, / The moon behind the hill.

'The Moon behind the Hill'

**Kenealy, Edward Vaughan** 1819-1880

2 What is an Irishman but a mere machine for converting potatoes into human nature? *Table-Talk*

**Kennelly, Brendan** *b.* 1936

3 . . . morning steps like a laughing girl / Down from the Dublin hills.

'Getting Up Early'

4 My dark fathers lived the intolerable day / Committed always to the night of wrong. 'My Dark Fathers'

5 The green plant withered by an evil chance. Ib.

6 And yet upon the sandy Kerry shore / The woman once had danced at ebbing tide / Because she loved flute music. Ib.

**Kenney, James** 1780-1849

7 The summer bloom will fade away, / And will no more be seen; / These flowers, that look so fresh and gay, / Will not be ever green — / For the green leaves all turn yellow.

'The Green Leaves All Turn Yellow'

**Kettle, Thomas** 1880-1916

8 My only programme for Ireland consists, in equal parts, of Home Rule and the Ten Commandments. My only counsel to Ireland is, that in order to become deeply Irish, she must become European. 'Apology'

9 William Murphy is a humane man, known for his personal honour and charity; a 'good employer' as it is called, a successful captain of enterprise, an insensitive imagination, in short, a very dangerous opponent.

'Labour and Civilization'

10 Picturesque, eloquent, prophetic, at once dictatorial and intimate, he [James Larkin] was, as he might say himself, the very man for the job. Ib.

11 The Dublin worker is not a natural revolutionary, but he is a natural soldier. Ib.

12 It is with ideas as with umbrellas, if left lying about they are peculiarly liable to change of ownership.

Quoted in his wife's *Memoir*

13 It [the RIC] was formerly an army of occupation. Now, owing to the all but complete disappearance of crime, it is an army of no occupation. Ib.

14 Life is a cheap *table d'hôte* in a rather dirty restaurant, with time changing the plates before you've had enough of anything. Ib.

15 The Catholics take their beliefs *table d'hôte* and the Protestants theirs *à la carte*. Ib.

16 Ireland is a small but insuppressible island half an hour nearer the sunset than Great Britain.

'On Crossing the Irish Sea'

17 Ireland has been finally conquered at least three times; she has died in the last

ditch repeatedly; she has been a convict in the dock, a corpse on the dissecting-table, a street-dog yapping at the heels of Empire, a geographical expression, a misty memory. And with an obtuseness to the logic of facts which one can only call mulish, she still answers, 'Adsum.'
Ib.

1 Know that we fools, now with the foolish dead, / Died not for the flag, nor King, nor Emperor, / But for a dream, born in a herdsman's shed, / And for the secret Scripture of the poor.
'To My Daughter Betty, the Gift of God'

**Kierkegaard, Søren Aabye** 1813-1855

2 If I did not know that I was a true Dane, I might almost be tempted to suppose I was an Irishman in order to explain the contradictions at work within me. For the Irish have not the heart to baptize their children completely, they want to preserve just a little paganism and whereas a child is normally completely immersed, they keep his right arm out of the water so that in after life he can grasp a sword and hold a girl in his arm.
(Trans. Alexander Dru) *Journal*, 1840

**Kilroy, Thomas** *b.* 1934

3 But when the riots stopped business came back better than ever. That was when they knew they had beaten him, when they saw the circulation of money come back over the counters, like blood, while he withered away in the dilapidated Presbytery. They saw their new prosperity like a sign from the Almighty. *The Big Chapel*

4 Georgian! Balls to you and your Georgian! Where were the likes of you and me, Kelly, when they were building your Georgian?
*The Death and Resurrection of Mr Roche*

5 I don't go back at all now. Y'know I used to like going back at Christmas. Walking to the parish church for Midnight Mass with white frost on the road and ice in the drains. They liked that, the young brothers. The cut of my suit. My white shirt. It was a sort of white Christmas, if you see what I mean. All clean collars and long, white candles. Ib.

**Kinsella, Thomas** *b.* 1928

6 Around the corner, in an open square, / I came upon the sombre monuments / That bear their names: MacDonagh and McBride, / Merchants; Connolly's Commercial Arms. 'A Country Walk'

7 The phantoms of the overhanging sky / Occupied their stations and descended; / Another moment, to the starlit eye, The slow, downstreaming dead, it seemed, were blended / One with those silver hordes, and briefly shared / Their order, glittering. And varied barrenness as toward its base / We glided – blotting heaven as it towered – Searching the darkness for a landing place. 'Downstream'

8 Now plainly in the mirror of my soul / I read that I have looked my last on youth / And little more; for they are not made whole / That reach the age of Christ. 'Mirror in February'

9 In slow distaste / I fold my towel with what grace I can, / Not young and not renewable, but man. Ib.

10 I only know things seem and are not good. 'Nightwalker'

11 I scoop at the earth, and sense famine, a first / Sourness in the clay. The roots tear softly. 'Ritual of Departure'

**Kipling, Rudyard** 1865-1936

1 Old Days! The wild geese are flighting, / Head to the storm as they faced it before! / For where there are Irish there's loving and fighting, / And when we stop either, it's Ireland no more.

'The Irish Guards'

2 What answer from the North? / One law, one land, one throne. / If England drive us forth, / We shall not fall alone.

'Ulster', 9 April 1912

**Kohl, Johann Georg** 1808-1878

3 It seems as if there were something peculiar in the nature and condition of Ireland that prevents her wounds from ever healing; she is constantly bleeding from a thousand wounds and sores; and though still clinging to life with too much tenacity entirely to die away, she never at any moment possesses energy enough completely to achieve her freedom, or restore herself to a more healthy state of existence.

1842, quoted in Maxwell, *The Stranger in Ireland*

# L

**Lalor, James Fintan** 1807-1849

1 The land question contains and the legislative does *not* contain the materials from which victory is manufactured. Letter, *Irish Felon*, 24 June 1848

2 And such a question there is in the land — ages have been preparing it. An engine ready-made, one that will generate its own steam without cost or care – a self-acting engine, if once the fire be kindled. . . . Repeal had always to be dragged. This I speak of will carry itself — as the cannon ball carries itself down the hill. Ib.

3 The principle I state, and mean to stand upon, is this, that the entire ownership of Ireland, moral and material, up to the sun, and down to the centre, is vested of right in the people of Ireland. Ib.

4 Who strikes the first blow for Ireland? Who draws first blood for Ireland? Who wins a wreath that will be green for ever? *Irish Felon*, 22 July 1848

**Lambert, Nannie** late 18th Century

5 What is a gentleman? It is a thing / Decked with a scarf-pin, a chain, and a ring, / Dressed in a suit of immaculate style, / Sporting an eye-glass, a lisp, and a smile. 'What is a Gentleman?'

**Landor, Walter Savage** 1775-1864

6 Ireland never was contented . . . / Say you so? You are demented. / Ireland was contented when / All could use the sword and pen, / And when Tara rose so high / That her turrets split the sky, / And about her courts were seen / Liveried angels robed in green, / Wearing by St Patrick's bounty, / Emeralds big as half the county. 'The Last Fruit Off an Old Tree'

**Lane, Denny** 1818-1896

7 On Carrigdhoun the heath is brown, / The clouds are dark o'er Ardnalee, / And many a stream comes rushing down / To swell the angry Ownabwee. 'Lament of the Irish Maiden'

**Larkin, James** 1876-1947

8 We are going to make this a year to be spoken of in the days to come . . . . There is a great dawn for Ireland. Speech, May 1913

9 This is not a strike, it is a lock-out of the men who have been tyrannically treated by a most unscrupulous scoundrel . . . . By the living God, if they want war, they can have it. Speech, 26 August 1913

10 I am going to O'Connell Street on Sunday. I am going there alive or dead,

and I depend on you to carry me out if I'm dead. Speech at burning of police notice banning meeting at Liberty Hall, 29 August 1913

**Larminie, William** 1850-1899

1 Who were the builders? Question not the silence / That settles on the lake for evermore. 'The Nameless Doon'

2 Someone murdered / We know, we guess; and gazing upon thee, / And, filled by the long silence of reply, / We guess some garnered sheaf of tragedy. Ib.

**Lavery, Sir John** 1856-1941

3 I have felt ashamed of having spent my life trying to please sitters and make friends instead of telling the truth and making enemies. *Autobiography*

**Lavin, Mary** *b.* 1912

4 '. . . isn't it strange that a love that was unrealized should have given such joy?' he said quietly. 'Yes, yes,' she said gratefully. Then she closed the door behind them. 'And such pain.' 'The Cuckoo-Spit'

5 Like a rock in the sea, she was islanded by fields, the heavy grass washing about the house, and the cattle wading in it as in water. 'In the Middle of the Fields'

6 That dunghill isn't doing anyone any harm, and it's not going out of where it is as long as I'm in this house. 'Lilacs'

7 Under a weight of bitterness too great to be borne his face was pressed into the wet leaves, and when he gulped for breath, the rotted leaves were sucked into his mouth. 'A Memory'

**Lawless, Hon. Emily** 1845-1913

8 See us, cold isle of our love! / Coldest, saddest of isles — / Cold as the hopes of our youth, / Cold as your own wan smiles. 'Clare Coast — Circa 1720'

9 There's famine in the land, its grip is tightening still! / There's trouble, black and bitter, on every side I glance, / There are dead upon the roadside, and dead upon the hill, / But my Jamie's safe and well away in France. 'An Exile's Mother'

10 Wave follows wave into the same old sea. 'To —— Aged 22'

**Ledwidge, Francis** 1891-1917

11 'But in the lonely hush of eve / Weeping I grieve the silent bills.' / I heard the Poor Old Woman say / In Derry of the little hills. 'Lament for the Poets: 1916'

12 He shall not hear the bittern cry / In the wild sky, where he is lain, / Nor voices of the sweeter birds / Above the wailing of the rain. 'Lament for Thomas MacDonagh'

13 And then three syllables of melody / Dropped from a blackbird's flute, and died apart. 'A Twilight in Middle March'

**Le Fanu, Joseph Sheridan** 1814-1873

14 Her soft cheek was glowing against mine. 'Darling, darling,' she murmured. 'I live in you; and you would die for me, I love you so.' 'Carmilla'

15 And all the girls liked him, for he could spake civil / And sweet when he chose it, for he was the divil, / And there wasn't a girl from thirty-five undher, / Divil a matter how crass, but he could come round her. 'Phaudrig Crohoore'

16 Your swords they may glitter, your carbines go bang, / But if you want hangin', but if you want hangin' it's yourself you must hang. / To-night he

is sleeping in Aherloe Glin / An' the divil's in the dice if you catch him again.
'Shamus O'Brien'

**Le Fanu, William Robert** 1816-1894

1 After a stay of about three weeks in Ireland, the king embarked for England at Dunleary, then little more than a fishing village, but now, under its new name, 'Kingstown' which George IV then gave it, one of the most flourishing towns in Ireland.
*Seventy Years of Irish Life*

2 . . . if nothing untoward arises to retard its prosperity, if (is the hope too sanguine?) Ireland can cease to be 'the battlefield of English parties', it will, I trust ere many years, be as happy and contented as any part of our good Queen's dominions. Ib.

**Leitch, Maurice** *b.*1933

3 I began to think about Catholics, not about Catholics I know because I don't really know any, but about them in general. Anything I found out about them has been second-hand, because, living in a community like this, one where the proportions are seventy-five for us, twenty-five for *them* (an inflammable mixture), division starts early – separate housing-estates, then separate schools, separate jobs, separate dances, separate pubs . . . a people with a past and no interest in the present.
*The Liberty Lad*

4 The Protestant ruling majority. An ugly race. In-breeding? No poet will ever sing for them — of them.
*Poor Lazarus*

**Lemass, Sean Francis** 1899-1971

5 We ask Deputies in this House . . . to co-operate with us in abolishing the memory of past dissensions, in wiping out the recollection of the hatred, the bitterness and the jealousies that were created in this country after the Civil War. Maiden speech, Dáil Éireann, 11 October 1927

6 The historic task of this generation is to secure the economic foundation of independence.
Dáil Éireann, 3 June 1959

7 Unity has got to be thought of as a spiritual development which will be brought about by peaceful, persuasive means. 'Sean Lemass looks back', *The Irish Press*, 28 January 1969

**Lenehan, Joseph R.** *b.*1916

8 If we enter the Common Market in two years there will not be a snail on our walls, a frog in our pools or a fish in our bays. *The Irish Times*, 'This Week They Said', 10 July 1971

**Leonard, Hugh (John Keyes Byrne)** *b.* 1926

9 All I ever seemed to get was the kind of girl who had a special dispensation from Rome to wear the thickest part of her legs below the knees. *Da*

10 When you can see the Mountains of Mourne, that's a sure sign it'll rain. Yis, the angels'll be having a pee. Ib.

11 My grandmother made dying her life's work. *Home Before Night*

12 [His da] looked at Jack on the edge of the big double bed, and said: 'Do you know what I'm going to tell you? The Kerry Blue and the alsatian is treacherous animals.' Ib.

13 The climate is temperate, the birthrate relentless and the mortal . . . the mortality rate is consistent with the national average. *A Life*

1 'And see undrugged in evening light the decent inn of death.' It isn't a decent inn, Mary. When you get up close it's a kip. Ib.

**Leslie, Sir Shane** 1885-1971

2 In the Middle Ages it was claimed to mark the meeting of three dioceses, Derry, Raphoe, Clogher.
'St Patrick's Purgatory'

3 St Joseph, St Peter, St Paul / Encounter the rain that it stops: / St Patrick whatever befall / Keep an eye on the state of the crops. / St Andrew, St John, and St James, / Preserve us from deluge and floods: / If the Fiend takes to watery games / Have pity at least, on the spuds. 'Prayers for Fine Weather'

**Letts, Winifred M.** 1882-*c.*1950

4 A soft day, thank God! / A wind from the south / With a honeyed mouth.
'A Soft Day'

**Lever, Charles** 1806-1872

5 Bad luck to this marching, / Pipeclaying and starching, / How neat one must be / to be killed by the French!
'Bad Luck to This Marching'

6 Did you hear of the Widow Malone, ohone! / Who lived in the town of Athlone? / O she melted the hearts / Of the swains in them parts, / So lovely, the Widow Malone.
'The Widow Malone'

**Lewis, Cecil Staples** 1898-1963

7 There is wishful thinking in Hell as well as on earth. *The Screwtape letters*

8 She's the sort of woman who lives for others — you can always tell the others by their hunted expression. Ib.

**Lloyd, George David, 1st Earl of Dwyfor** 1863-1945

9 Any attempt at [Ireland's] secession will be fought with the same resolve as the Northern States of America put into the fight against the Southern States.
House of Commons, 22 December 1919

10 If I send this letter it is war, and war within three days.
Threat during Treaty negotiations, 5 December 1921

**Locke, John** 1847-1889

11 Th' anam an Dhia but there it is — / The dawn on the hills of Ireland! / God's angels lifting the night's black veil / From the fair, sweet face of my sireland! / O Ireland isn't it grand you look — / Like a bride in her rich adornin'? / And with all the pent-up love of my heart / I bid you the top of the mornin'! 'The Exile's Return'

**Longley, Michael** *b.* 1939

12 I extend the sea, its idioms. 'Circe'

13 I am lying with my head / Over the edge of the world, / Unpicking my whereabouts / Like the asylum's name / That they stitch on the sheets.
'Journey out of Essex, or John Clare's Escape from the Madhouse'

14 A knife thrower / hurling himself, a rainbow / fractured against / the plate glass of winter. 'Kingfisher'

15 And did we come into our own / When, minus muse and lexicon, / We traced in August sixty-nine / Our imaginary Peace Line / Around the burnt-out houses of / The Catholics we'd scarcely loved, / Two Sisyphuses come to budge / The sticks and stones of an old grudge.
'Letter to Derek Mahon'

**Lover, Samuel** 1797-1868

1 When first I saw sweet Peggy, / 'Twas on a market day, / A low-backed car she drove, and sat / Upon a truss of hay.

'The Low-Backed Car'

2 'Now Rory, leave off, sir; you'll hug me no more; / That's eight times to-day that you've kissed me before.' / 'Then here goes another,' says he 'to make sure, / For there's luck in odd numbers,' says Rory O'More.

'Rory O'More'

3 At Glendalough lived a young saint, / In odour of sanctity dwelling, / An old-fashioned odour, which now / We seldom or never are smelling.

'St Kevin'

4 Andy Rooney was a fellow who had the most singularly ingenious knack of doing everything the wrong way; disappointment waited upon all affairs in which he bore a part, and destruction was at his fingers end; so the nickname the neighbours stuck upon him was Handy Andy, and the jeering jingle pleased them. *Handy Andy*

**Luce, Arthur Aston** 1882-1977

5 He lived the good life, and he cast a lovely line. *Fishing and Thinking*

**Lucey, Cornelius, Bishop of Cork and Ross** 1902-1982

6 The people before us didn't rat on their children for the sake of Protestant schooling, land or soup; surely we won't for the sake of easy sex.

*The Irish Times*, 'This Week They Said', 1 May 1971

**Lynch, Jack** *b.* 1917

7 It is evident also that the Stormont government is no longer in control . . . the Irish government can no longer stand by and see innocent people injured and perhaps worse.

Television address, 13 August 1969, as given in *Speeches and Statements*, 1972. Video-tape records the phrase 'stand *idly* by'.

8 I have never and never will accept the right of a minority who happen to be a majority in a small part of the country to opt out of a nation.

*The Irish Times*, 'This Week They Said', 14 November 1970

9 I would not like to leave contraception on the long finger too long.

Ib., 23 May 1971

**Lynd, Robert Wilson ('Y.Y.')** 1879-1949

10 Galway is Irish in a sense in which Dublin and Belfast and Cork and Derry are not Irish but cosmopolitan. Its people, their speech, their dress, their swarthy complexions, their black hair, their eyes like blue flames, excite the imagination with curious surmises. Galway city – technically, it is only Galway town – is to the discoverer of Ireland something like what Chapman's *Homer* was to Keats. It is a clue, a provocation, an enticement.

'Galway of the Races'

11 What I especially like about Englishmen is that after they have called you a thief and a liar and patted you on the back for being so charming in spite of it, they look honestly depressed if you fail to see that they have been paying you a handsome compliment.

'Irish and English'

**Lysaght, Edward** 1763-1810

12 Ye gods! my wishes are confin'd / To— health of body, peace of mind, / Clean linen, and a guinea!

'Clean Linen and a Guinea'

# M

**Mac Ambróis, Seán**
fl. early 19th Century

1 Dá mbeinn fhéin in Airdí Chuain, / In aice an tsléibhe úd tá i bhfad uaim, / B'annamh liom gan dul ar cuairt, / Go Glenn na gCuach Dé Domhnaigh.

'Dá mbeinn fhéin in Airdí Chuain'

*O would I were in Ardicoan / Beside the hill above my home, / To the Cuckoos' Glen I'd often stroll / To spend the holy day.*

**Macaulay, Thomas Babington** 1800-1859

2 When the historian of this troubled reign turns to Ireland, his task becomes peculiarly difficult and delicate. His steps – to borrow a fine image used on a similar occasion by a Roman poet – are on the thin crust of ashes beneath which the lava is still flowing.

*History of England from the Accession of James* II

3 The rebellion of the aboriginal race has excited in England a strong religious and national aversion to them .... On those who resisted he [Cromwell] had made war as the Hebrews made war on the Canaanites. Drogheda was as Jericho; and Wexford as Ai. To the remains of the old population the conqueror granted a peace, such as that which Israel granted to the Gibeonites. He made them hewers of wood and drawers of water.

'Sir William Temple', *Literary Essays*

**MacBride, Maud Gonne** 1866-1953

4 More and more I realized that Ireland could rely only on force, in some form or another, to free herself.

'A Servant of the Queen'

5 The little stones on which the feet of Cathleen have rested disappear in the dark loneliness of the night .... It is blessed to have been for a moment one of those little stones. Ib.

**MacCarthy, Denis Florence** 1817-1882

6 The pillar towers of Ireland, how wondrously they stand / By the lakes and rushing rivers, through the valleys of our land! / In mystic file, through the isle, they lift their heads sublime, / These gray old pillar temples — these conquerors of time!

'The Pillar Towers of Ireland'

**MacCormack, John** 1884-1945*

7 I've no intention of writing anything, not even of any sort — let alone memoirs. And it isn't laziness. My life is my own. Sure, I've said everything I can about things with my voice — what the hell's the use of writing about that?

Quoted in macLiammóir, *All for Hecuba*

**Mac Cuarta, Séamas Dall** 1647?-1733

1 Mo thuirse nach bhfuaireas bua ar m'amharc a dh'fháil / go bhfaicinn ar uaigneas uaisle an duillliúir ag fás; / cuid de mo ghruaim nach gluaisim ag cruinniú le cách, / le seinm na gcuach ar bhruach na gcoilleadh go sámh.

'Fáilte Don Éan'

*Alas, I have lost all hope of going, my sight regained, / To see the beautiful foliage growing in desolate places, / And it adds to my woe to know I can never join the trail / When the cuckoo intones its peaceful notes in the woodland glades.* 'Welcome, Sweetest Bird'

2 Is iomaí cúirt agus caisleán laidir / ina raibh mé ag ráfladh is ag déanamh spóirt, / Ach má théim go flaitheas, a Rí na nGrása, / cérbh fhearr 'mo thámh mé ná ag déanamh ceoil.

'Is Fada Mé 'Mo Luí'

*In many a court and strong fortress / I had good sport and chatted away; / And if you'll have me, O King of Heaven, / Wouldn't a song be better than a scowling face?* 'Long Have I Lain'

**MacCumhaigh, Art** 1738-1773

3 Ag Úr-Chill an Chreagáin chodail mé aréir faoi bhrón, / is le héirí na maidne tháinig ainnir fá mo dhéin le póig, / bhí gríosghrua ghartha aici agus loinir ina céibh mar ór, / is gurbh é íocshláinte an domhain bheith ag amharc ar an ríoghain óig. 'Úr-Chill An Chreagáin'

*By the churchyard of Creagan in sorrow last night I slept / and at dawning of day a maiden came up with a kiss. / She had ember-bright cheeks and a light in her locks like gold / — it would cure the world's ills to behold that young princess.*

'The Churchyard of Creagan'

**MacDermot, Frank** 1886-1975

4 Just as nature abhors a vacuum, I suggest that statesmanship should avoid an ambiguity . . . If we want to be out of the British Commonwealth, let us say so and go out of it like men . . . Do not let us behave like guttersnipes. Politically, we are a young nation. Let us form the habit of thinking rather of our opportunities than of our rights. The lunatic asylums and the bankruptcy courts are the destiny of individuals who brood too much over their rights.

On Constitution
(Removal of Oath) Bill,
Dáil Éireann, 20 April 1932

5 A thing called a country cannot be formed in Ireland until we purge our minds of childishness and purge our minds of malice, and cease to have the impulse to call all those opposed to us traitors, Englishmen, Freemasons, and other things of that kind. Ib.

**MacDonagh, Donagh** 1912-1968

6 Dublin made me and no little town / With the cattle closing in on its streets.

'Dublin Made Me'

7 I disclaim all fertile meadows, all tilled land / The evil that grows from it and the good, / But the Dublin of old statues, this arrogant city, / Stirs proudly and secretly in my blood. Ib.

8 Going to Mass last Sunday my true love passed me by, / I knew her mind was altered by the rolling of her eye.

'Going to Mass Last Sunday'

9 Here in a year when poison from the air / First withered in despair the growth of spring / Some skull-faced wretch whom nettle could not save / Crept on four bones to his last scattering.

'The Hungry Grass'

1 This soft land quietly / Engulfed them like the Saxon and the Dane — / But kept the jutted brow, the slitted eye; / Only the faces and the names remain.
'A Warning to Conquerors'

2 We are three old ladies from Hades.
'Song of the Fates', *Happy As Larry*

3 WIDOW: The pounds of tobacco you stuff in your pipe / May solace a moment, an hour or a day / But when they are smoked you are left with your pipe / And the pleasure and solace are merely hearsay; / But a woman that's healthy and loving and young / Gives pleasure for months or a year, or a life, / When the throat's harsh with smoke she's still sweet to the tongue / So who'd choose tobacco in place of a wife? *Happy As Larry*

4 JUSTICE: Oh, *tá, tá*; I mean *seadh, seadh*; / My Irish is gone with my Algebra, / But there was a time when I wore the ring / With *An t-Athair Peadar* and *An Craoibhinn Aoibhinn.*
*Step-in-the-Hollow*

5 JUSTICE: To be a swaggering youngster for an hour / I could abandon money, place and power; / I'd give up all I have without a pain / To tramp it barefoot and be in love again . . . / But still that louser's gone — I can't complain. Ib.

**MacDonagh, Thomas** 1878-1916

6 Oh, you're my husband right enough, / But what's the good of that? / You know you never were the stuff / To be the cottage cat. 'John-John'

**MacDonogh, Patrick** 1902-1961

7 Oh, she walked unaware of her own increasing beauty / That was holding men's thoughts from market or plough.
'She Walked Unaware'

**MacGill, Patrick** 1890-1963

8 Brian O'Lynn and his last hour was due. / 'Repent or St Peter will not let you through!' / 'I've a trick up my sleeve if he won't let me in, / So give me a jemmy', said Brian O'Lynn.
'Brian O'Lynn'

9 I speak with the proud tongue of the people who were / And the people who are, / The worthy of Ardara, the Rosses and Inishkeel, / My kindred.
'Dedication'

10 Meenarood and Kilfinnan, / Cleengarra and Crinnan, / That slope to the salt seastrand — / Gortmeera, Kingarrow, / Drimeeney, Falcarragh / But the best is my own townland.
'In the Parish'

11 Tirconail! / On the hem of the royal Hill, the Hill of Aileach, / I stood.
'Tirconail'

12 Bad cess to the boats! for it's few they take back of the many they take away.
*Children of the Dead End*

13 God's choice about the company He keeps and never comes near Derry.
*The Rat Pit*

**Mac Giolla Gunna, Cathal Buí**
*c.* 1680-1756

14 A Íosa, a Spioraid Naofa, a Athair, agus a Uain, / A thug fíorfhuil do thaoibhe dár gceannach go cruaidh, / Bí im dhídean, bí im smaointí, bí ar m'aire gach uair, / Más suí dhom, más luí dhom, más seasamh, más suan.
'Aithreachas Chathail Bhuí'

*Jesus, Father, Holy Spirit and Lamb, / Who shed Thy healing blood on the bitter tree, / Protect me, I pray, for Thou*

*knowest how frail I am, / And may I, awake or asleep, be guided by Thee.*
'The Repentance of Cathal Buí'

1 A bhonnáin bhuí, is é mo léan do luí, / Is do chnámha sínte tar éis do ghrinn, / Is ní easpa bídh ach díobháil dí / A d'fhág id luí thú ar chúl do chinn.
'An Bonnán Buí'

*O yellow bittern, I grieve to think / That your voice is still after all your crack; / And not lack of victuals but want of drink / Had left you stiff on the broad of your back.*
*'The Yellow Bittern'*

**MacGreevy, Thomas** 1893-1967

2 The brave stupidity of soldiers, / The proud stupidity of soldiers' wives.
'Homage to Jack Yeats'

**MacGreil, Rev. Michael**

3 Violence inevitably leads to the peace of the graveyard. *The Irish Times*, 'This Week They Said', 15 May 1971

4 It is time that the Republic replaced the National Anthem with something more worthy of a civilised people, which could express sentiments of peace, justice and brotherhood instead of the gun and the barna baoil.
Ib., 7 April 1973

**Mac Grianna, Seosamh** *b.* 1900

5 Is óg i mo shaol a chonaic mé uaim é an ród sin a bhí le mo mhian, an bealach cas geal a raibh sleasa cnoc ar gach taobh de a ba deise ná aon chnoc dá bhfuil i gceol.
*Mo Bhealach Féin*

*I was very young when I first saw the road that matched my desire, a bright highway that wound between sloping hills more beautiful than any the poets have sung.* *'My Own Road'*

6 Bailte bánbhreaca idir neoin bhig agus béal maidne. Ib.

*Glimmering villages glimpsed between dusk and daybreak.* Ib.

**MacHale, John,**
**Archbishop of Tuam** 1791-1881

7 For forty-six years the people of Ireland have been feeding those of England with the choicest produce of their agriculture and pasture; and while they thus exported their wheat and their beef in profusion, their own food became gradually deteriorated in each successive year, until the mass of the peasantry was exclusively thrown on the potato. Letter to Lord John Russell, 15 December 1846

**MacIntyre, Tom** *b.* 1933

8 Sunrise will find us / But sunrise won't tell / That Love lacks surveillance / On sweet Killen Hill.
'On Sweet Killen Hill', after the Irish of Peadar O Doirnín

**Macken, Walter** 1916-1967

9 The bailiffs! Well, now, isn't he a great one for the jokin', a Christian man like him that's never outa church or chapel and his face always stuck in the Lives a the Saints, God bless'm, teh be jokin' about the bailiffs? Wouldn't he put the heart crossways in yeh with the lovely sinse a humour he has?
*Mungo's Mansions*

10 Sweet water and space and a sound bottom to sail to freedom.
Cry of ship's agents in Cork in *The Silent People*

**MacKenna, Stephen** 1872-1934

11 [The Turko-Grecian War] was like waiting for a train in Mullingar. Attrib.

**Macklin, Charles** 1690-1797

1 SIR PERTINAX MACSYCOPHANT: . . . for I observed, sir, that beauty is, generally, — a proud, vain, saucy, expensive, impertinent sort of a commodity.
EGERTON: Very justly observed.
SIR PERTINAX: And therefore, sir, I left it to prodigals and coxcombs that could afford to pay for it; and in its stead, sir, mark! — I looked out for an ancient, weel-jointured, superannuated dowager; a consumptive, toothless, phthisicky, wealthy widow; or a shriveled, cadaverous piece of deformity, in the shape of an izzard [the letter Z]; or an appersi-and-or [the ampersand &], in short, ainything that had the siller — the siller for that, sir, was the north star of my affections.
*The Man of the World*

**macLiammóir, Micheál** 1899-1978

2 Skirts were shorter than ever and the legs of the ladies of Cork were bright pink. *All for Hecuba*

3 . . . malicious fate had thrown me into the company of Padraic Ó Conaire, already a great friend under whose influence I had changed my Munster Irish into Connacht and adopted a battered black hat, a heavy stick, and a taste for whiskey, none of which things really belonged to myself. Ib.

4 The Irish writer of English, practising his art and drawing his inspiration where and whence he will, and reaping the fruits of his labour at a future time and probably in some distant land, has no such gloomy problem. At worst his book, having appeared and been duly banned by his compatriots, is still in existence; he can fish it out of a drawer or refer to his British or American readers to bear witness to what he has done.

But with the actor it is different: we are born at the rise of the curtain and we die with its fall, and every night in the presence of our patrons we write our new creation, and every night it is blotted out forever; and of what use is it to say to audience or to critic, 'Ah but you should have seen me last Tuesday?'
'Hamlet in Elsinore', *The Bell*, October 1952

5 Tá genius ag baint leis an tír seo againne agus tallan ar bith níl aici. Sin agaibh rún a scéil thruamhéiligh agus fáth na bua atá faighte aici ar lucht a scriosta.
*Ceo Meala Lá Seaca*

*There is a genius to be found in this country of ours, but no talent. That is the secret of her tragic history and the explanation of the hold that she has won over her conquerors.*
*A Honey Mist on a Day of Frost*

6 *February* 4, 1949: Hilton, smoking gigantic cigar, said film-making will be good for me as I'll be forced to *think* rather than to *frame about*, a phrase I do not find in good taste.
*Put Money in Thy Purse*

7 *March* 5, 1950: Tea with Madam Gonne MacBride . . . . Her heroic and now cavernous beauty, made sombre by the customary black draperies she wears, is also illumined by an increasing gentleness and humour; she has now what seemed a faint, far-away amusement at life. Ib.

8 *Belfast: April* 12, 1949: Impossible to fathom why I like this city but I do. Admittedly a cold, ugly sort of place even in this radiant northern April, its setting of windy mountains and dark shipyards blotched with fin-de-siècle mansions and fussy streets full of plate-glass and cake shops and trams, but

there is something about it all, its fantastic practicability, its bleak, bowler-hatted refusal of the inevitable.
Ib.

1 *April* 17, 1949: Irish Republic tonight at midnight. H[ilton Edwards] piously thanked God that England was free at last from 700 years of Irish domination.
Ib.

**MacMahon, Bryan** *b.* 1909

2 In Ireland, all you need to make a story is two men with completed characters — say, a parish priest and his sexton.
'The Cat and the Cornfield'

3 As I watched her she viced a mackerel by the gills and ran it through the O of the thumb and forefinger. Well for one thing the end of the world would put a stop to that sleazy antic.
'The End of the World'

4 The mountains were thrown higgledy-piggledy into the distance where the sea was. The white dusty road wound round the near flank of the valley and then fell gracefully away to the one-arched bridge below. Among the few tufted oaks beyond the bridge the church lurked. A cluster of thatched houses crouched about it. Bird song had shrivelled and died.
'Evening in Ireland'

**MacManus, Francis** 1909-1965

5 . . . there were crucifixes, big and small, of wood and metal, hanging on the wooden partition between the crowded gaudy oleographs of martyrs and mystics, all seeking eagerly with their rolled-up eyes for the release of the soul from hateful and hated bodies.
*The Fire in the Dust*

6 My body seems to respond to the movement of the river once more, and it is a movement that I cannot dam for one instant as it gathers momentum, charges through me, curves, drops, slides, races and foams out into the black leagues of the sea. Yes. She's like the river.
*Flow On, Lovely River*

7 When I lifted my eyes beyond the little houses, and saw Camp Hill that had been ours, the world seemed at a standstill and nobody was alive but myself and God Almighty.
*This House Was Mine*

8 Ireland's a door where the living collogue with the dead.
'Praise God for Ireland'

9 Why don't Irishmen forsake the eternal bogs and bleak mountain roads — all part of a small, narrow, and even romantic view of Ireland.
*Watergate*

**MacManus, Michael Joseph** 1888-1951

10 But my work is undistinguished / And my royalties are lean / Because I never am obscure / And not at all obscene.
'An Author's Lament'

11 Some Connacht garb around me clings, / Some savage strain, an uncouth air; / I'd rather hear the fiddle strings / Of tinker folk at Galway Fair.
'Ballade of a Dublin Salon'

12 Father Pat he banged the pulpit, / Said the devil's work must cease, / Banned the gathering and the Pattern / And the breaking of God's peace.
'The Pattern'

•

**MacNamara, Brinsley, (John Weldon)** 1890-1963

13 Yet were the people gripped, for no other reason than because it was a play about Robert Emmet. Indeed, Michael Dempsey need not have gone to such pains to give a great performance. Merely to have stood there on the very middle of the stage in his top boots with

gold tassels, white trousers and black cut-away coat, his arms folded, and a lock of hair brushed down upon his forehead, would have been quite sufficient. In fact from one aspect of Ballycullen's point of view, the whole thing was quite unnecessary. The drunken ballad-singers had told them all they wanted to know about Robert Emmet, and this was how they had always seen Robert Emmet dressed up in a picture. *The Clanking of the Chains*

1 On a Sunday morning the procession they formed was like a flock of human crows. And the noise they made was a continual caw of calumny.
*The Valley of the Squinting Windows*

**MacNeice, Louis** 1907-1963

2 In my childhood trees were green / And there was plenty to be seen. / *Come back early or never come.*
'Autobiography'

3 My father made the walls resound, / He wore his collar the wrong way round. / *Come back early or never come.* Ib.

4 . . . the voodoo of the Orange bands / Drawing an iron net through darkest Ulster. 'Autumn Journal XVI'

5 Up the Rebels, To Hell with the Pope, / And God Save – as you prefer – the King or Ireland. Ib.

6 Why should I want to go back / To you, Ireland, my Ireland? / The blots on the page are so black / That they cannot be covered with shamrock. / I hate your grandiose airs, / Your sob-stuff, your laugh and your swagger, / Your assumption that everyone cares / Who is the king of your castle. Ib.

7 It's no go my honey love, it's no go my poppet; / Work your hands from day to day, the winds will blow the profit. / The glass is falling hour by hour, the glass will fall for ever, / But if you break the bloody glass you won't hold up the weather. 'Bagpipe Music'

8 Down there at the end of the melancholy lough / Against the lurid sky over the stained water / Where hammers clang murderously on the girders / Like crucifixes. 'Belfast'

9 I was born in Belfast between the mountains and the gantries / To the hooting of lost sirens and the clang of trams: / Thence to Smoky Carrick in County Antrim / Where the bottle-neck harbour collects the mud which jams / The little boats beneath the Norman castle. 'Carrickfergus'

10 This was never my town, / I was not born nor bred / Nor schooled here and she will not / Have me alive or dead / But yet she holds my mind with her seedy elegance.
'Dublin', *The Closing Album*

11 O the crossbones of Galway, / The hollow grey houses, / The rubbish and sewage, / The grass-grown pier, / And the dredger grumbling / All night in the harbour: / The war came down on us here. 'Galway', ib.

12 I come from an island, Ireland, a nation / Built upon violence and morose vendettas. 'Eclogue from Iceland'

13 Time was away and somewhere else, / There were two glasses and two chairs / And two people with the one pulse / (Somebody stopped the moving stairs): / Time was away and somewhere else.
'Meeting Point'

1 The sunlight on the garden / Hardens and grows cold, / We cannot cage the minute / Within its net of gold, / When all is told / We cannot beg for pardon.
'The Sunlight on the Garden'

2 World is crazier and more of it than we think, / Incorrigibly plural. I peel and portion / A tangerine and spit the pips and feel / The drunkenness of things being various. 'Snow'

3 Trains came threading quietly through my dozing childhood.
'Trains in the Distance'

4 I give you the disproportion between labour spent / And joy at random; the laughter of the Galway sea / Juggling with spars and bones irresponsibly, / I gave you the Liffey and the vast gulls, / I give you fuchsia hedges and the whitewashed walls. 'Train to Dublin'

5 I give you the smell of Norman stone, the squelch / Of bog beneath your boots, the red bog-grass, / The vivid chequer of the Antrim hills, the trough of dark / Golden water for the cart-horses, the brass / Belt of serene sun upon the lough. Ib.

6 I would call you to book / I would say to you, Look; / I would say, This is what you have given me / Indifference and sentimentality / A metallic giggle, a fumbling hand, / A heart that leaps to a fife band. 'Valediction'

7 Therefore I resign, good-bye the chequered and the quiet hills / The gaudily-striped Atlantic, the linen-mills / That swallow the shawled file, the black moor where half / A turf-stack stands like a ruined cenotaph; / Good-bye your hens running in and out of the white house / Your absent-minded goats along the road, your black cows / Your greyhounds and your hunters beautifully bred / Your drums and your dolled-up Virgins and your ignorant dead. Ib.

8 In doggerel and stout let me honour this country / Though the air is so soft that it smudges the words.
'Western Landscape'

**MacNeill, Eoin** 1867-1945

9 We must remember that what we call our country is not a poetical abstraction, as some of us . . . are sometimes apt to imagine . . . There is no such person as Caitlin Ni Uallachain or Roisin Dubh or the Sean-bhean Bocht, who is calling us to serve her. What we call our country is a concrete and visible reality. Memorandum to Irish Volunteers, February 1916

10 I wish it then to be clearly understood that under present conditions I am definitely opposed to any proposal that may come forward involving insurrection. Ib.

**MacSwiney, Terence** 1879-1920

11 O my God, I offer my pain for Ireland. She is on the rack.
Letter from Brixton Prison, 5 October 1920

**Maginn, William** 1793-1842

12 You've heard, I suppose, long ago, / How the snakes, in a manner most antic, / He marched to the County Mayo, / And trundled them into th'Atlantic. 'St Patrick of Ireland'

13 . . . not to use water for drink, / The people of Ireland determine / With mighty good reason, I think, / Since St Patrick has filled it with vermin / And vipers and other such stuff! Ib.

1 When a man is drunk, it is no matter upon what he has got drunk.
*Thoughts and Maxims*

2 The safety of women consists in one circumstance — men do not possess at the same time the knowledge of thirty-five and the blood of seventeen. Ib.

**Maguire, Tom** 1870-?

3 The struggle is over, the boys are defeated, / Old Ireland's surrounded with sadness and gloom, / We were defeated and shamefully treated, / And I, Robert Emmet, awaiting my doom.
'Bold Robert Emmet'

4 Bold Robert Emmet, the darling of Erin, / Bold Robert Emmet will die with a smile, / Farewell companions both loyal and daring, / I'll lay down my life for the Emerald Isle. Ib.

**Mahaffy, Sir John Pentland** 1839-1919

5 If Berkeley and Swift, Goldsmith and Sheridan, Grattan and Burke, had been compelled to write in Irish for the sake of official promotion, or to soothe national sensibilities, not only would the English-speaking world but Ireland herself, have suffered unreasonable damage. 'The Modern Babel', *Nineteenth Century*, 1896

6 In Ireland the inevitable never happens and the unexpected constantly occurs.

7 An Irish Bull is always pregnant.

8 An Irish Atheist is one who wishes to God he could believe in God.

9 Nemo repente fuit turpissimus [*No one ever sank to the depths of evil all at once*]: it takes forty years to become a Senior Fellow of Trinity College, Dublin. Epigrams attrib.

**Mahony, Francis Sylvester, ('Father Prout')** 1804-1866

10 The town of Passage / Is both large and spacious, / And situated / Upon the say. / 'Tis nate and dacent / And quite adjacent / To come from Cork / On a summer's day.
'The Attractions of a Fashionable Irish Watering-Place'

11 With deep affection / And recollection / I often think of / Those Shandon Bells / Whose sounds so wild would / In the days of childhood / Fling round my cradle / Their magic spells.
'The Bells of Shandon'

**Máire (Séamus Ó Grianna)** 1891-1969

12 'A Shéimí, goidé an cineál tithe iad sin,' ar sise, ag amharc ar na néalta, 'atá os cionn luí na gréine?' 'Tá,' arsa Séimí, 'sin caisleáin óir a bhfuil na daoine beaga ina gcónaí iontu . . . .'
*Caisleáin Óir*

*'Seimi, what kind of houses are those,' said she looking at the clouds, 'the ones in the sunset?' 'Those are the golden castles where the fairies live' said Seimi.*
*Golden Castles*

13 'Tá sé fuar,' arsa an seanduine. 'Is é atá,' arsa Séimí, 'fuar, fuar.' Ib.

*'It's cold,' said the old man. 'Yes, indeed! Cold, cold.'* Ib.

14 'Níl a fhios agam,' ar sise, 'an bhfóirfeadh bríste Mhicí duit — grásta ó Dhia ar Mhicí!' *Cioth is Dealán*

*'I wonder,' said she, 'would Mici's trousers fit you? — God rest his soul.'*
*Sunshine and Shower*

**Malachy, St** 1094-1148

15 Habete curam mei; ego vestri, si licuerit, non obliviscar. Licebit autem.

Credidi in Deum, et omnia possibilia credenti, Amavi Deum, amavi vos, et caritas nunquam excidit.

Dying words, as recorded by St Bernard of Clairvaux, in *Patrologia Latina*

*Look after me; I, if I am able, will not forget you. That much will be permitted. I have believed in God and all is possible to the believer. I loved God, I have loved you and love will never fail.*

*Patrologia Latina*

**Mangan, James Clarence** 1803-1849

1 I saw her once, one little while, and then no more: / 'Twas Eden's light on Earth a while, and then no more.

'And Then No More'

2 Solomon! where is thy throne? It is gone in the wind. / Babylon! where is thy might? It is gone in the wind. / All that the genius of Man hath achieved or designed / Waits but its hour to be dealt with as dust by the wind.

'Gone in the Wind'

3 The language of Erin is brilliant as gold; / It shines with a lustre unrivalled of old. / Even glanced at by strangers by whom 'tis unknown / It dazzles their eyes with a light all its own!

'The Irish Language'

4 I am Mac-Liag, and my home is on the Lake: / Thither often, to that palace whose beauty is fled, / Came Brian, to ask me, and I went for his sake, / O, my grief! that I should live, and Brian be dead! / Dead, O Kinkora! 'Kinkora'

5 . . . the moon is very thin and cold.

'The Lover's Farewell'

6 Roll forth, my song, like the rushing river / That sweeps along to the mighty sea; / God will inspire me while I deliver / My soul of thee!

'The Nameless One'

7 My eyes are filmed, my beard is grey, / I am bowed with the weight of years; / I would I were stretched in my bed of clay, / With my long-lost youth's compeers. / For back to the Past, though the thought brings woe, / My memory ever glides — / To the old, old time, long, long ago, / The time of the Barmecides. 'The Time of the Barmecides'

8 I hate thee, Djaun Bool, / Worse than Marid or Afrit, / Or corpse-eating Ghool. 'To the Ingleezee Khafir'

9 Twenty years ago, alas! – but stay – / On my life, 'tis half-past twelve o'clock! / After all, the hours *do* slip away – / Come, here goes to burn another block! / For the night, or morn, is wet and cold; / And my fire is dwindling rather low – / I had fire enough, when young and bold / Twenty golden years ago.

'Twenty Golden Years Ago'

10 O woman of Three Cows, agra! don't let your tongue thus rattle! / O, don't be saucy, don't be stiff, because you may have cattle. / I have seen – and, here's my hand to you, I only say what's true – / A many a one with twice your stock not half so proud as you.

'The Woman of Three Cows'

**Markievicz, Countess Constance** 1868-1927

11 Armed for the battle, kneel we before Thee / Bless Thou our banners, God of the brave!

'A Battle Hymn'

12 I have seen the stars.

Conclusion of Treaty speech, 1922, quoted in O'Faoláin, *Constance Markievicz*

**Marsh, Archbishop Narcissus** 1638-1713

1 . . . we must always treat them [dissenters] with the spirit of meekness and love else our labour will be but lost upon them. For Haughtiness and Bitterness of spirit do but incense and provoke, and is rather to drive men out of the church, than to bring any into it.

Charge given to clergy on his primary visit to St Patrick's, Dublin, 27 June 1649

2 All Graduats and Gentlemen shall have free access to the said Library on the Dayes and Houres before determined, Provided They behave Themselves well, give place and pay due respect to their Betters, But in case any person shall carry Himself otherwise (which We hope will not happen) We order Him to be excluded, if after being admonished He does not amend His manners.

Rules for Marsh's Library, 1704

**Marshall, Rev. William Frederick** 1882-1959

3 As long as the silver Foyle runs deep, / And Dungannon sits on the hill.

'Goordaspoore'

4 I'm livin' in Drumlister / An' I'm gettin' very oul', / I have to wear an Indian bag / To save me from the coul'. / The deil a man in this town lan' / Wos claner raired nor me, / But I'm livin' in Drumlister / In clabber to the knee.

'Me an' Me Da'

5 . . . her face wos like a gaol dure / With the bowlts pulled out. Ib.

6 When weemin gets wicked they're tarra, / Ye'll not intherfair if yir wise, / For ten townlan's wudn't settle / The birl that two weemin can rise.

'The Runaway'

**Martyn, Edward** 1859-1924

7 The wild heath has broken out again in the heather field. *The Heather Field*

**Marvell, Andrew** 1621-1678

8 And now the Irish are ashamed / To see themselves in one year tamed.

'An Horation Ode upon Cromwell's Return from Ireland'

**Marx, Karl** 1818-1883

9 The task of the 'International' [Workingmen's Association] is everywhere to put the conflict between England and Ireland in the foreground, and everywhere to side openly with Ireland. The special task of the Central Council in London is to awaken a consciousness in the English workers that for them the national emancipation of Ireland is no question of abstract justice or human sympathy but the first condition of their own emancipation.

Letter to Meyer and Vogt, 9 April 1870

**Maturin, Charles Robert** 1782-1824

10 The burning waves boomed over his sinning head and the clock of eternity rung out its awful chime — 'Room for the soul of the Wanderer!' and the waves of the ocean answered, as they lashed the admantine rock, — 'There is room for more!' *Melmoth the Wanderer*

**Maxwell, William Hamilton** 1792-1850

11 The town of Ballinasloe is seated upon a river, the name of which I neglected to inquire. It is much frequented by saints and cattle-dealers, carries on a smart trade in sheep and proselytes, and Bibles and bullocks are 'thick as leaves on Vallombrosa' . . . pigs and popery are prohibited. *Wild Sports of the West*

**Mayne, Rutherford**
(Samuel John Waddell) 1878-1967

12 Of course in a breach of promise letters are a great help. A great help. I'm very

glad, however, just for your sister's sake, that she never wrote any to John. Imagine them reading out the love letters in the open court, and all the servant boys gaping and laughing.

*The Drone*

1 Do you think them proud city folk will listen to his poor ould ballads with the heart of the boy singing through them. It's only us – it's only us, I say, as knows the long wild nights, and the wet and the rain and the mist of nights on the boglands – it's only us I say could list to him in the right way; and ye knowed, right well ye knowed, that every string of his fiddle was keyed to the crying of your own heart.

*The Turn of the Road*

**McAteer, Edward** *b.* 1914

2 If another hand than ours does embark upon the terrible work we all fear this week, be right sure this means the raising of the curtain on the last terrible act of the age-old Irish drama.

*The Irish Times*, 'This Week They Said', 16 August 1969

3 We have this London word in our name since 1613 — and really we have never got used to it.

Proposing to amend the name Londonderry, ib., 26 May 1973

**McBurney, William** *c.* 1844-*c.* 1892

4 At the siege of Ross did my father fall, / And at Gorey my loving brothers all. / I alone am left of my name and race; / I will go to Wexford and take their place.

'The Croppy Boy'

**McCabe, Eugene** *b.* 1930

5 Dig out the badger . . . blind him with lime . . . jeer and cudgel . . . split his belly . . . spike him to a tree, or any man that cuts his way up from what *they* are to what *I* am . . . That's their religion. . . . Well by Christ I'll not be fed to scaldcrows. . . I'll bury every last man of them. . . I'll out-buy . . . out-crop . . . out-credit . . . *King of the Castle*

6 Ever ass yourself — what's a woman for? Scrape plates, twig floors – look at rocks and heather, eat, cook, sleep, drink, empty pots, feed men – and hens, talk with a hired girl, confess on Saturday, pray of a Sunday, and think of sin all day Monday? Ib.

**McCall, Patrick Joseph** 1861-1919

7 At Boolavogue, as the sun was setting, / O'er the bright May meadows of Shelmalier, / A rebel hand set the heather blazing / And brought the neighbours from far and near. / Then Father Murphy, from old Kilcormack, / Spurred up the rocks with a warning cry; / 'Arm! Arm!' he cried, 'for I've come to lead you, / For Ireland's freedom we fight or die.' 'Boolavogue'

8 What's the news? What's the news? O my bold Shelmalier, / With your long-barrelled gun of the sea?

'Kelly of Killane'

**McCann, Michael Joseph** 1824-1883

9 Many a heart shall quail / Under its coat of mail; / Deeply the merciless foeman shall rue, / When on his ear shall ring / Borne on the breeze's wing / Tir Connell's dread war-cry, 'O'Donnell Aboo!' 'O'Donnell Aboo!'

**McDyer, Rev. James** *b.* 1911

10 You cannot wait until the people are ready for socialism. It may have to be forced on them as it was forced upon us in Glencolumbkille.

*The Irish Times*, 'This Week They Said', 14 November 1970

**McFadden, Roy** *b.* 1922

1 . . . every road in Ulster veined my heart. 'Cuchulainn'

2 There are more familiar ways of falling out of life. 'Elegy for the Dead of the *Princess Victoria*'

**McGee, Thomas D'Arcy** 1825-1868

3 Long, long ago, beyond the misty space / Of twice a thousand years, / In Erin old there dwelt a mighty race, / Taller than Roman spears. 'The Celts'

4 He came from the North, and his words were few / But his voice was kind and his heart was true. 'The Man of the North Countrie'

**McGrath, Joseph** 1887-1966

5 It is bad that unemployment money should be paid at all . . . This unemployment scheme is purely an English scheme. Unemployment Problem, Dáil Éireann, 20 October 1922

**McLaverty, Michael** *b.* 1907

6 . . . there were the green spires of Ardoyne where the sinners brought their great sins to the Passionists, there was the stumpy spire of the Monastery, and farther along in the heart of the city, sticking high above the smoke, were the sharp spires of St Peter's. *Call My Brother Back*

7 Supposin' ye got all the Orange sashes and all the Green sashes in this town and ye tied them round loaves of bread and flung them over Queen's Bridge, what would happen? . . . The gulls – the gulls that fly in the air, what would they do? They'd go for the bread! But *you* – the other Gulls – would go for the sashes every time! Ib.

8 Stone is lasting: all life ends in death, but stone lives on. It was more lasting than all their children. They needn't chaff him any more about his name dying with neither chick nor child to leave behind him! 'Stone'

9 A moss-cheeper, swaying on a reed like a mouse, filled the air with light cries of loneliness. 'The Wild Duck's Nest'

**McNamara, Gerald, (Harry C. Morrow)** 1866-1938

10 GRANIA *(shocked)*: The Hiberniana! but are not all the people in Erinn Hibernians?
THOMPSON: In sowl they're not.
GRANIA: Are all the people in Portadown Hibernians?
THOMPSON: Talk sense, woman dear. *Thompson in Tir-na-nOg*

**McQuaid, John Charles, Archbishop of Dublin** 1895-1973

11 To speak of a right to contraception on the part of an individual . . . is to speak of a right that cannot even exist. *The Irish Times*, 'This Week They Said', 3 April 1971

**Meagher, Thomas Francis** 1823-1867

12 The soldier is proof against an argument but he is not proof against a bullet. Speech, Dublin, 28 July 1846

13 Be it in the defence, or be it in the assertion of a people's liberty, I hail the sword as a sacred weapon. Ib.

**Medico-Social Research Board**

14 Since the Famine Ireland has controlled its population growth by three measures: celibacy, late marriage and emigration. Annual Report, *The Irish Times*, 'This Week They Said', 8 May 1971

**Meredith, George** 1828-1909

1 'Tis Ireland gives England her soldiers, her generals too. *Diana of the Crossways*

**Merriman, Brian** 1749-1803

2 Ba ghnáth mé ag siúl le ciumhais na habhann / ar bháinseach úr 's an drúcht go trom, / in aice na gcoillte, i gcoim an tslé, / gan mhairg, gan mhoill, ar shoilse an lae. *Cúirt an Mheán Oíche*

*I often went to the edge of the pool / Through verdant meadows of heavy dew / Where trees grew tall by the wall of hills, / Carelessly sauntering in the dawn's first glint.*

*The Midnight Court*

3 Ní labharfadh focal dá mb'obair an oíche / is thabharfadh cothrom do stollaire bríomhar, / go brách ar siúl nár dhiúltaigh riamh é / ar chnámh a cúil 's a súile iata. Ib.

*She wouldn't whine after a night's hard labour / But still be on fire for the wildest of games, / And never decline to lie unclothed / On the flat of her spine with her eyelids closed.* Ib.

4 Scaras lem néall, do réidheas mo shúile / is phreabas de léim ón bpéin im dhúiseacht! Ib.

*I opened my eyes as I writhed in pain, / The ghosts took flight — I was wide awake!* Ib.

**Mhac an tSaoi, Máire** *b.* 1922

5 Ach tagann an fhearthainn de ghualainn na gaoithe / Droim máma isteach . . . / Féach nach in aisce a baisteadh ort Bríde — / Ní fuacht go hearrach!

'Amhrán Feabhra'

*But the rain is carried in on the back of the wind / Down from the gap in the hills . . . / How well you were christened after St Brigid — / As cold as the first day of spring!* 'February Song'

**Michael, Friar** 14th Century

6 This worldis loue is gon awai / So dew on grasse in somcris dai, / Few ther beth, weilawai, / That louith goddis lore.

*This world's love is gone away / As dew from grass on summer day / Few there be, alas / That love the words of God.*

'Sweet Jesus'

**Mill, John Stuart** 1806-1873

7 Ireland is not an exceptional country but England is. Irish circumstances and Irish ideas as to social and agricultural economy are the general ideas of the human race; it is English circumstances and English ideas that are peculiar. Ireland is in the main stream of human existence and human feeling and experience; it is England that is one of the lateral channels. If we are to be guided by experience in legislating for Ireland, it is continental rather than English experience we ought to consider, for it is on the Continent, and not in England, that we find anything like similarity of circumstances.

On Fortescue's Land Bill, House of Commons, 17 May 1866

**Milligan, Alice** 1880-1953

8 The Donegal border comes so near to Derry city that we had only to take the road that runs north and go along it for some twenty minutes; then passing a boundary stone we knew that we had reached the enchanted ground. Once in the territory of the Gael life seemed to hold possibilities that were out of question in the realm of Derry of the Londoners. *The Shan Van Vocht*

9 In Cavan of the little lakes, / As I was walking with the wind, / And no one

seen beside me there / There came a song into my mind.
'A Song of Freedom'

1 'Come in! for it is growing late, / And the grass will wet ye! / Come in or when it's dark / The Fenians will get ye.' 'When I was a Little Girl'

**Milliken, Richard Alfred** 1767-1815

2 The groves of Blarney / They look so charming, / Down by the purling / Of sweet, silent brooks.
'The Groves of Blarney'

**Mitchel, John** 1815-1875

3 Good night, then, Ireland and Irish tumults, strugglings and vociferations, quackery, puffery and endless talk.
*Jail Journal*

4 I know that all weakness is past, and that I am ready for my fourteen years' ordeal, and for whatever the same may bring me — toil, sickness, ignominy, death. Ib.

5 He [Daniel O'Connell] was a lawyer; and never could come to the point of denying and defying all British law. He was a Catholic . . . and would not see that the Church has ever been the enemy of Irish Freedom. Ib.

6 An exile in my circumstances is a branch cut from its tree; it is dead but it has an affectation of life. Ib.

7 O'Connell was, next to the British government, the worst enemy Ireland ever had — or rather the most fatal friend. *The Last Conquest of Ireland*

**Mitchell, Susan Langstaff** 1866-1926

8 Jove thunders from Olympus, and Moore from Ely Place, / I damn respectability, and call it a disgrace;
*Aids to Immortality of Certain Persons*

9 But W B was the boy for me — he of the dim, wan clothes; / And – don't let on I said it – not above a bit of pose; / And they call his writing literature, as everybody knows. Ib.

**Molloy, James Lynam** 1837-1909

10 Time goes on and the happy years are dead, / And one by one the merry hearts are fled; / Silent now is the wild and lonely glen / Where the bright glad laugh will echo ne'er again.
'The Kerry Dance'

11 As I'm sitting all alone in the gloaming, / The shadows of the past draw near, / And I see the loving faces round me / That used to glad the old stone pier.
'Bantry Bay'

**Molloy, Michael Joseph** *b.* 1914

12 The Wood of the Whispering they do call this wood on account of all the courting couples that used to be in it some years ago before all the lads and girls went foreign.
*The Wood of the Whispering*

**Monk, Hon. Mrs** 1677-1715

13 O'er this marble drop a tear; / Here lies fair Rosalinde. / All mankind was pleased with her / And she with all mankind. 'Fair Rosalinde'

**Montague, John** *b.* 1929

14 Naturally, we fall from grace. / Mere humans, we forget what light / Led us, lonely, to this place. 'Blessing'

15 In cabin / and field, they still / speak the old tongue. / You may greet no one. / To grow / a second tongue, as / harsh a humiliation / as twice to be born. / Decades later / that child's grandchild's / speech stumbles over lost / syllables of an old order. 'A Grafted Tongue'

1 Like Dolmens Round My Childhood, the Old People Title of poem

2 All around, shards of a lost tradition; / From the Rough Field I went to school / In the Glen of the Hazels.
'A Severed Head'

3 The whole landscape a manuscript / We had lost the skill to read, / A part of our past disinherited; / But fumbled, like a blind man, / Along the fingertips of instinct. Ib.

4 Puritan Ireland's dead and gone, / A myth of O'Connor and Ó'Faoláin.
'The Siege of Mullingar, 1963'

**Moore, George Augustus** 1852-1933

5 *Scene:* A great family coach, drawn by two powerful country horses, lumbers along a narrow Irish road. The ever-recurrent signs — long ranges of blue mountains, the streak of bog, the rotting cabin, the flock of plover rising from the desolate water.
*Confessions of a Young Man*

6 Art must be parochial in the beginning to become cosmopolitan in the end.
*Hail and Farewell I: Ave*

7 Ireland is a little Russia in which the longest way round is the shortest way home, and the means more important than the end. Ib.

8 His [Douglas Hyde] volubility was extreme as a peasant's come to ask for a reduction in rent. It was interrupted, however, by Edward [Martyn] calling on him to speak in Irish, and then a torrent of dark, muddied stuff flowed from him, much like the porter which used to come up from Carnacun to be drunk by the peasants on Midsummer nights when a bonfire was lighted. It seemed to me a language suitable for the celebration of an antique Celtic rite, but too remote for modern use. It had never been spoken by ladies in silken gowns with fans in their hands. Ib.

9 There is a lake in every man's heart . . . and he listens to its monotonous whisper year by year, more and more attentive until at last he ungirds.
*The Lake*

10 Acting is therefore the lowest of the arts, if it is an art at all.
*Mummer-Worship*

11 We all did something, but none did what he set out to do. Yeats founded a realistic theatre, Edward emptied two churches – he and Palestrina between them – and I wrote *The Untilled Field,* a book written in the beginning out of no desire of self-expression, but in the hope of furnishing the young Irish of the future with models.
Preface, *The Untilled Field*

12 There is an unchanging, silent life within every man that none knows but himself, and his unchanging silent life was his memory of Margaret Dirken. The bar-room was forgotten and all that concerned it, and the things he saw most clearly were the green hillside, and the bog-lake and the rushes about it, and the greater lake in the distance, and behind it the blue line of wandering hills. 'Home Sickness', ib.

13 . . . he did not feel he was a free soul until the outlines of Howth began to melt into the grey drift of evening. . . . If he stayed he would have come to accept all the base moral coinage in circulation; and he stood watching the green waves tossing in the mist, at one moment ashamed of what he had done, and the next overjoyed that he had done it. 'The Wild Goose', ib.

**Moore, Thomas** 1779-1852

1 At the mid-hour of night, when stars are weeping I fly / To the lone vale we loved, when life shone warm in thine eye.
'At the mid-hour . . .' *Irish Melodies*

2 Avenging and bright fall the swift sword of Erin, / On him, who the brave sons of Usna betrayed.
'Avenging and Bright', ib.

3 Believe me, if all those endearing young charms, / Which I gaze on so fondly today. / Were to change by to-morrow, and fleet in my arms, / Like fairy-gifts fading away ! / Thou wouldst still be adored, as this moment thou art, / Let thy loveliness fade as it will, / And around the dear ruin each wish of my heart / Would entwine itself verdantly still.
'Believe me', ib.

4 Oh! the heart that has truly loved, never forgets, / But as truly loves on to the close;
Ib.

5 Dear Harp of my Country! in darkness I found thee, / The cold chain of silence had hung o'er thee long.
'Dear Harp of my Country', ib.

6 Erin, the tear and the smile in thine eyes / Blend like the rainbow that hangs in the skies; / Shining through sorrow's stream, Sadd'ning through pleasure's beam / Thy suns, with doubtful gleam, weep while they rise.
'Erin the Tear . . .', ib.

7 You may break, you may ruin the vase, if you will; / But the scent of the roses will hang round it still!
'Farewell! But Whenever', ib.

8 When around thee dying, / Autumn leaves are lying / Oh, then remember me.
'Go Where Glory Waits Thee', ib.

9 Has sorrow thy young days shaded, / As clouds o'er the morning fleet? / Too fast have those young days faded, / That even in sorrow were sweet?
'Has Sorrow Thy Young Days Shaded?', ib.

10 How sweet the answer Echo makes / To music at night – To music at night / When roused by lute or horn, / She wakes – she starting wakes, / And far away o'er lawns and lakes, / Goes answering light – goes answering light.
'How Sweet the Echo', ib.

11 Each wave that we danced on at morning ebbs from us, / And leaves us, at eve, on the bleak shore alone.
'I Saw from the Beach', ib.

12 Give me back, give me back the wild freshness of Morning, / *Her* clouds and her tears are worth Ev'ning's best light.
Ib.

13 It is not the tear at this moment shed, / When the cold turf has just been laid o'er him, / That can tell how beloved was the soul that's fled / Or how deep in our heart we deplore him.
'It Is Not the Tear', ib.

14 Lay his sword by his side – it has served him too well, / Not to rest near his pillow below.
'Lay His Sword by His Side', ib.

15 Sweeter 'tis to gaze upon / My Nora's lid that seldom rises; / Few her looks, but ev'ry one, / Like an unexpected light surprises!
'Lesbia Has a Beaming Eye', ib.

1 On Lough Neagh's bank, as the fisherman strays, / When the clear cold eve's declining, / He sees the round towers of other days / In the wave beneath him shining!

'Let Erin Remember', ib.

2 My gentle Harp! once more I waken / The sweetness of thy slumb'ring strain; / In tears our last farewell was taken, / And now in tears we meet again.

'My Gentle Harp', ib.

3 Oh! Arranmore, loved Arranmore, / How oft I dream of thee, / And of those days when by thy shore, / I wandered young and free. / Full many a path I've tried, since then, / Through pleasure's flow'ry maze, / But ne'er could find the bliss again / I felt in those sweet days.

'Oh! Arranmore, Loved Arranmore', ib.

4 Oh! blame not the Bard, if he fly to the bowers / Where Pleasure lies carelessly smiling at Fame; / He was born for much more, and in happier hours, / His soul might have burned with a holier flame. 'Oh! Blame Not the Bard', ib.

5 Sad, silent, and dark, be the tears that we shed, / As the night dew that falls on the grass o'er his head.

'Oh, Breathe Not His Name', ib.

6 . . . there's nothing half so sweet in life / As love's young dream.

'Oh! The Days Are Gone', ib.

7 Quick! we have but a second, / Fill round the cup, while you may; / For Time, the churl, hath beckoned, / And we must away — away.

'Quick! We Have but a Second', ib.

8 Remember the glories of Brian the brave, / Tho' the days of the hero are o'er; / Tho' lost to Mononia and cold in the grave, / He returns to Kinkora no more! 'Remember the Glories of Brian the Brave', ib.

9 Rich and rare were the gems she wore, / And a bright gold ring on her wand she bore; / But oh! her beauty was far beyond / Her sparkling gems and snow-white wand. 'Rich and Rare', ib.

10 Sir Knight! I feel not the least alarm; / No son of Erin will offer me harm; / For tho' they love woman and golden store, / Sir Knight, they love honour and virtue more!' Ib.

11 She is far from the land where her young hero sleeps, / And lovers around her are sighing; / But coldly she turns from her gaze, and weeps / For her heart in his grave is lying! 'She Is Far', ib.

12 She sings the wild songs of her dear native plains, / Ev'ry note which he loved awaking — / Ah little they think, who delight in her strains, / How the heart of the Minstrel is breaking! Ib.

13 Silent, O Moyle! be the roar of thy water, / Break not, ye breezes! your chain of repose, 'Silent, O Moyle!', ib.

14 When shall the Swan, her death-note singing, / Sleep with wings in darkness furl'd? / When will Heav'n, its sweet bell ringing, / Call my spirit from this stormy world? Ib.

15 Sweet Innisfallen, fare thee well, / And oft may light around thee smile / As soft as on that ev'ning fell, / When first I saw thy fairy isle!

'Sweet Innisfallen', ib.

16 The harp that once, thro' Tara's halls, / The soul of Music shed, / Now hangs as mute on Tara's walls / As if that soul

were fled: — / So sleeps the pride of former days, / So glory's thrill is o'er / And hearts that once beat high for praise, / Now feel its pulse no more!
'The Harp That Once', ib.

1 There is not in the wide world a valley so sweet / As that vale in whose bosom the bright waters meet.
'The Meeting of the Waters', ib.

2 The Minstrel fell! – but the foeman's chain / Could not bring that proud soul under; / The harp he loved ne'er spoke again, / For he tore its chords asunder.
'The Minstrel Boy', ib.

3 And said, 'No chains shall sully thee, / Thou soul of love and bravery! / Thy songs were made for the pure and free, / They shall never sound in slavery.'
Ib.

4 My only books / Were Woman's looks, / And Folly's all they taught me.
'The Time I've Lost', ib.

5 I look'd for the lamp which, she told me, / Should shine, when her Pilgrim return'd, / But tho' darkness began to infold me, / No lamp from the battlements burn'd!
'The Valley Lay Smiling', ib.

6 Then awake! the heavens look bright, my dear; / 'Tis never too late for delight, my dear; / And the best of all ways to lengthen our days / Is to steal a few hours from the night, my dear!
'The Young May Moon', ib.

7 Tho' humble the banquet to which I invite thee, / Thou'lt find there the best a poor bard can command: / Eyes, beaming with welcome, shall throng round to light thee, / And Love serve the feast with his own willing hand.
'Though Humble the Banquet', ib.

8 To the gloom of some desert, or cold rocky shore, / Where the eye of the stranger can haunt us no more, / I will fly with my Coulin, and think the rough wind / Less rude than the foes we leave frowning behind.
'Though the Last Glimpse of Erin', ib.

9 'Tis the last rose of summer, / Left blooming alone; / All her lovely companions are faded and gone.
'Tis the Last Rose of Summer', ib.

10 When he who adores thee has left but the name / Of his fault and his sorrow behind.
'When He Who Adores Thee', ib.

11 When in death I shall calm recline, / O bear my heart to my mistress dear / Tell her it lived upon smiles and wine / Of the brightest hue, while it lingered here.
'When In Death I Shall Calm Recline', ib.

12 Oh! how welcome breathes the strain, / Wak'ning thoughts that long have slept — / Kindling former smiles again / In faded eyes that long have wept.
'When Through Life Unblest We Rove', ib.

13 I never nursed a dear gazelle, / To glad me with its soft black eye, / But when it came to know me well, / And love me, it was sure to die.
*Lalla Rookh*

14 I am strongly inclined to think that, in a race into future times . . . those little ponies, the *Melodies*, will beat the mare, *Lalla*, hollow.
Letter to Thomas Longman, 23 November 1837

15 Oft in the stilly night, / Ere Slumber's chain has bound me, / Fond Memory brings the light / Of other days around me; / The smiles, the tears, of

boyhood's years, / The words of love then spoken; / The eyes that shone, / Now dimmed and gone, / The cheerful hearts now broken!

'Oft in the Stilly Night', *National Songs*

1 I feel like one / Who treads alone / Some banquet-hall deserted, / Whose lights are fled, / Whose garlands dead / And all but he departed. Ib.

**Moran, David Patrick** 1871-1936

2 Since Grattan's time every popular leader, O'Connell, Butt, Parnell, Dillon and Redmond, has perpetuated this primary contradiction. They threw over Irish civilisation whilst they professed – and professed in perfectly good faith – to fight for Irish nationality. *The Philosophy of Irish Ireland*

3 *Shoneens:* apers of English manners; *Sour-faces:* Protestants; *West-Britons:* Anglo-Irish; *The Hairy Fairy:* AE (George Russell).

Ib., *passim*

**Morgan, Lady, (Sydney Owenson),** 1783-1859

4 Who dares inhale her mouth's spicy gale / Must die by the breath of Kate Kearney. 'Kate Kearney'

5 Lady Singleton had, however, something to blame or rectify with every step she took. At Belfast where they remained a day, she proved as she stood on the bridge, that it should have been erected upon twenty arches instead of twenty-one . . . that the canal which connects the harbour with Lough Neagh was formed against every principle and system of inland navigation. At Carrickfergus where they were shown the spot on which King William landed, she discovered he had chosen the worst place on the coast. *O'Donnell*

**Moriarty, David, Bishop of Kerry** 1814-1877

6 When we look down into the fathomless depths of the Fenian conspiracy we must acknowledge that eternity is not long enough nor hell hot enough for such miscreants. Sermon, February 1867

**Mozeen, Thomas** 18th Century

7 In seventeen hundred and forty-four / The fifth of December, I think 'twas no more, / At five in the morning by most of the clocks, / We rode from Kilruddery in search of a fox.

'The Kilruddery Hunt'

**Mulcahy, General Richard** 1886-1971

8 We have lost two people who were the leaders, and to whom we looked as the leaders of the future, one of them the sower who lived in Ireland, and the other the greatest reaper the country has ever had. . . . We have first and foremost to implement the Treaty . . . made by, among others, these two Chieftains whom we have lost.

Referring to Griffith and Collins in a speech proposing W. T. Cosgrave as President of Dáil Éireann, 9 September 1922

9 . . . unless we take very stern measures, we will not throw back the tide of lawlessness and the tide of lust and loot that some mad political leaders have stirred up in their train in this country.

On Military Executions, Dáil Éireann, 17 November 1922

**Mulchineck, William** 1820-1864

10 A curse for the cold, a cup for the bold, / A smile for the girls we love; / And for him who'd bleed in his country's need / A home in the skies above.

'Fill High Tonight'

11 Tho' lovely and fair as the rose of the summer, / Yet 'twas not her beauty

alone that won me, / Oh, no, 'twas the truth in her eyes ever beaming / That made me love Mary, the Rose of Tralee.
'The Rose of Tralee'

**Muldoon, Paul** *b.* 1951

1 A girl who would never pass out of fashion / So long as there's an 'if' in California. 'Immram'

2 I know that eternal interim; / I think I know what they're waiting for / In Tyrone, Fermanagh, Down and Antrim. 'Lull'

3 Old miners at Coalisland / Going into the ground. Swinging, for fear of the gas, / The soft flame of a canary. 'Ma'

4 We might yet claim that it sprang from earth / Were it not for the afterbirth / Trailed like some fine, silk parachute, / That we would know from what heights it fell. 'Mules'

**Mulkerns, Val** *b.* 1925

5 There were trees too and green lawns passing the railings to your left before you swung right at Elvery's where the elephant was. You could look into the elephant's small eyes which were about level with your own and feel at times that a stretched out hand could touch the tassels of his headgear.
'The Sisters', Antiquities

6 'It's not a fair world love,' said my father, 'but it's not the end of the world either. We'll have a lot of good times yet.'

But he knew what I knew, that the good times were all gone. For the foreseeable future, at any rate.
'A Cut above the Rest', ib.

7 Sorry, yes, but you'll go on waiting for a celibate churchman in Mother Rome to change his mind again, won't you? How long is it going to take him to realise that though he may have spoken, the people of God have long passed out of earshot?
'Humanae Vitae', *An Idle Woman*

8 I was fourteen, and abruptly at the end of the holidays some soft, almost physical appendage of childhood seems to have fallen away, like the tail of a tadpole, and I would never be quite the same again. 'Home for Christmas', ib.

9 It is a strange country. Let it once grip a traveller and it will not leave go until he is sucked dry, and the people can be like that too. They are hard and humorous and often beautiful, but difficult to know. 'A Peacock's Cry'

10 Howth was a seal floating darkly in the sun, dreaming of mists and lost heroes.
*A Time Outworn*

**Murdoch, Iris** *b.* 1920

11 I think being a woman is like being Irish. . . . Everyone says you're important and nice but you take second place all the same. *The Red and the Green*

**Murphy, Michael John** *b.* 1913

12 Three things one should do every year — listen to a storyteller at a fireside, give a hand in a corn harvest field, and climb an Irish mountain. *Mountain Year*

13 The folklore collector knows he has to spend months, even years, with one mind. *Tyrone Folk Quest*

**Murphy, Nicholas P.** *d.* 1914

14 When he arrived at his destination, he paused at the door, and looked up at the signboard. The artist who had inflicted this atrocity on the establishment has passed away, and, as nothing but good may be said about the dead, the design will be here merely reproduced without

any accompanying criticism.

dAnIELmaCk
inthErTainminT
formAn an Baste

*A Corner in Ballybeg*

**Murphy, Richard** *b.* 1927

1 The wind began to play, like country fiddlers / In a crowded room, with nailed boots stamping / On the stone cottage floor, raising white ashes. / The sea became a dance.

'The Cleggan Disaster'

2 If words were banknotes, he would filch a wad; / If they were pheasants, they'd be in the pot / For breakfast, or if wrens he'd make them king.

'The Reading Lesson'

3 But tonight we stay, drinking with people / Happy in the monotony of boats. 'Sailing to an Island'

4 Lever and Lover, Somerville and Ross / Have fed the same worm as Blackstone and Gibbon, / The mildew has spotted *Clarissa's* spine / And soiled the *Despatches of Wellington.*

'The Woman of the House'

**Murphy, Seamus** 1907-1975

5 With hammer, mallet and chisel we have shaped and fashioned rough boulders. We often curse our material and often we speak kindly to it . . . We try to impose ourselves on it, but if we know our material and respect it we will often take a suggestion from it, and our work will be the better for it. *Stone Mad*

**Murphy, Thomas Bernard** *b.* 1935

6 Heeding that hussy of a clotty of a plótha of a streleen of an ownshock of a lebidjeh of a girleen that's working above in the bank.

*A Crucial Week in the life of a Grocer's Assistant*

7 . . . from unexchanged glances it was plain, that twixt my ma and he, all was not well. *The Morning after Optimism*

8 What's right in a country when the land goes sour? What is a woman with children when nature lets her down?

*Famine*

9 God made the world, right? And fair play to him. What has he done since? Tell me. Right, I'll tell you. Evaporated himself. When they painted his toenails and turned him into a church, he lost his ambition, gave up learning, stagnated for a while, then gave up even that, said fuck it, forget it, and became a vague pain in his own and everybody else's arse. *The Sanctuary Lamp*

10 The number of times I've had to pretend I'm some money-grabbing gombeen man or they wouldn't believe me. The number of times I've had to pretend I'm some thick fast-talking flash Harry for fear they would believe me, and in their fear maybe kick me to death. *The White House*

**Murphy, William Martin** 1844-1919

11 I am not the leader of the employers, although I have been called the leader. I seem to have gained a great deal of notoriety, but I have had greatness thrust upon me. September 1913

**Murray, Thomas Cornelius** 1873-1959

12 The stars will wither in the skies before I forgive you. *Michaelmas Eve*

13 Hearing the cows gadding in the heat and they making a little boom of thunder with their hoofs on the sod and myself in a little room under the roof no better than a breathing corpse.

*Autumn Fire*

**Na gCopaleen, Myles,**
**(Brian O'Nolan, Flann O'Brien)**
1911-1966

1 Is amhlaidh abhí: / 1 doineann na dúiche ró-dhoineanta; / 2 bréantas na dúiche ró-bhréan; / 3 bochtanas na dúiche ró-bhocht; / 4 gaelachas na dúiche ró-ghaelach; / 5 seanchas na sean ró-sheanda. *An Béal Bocht*

*It was like this in the place: / 1 the foulness of the weather was too foul; / 2 the fetidness of the fetor was too fetid; / 3 the poverty of the poor was too pauperish; / 4 the Hibernianism of the Hibernians was too Hibernicised; / 5 the antiquity of the antiquaries was too antique.* *The Poor Mouth*

2 'A Ghaela,' adúirt sé, 'cuireann sé gliondar ar mo chroí Gaelach a bheith annso iniu ag caint Gaeilge libh-se ar an fheis Ghaelaí seo i lár na Gaeltachta.' Ib.

*'Fellow Gaels,' he said, 'it warms the cockles of my Gaelic heart to be here today talking Gaelic to you at this Gaelic feis in the most Gaelic part of the Gaeltacht.'* Ib.

3 'Níl mé ach go measardha,' arsa Jams, 'agus níl Gaeilg ar bith agam ach Gaeilg Chúige Uladh.' Ib.

*'My health is only middling,' said Jams, 'and I can only speak Ulster Irish.'* Ib.

4 Bhíodh aibhneacha mhóra ag gluaiseacht béal dorais agus má sciobadh uainn a raibh de phrátaí ins an ghort againn, is minic go raibh iasc le fáil ar thaobh an bhealaigh. Ib.

*Great rivers washed by our door and if they swept away all the potatoes out of our field itself, sure there were often fish to be had at the roadside.* Ib.

5 Ní dóigh liom go mbeidh mo leithéid arís ann. Ib.

*I do not believe that there will ever be the like of me again.* Ib.

6 Cruiskeen Lawn is 10 years old today; as a long-term feat of denunciation and abuse I do not think it has ever been equalled; certainly it has never been surpassed. *The Irish Times,* 'Cruiskeen Lawn', 23 October 1950

7 The Brother. / The Plain People of Ireland. / Sir Myles na gCopaleen. / The Man who spoke Irish at a Time when it was neither Profitable nor Popular. Ib., *passim*

**Nichevo, (Robert Maire Smyllie)**
1894-1954

1 Most Corkmen know a lot; but this one knew everything. I tried many times to catch him out on some bit of esoteric information but it was no use. Invariably he was ready for me, and whether it was some abstruse point in Canon Law, the history of the Babylonian civilisation, the multifarious uses of the Soya Bean, or even how to make drisheens, he could hold forth for a couple of hours and never become boring. *Carpathian Days – and Nights*

**Ní Chuilleanáin, Eiléan** *b.* 1942

2 If there was a single / Streak of decency in these waves now, they'd be ridged / Pocked and dented with the battering they've had. 'The Second Voyage'

3 Walking in a library door is like / Being raped by an army. 'Trinity New Library'

**Northern Ireland Tourist Board**

4 Shooting is a popular sport in the countryside . . . Unlike many other countries, the outstanding characteristic of the sport has been that it is not confined to any one class.
*New Statesman*, 29 August 1969

**Norton, Caroline Elizabeth Sarah**
1808-1877

5 The Arab's Farewell to His Steed
Title of poem

# O

**O'Brien, Conor Cruise** *b.* 1917

1 Irishness is not primarily a question of birth or blood or language; it is the condition of being involved in the Irish situation, and usually of being mauled by it. 'Irishness', *New Statesman*, January 1959

2 Man watches his history on the screen with apathy and an occasional passing flicker of horror or indignation.
*The Irish Times*, 'This Week They Said', 16 July 1969

3 If I saw Mr Haughey buried at midnight at a cross-roads, with a stake driven through his heart – politically speaking – I should continue to wear a clove of garlic round my neck, just in case.
*Observer*, 10 October 1982

**O'Brien, Edna** *b.* 1936

4 Irish, cottage, typical, pink cheeks, came to be a nurse in London, loved by all the patients, loved being loved, ran from the operating theatre because one of the patients, who had a cancer, was just opened and closed again, met a man who liked the nursemaid in me, married him in registry office, threw away the faith, one son soon after. Over the years the love turned to something else and we broke up. Exit the nice girl.
*August Is a Wicked Month*

5 Oh, God, who does not exist, you hate women, otherwise you'd have made them different.
*Girls in their Married Bliss*

6 Upstairs she lay awake and planned a new heroic life for herself. She would expiate all her sins by sinking into domesticity . . . She would put her lily hand down into sewerages and save him the trouble of lifting out the ooze, and hairs, and grey slime that resulted from their daily lives. Ib.

7 Dawn, day, dark, frost, cloud, sprinkling, icicle, a fall of snow, bare places covered over, sparrows and red wings, daisy, hollyhock, wall marigolds. . . Ah ye world that I hold dear, soon now you will be slipping away.
*Johnny I Hardly Knew You*

8 Will you for Chrissake stop asking fellas if they read James Joyce's *Dubliners*. They're not interested. They're out for the night. Eat and drink all you can and leave James Joyce to blow his own trumpet. *The Lonely Girls*

9 Oh shadows of love, inebriations of love, foretastes of love, trickles of love, but never yet the one true love. *Night*

**O'Brien, Flann**
**(Myles na gCopaleen, Brian O'Nolan)**
1911-1966

1 The Pooka MacPhillimey, a member of the devil class, sat in his hut in the middle of a firwood meditating on the nature of the numerals and segregating in his mind the odd ones from the even.
*At Swim-Two-Birds*

2 *Quality of rasher in use in household:* Inferior, one and two the pound. Ib.

3 The College is outwardly a rectangular plain building with a fine porch where the midday sun pours down in summer from the Donnybrook direction, heating the steps for the comfort of the students. Ib.

4 . . . we filled up the loneliness of our souls with the music of our two voices, dog-racing, betting and offences against chastity being the several objects of our discourse. Ib.

5 When money's tight and is hard to get / And your horse has also ran, / When all you have is a heap of debt — / A PINT OF PLAIN IS YOUR ONLY MAN. Ib.

6 Come all ye lads and lassies prime / From Macroom to Strabane, / And list to me till I say my rhyme / THE GIFT OF GOD IS A WORKIN' MAN. Ib.

7 I dedicate these pages to my guardian angel, impressing upon him that I'm only fooling and warning him to see to it that there is no misunderstanding when I go home.
Dedication, *The Dalkey Archive*

8 Into his mind came that other book, *Portrait of the Artist.* Here had been renunciation of family, faith, even birthland and that promise of silence, exile and cunning. What did there seem to be here? The garrulous, the repatriate, the ingenuous.
*The Dalkey Archive*

9 It is not that I half knew my mother. I knew half of her: the lower half — her lap, legs, feet, her hands and wrists as she bent forward. *The Hard Life*

10 They say piety has a smell, Mr Collopy mused, half to himself. It's a perverse notion. What they mean is only the absence of the smell of women. Ib.

11 A humble Jesuit would be like a dog without a tail or a woman without a knickers on her. Ib.

12 Well, damn the cardboard shields the Dominicans used in Spain, those blood-stained bowsies. Ib.

13 The gross and net result of it is that people who spend most of their natural lives riding iron bicycles over the rocky roadsteads of this parish get their personalities mixed up with the personalities of their bicycles as a result of the interchanging of the atoms of each of them and you would be surprised at the number of people in these parts who are nearly half people and half bicycles.
*The Third Policeman*

**O'Brien, Kate** 1897-1974

14 . . . she grew into that kind of nun who will never have to trouble about the vow of poverty, because poverty is attractive to her fastidiousness; who had looked chastity in the eyes with exaggerated searching, and finding in it the perverse seduction she needed at a moment of flight from life, accepts it once and for all with proud relief, but who will have to wrestle with obedience. *The Land of Spices*

1 Denis and Anne danced the discreet waltz of their day, danced it with a beautiful grave precision, with perfect circumspection, with composed and masklike faces. But to the alert nerves of the lookers-on, it was as if what they did was shameless. *Without My Cloak*

**O'Brien, Kate Cruise** *b.* 1948

2 University students are rarely able to cope with universals and death is the most embarrassing universal.
'Henry Died', *A Gift Horse*

**Ó Brolchán, Mael Ísu** *d.* 1086

3 A Chrínóc, cubaid do cheól, / cencobat fíróc, at fíal; / ro mósam túaid i tír Néill / tan do-rónsam feis réid ríam.

*Crionog, it is proper to sing of you; even though you are no longer young, you are chaste. We grew up in the north, in Ulster, at the time when we slept sweetly together.*
*Mael Ísu Finds His Psalter Again*

4 Rop sí m'aes tan ro fóis lem, / a bé níata in gaesa grinn, / daltán clíabgan caem nád cam / maccán mall secht mblíadan mbinn.

*When you slept with me, valiant maiden of the sharp wisdom, I was a pure-hearted, quiet, uncomplicated lad, a gentle boy of seven sweet years.* Ib.

**Ó Bruadair, Dáibhí** *c.* 1625-1698

5 D'aithle na bhfileadh n-uasal / truaghsan timheal an tsaoghail
'D'aithle Na Bhfileadh — do chlainn Chon Connacht Ui Dhalaigh'

*The high poets are gone / And I mourn for the world's waning.*
*'The High Poets Are Gone; For the Family of Cuchonnacht O Dalaigh'*

**O'Byrne, Dermot (Sir Arnold Bax)** 1883-1953

6 O write it up above your hearth / And troll it out to sun and moon, / To all true Irishmen on earth / Arrest and death come late and soon.
'A Dublin Ballad – 1916'

7 We're free to sentimentalize / By corners where the martyrs fell. Ib.

**Ó Cadhain, Máirtín** 1906-1970

8 Ní mé ar Áit an Phuint nó na Cúig Déag atá mé curtha? *Cré na Cille*

*I wonder am I buried in the Pound section or in the Fifteen Shilling section?*
*Graveyard Clay*

9 Is mise Stoc na Cille. Éistear le mo ghlór! Caithfear éisteacht . . . Ib.

*I am the Graveyard Trumpet. Listen to my voice! You must listen . . .* Ib.

10 Tháinig an gnáthghalar Gaelach, scoilteadh.
'Conradh na Gaeilge agus an Litríocht'
*The Gaelic League Idea*

*They succumbed to the chronic weakness of the Irish, and split.*
'The Gaelic League and Literature', *The Gaelic League Idea*

**O'Casey, Sean** 1880-1964

11 When the employers sacrifice wan victim, the Trades Unions go one betther be sacrificin' a hundred.
*Juno and the Paycock*

12 There'll never be any good got out o' him so long as he goes with that shoulder-shruggin' Joxer. I killin' meself workin', and he sthruttin about from mornin' till night like a paycock! Ib.

1 The foreman at Killester — oh yis, yis. He's an oul' butty o' mine — oh, he's a darlin' man, a darlin' man. Ib.

2 An' as it blowed an' blowed, I ofen looked up at the sky an' assed meself the question — what is the stars, what is the stars? Ib.

3 Joxer's song, Joxer's song — give us wan of your shut-eyed wans. Ib.

4 It's a sad journey we're goin' on, but God's good, an' the Republicans won't always be down. Ib.

5 Sacred Heart of the Crucified Jesus, take away our hearts o' stone . . . an' give us hearts o' flesh! . . . take away this murdherin hate . . . an' give us Thine own eternal love! Ib.

6 I always knew you were a prognosticator an' a procrastinator! Ib.

7 The last o' the Mohicans. . . . The blinds is down, Joxer, the blinds is down. Ib.

8 I'm tellin' you . . . Joxer . . . th' whole worl's . . . in a terr . . . ible state o' . . . chassis. Ib.

9 As far as I can see, the Polis as Polis, in this city, is null and void. Ib.

10 It's only a little cold I have; there's nothing derogatory wrong with me. *The Plough and the Stars*

11 That's all dope, comrade; th' sort o' thing that workers are fed on to be th' Boorzwawzee. Ib.

12 Here we have bishops, priests and deacons, a Censorship Board, vigilant librarians, confraternities and sodalities, Duce Maria, Legions of Mary, knights of this Christian order and knights of that one, all surrounding the sinner's free-will in an embattled circle. . . . The banning of bombs is more to the point than the banning of books, and Christians should know this better than anyone. *The Irish Times*, 8 June 1957

**Ó Conaire, Pádraic** 1882-1928

13 Bhí sean scian lena thaobh, sean scian mhaol mhanntach, agus is léi a maraíodh é . . . ach ba bheag an ceapadh a bhí ag mo chara bocht go loiceadh an piostal úd a cheannaigh sé ón mairnéalach air — Ach nár loic an saol? *Deoraíocht*

*There was an old knife beside him, a blunt and jagged old knife, and it was with it that he had been killed . . . but my poor friend had never expected that the pistol he bought from the sailor would let him down — But hadn't life let him down?* *Exile*

14 An oíche úd ar imigh Nóra d'fheicfeá seanfhear istigh i mbád iascaireachta dá mbeifeá ar chéibh Ros Dhá Loch. Bhí soitheach tara lena thaobh agus é ag milleadh an ainme a bhí ar an mbád. Má mhill féin, níor éirigh leis an t-ainm úd a scriosadh amach óna chroí. Ainm a iníne bhí aige ar a bhád. 'Nora Mharcais Bhig'

*If you had been on the quay at Rossdalough that night after Nora had gone, you would have seen an old man in a fishing boat. He had a pot of tar beside him and he was obliterating the name of the boat. He could do that, but he was unable to efface the name from his heart. He had named the boat after his daughter.* 'Little Marcus's Nora'

**O'Connell, Daniel** 1775-1847

15 I know that the Catholics of Ireland still remember they have a country, and that

they would never accept any advantages as a sect that would destroy them as a people. Speech against Act of Union, 13 January 1801

1 The hospitality of an Irishman is not the running account of posted and ledgered courtesies, as in other countries; it springs, like all his qualities, his faults, his virtues, directly from his heart.

Speech against Marquess of Headfort, July 1804

2 The Union was therefore a manifest injustice, and it continues to be unjust to this day. It was a crime, and it must still be criminal unless it shall be ludicrously pretended that crime, like wine, improves by old age, and that time mollifies injustice and innocence.

Repeal Speech, 1809

3 The President [of a proposed Catholic Relief Commission] would be Orange Peel who had been sent over here before getting rid of the foppery of perfumed handkerchiefs and thin shoes.

Speech to Catholic Board, 28 February 1813

4 Our liberties were not lost in any disastrous battle; our rights were not won from us in any field of fight. No, our ancestors surrendered upon capitulation — on the faith of a solemn treaty which stipulated for Ireland liberty of conscience. The treaty was ratified, passed the great seal of England; it was observed – yes, observed according to English fidelity! – for just seven weeks.

Speech against the Veto, 29 August 1815

5 I said, 'Miss O'Connell' (she was also an O'Connell) 'are you engaged?' She replied, 'I am not!' I said, 'Then will you engage yourself to me?' 'I will,' was her reply; and I said I would devote my life to make her happy. She deserved that I should. She gave me thirty-four years of the purest happiness that man ever enjoyed.' On the death of his wife, 31 October 1836

6 Hurrah for the darling little queen . . . she has shown great firmness and excellent heart. Letter to Dr MacHale, Archbishop of Tuam, 10 May 1839

7 I will never get half credit enough for carrying Emancipation, because posterity never can believe the species of *animals* with which I had to carry on my warfare with the common enemy. It is crawling slaves like them that prevent our being a nation.

Letter to P. V. Fitzpatrick, 14 May 1839

8 My beagles never cease their cry until they catch their game.

Answer to Leigh Hunt when he compared the Repeal cry to that of the Derrynane beagles, December 1842

9 Thank God, I'll have the privilege of knocking down any man that now calls me, 'My Lord.'

On giving up the Lord Mayorship of Dublin, 1842

10 Not for all the universe contains would I, in the struggle for what I conceive my country's cause, consent to the effusion of a single drop of human blood, except my own. Speech, 28 February 1843

11 There is not a human being so stultified as to think the English Parliament will do anything for Ireland. I would walk from here to Drogheda and back to see the man who is blockhead enough to expect anything except injustice from an English Parliament.

Speech at Trim, 16 March 1843

1 I am the hired servant of Ireland, and I glory in my servitude.

Letter, February 1848

2 I am sufficiently utilitarian not to regret its [the Irish language] gradual abandonment. A diversity of tongues is no benefit; it was first imposed upon mankind as a curse, at the building of Babel. It would be of great advantage to mankind if all the inhabitants of the Earth spoke the same language. Therefore though the Irish language is connected with many recollections that twine around the hearts of Irishmen, yet the superior utility of the English tongue, as the medium of all modern communication, is so great that I can witness without a sigh the gradual disuse of Irish.

Attrib. by O'Neill Daunt, *Personal Recollections of Daniel O'Connell*

3 Was it not a live fly that was in the dead man's mouth when his hand was placed on the will?

During cross-questioning of a witness who claimed that a testator had *life in him* when he signed the will. Attrib.

4 Peel's smile was like the silver plate on a coffin.

Attrib.

## O'Connor, Frank (Michael O'Donovan) 1903-1966

5 The greatest oak in the forest had crashed; it seemed as if it must destroy all life in its fall. It did destroy the Sinn Fein movement and all the high hopes that were set in it, and a whole generation of young men and women for whom it formed a spiritual centre.

*The Big Fellow*

6 The writer should never forget that he is also a reader, though a prejudiced one, and if he cannot read his own work a dozen times he can scarcely expect a reader to look at it twice.

*The Lonely Voice*

7 Yeats was one of the most devious men I have ever known, and I deliberately mocked at his deviousness as he mocked at my simple-mindedness, probably with equal justification.

*My Father's Son*

8 My fight for Irish freedom was of the same order as my fight for other sorts of freedom. Still, like Dolan's ass, I went a bit of the way with everybody, and in those days everybody was moving in the same direction.

*An Only Child*

9 The officers in the barracks played proper cricket, and on summer evenings I used to go and watch them, like one of the souls in Purgatory watching the joys of Paradise.

'The Idealist'

10 I hope he'll give you the penitential psalms, you dirty little caffler.

'First Confession'

11 'Father,' I said, feeling I might as well get it over while I had him in good humour, 'I had it all arranged to kill my grandmother.'

Ib.

12 His treachery had made two parts of him. He had become a man. But the idea gave him singularly little comfort.

'First love'

13 And suddenly Farranchreesht, the bare bogland with the hump-backed mountain behind, the little white houses and the dark fortifications of turf that made it seem like the flame-blackened ruin of some mighty city, all was lit up in their minds.

'In the Train'

1 The hearse stopped at the foot of the lane that led to the roofless cabin just as she had pictured it to herself in the long nights, and Pat, looking more melancholy than ever, turned to the waiting neighbours and said: 'Neighbours, this is Abby, Batty Heige's daughter, that kept her promise to ye at the end of all.'

'The Long Road to Ummera'

**O'Connor, John** 1920-1960

2 The Row in which the Coyle's house stood was on a higher level than the others, which flooded more quickly, a regrettable fact acknowledged by the mill-owners, and accounting for the reduction in rents of the lower houses.

*Come Day – Go Day*

3 The rain still fell heavily, driving down between the gleaming, chimney shadowed rooftops, but the darkness in the air was beginning to lift, as a white, glowing patch spread slowly in the sky above the Asylum trees. For a while everything was silent, except for the whisper of the rain and a faint, almost inaudible hum from the now empty Mill.

Ib.

**O'Connor, P[ower] T[homas]** 1848-1929

4 The Belfast Quasimodo to the Irish Esmeralda. [Description of Joe Biggar.]

*Memoirs of an Old Parliamentarian*

5 It may be that with him [Isaac Butt] as with so many others that the pursuit of pleasure was but the misnomer for the flight from despair.

Ib.

**Ó Criomhthainn, Tomás** 1856-1937

6 Thugas iarracht ar mheon na ndaoine a bhí i mo thimpeall a chur síos chun go mbeadh a dtuairisc inár ndiaidh, mar ná beidh ár leithéidí arís ann.

*An tOileánach*

*I have tried to describe the mind and character of the people I knew so that some memorial of them might remain, for there will never be the like of us again.*

*The Islandman*

**O'Curry, Eugene** 1796-1862

7 . . . your soft pleasant converse / Hath deprived me of heaven.

'Do You Remember That Night?' – from the Irish.

**Ó Direáin, Máirtín** *b.* 1910

8 Is é a dhighnit a loime.

'Crainn Oiche Seaca'

*Its bareness is its dignity.*

'Trees on a Frosty Night'

9 Luigh ar do chranna foirtil / I gcoinne mallmhuir is díthrá, / Coigil aithinne d'aislinge, / Scaradh léi is éag duit.

'Cranna Foirtil'

*Pull on your sturdy oars / Against the spring tide and the neap: / Cherish the living coal of your vision, / If you part with it, you perish.*

'Sturdy Oars'

10 Mórchuid cloch is gannchuid cré / Sin é teist an scéird-oileáin.

'Cuimhne an Domhnaigh'

*Wealth of stone and dearth of clay, / Signature of the rugged island.*

'Remembering Sunday'

11 Chím mar chaith an chloch gach fear / Mar lioc ina cló féin é.

Ib.

*I see how the rock has worn each man down / And compressed him into a featureless plate of stone.*

Ib.

12 Beidh cuimhne orainn go fóill; / Beidh carnán trodán / Faoi ualach deannaigh / Inár ndiaidh in Oifig Stáit.

'Stoite'

*We will be remembered yet; / We will leave a heap of files / Thick with dust / Lying in a government office.*
'Uprooted'

**O'Donnell, Frank Hugh** 1848-1916

1 Yeats's occult mission, it seemed, was to celebrate the wedding of Madame Blavatsky and Finn Mac Cumhail.
'The Stage Irishman of the Pseudo-Celtic Drama'

**O'Donnell, John Francis** 1837-1874

2 The free fold of her garments' damask grain / Fashioned a hieroglyph upon the floor. 'Where?'

**O'Donovan, Harry** 1896-1973

3 MRS MULLIGAN *(Picks up turkey)*: The end of a mis-spent life.
MCGUIRK (Poultry Salesman): It's a beauty.
MULL.: I know. But I want it for eatin' not for classical dancin'.
MCGUIRK: I killed that myself.
MULL.: Yeh coward: yeh struck an oul' man. What were yeh doin' with it . . . racin' it at Harold's Cross?
MCGUIRK: I kill all me own birds.
MULL.: Yeh never killed that wan. It's a clear case of suicide.
'Buying a Turkey' – a sketch for Jimmy O'Dea as 'Mrs Mulligan'

**O'Donovan, Jeremiah 'Gerald'** 1871-1942

4 The Carmelites will do their best to get him. He would be wasted with them — the boy ought to be a scholar, not a pulpit wind-bag. *Father Ralph*

5 'There's no use asking you to smoke,' he said. 'It's a dirty habit,' Father Mahon said, spitting at the fire.
*Waiting*

**O'Donovan Rossa, Jeremiah** 1831-1915

6 My prison chamber now is iron-lined, / An iron closet and an iron blind, / But bars, and bolts, and chains can never bind / To tyrant's will the freedom-loving mind. 'My Prison Chamber'

7 I cannot yet conceive how any Irishman can be considered an Irish patriot who will sing out to his people, either in prose or verse, that it is impossible to free Ireland from English Rule. [About Tom Moore.] *Recollections*

8 Gladstone starved me till my flesh was rotten for want of nourishment, Gladstone chained me with hands behind my back for thirty-five days at a time, Gladstone leaped upon my chest, while I lay on the flat of my back in a black-hole cell in his prison. Peori [Italian revolutionary] didn't experience such treatment as that in the Italian prison. Yet the great Englishman could cry out his eyes for him. No wonder those eyes of his got sore in the end. Ib.

9 I am ever ready to do my utmost to promote the cause and acquire the reality of nationality . . . but . . . I don't believe the Saxon will ever relax his grip except by the persuasion of cold lead and steel.
Letter, quoted in Kee, *The Green Flag*

**O'Duffy, Eimar Ultan** 1893-1935

10 There was a Philosopher once who lived in a little room in a tumbledown house in a back lane off Stonybatter; which is not a place plentiful in philosophers, for the reason that the folk there are too busy picking up half a living to have time for the cultivation of wisdom.
*King Goshawk and the Birds*

11 Dublin has reason to be proud of Easter Week, for the gay, shabby, majestic old city bore herself bravely during her six days agony. *The Wasted Island*

**O'Duffy, General Eoin** 1892-1944

1 The only pleasure in freedom is fighting for it. Dáil Éireann, 17 December 1921

2 The National Guard being a non-military or civil organization there will be no military equipment of any kind. Blue is adopted as the organization's colour for flags, shirts, ties, badges etc. just as sports clubs adopt a distinctive blazer or jersey. Any organization may adopt a special colour without infringing the law. Speech, 21 July 1933

**Oengus, The Culdee** *fl.* 800-850

3 Na mórshlébe andaig ro tesctha co rinnib; do-rónta co lléce slébe donaib glinnib.

*The great hills of evil have been cut down with spear-points, while the glens have been made into hills.*

*'The Downfall of Heathendom'*

**Ó Faoláin, Sean** *b.* 1900

4 That was why we chose the name of 'The Bell'. Any other equally spare and hard and simple word would have done, any word with a minimum of associations. Editorial to first number of *The Bell*, October 1940

5 Our sins are tawdry, our virtues childlike, our revolts desultory and brief, our submissions formal and frequent. In Ireland a policeman's lot is a supremely happy one. God smiles, the priest beams, and the novelist groans. 'The Dilemma of Irish Letters', *The Mouth*, December 1949

6 I was in fact exactly forty-six years old before I finally abandoned the faith of my fathers, and, under the life-loving example of Italy, became converted to Roman Catholicism.

'A Portrait of the Artist as an Old Man', *Irish University Review*, Spring 1976

7 . . . wherever the clouds occluded the ruthless sun I felt my senses at once leap in whatever part of me belongs irrevocably to this island of dark green brooding under a sky that is one vast pearl.

*Vive Moi!*

**O'Flaherty, Liam** 1897-1984

8 'Níl braon de mo chuid fola ionat,' a bhéic an t-athair agus é ag gabhail thart isteach ar an tsráid. 'Le do mháthair a chuaigh tú, a ruidín fánach leisciúil.'

'An Buille'

*'There's not a drop of my blood in you,' roared the father as he went into the yard. 'You took after your mother, you useless, lazy little good-for-nothing.'*

'The Blow'

9 . . . then just as suddenly her anger vanished like a puff of smoke, and she burst into wild tears, wailing: 'My children, oh, my children, far over the sea you will be carried from me, your mother.' And she began to rock herself and she threw her apron over her head.

'Going into Exile'

10 She was dead within a week. Wise old women that followed her corpse to the grave said that a convent was the proper place for such frail beauty.

'The Mermaid'

11 Man is a born liar. Otherwise he would not have invented the proverb, 'Tell the truth and shame the devil.'

*Shame the Devil*

12 Then the sniper turned over the dead body and looked into his brother's face.

'The Sniper'

**Ó Floinn, Criostóir** *b.* 1927

13 Tá nós an tsagart paróiste agat fós — gach scéim agus plean as do stuaim féin gan comhairle a ghlacadh le aon duine eile. 'Cóta Bán Chríost'

*You still behave like a parish priest — every move is made off your own bat without consulting anyone else.*

'Christ's White Garment'

**O'Hagan, John** 1822-1890

1 Too long our Irish hearts we schooled / In patient hope to bide, / By dreams of English justice fooled / And English tongues that lied. / That hour of weak delusion's past — / The empty dream has flown: / Our hope and strength, we find at last, / Is in Ourselves Alone.

'Ourselves Alone'

**Ó hAimhirgín, Osborn (Bergin)** 1872-1950

2 'Trí tréithe do dhaingnigh sinn,' / D'fhreagair Caoilte ciallmhar. / 'Gloine ár gcroí agus neart ár ngéag, / Is beart do réir ár mbriathar.'

'Trí Tréithe Na Féinne'

*'Three things', said Caoilte, 'gave the Fianna / Their confidence and pride, / Pure heart, sinewy arm / And deed that followed word.'*

'The Three Traits of the Fianna'

**O Hifearnáin, Liam** 1720-1760

3 I ngleannta séimhe na héigse bhím, / I bhfanntais péine i ngéibh gach laoi; / An tseangbhean ghlé ba bhéasach gnaoi / Do scanraigh mé, pé in Éirinn í.

'Pé in Éirinn Í'

*Pensive I stray through vales of dream, / Oppressed with pain, and faint I see / The gentle maid whose face has been / My endless bane, who e'er she be.*

**O'Higgins, Kevin Christopher** 1892-1927

4 Many would like to do with the British what we read that Brian Boru did with the Danes, not far from here. But we did not do it. We were not able to do it.

Bill to enact a Constitution,
Dáil Éireann, 18 September 1922

5 His [Erskine Childers'] programme is a negative programme, a purely destructive programme, and it will be victory to him and his peculiar mind if he prevents the government coming into existence. He has no constructive programme and so he keeps steadily, callously and ghoulishly on his career of striking at the heart of this nation.

On Standing Order 54,
Dáil Éireann, 27 September 1922

6 Men are standing in the path today, armed men, saying to the masked men of this nation, you must not take a certain course. That is a position which never has been conceded here. . . . Some men must be allowed to work that Treaty Settlement.

On the Re-establishment of
Civic Administration, Dáil Éireann,
29 September 1922

7 Now the life of this nation and the honour of this nation is worth the lives of many individuals. And we, in grave consultation and in grave council, have decided that if it is necessary to take the lives of many individuals then the lives of many individuals will be taken.

On Military Executions,
Dáil Éireann, 17 November 1922

8 These people [the Ulster Unionists] are part and parcel of the nation, and we being the majority and strength of the country . . . it comes well from us to make a generous adjustment to show that these people are regarded, not as alien enemies, not as planters, but that we wish them to take their share of its responsibilities.

Speech in Dáil Éireann, 1922

9 People, after all, must live, must order their lives either by law or by the strong hand; by the quick draw on the gun, the light finger and the sure eye; or by rules

made by their own representatives in their Parliament.

Enforcement of Law (Occasional Powers) Bill, Seanad Éireann, 8 February 1923

1 When I think of the hardship involved in only having seven hours to drink on a Sunday my soul shudders.

Intoxicating Liquor Bill, Dáil Éireann, 23 March 1927

2 The Party that was to end Partition, the Party that was to halve taxation, the Party that was to have every man sitting down under his own vine tree smoking a pipe of Irish-grown tobacco are not here today.

Dáil Éireann, 23 June 1927, commenting on the failure of Fianna Fáil to take up its seats.

**O'Keefe, John** 1747-1833

3 Amo, amas, I love a lass, / As cedar tall and slender; / Sweet cowslip's grace / Is her nominative case, / And she's of the feminine gender.

'The Agreeable Surprise'

4 I am a friar of orders grey: / As down the valley I take my way, / I pull not blackberry, haw, or hip, / Good store of venison does fill my scrip; / My long bead-roll I merrily chaunt, / Wher'er I walk no money I want; / And why I'm so plump the reason I'll tell — / Who leads a good life is sure to live well. / What baron or squire / Or knight of the shire / Lives half so well as a holy friar!

'The Friar of Orders Grey'

5 Fat, fair and forty. *Irish Minnie*

6 You should always except the present company. *The London Hermit*

**O'Kelly, Patrick** 1754-?

7 May Beef, or Mutton, Lamb or Veal / Be never found in Doneraile / But Garlic soup and curvy kale / Be still the food for Doneraile.

'The Curse of Doneraile'

**O'Kelly, Seumas** 1880-1918

8 We must take some things in this world by instalments, and at the last leave a lot of reckoning to the Almighty. *Hillsiders*

9 Both old men had the air of those who had been unexpectedly let loose. For a long time they had lurked somewhere in the shadows of life, the world having no business for them, and now, suddenly, they had been remembered and called forth to perform an office which nobody else on earth could perform. *The Weaver's Grave*

**Ó Laoghaire, Peadar** 1839-1920

10 Dá mba ná béadh agam acht an Ghaeluinn anois, ní tabharfaí aon toradh ann pé olc maith a bhéadh sé agam. Agus dá mba ná béadh agam acht an Béarla, ní fhéadfainn aon úsaid a dhéanamh de chun na Ghaeluinne do shaothrú pé olc maith a bhéadh sé agam.

*Mo Sgéal Féin*

*If I could speak only in Irish, nobody nowadays would notice whether I spoke well or badly. And if I could speak only in English, whether well or badly, I wouldn't be able to make any use of it to reclaim Irish.* *My Story*

11 Measaim nách misde dhom stad anso, agus a rádh mar a deireadh lucht scéalaíochta in Éirinn fadó: 'Gonadh é sin mo scéal-sa go nuige sin.' Ib.

*I think I should stop there, and announce as did the storytellers in Ireland long ago: 'Thus far, then, my tale.'* Ib.

**O'Leary, Ellen** 1831-1889

1 He fell asleep and woke in heaven / Ere I knew he was dead; / Yet why should I my darling rue? / He was to God and Ireland true. 'To God and Ireland True'

**O'Leary, John** 1830-1907

2 Parnell may be the Uncrowned King of Ireland; he is not the infallible Pope of Rome.
Address at Mullinahone, August 1885

3 It is one amongst the many misfortunes of Ireland that she has never yet produced a great poet.
Lecture in Cork, February 1886

4 There are certain things a man must not do to save a nation . . . To cry in public.
In conversation with W. B. Yeats

**O'Leary, Joseph** 1790-1850

5 Whisky, drink divine! / Why should drivelers bore us / With the praise of wine / While we've thee before us?
'Whisky, Drink Divine'

**O'Mahony, John** 1816-1877

6 Ere long there shall be an Irish Army on the Irish hillsides ready to battle for Irish independence and drive back from the green and sacred Isle of Erin those ruthless tyrants who have desolated our homes and driven us wandering exiles over the whole earth.
Quoted in Kee, *The Green Flag*

**Ó Muineacháin, Diarmuid**

7 Na daoine is lú ciall i n-Éirinn / Daoine gan Bhéarla gan Ghaeluinn.

*They are the stupidest people in Ireland, / Whose English is broken and whose Irish is faulty.*

**O'Neill, Hugh, 2nd Earl of Tyrone** 1550-1616

8 We have received your letter, and what we make out from it is that you offer nothing but sweet words and procrastination. For our part in the matter, whatever man would not be on our side and would not spend his efforts for the right, we take it that that is a man against us. For this reason, wherever you yourself are doing well, hurt us as much as you are able, and we shall hurt you to the best of our ability, with God's will. Letter to Sir John McCoughleyn, 6 February 160c

**O'Neill, Mary Davenport** 1875-1967

9 I know a town tormented by the sea, / And there time goes slow / That the people see it flow / And watch it drowsily. 'Galway'

10 This town is eaten through with memory / Of pride and thick red Spanish wine and gold / And a great come and go. Ib.

**O'Neill, Moira (Agnes M. Skrine)** *c.* 1870-?

11 All the gold in Ballytearim is what's stickin' to the whin.
'The Boy from Ballytearim'

12 Over here in England I'm helpin' wi' the hay, / An' I wisht I was in Ireland the livelong day; / Weary on the English hay and sorra take the wheat! / Och, Corrymeela an' the blue sky over it! 'Corrymeela'

13 I hope this finds all well at home, as it leaves me at present.
'The Emigrant's Letter'

14 Sure he's five months old, an' he's two foot long — Baby Johneen. 'Johneen'

1 Oh, think o' my fate when ye dance at a fair, / In Rachray there's no Christianity there.

'The Rachray Man'
(Rachray is Rathlin Island off North Antrim.)

**O'Neill, Terence,**
**Lord O'Neill of the Maine** *b.* 1914

2 We cannot be part of the United Kingdom merely when it suits us. . . . Is a freedom to pursue the un-Christian path of communal strife and sectarian bitterness really more important to you than all the benefits of the British welfare state?

Television address, 9 December 1968

3 I have tried to break the chains of ancient hatreds. I have been unable to realise during my period of office all that I had sought to achieve. Whether now it can be achieved in my life-time I do not know. But one day these things will be and must be achieved.

Television resignation address, 28 April 1969

4 It is frightfully hard to explain to a Protestant that if you give Roman Catholics a good job and a good house, they will live like Protestants, because they will see neighbours with cars and television sets.

They will refuse to have eighteen children, but if the Roman Catholic is jobless and lives in a most ghastly hovel, he will rear eighteen children on national assistance. . . .

If you treat Roman Catholics with due consideration and kindness they will live like Protestants, in spite of the authoritative nature of their Church.

Radio interview quoted in *Belfast Telegraph*, 5 May 1969

5 How could Southern Ireland keep a bridal North in the manner to which she is accustomed?

*The Irish Times*, 'This Week They Said', 16 January 1971

**Orange Ballads and Songs**
19th Century

6 So praise God, all true Protestants, and I will say no further, / But had the Papists gain'd the day there would have been open murder. 'The Boyne Water'

7 And soon the bright Orange put down the Green Rag, / Down, down, Croppies lie down.'

'Croppies Lie Down'

8 Then Orangemen remember King William, / And your fathers who with him did join, / And fought for our glorious deliverance / On the green, grassy slopes of the Boyne.

'The Green, Grassy Slopes of the Boyne'

9 A it stands for Aughrim, where blood flowed on the plain, / B is for Boyne Water, where bones do still remain, / C is for Culmore, where crossing it we had our falls, / D I'm sure you all know well, our Maiden Derry's Walls.

'The Orange ABC'

10 Then heigho the lily-o / The royal, loyal lily-o / There's not a flower in Erin's bower / Can match the Orange lily-o. 'The Orange Lily-o'

11 So, all true blues, come fill your glass, a better toast will ever pass, / We'll drink unto the lovely lass, the Orange Maid of Sligo. 'The Orange Maid of Sligo'

12 Scarlet Church of all uncleanness, / Sink thou to the deep abyss, / To the orgies of obsceneness, / Where the hell-bound furies hiss; / Where thy father Satan's eye / May hail thee, blood-stained Papacy. 'The Papacy'

1 The Protestant boys are loyal and true, / Stout-hearted in battle, and stout-handed too. 'The Protestant Boys'

2 It's old but it is beautiful / Its colours they are fine. 'The Sash My Father Wore'

**Ó Rathaille, Aogán** 1670-1726

3 Is iomaí marbh do mharaigh an marbh so fútsa, a líog! / Is mairg don mharbh so mhairfeadh le rún a chroí, / Marbh do mharaigh na mairbh is nár iontaigh slí / Is is marbh é an marbh so in Acheron suíte síos. 'Fé Lár na Leice Seo'

*Many dead did he do to death, this dead man under the headstone, / Doomed after death is this dead man and his deadly heart's designs, / This dead man did the dead to death and death did not deter him, / This dead man has gone to his death in the deadly swamps of Acheron.* 'Under this Headstone'

4 Gile na gile do chonnarc ar slí in uaigneas, / Criostal an chroistail a goirmroisc rinn-uaine, / Binneas an bhinnis a friotal nár chríonghruama, / Deirge is finne do fionnadh 'na gríosghruannaibh. 'Gile na Gile'

*Brightness of brightness I've seen on the way, lonely, / Shining of shining blue-greens in her gaze glowing, / Fineness of fineness her speech like the waves' motion, / Fireflush and whiteness compete in her face boldly.* 'Brightness of Brightness'

5 Caiseal gan cliar, fiailteach ná macraí ar dtúis / is beanna-bhruig Bhriain ciarthuilte 'mhadraíbh úisc, / Ealla gan triair triaithe de mhacaibh rí Mumhan, / fá deara dhom triall riamh ort, a Vailintín Brún. 'Vailintín Brún'

*Cashel without guests, rest-house abandoned and fire out, / Packs of dark hounds growling on the battlements of Brian's tower, / Duhallow without chief, leaderless the Dalcassian line now, / These commanded me to this visit, Valentine Brown.* 'Valentine Brown'

**Ó Reachtabhra, Antoine / Raifteirí** 1784-1835

6 Anois teacht an Earraigh beidh an lá dul chun síneadh, / Is tar éis na Féil Brighde ardóidh mé mo sheol, / Ó chuir mé i mo cheann é ní stopfaidh mé choíche / Go seasfaidh mé síos i lár Chontae Mhuigheo. 'Cill Aodáin'

*Now with the coming of Spring, the day is beginning to stretch, / And after the feast of St Brigid I'll rise up and go, / Since the notion came into my head I'll not even stop for a second / Till I set my foot down in the middle of County Mayo.*

7 Mise Raifteirí, an file, / lán dóchas is grá / le súile gan solas, / le ciúineas gan crá, / 'dul siar ar m'aistear / le solas mo chroí, / fann agus tuirseach / go deireadh mo shlí. 'Mise Raifteirí'

*I am Raftery the poet, / Full of hope and love, / My eyes are sightless, / I am filled with peace. / I travel westward / By the light of my heart / Faint and weary / Till the end of the way.* 'I Am Raftery'

**O'Reilly, John Boyle** 1844-1890

8 'You gave me the key of your heart, my love; / Then why did you make me knock?' / 'Oh that was yesterday, saints above! / And last night — I changed the lock!' 'Constancy'

9 May no weak race be wronged, and no strong robber feared / To oppressors more hateful, to slaves more endeared, / Till the world comes to know that the test of a cause / Is the hatred of tyrants and Erin's applause. 'Erin'

1 Ireland is a fruitful mother of genius, but a barren nurse. 'Watchwords'

**Ó Ríordáin, Seán** 1917-1977

2 Is níl laistigh d'aon daoirse / Ach saoirse ó'n daoirse sin. 'Daoirse'

*And only the unfree / Can know what freedom is.* 'Lack of Freedom'

3 Níl éinne beo nach bhfuair oileán, / Is trua a chás má thréig.
'Oileán agus Oileán Eile'

*Each of the living has found an island, / He who has left it is lost.*
'The Two Islands'

4 Níor saolaíodh mé gur cailleadh é, / Is mó mé i mise amháin, / Cailltear le gach focal mé, / Ach éiríonn le gach anáil
'Rian na gCos'

*'I' wasn't born until 'I' died, / Many 'I's preceded my death, / The old 'I' dies with every word, / The new 'I' rises with each breath . . .* 'Footprints'

**Ormsby, Frank** *b.* 1947

5 We persevere from habit, when we try / These days our hope's mechanical, we trust / To accident. We are selective / No longer, the full hundred crosses / Filling the sky. 'Spot the Ball'

6 Unbowed I claim my rights — to herd alone, / and be accepted. 'Sheepman'

**Orpen, Sir William** 1878-1931

7 . . . old Ireland that Romantic Lady who slumbered and dreamt her way along to the music of the laughter and tears of her people.
*Stories of Old Ireland and Myself*

8 LANE'S COMMITTEE:
We want some of your money /
For Manet and Monet.
THE SUBSCRIBERS:
Sure we haven't got any for Monet and Manet.
[Of the Lane Pictures Committee] Ib.

**Orr, James** 1770-1816

9 The savage loves his native shore, / Though rude the soil and chill the air.
'The Irishman'

10 . . . who a friend or foe can act / So generous as an Irishman? Ib.

**Orr, William** 1768-1797

11 I am no traitor; I die a persecuted man for a persecuted country.
Speech from gallows, Carrickfergus

**Orthanach, Bishop** ? -840

12 Slán seiss, a Brigit co mbúaid / for grúaid Lifi lir co tráig; / is tú banfhlaith buidnib slúaig / fil for clannaib Cathaír Máir.

*Sit safely, Brigit, in triumph on Liffey's cheek to the strand of the sea; you are the princess with ranked hosts above the children of Cathaír Mór.*
'To St Brigit'

**O'Ryan, Jeremiah** 17? -1855

13 I am no Rogue, no Ribbonman, / No Croppy, Whig, or Tory, O; / I'm guilty not of any crime / Of petty or high thraison, O.
'The Peeler and the Goat'

**O'Shaughnessy, Arthur William Edgar** 1841-1881

14 We are the music makers, / We are the dreamers of dreams. 'Ode'

15 . . . three with a new song's measure / Can trample an empire down. Ib.

**Ó Súileabháin, Muiris** 1904-1950

1 Níl aon bhaol ná gur breá í an oíge, cé go bhfuil sí fá réim agamsa fós agus ní thagann ciall roimh aois.

*Fiche Blian Ag Fás*

*There's no doubt it's great to be young, though I say it as shouldn't, for I am still in the flower of my youth and wisdom comes only with age.*

*Twenty Years A-Growing*

2 Mhuise ba mhór é ár ndochma roimh an scoil — ach ní galar aenne amháin é, is é mo thuairim. Ib.

*Indeed, we were most reluctant to attend school — but there's many who feel like that, I'd say.* Ib.

3 'Nach fearr ná san an dá theanga bheith aige?' arsa m'athair – 'agus rud eile atá sa scéal, níl fhios agat cad é an chuma go n-iontóidh Éire amach fós – béidir go raghadh an teanga iasachta fé chois.' Ib.

*'Isn't he better off being able to speak both languages?', said my father, 'and as well as that, you don't know how Ireland may yet turn out — perhaps the language of the stranger will be the one to go under.'* Ib.

**Ó Súilleabháin, Eoghan Rua** 1748-1784

4 Ceo draíochta i gcoim oíche do sheol mé / trí thíorthaibh mar óinmhid ar strae, / gan príomhcharaid díograis im chóngar / 's mé i gcríochaibh tar m'eolas i gcéin. 'Ceo Draíochta'

*Through the deep night a magic mist led me / like a simpleton roaming the land, / no friend of my bosom beside me, / an outcast in places unknown.*

*'A Magic Mist'*

**Ó Súilleabháin, Tadhg Gaelach** 1715-1795

5 Gile mo chroí do chroí-se, A Shlánaitheoir, / is ciste mo chroí do chroí-se a dháil im chomhair; / ós follas gur líon do chroí dem ghrá-sa, a stóir, / i gcochall mo chroí do chroí-se fág i gcomhad. 'Duain Chroí Íosa'

*The light in my heart, O Saviour, is Thy heart, / the wealth of my heart, Thy heart poured out for me. / Seeing that Thy heart, Love, filled with love for me / leave Thy heart in keeping, hooded in mine.* 'A Poem to the Heart of Jesus'

**O'Sullivan, Seamus**
**(James Sullivan Starkey)** 1879-1958

6 And women with petticoats coloured like flame / And little bare feet that were blue with cold, / Went dancing back to the age of gold. 'A Piper'

# P

**Paisley, Rev. Ian Richard Kyle** *b.* 1926

1 As almost every accusation possible has already been hurled at the preacher any further attacks will be worn-out venom. Introduction, *Paisley: The Man and his Message*

2 But the Bible says there is none righteous. The old Pope too. He is not righteous either. You would think to hear some people talk that he was the next thing to God Almighty. 'Four Black Roman Nones', ib.

3 The Devil in a Pigskin Swimsuit Title of sermon, ib.

4 The Pigs that Got the Permanent Waves Ib.

5 You cannot talk peace until the enemy surrenders, and the enemy is the Roman Catholic Church. *The Irish Times*, 'This Week They Said', 23 August 1969

6 The Catholics have been interfering in Ulster affairs since 1641. Ib., 30 August 1969

7 The Roman Catholic Church is getting nearer to Communism every day. Ib., 13 September 1969

8 God has been our help in 1641, 1688, 1690, 1798, 1912, and 1920, and he will not fail us in the future. Ib., 2 October 1971

9 Mr Faulkner has sat down with the greatest IRA man of them all – Jack Lynch. Ib., 29 January 1972

10 I have reason to believe that the fowl-pest outbreaks are the work of the IRA. Ib., 1 December 1973

11 We do not accept the word of the slanderous bachelor who lives on the banks of the Tiber. *The Irish Times*, 'Sayings of the Year', 31 December 1974

**Parish Priest of Dingle, Co. Kerry**

12 Socialism is worse than Communism. Socialism is a heresy of Communism. Socialists are a Protestant variety of Communists. Sermon, June 1969, prior to General Election; quoted in Cruise O'Brien, *States of Ireland*

**Parish Priest of Roundwood, Co. Wicklow**

13 Parnellism is a simple love of adultery and all those who profess Parnellism profess to love and admire adultery. They are an adulterous set, their leaders are open and avowed adulterers, and

therefore I say to you, as parish priest, beware of these Parnellites when they enter your house, you that have wives and daughters, for they will do all they can to commit these adulteries, for their cause is not patriotism – it is adultery – and they back Parnellism because it gratifies their adultery.

Sermon, 19 June 1892,
quoted in Kee, *The Green Flag*

**Parnell, Charles Stewart** 1846-1891

1 A fair rent is a rent the tenant can reasonably pay according to the times, but in bad times a tenant cannot be expected to pay as much as he did in good times three or four years ago. . . . You must show the landlords that you intend to keep a firm grip of your homesteads.

Westport, 8 June 1879

2 When a man takes a farm from which another has been evicted, you must show him in the streets of the town, you must show him in the fair and in the market-place, and even in the house of worship, by leaving him severely alone, by putting him into moral Coventry, by isolating him from his kind as if he was a leper of old — you must show him your detestation of the crime he has committed, and you may depend upon it that there will be no man so full of avarice, so lost to shame, as to dare the public opinion of all right-thinking men and to transgress your unwritten code of laws.

Speech at Ennis, 18 September 1880

3 Captain Moonlight [agrarian outrage] will take my place.

When asked in October 1881 what would happen were he arrested.

4 We cannot under the British Constitution ask for more than the restitution of Grattan's Parliament, but no man has the right to fix the boundary of the march of a nation. No man has the right to say to his country, 'Thus far shalt thou go and no further', and we have never attempted to fix the *ne plus ultra* to the progress of Ireland's nationhood and we never shall.

Speech at Cork, 21 January 1885

5 Ireland has been knocking at the English door long enough with kid gloves, and now she will knock with a mailed hand.

Speech in private during 1885 election at Liverpool, recalled in *Tuam Herald* obituary by William O'Malley

**Patrick, Bishop of Dublin**
*fl.* 1074-1084

6 Continet hec hominis cuiusdam terra sepulcrum / Femineas turbas fallentis more doloso / Ille etenim numerum ingentem uiolauit earum: / Fine tamen fuerat felici crimina deflens. / Ergo modo miro mulier, si uiderit illud, / Pedere vel ridere solet cernendo sepulcrum: / Tormine iam resonat quod si non rideat illa.

*de mirabilibus Hibernie, xiii*

*This land holds also the tomb of a man / Who deceived in treacherous wise hosts of women. / For he raped them in countless numbers: / But at the end he wept for his crimes and found peace. / Wondrous to tell, any woman that sees this tomb / Breaks wind or laughs as soon as she lays eyes upon it: / Loudly it rumbles if she does not laugh.*

*On the Wonders of Ireland,*
trans. Aubrey Gwynn.

7 Perge carina / Per mare longum: / Christus in undis / Sit tibi ductor, / Remige tuto / Sidere sudo.

*Liber sancti Patricii episcopi: Prologus*

*Onward, my barque, / Through the long sea! / Christ on the water / Be thy steersman / With sure oar / And a clear sky!*

*The Book of Holy Patrick the Bishop: Prologue*, trans. Aubrey Gwynn.

**Patrick, St** ? - 490

1 Ego Patricius peccator rusticissimus et minimus omnium fidelium et contemptibilissimus apud plurimos.

*Confessio*

*I am Patrick, a sinner, the least learned of men, least of all the faithful, most worthless in the eyes of many.*

*Confessions*

2 . . . uide in visu noctis uirum uenientem quasi de Hiberione, cui nomen Victoricus, cum epistolis innumerabilibus, et dedit mihi unam ex his et legi principium epistolae continentem 'Vox Hiberionacum', et cum recitabam principium epistolae putabam ipso momento audire uocem ipsorum . . . et sic exclamauerunt quasi ex uno ore: 'Rogamus te, (sancte) puer, ut uenias et adhuc ambulas inter nos.' Ib.

*I saw in a dream a man called Victor who seemed to be from Ireland and had many letters. He gave me one and I read the opening words, 'The voice of the Irish.' And as I read the beginning I seemed at that moment to hear the voice of those people . . . They cried as with one voice, 'We beg you, holy youth, come and walk once more among us.'*

Ib.

3 Christ with me, Christ before me, Christ behind me, Christ on my right, Christ on my left, Christ when I lie down, Christ when I sit down, Christ when I arise, Christ in the heart of every man who thinks of me, Christ in the mouth of every one who speaks of me, Christ in every eye that sees me, Christ in every ear that hears me.

'The Deer's Cry, otherwise known as 'The Breastplate', attrib. St Patrick, trans: Kuno Meyer

**Patterson, Johnny** 1840-1889

4 She was just the sort of creature, boys, that nature did intend / To walk right through the world, my boys, without the Graecian bend, / Nor did she wear a chignon, I'd have you all to know, / And I met her in the garden where the praties grow.

'The Garden Where the Praties Grow'

5 Those days in our hearts we will cherish, / Contented, although we were poor, / And the songs that were sung in the days we were young, / On the stone outside Dan Murphy's door!

'The Stone Outside Dan Murphy's Door'

6 Shake hands with all the neighbours, / And kiss the colleens all. / You're as welcome as the flowers in May, / Back home to Donegal.

'Shake Hands With Your Uncle Dan'

7 Oh, the old turf fire, / And the hearth swept clean, / There is no one so contented / As myself and Paddy Keane; / With the baby in the cradle, / You can hear her grannie say: / 'Won't you go to sleep, alanna, / While I wet your daddy's tay.' 'The Old Turf Fire'

**Pearse, Patrick Henry** 1879-1916

8 Dá gcaillfí an Ghaeilge chaillfí Éire.

*If Irish were to be lost Ireland would perish.* *An Barr Buadh*, 4 May 1916

9 When the seven men met in O'Connell Street to found the Gaelic League they were commencing . . . not a revolt but a revolution. The Coming Revolution, November 1913

1 Since the wise men have not spoken, I speak that am only a fool. 'The Fool'

2 I have squandered the splendid years that the Lord God gave my youth / In attempting impossible things, deeming them alone worth the toil. Ib.

3 And though I grudge them not, I weary, weary / Of the long sorrow — And yet I have my joy: / My sons were faithful and they fought. 'The Mother'

4 A French writer has paid the English a very well-deserved compliment. He says they have never committed a useless crime.
'The Murder Machine', 1916

5 Life springs from death and from the graves of patriot men and women spring living nations. The Defenders of this Realm have worked well in secret and in the open. They think that they have pacified Ireland. They think that they have purchased half of us and intimidated the other half. They think that they have foreseen everything, think they have provided against everything; but the fools, the fools, the fools, they have left us our Fenian dead, and while Ireland holds these graves Ireland unfree shall never be at peace.
Oration at graveside of O'Donovan Rossa, 1 August 1915

6 There are in every generation those who shrink from the ultimate sacrifice, but there are in every generation those who make it with joy and laughter and these are the salt of the generations.
Robert Emmet Commemoration Address, Brooklyn, New York, 2 March 1914

7 What I mean by an Irish school is a school that takes Ireland for granted.
*The Story of a Success*, 1909

8 The object of Na Fianna Éireann is to train the boys of Ireland to fight Ireland's battle when they are men.
*To the Boys of Ireland*, February 1914

9 The beauty of the world hath made me sad / This beauty that will pass.
'The Wayfarer'

10 Fornocht do chonnach thú / A áille na háille. / Is do dhallas mo shúil / Ar eagla go stánfainn. 'Fornocht do chonac thú'

*Naked I saw thee, / O beauty of beauty, / And I blinded my eyes / For fear I should fail.* Trans. by Pearse

11 Do thugas mo ghnúis / Ar an ród so romham / Ar an ngníomh do chím / Is ar an mbás do gheobhad. Ib.

*I have turned my face / To this road before me / To the deed that I see / And the death I shall die.* Ib.

12 Mise Éire – Sine me ná an Chailleach Béarra. / Mór Mo Ghlóire – Mé do rug Cú Chulainn cróga. / Mór Mo Náire – Mo chlann féin do dhíol a máthair. / Mise Éire – Uaigní mé ná an Chailleach Béarra. 'Mise Éire

*I am Ireland: I am older than the Old Woman of Beare. / Great my glory: I that bore Cuchulainn the valiant. / Great my shame: My own children that sold their mother. / I am Ireland: I am lonelier than the Old Woman of Beare.*
Trans. by Pearse

**Pepys, Samuel** 1633-1703

13 Mr Butler was now all full of his high discourse in praise of Ireland. . . . But so many lies I never heard in praise of anything as he told of Ireland.
*Diary*, 28 July 1660

**Petrie, George** 1790-1866

1 Do you remember that night / That you and I were / At the foot of the rowan-tree / And the night drifting snow? / Your head on my breast, / And your pipe sweetly playing? / Little thought I that night / That our love ties would loosen! 'Do You Remember that Night?', from the Irish

**Phelan, James Leo 'Jim'** 1895-1960

2 The Irish have a word for it. The small-town merchant who gradually achieves a stranglehold on his neighbours is called a gombeen-man. Gomba, in Gaelic, means vaguely a bit or a scrap. Gombeen is the diminutive. A textbook of economics might well be condensed into the single word.
'Bell Wether', *Bog Blossom Stories*

3 At midnight on the Monday the Governor . . . came in my cell and read a long paper to me. I was respited, would go to penal servitude for life . . . Now I was finished with walking the roads. There's not much room to walk, in a cell twelve feet by seven.
*The Name's Phelan*

**Pigott, Richard** 1828-1889

4 Though I regret the accident of Lord Cavendish's death I cannot refuse to admit that Burke got no more than his deserts. Part of forged letter, ostensibly by Parnell

**Plunket, Lord William Conyngham** 1764-1854

5 For my own part, I will resist it to the last gasp of my existence and with the last drop of my blood, and when I feel the hour of my dissolution approaching, I will, like the father of Hannibal, take my children to the altar and swear them to eternal hostility against the invaders of their country's freedom.
Speech against Act of Union, 1800

**Plunkett, Edward John Morton Drax, 18th Baron Dunsany** 1878-1957

6 But I was growing impatient at being lectured at by a ghost, and was a little chilled by the mist. 'Are there such things as ghosts?' I asked then.
And a wind blew then, and the ghost was suddenly gone. 'We used to be,' it sighed softly. 'The Ghost of the Valley'

**Plunkett, James (Kelly)** *b.* 1920

7 Then the bells of St Patrick's, with their time-mellowed tongues, began to play a little tune. 'Dublin Fusilier'

8 For him sin abounded in the dusty places of the office, in his sweat of fear when the morning clock told him he was late again, in the obsequious answer to the official question, in the impulse which reduced him to pawing the hot and willing typist who passed him on the deserted stairs.
'The Eagle and the Trumpets'

9 The outlook was frightening; but it was better to walk in your bare feet. It was better to walk without shoes and barefooted than to walk without dignity. 'Weep for Our Pride'

**Plunkett, Joseph Mary** 1887-1916

10 The wind rose, the sea rose, / A wave rose on the sea, / Swelled with the mournful singing / Of a sad century.
'1847-1891'

11 I see His blood upon the rose / And in the stars the glory of His eyes.
'I See His Blood Upon the Rose'

**Plunkett, Sir Horace Curzon** 1854-1932

12 We have been too long a prey to that deep delusion, which, because the ills of the country we love were in the past largely caused from without, bids us to look to the same source for their cure.
*Ireland in the New Century*

**Plunkett, St Oliver** 1625-1681

1 Sagairt óir is cailís chrainn / Bhí le linn Phádraig in Éirinn; / Sagairt chrainn is cailís óir / I ndeire an domhain dearóil.

*Golden priests and wooden chalices / In Ireland, in Patrick's time; / Golden chalices and wooden priests / In this late wretched time.*

Attrib., Rev. Desmond Forristal, *Oliver Plunkett*

**Pope John Paul II (Karol Wojtyla)** *b.* 1920

2 Pervading nationalism imposes its dominion on man today in many different forms and with an aggressiveness that spares no one. . . . The challenge that is already with us is the temptation to accept as true freedom what in reality is only a new form of slavery.

Address in Phoenix Park, Dublin, 29 September 1979

3 I end, dear brothers and sisters, beloved sons and daughters of Ireland by recalling how divine providence has used this island on the edge of Europe for the conversion of the European continent.

Ib.

4 On my knees, I beg you to turn away from the paths of violence and to return to the ways of peace. You may claim to seek justice. I, too, believe in justice, and seek justice. But violence only delays the day of justice. Further violence in Ireland will only drag down to ruin the land you claim to love and the values you claim to cherish.

Address at Killineer, Drogheda, Co. Louth, 29 September 1979

5 Young people of Ireland, I love, you: Young people of Ireland, I bless you.

Address at Ballybrit Racecourse, Galway, 30 September 1979

6 May Ireland always continue to give witness before the modern world to her traditional commitment to the sanctity and the indissolubility of the marriage bond.

Address at Limerick, 1 October 1979

**Powell, Anthony** *b.* 1905

7 The Batallion was first stationed at Portadown, a town politically reliable, if scenically unromantic.

*Faces in My Time*, Vol. III of *Memoirs: To Keep the Ball Rolling*

**Power, Richard (Risteard De Paor)** 1928-1970

8 'Níl aon rud ar thalaimh an domhain comh huafásach le bás a fháil mar sin, i ngan fhios do dhuine ar bith.'

*Úll i mBarr an Ghéagain*

*'There's nothing on earth in the world so tragic as to die this way, unbeknownst to anyone at all.'* *Apple On The Treetop*

9 Cuma sa diabhal liom faoi na rialacha geilleagracha . . . tá beocht agus beatha san áit seo.

Ib.

*Screw the laws of economics . . . there is yet a world of living and of life in this back of beyond.*

Ib.

**Praegar, Robert Lloyd** 1865-1953

10 A young fellow had got into some minor trouble with the police, and the question of bail arose. 'Haven't you any near relations who would help you?' asked the magistrate. 'Haven't you any brothers?' 'I have, indeed, Your Worship; I have three brothers — two alive, and one in Belfast!'

*The Way That I Went*

11 I have wandered about Europe from Lapland to the Aegean Sea: but have always returned with fresh appreciation of my own land. I think that is as it should be.

Ib.

**Pueckler-Muskau, H. L. H. Von**
1785-1871

1 Before I visit the Giant's Causeway, I wished to see Ireland's Giant [when asked by Daniel O'Connell if he had been to the Causeway, Autumn 1828].

Quoted in Maxwell,
*The Stranger in Ireland*

**Redmond, John Edward** 1856-1918

1 The one great principle of any settlement of the Irish question must be the recognition of the divine right of Irishmen, and Irishmen alone, to rule Ireland.
Speech in Chicago, 18 August 1886

2 I say that the coast of Ireland will be defended from foreign invasion by her armed sons, and for this purpose armed Nationalists in the South will only be too glad to join arms with the armed Protestants in the North.
Speech in House of Commons, at outbreak of Great War, 3 August 1914

**Rhodes, Cecil John** 1853-1902

3 Resign – marry – return.
Cable to Parnell during O'Shea Scandal, December 1890

**Robinson, Lennox** 1886-1958

4 It is common knowledge that the leading newspapers employ as dramatic critics journalists who are excellent on a racecourse or a football field but who are hopelessly astray – or asleep – in the stalls of the Gaiety or the Abbey.
'A Young Man from the South'

**Roche, Sir Boyle** 1743-1807

5 Mr Speaker, if we once permitted the villainous French masons to meddle with the buttresses and walls of our ancient constitution, they would never stop nor stay, sir, till they brought the foundation stones tumbling about the ears of the nation. . . . Here, perhaps, sirs, the murderous Marshellaw men would break in, cut us to mincemeat, and throw our bleeding heads upon that table, to stare us in the face.
Speech on threatened French invasion in Irish House of Commons, 1796

6 I would have the two sisters [England and Ireland] embrace like one brother.
Speech favouring Act of Union, 1799

7 How could the sergeant-at-arms stop him in the rear, while he was catching him at the front? Could he like a bird be in two places at once? Attrib.

8 Why should we put ourselves out of our way to do anything for posterity; for what has posterity done for us? *(Laughter)* I apprehend you gentlemen have entirely mistaken my words, I assure the house that by posterity I do not mean my ancestors but those who came immediately after them. Attrib.

9 I smelt a rat; I see him forming in the air and darkening the sky; but I'll nip him in the bud. Attrib.

**Rodgers, William Robert** 1910-1969

1 There is a through-otherness about Armagh / Of tower and steeple, / Up on the hill are the arguing graves of the kings, / And below are the people. 'Armagh'

2 And he / His knees drawn up, his head dropped deep, / Curled like a question mark asleep. 'Christ Walking on the Water'

3 Mary Magdalene, that easy woman, / Saw, from the shore, the seas / Beat against the hard stone of Lent, / Crying, 'Weep, seas, weep / For yourselves that cannot dent me more. 'Lent'

4 Turn down the candid lamp / And draw the equal quilt / Over our naked guilt. 'The Net'

5 I am Ulster, my people an abrupt people / Who like the spiky consonants in speech Epilogue, *The Character of Ireland*

6 Tin cans, fricatives, fornication, staccato talk, / Anything that gives or takes attack, / Like Micks, Tagues, tinkers' gets, Vatican. / An angular people, brusque and Protestant, / For whom the word is still a fighting word. Ib.

7 Mine were not born with silver spoon in gob. Ib.

**Rolleston, Thomas William Hazen** 1857-1920

8 In a quiet water'd land, a land of roses, / Stands Saint Kieran's city fair; / And the warriors of Erin in their famous generations / Slumber there. 'The Dead at Clonmacnoise'

9 Darkly grows the quiet ivy, / pale the broken arches glimmer through; / Dark upon the cloister-garden / dreams the shadow of the ancient yew. 'The Grave of Rury'

**Rooney, William** 1872-1901

10 Nothing less than a miracle could give us at once Gaelic readers; and we must read something if we are to remain reasonable beings. The Anglo-Irish literature, which certainly mirrors the life of Ireland that is presently ours, provides us with the necessary material. It is not the perfection of Irish thought . . . but it is a saving salt that will secure the heart of the country from complete decay. Prose Writings

11 . . . the national ideal, which, rightly interpreted, ought to mean an Irish state governed by Irishmen for the benefit of the Irish people. Ib.

12 I give you 'The Gallant Old West', boys, / Where rallied our bravest and best, / When Ireland lay broken and bleeding, / Hurrah for the men of the West! 'The Men of the West'

**Ros, Amanda McKitterick** 1861-1939

13 Dear Lord, the day of eggs is here. 'Ode to Easter'

14 Holy Moses! Take a look! / Flesh decayed in every nook, / Some rare bits of brain lie here, / Mortal loads of beef and beer. 'On Visiting Westminster Abbey'

15 I don't believe in publishers. . . . I consider they're too grabby altogether. They love to keep the Sabbath and everything else they can lay their hands on. Letters

16 I expected to be talked about at the end of a thousand years. Attrib.

**Rowley, Richard**
**(Richard Valentine Williams)** 1877-1947

1 JOVE: There shall you wander / Amidst a barbarous people harsh of speech / And of fierce aspect, dwelling in huts of stone, / Seeing the sun but seldom, eating strange meats, / And never tasing wine, or fruits, or oil.
*Apollo in Mourne*

2 An' now, an oul' bachelor-man / D'ye know what I think? / That life's a dreich job at the best / Wantin' women an' drink. 'The Bachelor-man'

3 Terrible as an army with banners / The legions of labour, / The builders of ships, / Tramp thro' the winter eve.
'The Islandmen'

4 Great lads, the Tinkers O' Mourne / A thievinger people / Never was born.
'The Tinkers O' Mourne'

**Russell, Diarmuid** *b.* 1906

5 Everywhere in Irish prose there twinkles and peers the merry eye of a people who had little to laugh about in real life.
Introduction,
*The Portable Irish Reader*

**Russell, William George (AE)** 1867-1935

6 We hold the Ireland in the heart / More than the land our eyes have seen.
'On Behalf of Some Irishmen Not Followers of Tradition'

7 We would no Irish sign efface, / But yet our lips would gladlier hail / The first born of the Coming Race / Than the last splendour of the Gael. / No blazoned banner we unfold — / One charge alone we give to youth, / Against the sceptred myth to hold / The golden heresy of truth. Ib.

8 We referred a couple of months ago to Dungloe, in the far northwest of Donegal, where the gombeen man and the higgler, the only surviving contemporaries of the cave tiger, the plesiosaurus, and other primaeval monsters, still roved about picking the bones of their victims. The creature will soon be extinct, as the co-operative hunter has found his way into this remote region, and is shooting his swift arrows. Anyone who wants to see these survivors of the ferocious, man-devouring creatures which once wallowed in the primordial slime, had better make haste, and take the train to Dungloe, where they can still be stalked and their habits observed.
*Irish Homestead*, 5 January 1907

9 A literary movement: five or six people who live in the same town and hate each other. Attrib.

**Ryan, Desmond** 1893-1964

10 Mrs Marion Bloom bathing in her sexual reveries without breath or comma. *Remembering Sion*

# S

**Sarsfield, Patrick, Earl of Lucan** *d.* 1693

1 Sarsfield is the watchword — Sarsfield is the man. At Ballyneety, 11 August 1690, quoted in Lenihan, *Limerick, its History and Antiquities* 1866

2 Change kings and we will fight it over again with you. After Limerick, Attrib.

3 Would to God this was shed for Ireland. Attrib. last words, fighting for France at Landen.

**Savage-Armstrong, G. F.** 1846-1906

4 A'm proof the-night 'gen win' an' snaw, / A'll walk frae here tae Derry — / Though Noe's flood yince mair cam doon / A'd face it bowld and merry. 'The Shawlie'

**Sayers, Peig** 1873-1958

5 Seana-bhean isea mise anois, go bhfuil cos léi ins an uaigh is cos eile ar a bruach. *Peig*

*I am an old woman now, with one foot in the grave, and the other on its brink.* *Peig*

6 Dá mbeadh fhios agam go mbeadh a leath, ná a thrian, i ndán dom ní bheadh mo chroí ná m'intinn comh haerach ná comh misniúil is do bhí i dtosach mo shaoil. Ib.

*If I had known the half or the third of what was in store for me, neither my head nor my heart would have been as high-spirited and cheerful as they were when I was young.* Ib.

7 Is dócha ná beidh seana-bhean comh Gaelach liom ar an Oileán so go deo arís. Ib.

*I don't suppose there will ever be another old woman on this island as devoted to Irish as I was.* Ib.

**Scanlan, Michael** 1836-?

8 See who comes over the red-blossomed heather, / Their green banners kissing the pure mountain air. 'The Bold Fenian Men'

9 From mountain and valley, / 'Tis Liberty's rally — / Out and make way for the Bold Fenian Men! Ib.

10 . . . down the glen rode Sarsfield's men / And they wore the jackets green. 'The Jackets Green'

**Scottus, Sedulius** 9th Century

11 Nos tumidus Boreas vastat — miserabile visu — / Doctos grammaticos presbiterosque pios. 'Flamina Nos Borea'

*Ah woe! tumultuous Boreas has us all undone, / we learned teachers, yes, and pious priests.* 'The Arrival at Liège'

1 Aut lego vel scribo, doceo scrutorve sophiam. 'Aut Lego Vel Scribo'

*I read and write and teach, philosophy peruse.* 'Confession'

2 Nunc viridant segetes, nunc florent germine campi / Nunc turgent vites, est nunc pulcherrimus annus.
'Nunc Viridant Segetes'

*The crops are green and fields are all in flower, / budding the vine — the year now has its hour.*
'Request for Meat and Drink'

**Sechnall, St** *d.* 447

3 Audite, omnes amantes Deum, sancta merita / viri in Christo beati, Patricii episcopi, / quomodo bonum ob actum similatur angelis / perfectamque propter vitam aequatur apostolis.

*Hear ye, all that love God, of the merits / of a man blessed in Christ, Patrick the Bishop, / like to the angels because of his good works / and equal to the apostles in the sanctity of his life.*
'Hymn to St Patrick'

**Shakespeare, William** 1564-1616

4 'Tis like the howling of Irish wolves against the moon. *As You Like It*

5 An Irishman, a very valiant gentleman, i' faith. *Henry V*

6 MACMORRIS: . . . What ish my nation? is a villain, and a bastard, and a knave, and a rascal? What ish my nation? Who talks of my nation? Ib.

7 Now for our Irish wars: / We must supplant these rough rug-headed kerns, / Which live like venom where no venom else / But only they have privilege to live. *Richard II*

**Shaw, George Bernard** 1856-1950

8 . . . my sentimental regard for Ireland does not include the capital.
Preface to first novel, *Immaturity*

9 Even in Dublin, that city of tedious and silly derision, where men can do nothing but sneer, they no longer sneer at other nations.
'Interview' written entirely by Shaw in *The Evening Sun*, New York, 9 December 1911

10 At all events, as she, Ulster, cannot have the *status quo*, nothing remains for her but complete union or the most extreme form of Home Rule; that is, separation from both England and Ireland.
*New Statesman*, 7 June 1913

11 It is absolutely impossible to slaughter a man in this position without making him a martyr and a hero, even though the day before the rising he may have been only a minor poet.
Letter to *The Daily News*, London, 10 May 1916

12 An Irishman resorting to arms to achieve the independence of his country is only doing what Englishmen would do if it were their misfortune to be invaded and conquered by the Germans in the course of the war.
Letter, April 1916

13 His [Casement's] real offence is not merely that of being an Irishman but of being a nationalist Irishman.
'Shall Casement Hang?' letter – rejected by *The Times* – in *The Manchester Guardian*, 22 July 1916

1 So tear up your mourning and hang up your brightest colors in his honor; and let us all praise God that he had not to die in a snuffy bed of a trumpery cough, weakened by age, and saddened by the disappointments that would have attended his work had he lived.

Letter to Michael Collins' sister, Johanna, 24 August 1922

2 The British officer seldom likes Irish soldiers; but he always tries to have a certain proportion of them in his battalion, because, partly from a want of common sense which leads them to value their lives less than Englishmen do (lives are really less worth living in a poor country), and partly because even the most cowardly Irishman feels obliged to outdo an Englishman in bravery if possible, and at least to set a perilous pace for him, Irish soldiers give impetus to those military operations which require for their spirited execution more devilment than prudence.

Preface, *O'Flaherty V C*

3 She says all the English generals is Irish. She says all the English poets and great men was Irish. She says the English never knew how to read their own books until we taught them. She says we're the lost tribes of the house of Israel and the chosen people of God. She says that the goddess Venus, that was born out of the foam of the sea, came up out of the water in Killiney Bay off Bray Head. She says that Moses built the seven churches and that Lazarus was buried in Glasnevin. Ib.

4 I could not write the words Mr. Joyce uses: my prudish hands would refuse to form the letters. *Table Talk of G. B. S.*

5 An Irishman's heart is nothing but his imagination.

*John Bull's Other Island*

6 Your wits can't thicken in that soft moist air, on those white springy roads, in those misty rushes and brown bogs, on those hillsides of granite rocks and magenta heather. You've no such colors in the sky, no such lure in the distance, no such sadness in the evenings. Oh the dreaming! the dreaming! the torturing, heartscalding, never satisfying dreaming, dreaming, dreaming. Ib.

7 BROADBENT: Never despair, Larry. There are great possibilities for Ireland. Home Rule will work wonders under English guidance.

DOYLE: Tom why do you select my most tragic moments for your irresistible strokes of humor? Ib.

8 MALONE: When a country is full of food and exporting it, there can be no famine. Me father was starved dead, and I was starved out to America in me mother's arms. English rule drove me and mine out of Ireland.

*Man and Superman*

**Shee, Sir Martin Archer** 1769-1850

9 Dug from the tomb of taste-refining time, / Each form is exquisite, each block sublime, / Or good, or bad, – disfigured or depraved, – / All art is at its resurrection saved. 'Rhymes on Art'

**Sheehan, Canon Patrick Augustine** 1852-1913

10 No true Irishman sees a distinction between the battlefield and the scaffold. Both are fields of honour for our race.

*The Graves at Kilmorna*

11 It is all my own fault. I was too free with my tongue. I said in a moment of bitterness, 'What can a bishop do with a parish priest? He's independent of him.' It was not grammatical and it was not respectful. But the bad grammar and the impertinence were carried to his

Lordship, and he answered, 'What can I do? I can send him a curate who will break his heart in six weeks!'

*My New Curate*

**Sheehy-Skeffington, Francis** 1878-1916

1 [On being called a crank] . . . A crank is a small instrument that makes revolutions. Quoted in Edwards and Pyle, 1916: The Easter Rising

**Sheil, Richard Lalor** 1791-1851

2 Protestants, awake to a sense of your condition . . . disarray us by equality; instead of angry slaves make us contented citizens; if you do not tremble for the result.

Speech during Clare election, September 1828

3 A body of armed Orangemen fall upon and put to death a defenceless Catholic; they are put on trial, and when they raise their eyes and look upon the jury as they are commanded to do, they see twelve of their brethren in massacre.

Speech at Peneden Heath, Kent, October 1828

**Shelley, Percy Bysshe** 1792-1822

4 Oh, Ireland! thou emerald of the ocean, whose sons are generous and brave, whose daughters are honourable and frank and fair, thou art the isle on whose green shores I have desired to see the standard of liberty erected – a flag of fire – a beacon at which the world shall light the torch of Freedom!

*An Address to the Irish People,* 1812

**Sheridan, Richard Brinsley** 1751-1816

5 A circulating library in a town is as an ever-green tree of diabolical knowledge! It blossoms through the year!

*The Rivals*

6 She's as headstrong as an allegory on the banks of the Nile. Ib.

7 My valour is certainly going! — it is sneaking off! I feel it oozing out as it were at the palms of my hands! Ib.

8 Here's to the maiden of bashful fifteen; / Here's to the widow of fifty; / Here's to the flaunting extravagant quean; / And here's to the housewife that's thrifty. / Let the toast pass, — / Drink to the lass, / I'll warrant she'll prove an excuse for the glass.

'The School for Scandal'

**Shiels, George** 1886-1949

9 This country's going to hell at a hundred mile an hour. Petrol and pictures and potheen and jazz and dates and buses and bare legs and all sorts of foreign rascalities. You and I were content to toil and moil for a living, but the new breed wants to be well-paid, well-fed and idle. *The New Gossoons*

10 Ay, five guineas for looking at my tongue! I can look at my own tongue for less money. *The Passing Day*

**Simmons, James Stewart Alexander** *b.* 1933

11 For every year of life we light / a candle on your cake / to mark the simple sort of progress / anyone can make, / and then, to test your nerve or give / a proper view of death, / you're asked to blow each light, each year, / out with your breath. 'A Birthday Poem'

12 So do not think of helpful whores / as aberrational blots; / I could not love you half so well / without my practice shots. 'Cavalier Lyric'

13 I've made, while trying to tell no lies, / a noise to go with love.

'Lullaby for Rachael'

14 Poems are different. / Strange what crossings out, / what concentration it

takes / to be caught with my pants down. 'Photographs'

**Smith, Adam** 1723-1790

1 Without a union with Great Britain, the inhabitants of Ireland are not likely for many ages to consider themselves as one people. *Wealth of Nations*

**Smith, Frederick Edwin, Earl of Birkenhead** 1872-1931

2 A people [the Irish] so individual in its genius, so tenacious in love or hate, so captivating in its nobler moods.
Speech on Irish Treaty, House of Lords, 23 November 1920

**Smith, Sydney** 1771-1845

3 The moment the very name of Ireland is mentioned, the English seem to bid adieu to common feeling, common prudence, and common sense, and to act with the barbarity of tyrants, and the fatuity of idiots.
*Letters of Peter Plymley*, 1807

**Somerville and Ross – Edith Oenone Somerville** 1858-1949 and **Violet Martin Ross** 1862-1915

4 With the close of the 'seventies came the burst into the open of the Irish parliamentary party, in full cry. Like hounds hunting confusedly in covert, they had, in the hands of Isaac Butt, kept up a certain noise and excitement, keen, yet uncertain as to what game was on foot. From 1877 it was Parnell who carried the horn, a grim disdainful master, whose pack never dared get closer to him than the length of his thong; but he laid them on the line, and they ran like wolves. *The Martins of Ross*

5 'More rain coming,' said Mr Knox, rising composedly; 'you'll have to put a goose down these chimneys some day soon, it's the only way in the world to clean them.' 'Great-Uncle McCarthy', *Some Experiences of an Irish RM*

6 . . . my first November at Shreelane was composed of weather of which my friend Flurry Knox remarked that you wouldn't meet a Christian out of doors, unless it was a snipe or a dispensary doctor. Ib.

7 . . .the Quaker pursued at the equable gallop of a horse in the Bayeux Tapestry. 'In the Curranhilty Country', ib.

8 The dining-room at Aussolas Castle is one of the many rooms in Ireland in which Cromwell is said to have stabled his horse (and probably no one would have objected less than Mrs Knox had she been consulted in the matter.)
'Philippa's Fox-Hunt', ib.

9 There wasn't a day in the year you wouldn't get feeding for a hen and chickens on the floor [of old Mrs Knox's house, Aussolas]. Ib.

10 The very wind that blows softly over the brown acres of bog carries perfumes and sounds that England does not know: the women digging the potato-land are talking of things that England does not understand. The question that remains is whether England will ever understand. 'Children of the Captivity', *Some Irish Yesterdays*

11 An August Sunday afternoon in the north side of Dublin. Epitome of all that is hot, arid, and empty.
*The Real Charlotte*

12 Mrs Beattie had trawled Lismoyle and its environs with the purest impartiality: no one was invidiously omitted, not even young Redmond the solicitor's clerk, who came in thick boots and

a suit of dress clothes so much too big for him as to make his trousers look twin concertinas. Ib.

1 Christopher, having cut the grocer's cake, and found it was the usual conglomerate of tallow, saw-dust, bad-eggs, and gravel, devoted himself to thick bread and butter. Ib.

2 Yesterday as we left, an old spinster, daughter of the last owner, was at the door in a little donkey-trap. She lives near in an old castle and since her people died she will not go into the House, or into the enormous yard, or the beautiful old garden . . . She was a strange mixture of distinction and commonness, like her breeding . . . If we dared to write up that subject – !

Letter from 'Martin' to Edith, 18 March 1912, used as afterword to *The Big House of Inver*

**Spenser, Edmund** *c.* 1522-1599

3 Out of every corner of the woods and glens they came creeping forth upon their hands, for their legs could not bear them. They looked like anatomies of death; they spoke like ghosts crying out of their graves. Diary

4 [The Irish mantle] . . . a fit house for an outlaw, a meet bed for a rebel, and an apt cloak for a thief.

*A View of the Present State of Ireland*

5 In her [wandering prostitute] travel it is her cloak and safeguard and also a coverlet for her lewd exercise, and when she has filled her vessel, under it she can hide both her burden and her shame. Ib.

**Stanihurst, Richard** 1547-1618

6 Being moderately taken . . . it sloweth age, it strengtheneth youth, it helpeth digestion, it cutteth flegme, it abandoneth melancholie, it relisheth the heart, it lighteneth the mind, it quickeneth the spirits, it cureth the hydropsie, it healeth the strangurie, it pounceth the stone, it expelleth grauell, it puffeth away all ventositie, it keepeth and preserueth the head from whirling, the eies from dazeling, the toong from lisping, the mouth from maffling, the teeth from chattering, and the throte from ratling; it keepeth the weasan from stifling, the stomach from wambling, and the heart from swelling, the bellie from wirtching, the guts from rumbling, the hands from shivering and the sinewes from shrinking, the veines from crumpling, the bones from aking & the marrow from soaking.

*Aqua Vitae*

7 Vertuus living dyd I long relinquish, / Thy wyl and precepts misirablye scorning, / Grant toe mee, sinful pacient, repenting, / Helthful amendment. 'A Prayer to the Trinitie'

8 At the creeke of Bagganbun / Ireland was lost and wun!

Quoted in 'An Plaine and Perfect Description of Ireland' in Holinshed, *Chronicles*

9 One demanded merrily why Oneile that last was [Shane] would not frame himself to speak English? 'What,' quoth the other in a rage, 'thinkest thou that it standeth with Oneile his honor to writhe his mouthe in clattering English?' Ib.

**Steele, Sir Richard** 1672-1729

10 Though her mien carries much more invitation than command, to behold her is an immediate check to loose behaviour; to love her was a liberal education.

Of Lady Elizabeth Hastings, in *The Tatler*

1 The insupportable labour of doing nothing. Ib.

2 Reading is to the mind what exercise is to the body. Ib.

**Stephens, James** 1825-1901

3 The ardour of Young Ireland had evaporated as if it had never existed. 'Reminiscences' in *Weekly Freeman*, 13 October 1882

4 I was sure . . . that if another decade was allowed to pass without an endeavour of some kind or other to shake off an unjust yoke, the Irish people would sink into a lethargy from which it would be impossible . . . to arouse them. Ib., 9 February 1884

**Stephens, James** 1882-1950

5 . . . asking each other from what bluest blueness of blood / His daddy was squeezed, and the pa of the da of his dad? 'Blue Blood'

6 And the slack-jawed booby proved to the hilt that he / Was lout, son of lout, by old lout, and was da to a lout! Ib.

7 Now, with the coming in of the spring, the days will stretch a bit; / And after the Feast of Brigid I shall hoist my flag and go. 'The County Mayo', trans. of 'Cill Aodhan', see p. 128

8 May she marry a ghost and bear him a kitten, and may / The High King of Glory permit her to get the mange. 'A Glass of Beer'

9 A tree, a hill, a wind, a sky, / Where nothing ever passes by! 'Katty Gollagher'

10 I have looked him round and looked him through, / Know every thing that he will do / In such a case, and such a case; 'Nora Criona'

11 – Yesterday he gripped her tight / And cut her throat. And serve her right! Ib.

12 . . . straightway, like a bell, / Came low and clear / The slow, sad, murmur of far distant seas. 'The Shell'

13 Be green upon their graves, O happy Spring! / For they were young and eager who are dead! 'Spring 1916'

14 A woman is a branchy tree / And man a singing wind; / And from her branches carelessly / He takes what he can find. 'A Woman is a Branchy Tree'

15 I think the mountains ought to be / Taught a little modesty. 'The Paps of Dana'

16 Her mother seldom washed at all. She held that washing was very unhealthy and took the natural gloss off the face, and that, moreover, soap either tightened the skin or made it wrinkle. *The Charwoman's Daughter*

17 Personally Mrs Makebelieve did not admire policemen — they thought too much of themselves, and their continual pursuit of and intercourse with criminals tended to deteriorate their moral tone; also, being much admired by a certain type of woman, their morals were subjected to so continuous an assault that the wife of such a one would be worn to a shadow in striving to preserve her husband from designing and persistent females. Ib.

18 In a little city like Dublin one meets every person whom one knows within a few days. Around each bend in the road there is a friend, an enemy, a bore striding towards you. Ib.

1 Finality is death. Perfection is finality. Nothing is perfect. There are lumps in it. *The Crock of Gold*

2 I know her well, a big hat and no morals, a bankrupt's baggage! *Here Are Ladies*

**Sterne, Laurence** 1713-1768

3 They order, said I, this matter better in France. *A Sentimental Journey*

4 I had an affair with the moon, in which there was neither sin nor shame. Ib.

5 I wish either my father or mother, or indeed both of them, as they were in duty both equally bound to it, had minded what they were about when they begot me. *Tristram Shandy*

6 Digressions, incontestably, are the sunshine; – they are the life, the soul of reading! – take them out of this book, for instance, – you might as well take this book along with them; – one cold external winter would reign in every page of it; restore them to the writer; – and he steps forth like a bridegroom, – bids All-hail; brings in variety, and forbids the appetite to fail. Ib.

7 Heat is in proportion to the want of true knowledge. (Slawkenbergius's Tale) Ib.

8 The ancient Goths of Germany . . . had all of them a wise custom of debating everything of importance to their state; that is, – once drunk, and once sober: – Drunk, – that their councils might not want vigour; – and sober – that they might not want discretion. Ib.

9 If, when I was a schoolboy, I could not hear a drum beat, but my heart beat with it – was it my fault? Did I plant the propensity there? – Did I sound the alarm within, or Nature? (My uncle Toby's apologetical oration.) Ib.

10 My brother Toby, quoth she, is going to be married to Mrs Wadman. Then he will never, quoth my father, be able to lie diagonally in his bed again as long as he lives. Ib.

11 All womankind, continued Trim . . . from the highest to the lowest . . . love jokes; the difficulty is to know how they chuse to have them cut; and there is no knowing that, but by trying, as we do with our artillery in the field, by raising or letting down their breeches, till we hit the mark. – I like the comparison, said my uncle Toby, better than the thing itself. Ib.

**Stoker, Abraham ('Bram')** 1847-1912

12 The mouth, so far as I could see it under the heavy moustache, was fixed and rather cruel-looking, with peculiarly sharp white teeth; these protruded over the lips, whose remarkable ruddiness showed astonishing vitality in a man of his years. *Dracula*

13 It was like a miracle; but before our very eyes, and almost in the drawing of a breath, the whole body crumbled into dust and passed from our sight. Ib.

14 The Hill can hould tight enough! A man has raysons – sometimes wan thing and sometimes another–but the Hill houlds him all the same. *The Gombeen Man*

**Strong, Eithne** *b.* 1923

15 It is well that Alec is gone. Indeed I coldly killed him. Crime of frigidity. I see them looking at me, these gullible girls, wondering at my face. I have at last perfected the mask; its smiling ice is permanent. It pleases me to see the recoil in their faces. Soon the nuns' bell will ring. I will go to the mechanical

prayer, kneel in my stall, the veil hiding my silence. 'The Bride of Christ' *Patterns*

**Stuart, Francis** *b.* 1902

1 [Ireland] . . . where one must tacitly believe in the sacredness of property, in the sacredness of marriage, in the security of society, in the police force.
*The Pillar of Cloud*

**Sullivan, Alexander Martin** 1830-1884

2 Disaffection had disappeared. Nationality was unmentioned. Not a shout was raised. . . . The people no longer interested themselves in politics. Who went into or went out of parliament concerned them not. All was silence.
*The Story of Ireland*

**Sullivan, Timothy Daniel** 1827-1914

3 Deep in Canadian woods we've met, / From one bright island flown; / Great is the land we tread but yet / Our hearts are with our own. / And ere we leave this shanty small / While fades the Autumn day, / We'll toast Old Ireland! / Dear Old Ireland! / Ireland, boys, hurrah! 'Song From The Backwoods'

4 'Whether on the scaffold high, or in battlefield we die, / O what matter, when for Erin dear we fall!'
'God Save Ireland'

**Swift, Jonathan** 1667-1745

5 Satire is a sort of glass wherein beholders do generally discover everybody's face but their own.
Preface, *The Battle of the Books*

6 Instead of dirt and poison we have rather chosen to fill our hives with honey and wax; thus furnishing mankind with the two noblest of things, which are sweetness and light.
*The Battle of the Books*

7 A giddy son of a gun Ib.

8 A coming show'r your shooting corns presage. 'A Description of a City Shower'

9 Here various kinds by various fortunes led, / Commence acquaintance underneath a shed. / Triumphant Tories, and desponding Whigs, / Forget their feuds, and join to save their wigs. Ib.

10 Now Betty from her master's bed had flown, / And softly stole to discompose her own. 'A Description of the Morning'

11 Last week I saw a woman flayed, and you will hardly believe, how much it altered her person for the worse.
*Digression on Madness*

12 Big-endians and small-endians.
*Gulliver's Travels*

13 I cannot but conclude the bulk of your natives to be the most pernicious race of odious little vermin that nature ever suffered to crawl upon the surface of the earth. Ib.

14 And he gave it for his opinion, that whoever could make two ears of corn or two blades of grass to grow upon a spot of ground where only one grew before, would deserve better of mankind, and do more essential service to his country than the whole race of politicians put together. Ib.

15 He had been eight years upon a project for extracting sunbeams out of cucumbers, which were to be put into phials hermetically sealed, and let out to warm the air in raw inclement summers. Ib.

16 I often wished that I had clear, / For life, six hundred pounds a year; / A handsome house to lodge a friend; / A river at my garden's end.
'Imitation of Horace'

1 Principally I hate and detest that animal called man; although I heartily love John, Peter, Thomas, and so forth.

Letter to Alexander Pope, 29 September 1725

2 But you think . . . that it is time for me to have done with the world, and so I would if I could get into a better before I was called into the best, and not die here in a rage, like a poisoned rat in a hole. Letter to Viscount Bolingbroke, 21 March 1729

3 Long-winded schismatics shall rule the roast, / And Father Christmas mourn his revels lost.

'The Swan Tribe Club in Dublin'

4 The want of belief is a defect that ought to be concealed when it cannot be overcome. *Thoughts on Religion*

5 We have just enough religion to make us hate, but not enough to make us love one another.

*Thoughts on Various Subjects*

6 I have been assured by a very knowing American of my acquaintance in London, that a young healthy child well nursed is at a year old almost delicious, nourishing, and wholesome food, whether stewed, roasted, baked or boiled, and I make no doubt that it will equally serve in a fricassee, or a ragout. *A Modest Proposal*

7 I profess in the sincerity of my heart that I have not the least personal interest in endeavouring to promote this necessary work, having no other motive than the *public good of my country, by advancing our trade, providing for infants, relieving the poor, and giving some pleasure to the rich.* I have no children by which I can propose to get a single penny; the youngest being nine years old, and my wife past child-bearing. Ib.

8 Hail fellow, well met, / All dirty and wet: / Find out, if you can, / Who's master, who's man.

'My Lady's Lamentation'

9 I heard the late Archbishop of Tuam mention a pleasant observation of somebody's: 'that Ireland would never be happy until a law were made for burning anything that came from England, except their people and their coals.' *A Proposal for the Universal Use of Irish Manufacture*

10 Promises and pie-crust are made to be broken. *Polite Conversation*

11 I swear she's no chicken; she's on the wrong side of thirty, if she be a day. Ib.

12 O'Rourke's noble fare / Will ne'er be forgot, / By those who were there, / Or those who were not.

Out of the original Irish

13 Oh, would it please the gods to split / Thy beauty, size, and years, and wit, / No age could furnish out a pair / Of nymphs so graceful, wise and fair.

'On Stella's Birthday'

14 See, how the Dean begins to break: / Poor gentleman, he droops apace, / You plainly find it in his face: / That old vertigo in his head, / Will never leave him, till he's dead: / Besides, his memory decays, / He recollects not what he says; / He cannot call his friends to mind; / Forgets the place where last he din'd: / Plies you with stories o'er and o'er, / He told them fifty times before.

'Verses on the Death of Dr Swift, D.S.P.D.'

1 Fair LIBERTY was all his cry. Ib.

2 'He gave the little wealth he had / To build a house for fools and mad: / And show'd by one satiric touch, / No nation wanted it so much.' Ib.

3 High church, low steeple, / Dirty streets, proud people. About Newry, Co. Down, attrib.

4 I shall be like that tree, I shall die at the top. Attrib.

5 Good God! What a genius I had when I wrote that book.
Of *The Tale Of The Tub,* attrib.

6 Ubi saeva indignatio ulterius cor lacerare nequit.

*Where fierce indignation can no longer tear his heart.* Swift's epitaph

**Synge, John Millington** 1871-1909

7 The grief of the keen is no personal complaint for the death of one woman over eighty years, but it seems to contain the whole passionate rage that lurks somewhere in every native of the island. In this cry of pain the whole consciousness of the people seems to lay itself bare for an instant, and to reveal the mood of beings who feel their isolation in the face of a universe that wars on them with wind and seas. They are usually silent, but in the presence of death all outward show of indifference or patience is forgotten; and they shriek with pitiable despair before the horror of the fate to which they are doomed.
*The Aran Islands*

8 'A man who is not afraid of the sea will soon be drownded,' he said, 'for he will be going out on a day he shouldn't. But we do be afraid of the sea and we only do be drownded now and again.' Ib.

9 The sense of solitude was immense. I could not see or realize my own body, and I seemed to exist merely in my perception of the waves and of the crying birds, and the smell of the seaweed. Ib.

10 I remember coming out of St Patrick's, Sunday after Sunday, strained almost to torture by the music, and walking out through the slums of Harold's Cross as the lamps were being lit. Hordes of wild children used to play round the cathedral of St Patrick and I remember there was something appalling – a proximity of emotions as conflicting as the perversions of the Black Mass – in coming out suddenly from the white harmonies of the Passion according to St Matthew among this blasphemy of childhood.
*Autobiography*

11 Deirdre is dead, and Naisi is dead; and if the oaks and stars could die for sorrow, it's a dark sky and a hard and naked earth we'd have this night in Emain. *Deirdre of the Sorrows*

12 . . . the time a little stick would seem as big as your arm, and a rabbit as big as a bay horse, and a stack of turf as big as a towering church in the city of Dublin.
*In the Shadow of the Glen*

13 You'll be getting old and I'll be getting old, and in a little while, I'm telling you, you'll be sitting up in your bed . . . with a shake in your face, and your teeth falling, and the white hair sticking out round you like an old bush where sheep do be leaping a gap. Ib.

14 In the middle classes the gifted son of the family is always the poorest – usually a writer or artist with no sense for speculation – and in a family of peasants, where the average comfort is just over penury, the gifted son sinks

also, and soon is a tramp on the roadside. *In Wicklow and West Kerry*

1 This peculiar climate, acting on a population that is already lonely and dwindling, has caused or increased a tendency to nervous depression among the people, and every degree of sadness, from that of the man who is merely mournful to that of the man who has spent half his life in the madhouse, is common among the hills. Ib.

2 Anyone who has lived in real intimacy with the Irish peasantry will know that the wildest sayings and ideas in this play are tame indeed, compared with the fancies one may hear in any little hillside cabin in Geesala, or Carraroe, or Dingle Bay.

Introduction,
*The Playboy of the Western World*

3 When I was writing 'The Shadow of the Glen', some years ago, I got more said than any learning could have given me from a chink in the floor of the old Wicklow house where I was staying, that let me hear what was being said by the servant girls in the kitchen. Ib.

4 In a good play every speech should be as fully flavoured as a nut or apple. Ib.

5 Don't strike me. I killed my poor father, Tuesday was a week, for doing the like of that.

*The Playboy of the Western World*

6 It's that you'd say surely if you seen him and he after drinking for weeks, rising up in the red dawn, or before it maybe, and going out into the yard as naked as an ash-tree in the moon of May, and shying clods against the visage of the stars till he'd put the fear of death into the banbhs and the screeching sows. Ib.

7 Doesn't the world know you reared a black ram at your own breast, so that the Lord Bishop of Connaught felt the elements of a Christian, and he after eating it in a kidney stew. Ib.

8 I'm thinking you'll be a loyal young lad to have working around, and if you vexed me a while since with your leaguing with the girls, I wouldn't give a thraneen for a lad that hadn't a mighty spirit in him and a gamy heart. Ib.

9 Amn't I after seeing the love-light of the star of knowledge shining from her brow, and hearing words would put you thinking on the holy Brigid speaking to the infant saints. Ib.

10 Did you ever hear of the skulls they have in the city of Dublin, ranged out like blue jugs in a cabin of Connaught? Ib.

11 CHRISTY: Starting from you, is it? I will not, then, and when the airs is warming, in four months or five, it's then yourself and me should be pacing Neifin in the dews of night, the times sweet smells do be rising, and you'd see a little shiny, new moon, maybe sinking on the hills.

PEGEEN: And it's that kind of poacher's love you'd make, Christy Mahon, on the sides of Neifin, when the night is down?

CHRISTY: It's little you'll think if my love's a poacher's, or an earl's itself, when you'll feel my two hands stretched round you, and I squeezing kisses on your puckered lips, till I'd feel a kind of pity for the Lord God is all ages sitting lonesome in His golden chair. Ib.

12 Well, the heart's a wonder; and, I'm thinking, there won't be our like in

Mayo, for gallant lovers, from this hour today. Ib.

1 Wasn't it a shame I didn't bear you along with me to Kate Cassidy's wake, a fine, stout lad, the like of you, for you'd never see the match of it for flows of drink, the way when we sunk her bones at noonday in her narrow grave, there were five men, aye, and six men, stretched out retching speechless on the holy stones. Ib.

2 Ten thousand blessings upon all that's here, for you've turned me into a likely gaffer in the end of all, the way I'll go romancing through a romping lifetime from this hour to the dawning of the Judgement Day. Ib.

3 Oh my grief, I've lost him surely. I've lost the only Playboy of the Western World. Ib.

4 And, No, you said, for if you saw a crew / Of living idiots pressing round that new / Oak coffin – they alive, I dead beneath / That board – you'd rave and rend them with your teeth.

'A Question', *Poems & Translations*

5 Lord, confound this surly sister, / Blight her brow with blotch and blister, / Cramp her larynx, lung and liver, / In her guts a galling give her.

'The Curse', ib.

6 It's the life of a young man to be going on the sea, and who would listen to an old woman with one thing and she saying it over. *Riders to the Sea*

7 Michael has a clean burial in the far north, by the grace of Almighty God. Bartley will have a fine coffin out of the white boards, and a deep grave surely. What more can we want than that? No man at all can be living for ever and we must be satisfied. Ib.

8 In the greater part of Ireland, however, the whole people, from the tinkers to the clergy, have still a life, and a view of life, that are rich and genial and humorous. Preface, *The Tinker's Wedding*

9 The doctors say I'm a very interesting case and generally patronise my belly — to think that I used once to write 'Playboys', MacKenna, and now I'm just a bunch of interesting bowels!

Letter to Stephen MacKenna, 1908

# T

**Tandy, James Napper** 1740-1803

1 Strike on their blood-cemented thrones the murderers of your friends.

Proclamation at Rutland Island, Co. Donegal, 16 September 1798

**Tate, Nahum** 1652-1715

2 While shepherds watched their flocks by night, / All seated on the ground, / The angel of the Lord came down, / And glory shone around.

'While Shepherds Watched'

**Thompson, Sam** 1916-1965

3 There's nothing civilised about a mob, be it Protestant or Catholic. They can store their bigotry for a long time. They can spew it out in violence.

*Over the Bridge*

**Tierney, Michael** 1894-1975

4 The Corporate State must come in the end, in Ireland as elsewhere. Its inauguration need not be the work of any one political party, but the future is with those who honestly, intelligently and fearlessly will undertake its cause.

*United Ireland*, 16 December 1933

**Times, The,** early 19th century

5 Scum condensed of Irish bog, / Ruffian, coward, demagogue, / Boundless liar, base detractor, / Nurse of murders, treason's factor.

Broadside against Daniel O'Connell

**Todhunter, John** 1839-1916

6 But they never took him living in Aghadoe, Aghadoe; / With the bullets in his heart in Aghadoe, / There he lay, the head – my breast keeps the warmth where once 'twould rest – / Gone, to win the traitor's gold from Aghadoe!

'Aghadoe'

**Tomelty, Joseph** *b.* 1911

7 Two sins I remember. Once with Kathleen on the clover patch of the Forth of Tara. Weary of the warm harvest we lay together. Communion breads I ate from the vestry but they were unblessed. 'Twas hunger forced me. Fresh are the two sins for God to know. *All Souls' Night*

8 Folks are kinder in death than they are in life. Ib.

9 The port light always fascinated him. It had the warmth of a homely fire in its red glow. He could kneel on the desk, polishing its glass, peering into its red heart. It was to him the symbol of home, of a real home, with a wife, with children. *Red is the Port Light*

**Tone, Theobald Wolfe** 1763-1798

10 The emancipated and liberal Irishman, like the emancipated and liberal Frenchman, may go to Mass, may tell his

beads, or sprinkle his mistress with Holy Water. *An Argument on Behalf of the Catholics of Ireland*, 1791

1 An Irishman's first duty is to his country, his second is to his King, and both are now, and by God's blessing will, I hope, remain, united and inseparable. Ib.

2 To subvert the tyranny of our execrable government, to break the connection with England, the never-failing source of all our political evils and to assert the independence of my country — these were my objects. To unite the whole people of Ireland, to abolish the memory of all past dissensions and to substitute the common name of Irishman in place of the denominations of Protestant, Catholic and Dissenter — these were my means. *Autobiography*

3 That Ireland was not able of herself to throw off the yoke, I knew; I therefore sought for aid wherever it was to be found. Speech at Court Martial, 10 November 1798

4 I find I am but a bad anatomist.
Whispered to his doctor, after slashing windpipe instead of jugular, 12 November 1798

**Tonna, Charlotte Elizabeth** 1790-1846

5 . . . Derry's sons alike defy / Pope, traitor, or pretender; / And peal to heaven their 'prentice cry / Their patriot — 'No Surrender!'
'No Surrender'

6 Where Foyle his swelling waters / Rolls northward to the main, / Here, Queen of Erin's daughters, / Fair Derry fixed her reign; / A holy temple crowned her, / And commerce graced her street, / A rampart wall was round her, / The river at her feet; / And here she sat alone, boys, / And, looking from the hill, / Vowed the Maiden on her throne, boys, / Would be a Maiden still.
'The Maiden City'

**Tracy, Honor Lilbush Wingfield** *b.* 1913

7 On the church gate a hand-painted notice with two spelling mistakes announced that owing to the welcome presence of the Redemptorist Fathers in the town there would be no dance on Sunday. 'A Ferocious Anti-Clerical', *Mind You, I've Said Nothing*

8 X spent some time trying to persuade me that the local people were the meanest and most rapacious as well as the most ill-natured and evil-spoken in the whole of the country; and poured out his words with such despairing conviction that, if I had not heard similar claims made for every little Irish town I had ever known, he might almost have won me over. Ib.

9 The difficulty, indeed the impossibility, of writing about Ireland in such a way as to win the approval of Irishmen may arise from the ambiguity of their own feelings towards her. If she is criticized they are publicly furious and privately amused; if praised, they are outwardly pleased while inwardly condemning the writer as a fool.
'Forebodings', ib.

10 What we have to do, my dear brethren, is stay on the straight and narrow path between good and evil.
Fragment of sermon used as epigraph to *The Straight and Narrow Path*

**Trench, Richard Chenevix** 1807-1886

11 This winter eve how soft! how mild! / How calm the earth! how calm the sea! / The earth is like a weary child, / And ocean sings its lullaby. 'Elegy'

**Trench, William Steuart** 1808-1872

1 We can scarcely shut our eyes to the fact that the circumstances and feelings which have led to the terrible crime of murder in Ireland, are usually very different from those which have led to murder elsewhere . . . In Ireland that dreadful crime may almost invariably be traced to a wild feeling of revenge for the national wrongs, to which so many of her sons believe she has been subject for centuries.

*The Realities of Irish Life*

**Trevor, William (Cox)** *b.* 1928

2 No alcoholic liquor was ever served in the Ballroom of Romance, the premises not being licensed for this added stimulant. Mr Dwyer in fact had never sought a licence for any of his premises, knowing that romance and alcohol were difficult commodities to mix, especially in a dignified ballroom.

'The Ballroom of Romance', *The Distant Past*

3 It was against the background of the oatmeal shade and the oxen in the dawn that I, through the rails of the banisters on the upper landing, saw my father kissing Bridget at the end of one summer holiday.

'A Choice of Butchers', ib.

4 Now and again, he thought, he would drive slowly in to the town to buy groceries and meat with the money they had saved, and to face the silence that would sourly thicken as their own two deaths came closer and death increased in another part of their island . . . Because of the distant past they would die friendless. It was worse than being murdered in their beds.

'The Distant Past', ib.

5 At midnight he rose to make the journey to bed and found himself unsteady on his feet. People looked at him, thinking it disgraceful for a priest to be drunk in Jerusalem, with cigarette ash all over his clerical cloth.

'Death in Jerusalem', ib.

6 At that time she used to go for walks with a boy who whispered often that he loved her, until one night, behind the Electricity Works he had taken liberties with her unresisting body and afterwards had whispered nothing more at all.

*Mrs Eckdorf in O'Neill's Hotel*

**Tynan, Kenneth** 1927-1980

7 William Congreve is the only sophisticated playwright England has produced; and like Shaw, Sheridan, and Wilde, his nearest rivals, he was brought up in Ireland.

'The Way of the World', *Curtains*

**Ussher, Archbishop James** 1581-1656

1 How Adam and Eve Broke All the Commandments At Once

Title of sermon

**Ussher, Percival Arland** 1899-1980

2 *A* man does not die of love or his liver or even of old age; he dies of being a man. *U*nless you make every act of your life an erotic one, you are not fully alive.

*An Alphabet of Aphorisms*

3 Fifteen of the rebel leaders were executed; most of the other prisoners were released after only a few months' imprisonment or internment . . . When we think of Thiers' monstrous revenge after the Paris Commune, or the Bartholomew nights of Nazi Germany – or even of the Indian Mutiny – we cannot fairly accuse the British of great severity or vindictiveness on this occasion [aftermath of Easter Week].

*The Mind and Face of Ireland*

# W

**Waddell, Helen Jane** 1889-1965

1 I shall not go to heaven when I die, / But if they will let me be / I think I'll take the road I used to know / That goes by Shere-na-garagh and the sea.
'I Shall Not Go to Heaven'

2 Would you think Heaven could be so small a thing / As a lit window on the hills at night? Ib.

**Wadding, Luke** 1588-1657

3 Christmas Day is come; let's all prepare for mirth / Which fills the heav'ns.
'Christmas Day Is Come'

**Walker, Rev. George** 1618-1690

4 We were under so great necessity that we had nothing left unless we could prey upon one another: A certain fat gentleman conceived himself in the greatest danger, and fancying several of the garrison looked on him with a greedy eye, thought fit to hide himself for three days. . . . Our necessity of eating the composition of tallow and starch, did not only nourish and support us, but was an infallible cure of the looseness. *A True History of the Siege of Londonderry in* 1689

**Wall, Mervyn Eugene Welply** *b.* 1908

5 Your mother says you're rusticating in a ghastly midland village inhabited entirely by a savage peasantry and small shopkeepers more savage still.
*Leaves For The Burning*

6 Lucian began to think of the ubiquity of dogs in Ireland. Ib.

7 'Father, have you ever heard of the Warriors of the Cross?' '. . . one hears of them giving money to charity and presenting stained glass windows to churches. There was some mention of them lately, some generous donation.' 'Yes they all do that. They're very good at raising clouds of incense to cloak their real purpose.' *No Trophies Raise*

8 Forty Foot Gentlemen Only
Title of pamphlet

**Waller, John Francis** 1809-1894

9 Now coyly retiring, now boldly advancing, — / Search the world all around, from the sky to the ground, / No such sight can be found as an Irish lass dancing! 'Dance Light, For My Heart It Lies Under Your Feet'

10 Slower – and slower – and slower the wheel swings; / Lower – and lower – and lower the reel rings; / Ere the wheel and the reel stopped their ringing and moving, / Through the grove the young lovers by moonlight are roving.
'The Spinning Wheel'

**Walsh, Edward** 1805-1850

1 I met a maid in the greenwood shade / At the dawning of the day.

'The Dawning of the Day'

**Walsh, Louis John** 1880-1942

2 Here's to the Pope in Killybuck, and may there be strife between Orange and Green as long as Alexander McCracken has a bad farm of land to sell.

*The Pope in Killybuck*

**Watters, Eugene R.**
**(Eoghan Ó Tuairisc)** 1926-1982 ·

3 And a white rose against a brick wall in Drumcondra / Is simply a shattering thing.

'The Week-End of Dermot and Grace'

**Wharton, Thomas, 1st Marquis of** 1648-1715

4 Ho, Brother Teague, dost hear de Decree? / Lilli Burlero Bullena-la / Dat we shall have a new Debity / Lilli Burlero Bullena-la. 'A New Song, 1688'

**Whately, Richard,**
**Archbishop of Dublin** 1787-1863

5 Preach not because you have to say something, but because you have something to say. *Apophthegms*

6 Happiness is no laughing matter. Ib.

7 It is folly to expect men to do all that they may reasonably be expected to do. Ib.

8 Honesty is the best policy; but he who is governed by that maxim is not an honest man. Ib.

9 I thank the goodness and the grace / That on my birth have smiled, / And made me in these Christian days / A happy English child.

Attrib. Verse required to be recited daily in Irish national schools.

**White, Terence De Vere**
*b.* 1912

10 Not the least of her early disappointment had been to find that what was missing in wit and poetry in Dublin was more than made up for in mordant criticism . . . and she was puzzled by the way in which everyone of established reputation was compared to his disadvantage with someone of whom she had never heard. It was as if a pilgrim to Stratford was to hear that Edmund, the younger brother, and not William was the real genius of the Shakespeare family. . . . She began to suspect that it was the world's failure to recognise the Irish Edmunds that made for the disparagement of the Irish Williams.

*Lucifer Falling*

11 With their traditional love of freedom, the people of England encouraged and applauded revolution in France, Hungary and Italy, while hastening to suppress it in Ireland.

*The Road of Excess*

12 Fundamentally kind, he [Joe Biggar] had a capacity for making himself unpleasant, remarkable even in a native of his province. Ib.

**White, William John (Jack)** 1920-1980

13 Sarsfield and the siege-train, he thought, the Island of Saints and Scholars, the Famine Queen bejasus and the Fenian dead, bold Robert Emmet the darling of Erin and Kevin Barry gave his young life for the cause of libertee. *The Devil You Know*

14 He was a decent skin all the same, always the good word for an old friend; many's a one would never have a shoe to their foot only for him; no blushing violet mind you the same man, de mortuis nil, but all the same many a man done his bit for Ireland the

same time and never got nothing out of it. . . . He gave a beautiful silver cup all the same to the Faysh Keyhole; well he wasn't slow to put his hand in his pocket, not only had he plenty of it but what he had he made himself no thanks to anybody and good luck to him if there was more like him we wouldn't be where we are today, he was one of the real old crowd anyway; sure there's only a few of us left. *The Hard Man*

**Wilde, Lady ('Speranza')** 1820-1896

1 'A million a decade!' – of human wrecks, / Corpses lying in fever sheds – / Corpses huddled on foundering decks, / And shroudless dead on their rocky beds; / Nerve and muscle, and heart and brain, / Lost to Ireland — lost in vain. 'The Exodus'

2 Weary men, what reap ye? – 'Golden corn for the stranger.' / What sow ye? – 'Human corses that wait for the avenger.' / Fainting forms, hunger-stricken, what see ye in the offing? / 'Stately ships to bear our food away amid the stranger's scoffing'. Ib.

**Wilde, Oscar Fingal O'Flahertie Wills** 1854-1900

3 I never saw a man who looked / With such a wistful eye / Upon that little tent of blue / Which prisoners call the sky. 'The Ballad of Reading Gaol'

4 Yet each man kills the thing he loves. Ib.

5 . . . it is not sweet with nimble feet / To dance upon the air! Ib.

6 Anybody can be good in the country. 'The Critic as Artist'

7 As long as war is regarded as wicked, it will always have its fascination. When it is looked upon as vulgar, it will cease to be popular. Ib.

8 There is no sin except stupidity. Ib.

9 Art never expresses anything except itself. 'The Decay of Lying'

10 To love oneself is the beginning of a lifelong romance. *An Ideal Husband*

11 The truth is rarely pure, and never simple. *The Importance of Being Earnest*

12 To lose one parent, Mr Worthing, may be regarded as a misfortune; to lose both looks like carelessness. Ib.

13 Is this Miss Prism a female of repellent aspect, remotely connected with education? Ib.

14 No woman should ever be quite accurate about her age. It looks so calculating. Ib.

15 I can resist everything except temptation. *Lady Windermere's Fan*

16 CECIL GRAHAM: What is a cynic? LORD DARLINGTON: A man who knows the price of everything and the value of nothing. Ib.

17 There is only one thing in the world worse than being talked about, and that is not being talked about. *The Picture of Dorian Gray*

18 All her bright golden hair / Tarnished with rust, / She that was young and fair / Fallen to dust. 'Requiescat'

19 I hope that you have not been leading a double life, pretending to be wicked and being really good all the time. That would be hypocrisy. *A Woman of No Importance*

1 Moderation is a fatal thing, Lady Hunstanton. Nothing succeeds like excess. Ib.

2 You should study the Peerage, Gerald. It is the best thing in fiction the English have ever done. Ib.

3 I have nothing to declare except my genius. Attrib. New York Customs House

4 Work is the curse of the drinking classes. Attrib., quoted in Pearson, *Life of Oscar Wilde*

**Wilhelm II, Kaiser** 1859-1941

5 I would have liked to go to Ireland but my grandmother [Queen Victoria] would not let me. Perhaps she thought I wanted to take the little place. Quoted in H. Montgomery Hyde, *Carson*

**Williams, Richard D'Alton** 1822-1862

6 Hang the bard, and cut the punster, / Fling all rhyming to the deuce, / Take a business tour through Munster, / Shoot a landlord – be of use. 'Advice to a Young Poet'

7 They brought her to the city / And she faded slowly there – / Consumption has no pity / For blue eyes and golden hair. 'The Dying Girl'

**Wilson, John Crawford** 1825-?

8 Proud Caesar fell down right before him, / And grovelled his length as he lay; / Then he knelt to the Saint, to adore him, / But Fin-ma-Cool dragged him away. / He rose, seemed desirous to linger, / So Brian Boru bade him 'Go!' / Saint Patrick, he lifted his finger, / But Fin-ma-Cool lifted his toe. 'New Ode to St Patrick'

**Winstanley, John** 1678-1750

9 When Fatty walks the street, the paviors cry, / 'God bless you, sir!' and lay their hammers by. *On a Fat Man*

10 Imprimis, there's a table blotted; / A tattered hanging all bespotted; / A bed of Flocks as one may rank it / Reduc'd to rag and half a blanket. 'Inventory of the Furniture of a Collegian's Chamber'

11 Cries Celia to a reverend dean, / 'What reason can be given, / Since marriage is a holy thing, / That there are none in heaven?' / 'There are no women,' he reply'd; / She quick returns the jest; / 'Women there are, but I'm afraid / They cannot find a priest.' 'On Marriage'

**Wolfe, Charles** 1791-1823

12 Not a drum was heard, not a funeral note, / As his corse to the rampart we hurried. 'The Burial of Sir John Moore'

13 He lay like a warrior taking his rest, / With his martial cloak around him. Ib.

14 We carved not a line, and we raised not a stone – / But we left him alone in his glory! Ib.

**Woolf, Virginia** 1882-1941

15 We [Virginia and Leonard] have had a most garrulous time. We never stop talking. The Irish are the most gifted people in that line. After dinner the innkeeper comes in and sits down and talks till bedtime, perfect English, much more amusing than any London society. . . . We spent a night with the Bowens, where, to our horror we found the Connollys — a less appetising pair I have never seen out of the Zoo, and the apes are considerably preferable to Cyril. She has the face of a golliwog and they brought the reek of

Chelsea with them. . . . Elizabeth's home was merely a great stone box, but full of Italian mantelpieces and decayed 18th Century furniture, and carpets all in holes — however they insisted on keeping up a ramshackle kind of state, dressing for dinner and so on.

Letter to Vanessa Bell, Glenbeigh, Co. Kerry, 3 May 1934

1 Your letter followed me to the wilds of Galway. It [Ireland] is a lovely country, but very melancholy, except that people never stop talking. Now we're in Dublin and still talking — this time to the Aran Islanders who are here making a film [Robert J. Flaherty's *Man of Aran*].

Letter to Katherine Arnold-Forster, Russell Hotel, Dublin, 8 May 1934

# Y

**Yeats, Jack Butler** 1871-1957

1 Tony-we-have-the-good-thought-for-you-still. *In Sand*

2 The train was over half an hour behind its time and the Traveller complained to the Guard of the train; and the Guard spoke to him bitterly. He said, 'You must have a very narrow heart that wouldn't go down to the town and stand your friends a few drinks instead of bothering me to get away.' *Sligo*

**Yeats, John Butler** 1839-1922

3 Hope, the great divinity, is domiciled in America, as the Pope lives in Rome. *Essays*

4 I have just read a long novel by Henry James. Much of it made me think of the priest condemned for a long space to confess nuns. Quoted in Archibald, *John Butler Yeats*

5 A saint but born in Portadown [of AE]. Attrib.

**Yeats, William Butler** 1865-1939

6 All things can tempt me from this craft of verse: / One time it was a woman's face, or worse — / The seeming needs of my fool-driven land. 'All Things Can Tempt Me'

7 O Body swayed to music, O brightening glance, / How can we know the dancer from the dance? 'Among School Children'

8 Those images that yet / Fresh images beget, / That dolphin-torn, that gong-tormented sea. 'Byzantium'

9 The intellect of man is forced to choose / Perfection of the life, or of the work. 'The Choice'

10 Now that my ladder's gone, / I must lie down where all the ladder's start, / In the foul rag-and-bone shop of the heart. 'The Circus Animals' Desertion'

11 We were the last romantics – chose for theme / Traditional sanctity and loveliness; / Whatever's written in what poet's name / The book of the people; whatever most can bless / The mind of man or elevate a rhyme; / But all is changed, that high horse riderless, / Though mounted in that saddle Homer rode / Where the swan drifts upon a darkening flood. 'Coole Park and Ballylee, 1931'

12 The years like great black oxen tread the world, / And God the herdsman treads them on behind, / And I am broken by their passing feet. *The Countess Cathleen*

1 'A woman can be proud and stiff / When on love intent; / But Love has pitched his mansion in / The place of excrement; / For nothing can be sole or whole / That has not been rent.'
'Crazy Jane Talks with the Bishop'

2 I write it out in a verse — / MacDonagh and MacBride / And Connolly and Pearse / Now and in time to be, / Wherever green is worn, / Are changed, changed utterly: / A terrible beauty is born. 'Easter 1916'

3 I balanced all, brought all to mind, / The years to come seemed waste of breath, / A waste of breath the years behind / In balance with this life, this death. 'An Irish Airman Foresees his Death'

4 A shudder in the loins engenders there / The broken wall, the burning roof and tower / And Agamemnon dead.
'Leda and the Swan'

5 We had fed the heart on fantasies, / The heart's grown brutal from the fare; / More substance in our enmities / Than in our love; O honey bees, / Come build in the empty house of the stare.
'Meditations in Time of Civil War'

6 Think where man's glory most begins and ends, / And say my glory was I had such friends.
'The Municipal Gallery Revisited'

7 You have never seen her, Ah! Conchubar, had you seen her / With that high, laughing, turbulent head of hers / Thrown backward, and the bowstring at her ear, / Or sitting by the fire with those grave eyes / Full of good counsel as it were with wine, / Or when love ran through all the lineaments / Of her wild body – although she had no child, / None other had all beauty, queen or lover, / Or was so fitted to give birth to kings. *On Baile's Strand*

8 Out of Ireland have we come, / Great hatred, little room, / Maimed us at the start. / I carry from my mother's womb / A fanatic's heart.
'Remorse for Intemperate Speech'

9 That is no country for old men. The young / In one another's arms, birds in the trees / – Those dying generations – at their song, / The salmon falls, the mackerel-crowded seas, / Fish, flesh, or fowl, commend all summer long / Whatever is begotten, born and dies. / Caught in that sensual music all neglect / Monuments of unageing intellect.
'Sailing to Byzantium'

10 O sages standing in God's holy fire / As in the gold mosaic of a wall, / Come from the holy fire, perne in a gyre, / And be the singing-masters of my soul. / Consume my heart away; sick with desire / And fastened to a dying animal / It knows not what it is; and gather me / Into the artifice of eternity. Ib.

11 Turning and turning in the widening gyre / The falcon cannot hear the falconer; / Things fall apart; the centre cannot hold; / Mere anarchy is loosed upon the world, / The blood-dimmed tide is loosed, and everywhere / The ceremony of innocence is drowned; / The best lack all conviction, while the worst / Are full of passionate intensity.
'The Second Coming'

12 Was it for this the wild geese spread / The grey wing upon every tide; / For this that all the blood was shed, / For this Edward Fitzgerald died, / And Robert Emmet and Wolfe Tone, / All that delirium of the brave? / Romantic Ireland's dead and gone, / It's with O'Leary in the grave. 'September 1913'

1 When you are old and grey and full of sleep, / And nodding by the fire, take down this book, / And slowly read, and dream of the soft look / Your eyes had once, and of their shadows deep.

'When You Are Old'

2 This country will not always be an uncomfortable place for a country gentleman to live in, and it is most important that we should keep in this country a certain leisured class. I am afraid that Labour disagrees with me in that. On this matter I am a crusted Tory. I am of the opinion of the ancient Jewish book which says 'there is no wisdom without leisure'.

Damage to Property Bill, Seanad Éireann, 28 March 1923

3 I remember John Synge and myself being considerably troubled when a man, who had drowned himself in the Liffey, was taken from the river. He had in his pocket a copy of Synge's play 'Riders to the Sea' . . . I think you can leave the arts, superior or inferior, to the conscience of mankind.

Censorship of Films Bill, Seanad Éireann, 7 June 1923

4 I have been looking for a historical precedent for the remarkable fact that certain Englishmen . . . went over to Ulster . . . and armed the people at a time of entire peace and urged them . . . to use their arms against us . . . Edmund Burke drew attention to a very remarkable item in the Estimates . . . for the purchase of five gross of scalping knives . . . intended to be given to the American Indians that they might scalp the French.

On the Boundary Commission, Seanad Éireann, 12 October 1924

5 If you show that this country, Southern Ireland, is going to be governed by Catholic ideas and by Catholic ideas alone, you will never get the North . . . you will put a wedge into the midst of this nation . . . You are now going to act on the advice of men who do not express the poetical mind, but who express the religious mind . . . In the long warfare of this country with England the Catholic clergy took the side of the people, and owing to that they possess here an influence that they do not possess anywhere else in Europe . . . I am proud to consider myself a typical man of that minority. We, against whom you have done this thing, are no petty people. We are one of the great stocks of Europe. We are the people of Burke; we are the people of Grattan; we are the people of Swift, the people of Emmet, the people of Parnell. We have created the most of the modern literature of this country. We have created the best of its political intelligence. Yet I do not altogether regret what has happened.

Debate on Divorce, Seanad Éireann, 11 June 1925

6 . . . designs in connection with postage stamps and coinage may be described, I think, as the silent ambassadors on national taste.

Coinage Bill, Seanad Éireann, 3 March 1926

**Young, Arthur** 1741-1820

7 A landlord in Ireland can scarcely invent an order which a servant, labourer or cottar dares refuse to execute. Nothing satisfies him but an unlimited submission. *Tour in Ireland*

8 [Irish landlords] . . . lazy, trifling, inattentive, negligent, slobbering, profligate. Ib.

# Z

**Zozimus, (Michael Moran)** 1794-1846

1 I live in Faddle Alley / Off Blackpits near the Coombe / With my poor wife, Sally, / In a narrow dirty room.

Broadsheet, *c.*1830

2 O long life to the man who invinted potheen – / Sure the Pope ought to make him a martyr – / If myself was this moment Victoria, our Queen, / I'd drink nothing but whiskey and wather.

'In Praise of Potheen'

3 You put up your proclamation / Says the Dan Van Vought / To agitate Paddy's nation / Says the Dan Van Vought. / You put me in a cage / The people to enrage / But I'm once more on the stage / Says the Dan Van Vought.

Street song on imprisonment of Daniel O'Connell by T. B. C. Smith, legal adviser to Dublin Castle

4 Saint Patrick was a gintleman, he came of decent people, / In Dublin town he built a church, and upon't put a steeple; / His father was a Callaghan, his mother was a Brady, / His aunt was an O'Shaughnessy, his uncle was a Grady.

'Saint Patrick Was a Gintleman'

5 Ah, kind Christian, do not grudge / The sixpence promised on the brudge.

Cry to passers-by from his station on Carlisle, now O'Connell, Bridge

# *Index by subject*


**Abbey Theatre:** brought to the A.T. 29: 8
who are hopelessly astray — or asleep — in the stalls of the Gaiety or the A. 138: 4
**Abbeys:** land of ruined a. 30: 15
**Abroad:** We call upon our countrymen a. 69:11
**Abundance:** exporting . . . in the most prodigal a. 39:3
**Abuse:** a long-term feat of denunciation and a. 113:6
**Acclamation:** by the noise of the a. 34: 15
**Achieve:** unable to realise . . . all that I had sought to a. 127:3
**Act:** I must say an a. of nutrition 42: 12
the last terrible a. of the age-old Irish drama 102:2
**Acting:** a. cannot be played at 59: 10
a. is therefore the lowest of the arts 106: 10
when he was off he was a. 66: 13
**Actor:** with the a. it is different 95: 4
**Adapting:** live through a. themselves 33: 8
**Adhmad:** cad a dhéanfaimid feasta gan a.? 16: 5
**Adultery:** Parnellism is a simple love of a. 131: 13
**Advantage:** no one could question their a. 54: 3
**Adventurer:** every a. of feeble and ostentatious talents 60: 4
**Advice:** *Colmcille's a.* 25: 9
here's a nice bit of a. 22: 14
**Affection:** my one a. left me 40: 1
**Against:** we take it that there is a man a. us 126:8
**Agamemnon:** the broken wall, the burning roof and tower and A. dead 164:4
**Age:** it sloweth a., it strengtheneth youth, it helpeth digestion, it cutteth flegme 146: 6
no woman should ever be quite accurate about her a. 160: 14
**Aged:** the beauty of an a. face 38: 1
**Aghadoe:** Gone, to win the traitor's gold from a. 154: 6
**Agricultural:** an a. Irish girl 18: 9
**Aherloe:** To-night he is sleeping in A. Glin 87: 16
**Aid:** I therefore sought for a. wherever it was to be found 155: 3
**Aileach:** God bless royal A. 55: 6
the royal hill, the hill of A. 93: 11
**Aileen:** Aileen Aroon! 69: 4
**Áille:** Fornocht do chonnach thú / A á. na há. 134:10
**Ainm:** A. a iníne bhí aige ar a bhád 118: 14
go naomhaítear tráth d'a. 51: 15
**Air:** in the clear a. of the day 60: 1
though the a. is so soft 98: 8
**Airdí Chuain:** Dá mbeinn fhéin in A. C. 91: 1
**Aire:** bí ar m'aire gach uair 93: 14
**Airm:** léig dhíot th'a. 59: 13
**Airport:** splattered the a. runways 77:7
**Airs:** I hate your grandiose a. 97: 6
**Aislinge:** Coigil aithinne d'a. 121: 9
**Áit:** ó áit go háit ba bhreá mo shiúl 75: 2
**Álainn:** Acht chena is á. cech nderg 12: 3
**Alba:** dá mba liom A. uile. 14: 8
**Alcohol:** romance and a. were difficult commodities to mix, especially in a dignified ballroom 156: 2
**Ale:** have I made good a. 37: 3
I have fed purely upon a. 58:9
*Spanish a. shall give you hope* 17:3
**Algebra:** my Irish is gone with my a. 93:4
**Alice:** what A. and I did was to start screaming 38:6
**Alien:** not racy of the soil but rather a. 48:2
once a. here my fathers built their house 73:1
**Allegiance:** I . . . do solemnly swear a. 23:7
**Allegory:** as headstrong as an a. on the banks of the Nile 144:6
**Alone:** a small nation that stood a. 53:1
I feel like one / Who treads alone 110:1
Is in ourselves a. 124:1
Riding a., my lord! 49:10
**Ambition:** to gratify the a. of an old man in a hurry! 41:13
**Ameer:** Abdulla Bulbul A. 61:6
**Amendment:** Grant toe mee, sinful pacient, repenting, / helthful a. 146:7
**America:** a voice from A. shouted to liberty 61:1
**Amour:** l'amour propre professionel 32:6
**Anatomist:** I find I am but a bad a. 155:4
**Andy:** the nickname . . . stuck upon him was Handy A. 90:4
**Angel:** an a. chanced to fall 58:2

I dedicate these pages to my guardian angel **116:7**
the a. of death would be unlikely 77:6
**Angels:** God's a. lifting the night's black veil 89:11
*like to the a. because of his good works* 142:3
Liveried a. robed in green 86:6
the a.'ll be having a pee 88:10
**anger:** her a. vanished like a puff of smoke 123:9
**animal:** I hate and detest that a. called man 150:1
**animals:** the Kerry Blue and the Alsatian is treacherous a. 88:12
**Ankles:** the thickest a. in the world 30:13
**Anlann:** Is maith an t-a. an t-ocras. 25:6
**Anna:** tell me all about A. Livia! 78:6
**Annraoi:** magairle A., Rí 15:3
**Annus:** est nunc pulcherrimus a. 142:2
**Anthem:** time the Republic replaced the National A. 94:4
**Antrim:** hated aych other like the men of A. 76:7
the chief of the A. men . . . not appearing 73:14
The vivid chequer of the A. hills 98:5
to Smoky Carrick in County A. 97:9
**Ants:** if them a. hated . . . aych other 76:7
**Anvil:** *Any a. that is struck* 11:1
**Aonach:** Chuaigh mé chun a. 16:2
**Apple:** *It was I who plucked the a.* 10:11
*when the a. is ripe* 24:13
**Apples:** battered down with roasted a. 25:16
**Approve:** All I a. persists 58:8
**April:** All in the A. evening 73:7
**Arab:** The a's farewell to his steed 114:5
**Araby:** burns in glorious A. 50:7
**Ardara:** the worthy of A. 93:9
**Ardicoan:** *Oh I would I were in A.* 91:1
**Ardoyne:** there were the green spires of A. 103:6
**Argument:** the soldier is proof against an a. 103:12
**Arís:** Ní dóigh liom go mbeidh mo leithéid a. ann 113:5
**Aristocracy:** an absentee a. 54:2
**Arm:** 'A. and prepare to acquit yourselves like men' 39:11
'Arm! Arm!' he cried 102:7
they keep his right a. out of the water 84:2
**Armagh:** A: where two cathedrals sit 30:6
look north towards A. 81:10
Phelim Brady, the bard of A. 19:1
there is a through-otherness about A. 139:1
**Arm-chair:** Pats will buy me an a. 60:5
**Armed:** a. Nationalists in the South will join arms with a. Protestants in the North 138:2
when a fellow is faced by a. men 38:7
**Arms:** a right to resist that surrender in a. 41:8
Connolly's Commercial a. 84:6
defended successfully by your a. 52:7
progress from injuries to a. 67:9
resorting to a. to achieve the independence of his country 142:12
the only a. I allow myself to use 79:4
**Army:** Ere long there shall be an Irish a. on the Irish hillsides 126:6
formerly an a. of occupation 83:13
I've listed in the a. 19:6
like / Being raped by an a. 114:3
terrible as an a. with banners 140:3
the a. of the Crown 23:5
**Aroon:** Soggarth A. 27:4
**Arrangement:** we made an a. 69:14
**Arranmore:** Oh! A., loved A. 108:3
**Arrest:** a. comes soon or late 31:7
**Arses:** thus I relieve their timid a. 78:10
**Art:** All a. is at its resurrection saved 143:9
A. must be parochial in the beginning 106:6
A. never expresses anything except itself. 160:9
I think of what great a. removes 31:12
It is a symbol of Irish a. 79:10
**Artificer:** Old father, old a. 79:5
**Artists:** Her writers and a. to banishment 78:8
**Ashamed:** And now the Irish are a. 101:8
**Ashes:** His steps . . . are on the thin crust of a. 91:2
**Ass:** and a stable for the a. 62:1
**Asses:** Garvagh for a. 30:8
Riding on two Spanish a. 60:6
**Athair:** Ár n-A. áta ins na flaithis 51:15
**Atheist:** An Irish a. is one who wishes to God he could believe in God 99:8
Jew, Turk or a. 15:1
**Athlone:** who lived in the town of A. 89:6
**Atlantic:** trundled them into th' A. 98:12
**Attitude:** a mental and spiritual a. 56:4
**Auburn:** Sweet A., loveliest village 66:6
**Aughrim:** A it stands for A., where blood flowed on the plain 127:9
**August:** In A. the barley grew up 72:7
the grey warm evening of A. 78:4
**Autumn:** *A. is an excellent season for staying at home* 13:8
It was a rich night in A. 46:14
when around thee dying, / A. leaves are lying 107:8
**Auxie:** An A. man / A black-and-tan 50:3
**Avenging:** His a. hand is slow but sure 14:9
**Awake:** a., and make haste to be blest 54:14
A. thee, my Bessy 37:4
*May I, a. or asleep, be guided* 93:14

**Baby:** they boil the b.77:9
**Bachelor:** a b. is happy and he's free 62:1
An' now, an oul' b.-man / D'ye know what I think? 140:2
the slanderous b. who lives on the banks of the Tiber 131:11
**Back:** He would go b. where he belonged 82:13
I don't go b. at all now 84:5
it's few they take back 93:12
**Bacon:** cabbage, boiled / with b. 42:12
**Badge:** the worst b. of conquest 51:8

thy b. my patriot brother 61:5
**Badger:** Dig out the b. . . . blind him with lime 102:5
**Bádussa:** Do b. úair 14:1
**Baggage:** a big hat and no morals, a bankrupt's baggage! 148:2
**Bagganbun:** At the creeke of B. / Ireland was lost and wun! 146:8
**Bail:** and the question of b. arose 136:10
**Bailiffs:** teh be jokin' about the b. 94:9
**Bailte:** b. bánbhreaca 94:6
**Balfe, Michael:** Pupil of M. B.'s wasn't she? 79:15
**Ball:** First Paddy struck the b. 45:3
learning a step for Lanigan's b. 21:5
that evening at a b. 62:5
**Ballads:** listen to his poor ould b. 102:1
**Ballinasloe:** the town of B. is seated upon a river 101:11
**Ballinderry:** 'Tis pretty to be in B. 18:11
**Ballocks:** *the b. of Henry the Eighth* 15:3
**Ballroom:** No alcoholic liquor was ever served in the B. of Romance 156:2
**Ballyjamesduff:** Come back, Paddy Reilly, to B. 61:8
**Ballymurphy:** chalked up / in B. 72:10
**Ballytearim:** All the gold in B. is what's stickin' to the whin 126:11
**Baltinglass:** Near to the town of B. 17:8
**Banality:** what b. a man expresses 79:7
**Bangor:** It's six miles from B. 23:2
*the little rule of B.* 11:3
**Banks:** Along the b. of the Royal Canal 30:1
the verdant b. of Skreen 22:13
the winding b. of Erne 10:3
**Banners:** their green b. kissing the pure mountain air 141:8
**Banning:** the b. of bombs is more to the point than the b. of books 118:12
**Banshee:** like the b.'s lonely croon 40:10
**Banter:** An adept at b. 72:1
**Baptize:** not the heart to b. their children completely 84:2
**Bar:** he was bred at the b. 56:1
Ireland stands at your b. expectant 65:5
**Barbadoes:** in safe custody for the B. 48:3
**Bard:** Hang the b., and cut the punster 161:6
oh! blame not the b. 108:4
Phelim Brady, the b. of Armagh 19:1
the best a poor b. can command 109:7
**Bargain:** will anyone be satisfied with the b.?43:12
**Barley:** the b. grew up out of the grave 72:7
'the wind that shakes the b.' 80:4
**Barmecides:** the time of the B. 100:7
**Barony:** through the B. her features they were famous 61:10
**Barque:** *Onward my b., / through the long sea!* 132:7
**Barrack:** the Irish police b. is invariably clean 31:5
**Barricades:** would take to the b. 82:12
**Barry, Kevin:** K. B. gave his young life 23:11
**Bás:** Ar an ngníomh do chím / Is ar an mb. do gheobhad 134:11
comh huafásach le b. a fháil mar sin 136:8
ní bhfuighe mise b. duit 15:4
Triúr atá ag brath ar mo b. 15:7
**Baste:** inthertainmint for man and b. 111:14
**Battering:** pocked and dented with the b. they've had 114:2
**Battering-ram:** shall the prop. of Ireland become its b.-r. 40:12
**Battle:** Armed for the b., kneel we before thee 100:11
stout-hearted in b., and stout-handed too 128:1
the first blow is half the b. 66:15
**Battles:** let England fight her own b. 73:9
**Bay:** the French are in the b. 22:10
**Bayeux:** the equable gallop of a horse in the B. Tapestry 145:7
**Beag:** codail beagán beagán b. 14:3
**Beagles:** My b. never cease their cry until they catch their game 119:8
**Béal:** Is binn b. 'na thost 24:14
**Bealach:** an b. cas geal a raibh sleasa cnoc 94:5
**Bean:** an tseanbh. ghlé ba bhéasach gnaoi 124:3
Atá b. as-tír 12:11
A b. lán de stuaim 41:1
pós b. sléibhe 24:9
Seana-b. isea mise anois 141:5
**Beare:** *I am Ireland: I am lonelier than the Old Woman of B.* 134:12
**Béarla:** Agus dá mba ná béadh agam acht an B. 125:10
Daoine gan B. gan Ghaeluinn 126:7
**Bearra:** *I am the nun of B. Baoi* 13:12
**Beatha:** tá beocht agus beatha san áit seo 136:9
**Beautiful:** *everything red is b.* 12:3
It's old but it is b. 128:2
they are hard and humorous and often b. 111:9
**Beauty:** A convent was the proper place for such frail b. 123:10
are changed, changed utterly: A terrible b. is born 164:2
b. is generally, a proud, vain, saucy, expensive, impertinent sort of commodity 95:1
B. must fade away 69:4
But oh! her b. was far beyond 108:9
her heroic and now cavernous b. 95:7
her own increasing b. 93:7
*Naked I saw thee, / O b. of b.* 134:10
None other had all b., queen or lover / Or was so fitted to give birth to kings. 164:7
on her cheek a glow of b. 68:1
the b. of an aged face 38:1
the b. of the world hath made me sad 134:9
the long path where B. wends 65:8
they say that her b. / Was music in mouth 42:8
'twas not her b. alone that won me 110:11
your b. left a lining in it 32:1

**Beaverbrook, Lord:** what lord B. thought about Ireland 38:3
**Bed:** A b. of flocks as one may rank it / Reduc'd to rag and half a blanket 161:10
in a manger for his b. 9:5
I often laid in b. and prayed 22:9
Madge Going To B. On My Last Night At Home 63:7
My b. was the ground 37:3
Now Betty from her master's b. had flown 149:10
When I went to b. at night 20:9
will never . . . be able to lie diagonally in his b. again 148:10
**Beds:** Feather b. are soft 20:11
**Beef:** the Mullingar heifer was b. to the heels 21:10
**Beehive:** a kind of virginal b. 48:7
**Beetle:** *One b. will find out another* 25:14
**Beg:** have to be put with a bowl to b. 18:1
**Begot:** had minded what they were about when they b. me 148:5
**Begins:** b. where I say it b. 63:3
**Beithil:** é ron-ucais i mB. 31:9
**Belashanny:** to my native B. 10:3
**Belfast:** a B. of exorbitant virtue 48:11
All the politest young ladies of B. 57:5
At B. where they remained a day 110:5
B. . . . impossible to fathom why I like this city 95:8
B. owes us a mighty grudge 66:1
Dublin and B. and Cork and Derry are . . . cosmopolitan 90:10
I have three brothers — two alive, and one in B! 136:10
I was born in B. 97:9
May the lord in His mercy be kind to B. 47:11
O B., B., dear object of my love 40:12
the B. Quasimodo to the Irish Esmeralda 121:4
*utters a note above B. Lough* 11:9
*See also* 25:17
**Belief:** the want of b. is a defect that ought to be concealed 150:4
**Believe:** B. me if all those endearing young charms 107:3
**Believer:** *all is possible to the b.* 99:15
**Bell:** Soon the nuns' b. will ring. I will go to the mechanical prayer 148:15
straightway, like a b., / Came low and clear 147:12
that was why we chose the name of 'the B.' 123:4
When will Heav'n, its sweet b. ringing 108:14
**Bellewstown Hill:** at 'Tatter Jack Welsh' upon B.H. 19:2
**Below:** wants but little here b. 66:11
**Bells:** b. are booming down the bohreens 30:16
I often think of / Those Shandon Bells 99:11
still listen for the landward b. 72:17
the B. of St. Nicholas 23:8
the b. of St. Patrick's with their time-mellowed tongues 135:7
the b. of Shandon 23:8
the dead-bells chime! 50:8
**Berkeley, Bishop:** if B. and Swift . . . had been compelled to write in Irish 99:5
**Bés:** 'Is é a b.', ól Ísu 11:1
**Bessy:** Awake thee, my B. 37:4
**Best:** the b. lack all conviction while the worst / Are full of passionate intensity 164:11
**Bethlehem:** *It was He whom you bore in B.* 31:9
**Betray:** finds too late that men b. 67:1
**Betrayal:** Home Rule morally is a great b. 10:2
**Better:** has to be something b. than this 62:9
**Beware:** *b., my son, womankind* 44:14
**Bhig:** idir neoin b. agus béal maidne 94:6
**Bible:** their hatred of the B. 71:4
**Bicycles:** who are nearly half people and half b. 116:13
**Biggar, Joseph** 159:12 *See also* 121:4
**Bigotry:** the passion of b. 50:1
**Bill:** Whenever I see a Minister sitting for two years on a B. 46:9
**Bind:** bars and bolts and chains can never b. 122:6
**Binn:** Ceol ba b. ná do cheol 15:8
Is b. béal 'na thost 24:14
**Bird:** Could he like a b. be in two places at once? 138:7
**Birds:** a real nest of singing b. 43:11
I kill all me own b. 122:3
In Iveragh of the singing b. 43:6
Nor voices of the sweeter b. 87:12
she was a flock of b. 27:7
**Birl:** the b. that two weemin can rise 101:6
**Birth:** I thank the goodness and the grace / that on my b. have smiled 159:9
the land that gave them b. 50:5
they give b. astride of a grave 29:13
**Birthrate:** the b. [is] relentless 88:13
**Bishops:** Here we have b., priests and deacons 118:12
**Bite:** recover'd of the b. 66:12
**Bites:** I will never give you an opportunity of making two b. 41:5
**Bittern:** He shall not hear the b. cry 87:12
*O yellow b.* 94:1
**Bitterness:** a weight of b. too great to be borne 87:7
Haughtiness and B. of spirit do but incense and provoke 101:1
our b. and love 51:12
**Black:** and little b. men 39:8
little b. rose shall be red at last 53:2
my b. hills have never seen 81:10
*your darling b. head*| 16:4, 59:14
**Black-and-Tan:** a b-and-t / a thief 50:3
humble the pride of the bold b. and t. 23:9
**Blackbird:** *A b. from a yellow-heaped branch* 11:9
*beautiful b. of Doire an Chairn! 15*:8
dropped from a b's flute 87:13
If I was a b. 23:13
**Blackguardism:** my monosyllabic answer was 'b.' 73:11

**Blackguards:** stood in the midst of four b. 73:10
**Blackleg:** the false and dirty b. / Is the vilest beast of all 45:14
**Blackthorn:** I cut a stout b. 22:8
**Blades:** a thousand b. were flashing 40:10
**Blame:** something to b. or rectify with every step she took 110:5
who was there to b. us 61:10
**Blarney:** the groves of B. 105:2
**Blas:** tá b. gan ceart ag an Muimhneach 17:4
**Blather:** I believe all their b. 29:4
**Bleed:** for him who'd bleed in his country's need 110:10
for others' liberties they b. 50:5
**Blind:** steal a penny from a b. man 28:8
**Blinds:** the b. is down, Joxer, the b. is down 118:7
**Blood:** Asking each other from what bluest blueness of b. 147:5
come back over the counters like b. 84:3
consent to the effusion of a single drop of human b. 119:10
for this that all the b. was shed 164:12
I see His b. upon the rose 135:11
lapping up his b. 53:3
let its tears of b. evaporate 71:7
may their b. cease to flow 51:1
my hands are so free from b. 40:9
stirs proudly and secretly in my b. 92:7
that there should be a b. sacrifice 73:8
the b. which here has streamed 56:6
*'There's not a drop of my b. in you.'* 123:8
there were blossoms of b. on our sprigs of green 43:2
washing out our whole life work in a sea of b. 54:1
*Who shed Thy healing b.* 93:14
**Bloom:** Mr. Leopold B. ate with relish 79:12
Mrs. Marion B. bathing in her sexual reveries 140:10
**Blow:** defeated before a b. is struck 46:7
the first b. is half the battle 66:15
who strikes the first b. for Ireland? 86:4
**Blow-ins:** some of these are b. 47:2
**Blue:** the world is only a b. bag 49:2
upon that little tent of b. / which prisoners call the sky 160:3
**Blunders:** never b. of the heart 56:2
**Blush:** to b. and hang back 66:17
**Bó:** a fhíorscoth na mb. 16:9
Cailín deas crúite na mb. 19:7
Go réidh, a bhean na dtrí mbó! 16:1
**Board of Works:** or the Irish B. of W. 27:3
**Boast:** it is an idle b. 51:7
**Boat:** *he was obliterating the name of the b.*118:14
My b. is on the shore 36:5
**Boats:** Bad cess to the b.! 93:12
Happy in the monotony of the b. 112:3
the little b. beneath the Norman Castle 97:9
**Boccaccio:** girl before me, reading B. 36:5
**Bodenstown:** In B. Churchyard 51:4
**Body:** B. awaits the tolerance 54:8
he had taken liberties with her unresisting b. 156:6
health of b., peace of mind 90:12
My b. seems to respond to the movement of the river 96:6
the mind not less than the b. 67:4
the whole b. crumbled into dust and passed from our sight 148:13
**Bog:** *Cold is the night in the Great B.* 14:5
every b. its bones 30:7
It thrives through the b. 41:4
Scum condensed of Irish b., / Ruffian, coward, demagogue 154:5
the squelch / Of bog beneath your boots 98:5
**Bogland:** Across the b. blown 38:9
the bare b. with the hump-backed mountain behind 120:13
**Bogs:** Brown b. with black water 44:10
forsake the eternal b. 96:9
I rattled o'er the bogs 22:8
**Bohreens:** Bells are booming down the b. 30:16
**Boil:** they b. the baby 77:9
**Bombs:** the banning of b. is more to the point than the banning of books 118:12
**Bone:** I have no b. to pick with graveyards 29:3
**Bones:** Crept on four b. to his last scattering 92:9
every bog its b. 30:7
his b. were cold as clay 22:9
I'll lay my b. a while 73:3
the b. from aking and the marrow from soaking 146:6
the unemployment in our b. 51:12
**Bonnán:** A b. bhuí is é mo léan do luí 94:1
**Bonny:** b., b. Sliabh Gallion braes 22:11
painted rooms are b. 20:11
the b. boy was young 19:3
**Book:** A b. written out of no desire of self-expression 106:11
At worst his book . . . is still in existence 95:4
crazily tangled like the B. of Kells 72:17
If that couch could write a b. 63:4
that other b., *Portrait of the Artist* 116:8
When can a man get down to a b. in peace? 43:10
**Books:** My only b. / Were woman's looks 109:4
**Boolavogue:** At B., as the sun was setting 102:7
**Boot:** She'll get a b. up the transom 54:4
**Bootlaces:** have not taken away my b. 77:12
**Bootstraps:** the help of its own b. 64:8
**Booze:** this land of Popes and Pigs and B. 74:2
**Bord:** do cuireadh an B. Oideachais 74:6
**Boreas:** Nos tumidus B. vastat 141:11
**Boring:** he could hold forth for a couple of hours and never become b. 114:1
**Bosom:** how sweetly thy green b. rises 49:6
**Bothán:** b. deirrit díthreba 13:1
**Bouchaleen:** my own B. bawn! 82:11
**Boulders:** we have shaped and fashioned rough b. 112:5
**Boundary:** no man has the right to fix the b. of the march of a nation 132:4

**Bountiful:** My Lady B. 58:10
**Bowels:** now I'm just a bunch of interesting b.! 153:9
**Bowen, Elizabeth:** E.'s home was merely a great stone box, but full of Italian mantelpieces and decayed 18th century furniture 161:15
**Bower:** Will you come to the b. 19:9
**Bowl:** He held the b. aloft 79:9
**Boy:** as if they were going to kill a b. 40:9
Oh the bonny b. was young 19:3
the last of the Broths of a B. 57:6
**Boycott:** *are saying now to 'b.' someone* 60:2
**Boycotter:** ils disent à présent 'b.' 60:2
**Boyle, Edward:** For one glimpse of E. B. 21:12
**Boyne:** B is for B. water, where bones do still remain 127:9
On the green grassy slopes of the B. 127:8
reaching right back to the B. 76:3
**Boys:** All the servant b. gaping and laughing 101:12
the b. are defeated 99:3
the b. they all paid him a visit 21:13
to train the b. of Ireland to fight I.'s battle 134:8
We are the b. of Wexford 80:2
**Brady, Phelim:** then forget P. B., the Bard of Armagh 19:1
**Braes:** bonny, bonny Sliabh Gallion b. 22:11
**Brass:** if there was a wall of b. 30:11
**Brave:** Oh b. young men 59:16
**Breach:** in a b. of promise letters are a great help 101:12
**Breast:** to soothe a savage b. 45:9
**Breasts:** So he could feel my b. all perfume yes 80:1
**Breeches:** turned the colour of his leather b. 32:3
**Breed:** the new b. wants to be well-paid, well-fed and idle 144:9
**Breeding:** She was a strange mixture of distinction and commonness, like her b. 146:2
**Breffney:** the little waves of B. 67:7
**Brennan:** B. on the Moor 19:5
**Brewing:** like the b. of men 37:3
**Brian Boru:** Remember the glories of B. the brave 108:8
that I should live, and B. be dead! 100:4
what we read that B. B. did with the Danes 124:4
**Brick:** Red b. in the suburbs 47:11
**Bríde:** Féach nach in aisce a baisteadh ort B. 104:5
**Bride:** like a b. in her rich adornin' 89:11
who made a field for his b. 81:5
**Bridge:** All crossed over the b. together 17:6
On the b. of Toome today 38:11
**Bridges:** At two elegant b. 18:2
**Brigade:** Of the Irish B. 50:11
*Viva la,* the new B.! 50:12
**Bright:** All things b. and beautiful 9:3
*At the b. breaking of the day* 17:2
b. as a series of parasols 32:10
b. in the sun shone the emerald plain 31:2
b. with cozy homesteads 52:10
Inundher the b. new moon 69:3
the b. shillings of March 81:11
the heavens look b., my dear 109:6
With her hair as b. as seaweed 41:6
**Brightness:** *b. of b. I've seen on the way, lonely* 128:4
**Brigid:** After the Feast of B. I shall hoist my flag and go 147:7
*B., Patrick and Colmcille* 51:14
B., Patricius atque Columba 51:14
*How well you were christened after St. B.* 104:5
Slán seiss, a B. co mbúaid 129:12
**Brimstone:** b. on evil 59:8
**Bríste:** 'an bhfóirfeadh b. Mhicí duit' 99:14
**Britannia:** de Scotia ad B. 9:1
**Britain:** design for the separation of Ireland from B. 41:13
nearer the sunset than Great B. 83:16
proud of B.'s stand alone 53:1
will be Ireland and not Great B. 40:5
**British:** a link of the B. chain 67:8
denying and defying all B. law 105:5
If we want to be out of the B. Commonwealth 92:4
insolence of B. politicians 53:11
refusing to attend the B. parliament 69:11
to do with the B. what . . . Brian Boru did with the Danes 124:4
to kill the last link of B. supremacy 33:6
we cannot fairly accuse the B. of great severity or vindictiveness on this occasion 157:3
**Brogues:** In a bran new pair of b. 22:8
**Broke:** in fact the man was b. 62:5
**Brón:** Mo b. ar an bhfarraige 16:10
**Brooks:** Down by the purling / Of sweet, silent b. 105:2
**Brother:** Here our murdered b. lies 54:15
I would have the two sisters embrace like one b. 138:6
the B. / the Plain People of Ireland 113:7
turned over the dead body and looked into his b.s face 123:12
**Brothers:** At Gorey my loving b. all 102:4
**Broths:** the last of the B. of a Boy 57:6
**Brown:** B. bogs with black water 44:10
the b. wind of Connacht 38:9
the foot of the Sweet B. Knowe 21:7
*These commanded me to this visit, Valentine B.* 128:5
**Brún:** fá dheara dhom triall riamh ort, a Vailintín B. 128:5
**Buckshot:** more humane that b. be used 61:3
**Bud:** I smelt a rat; . . . I'll nip him in the b. 138:9
**Bugger:** is a savage b. 62:8
**Buí:** A bhonnáin b. 94:1
**Build:** We had to b. in stone for ever after 72:15
**Builders:** Who were the b.? 87:1
**Bull:** An Irish B. is always pregnant 99:7
**Bullet:** a b. may just as well have done the job 43:12
he is not proof against a b. 103:12
**Buried:** *Am I b. in the Pound section* 117:8
**Burke, Edmund:** E. B. drew attention to a very

remarkable item in the Estimates 165:4
**Burke, John:** J. B. remarked 73:12
**Burke, T. H.:** B. got no more than his deserts 135:4
**Burn:** to b. any scripture they found 71:4
will touch his image and b. 58:6
**Burns:** b. in glorious Araby 50:7
**Burnt:** *since you've b. the candle* 25:2
that they be b. and placed in a paper bag 29:8
**Bush:** you're a rag on every b. 33:3
**Business:** *What b. is that of anyone's?* 16:2
**Butt, Isaac:** every popular leader, O'Connell, B., Parnell, Dillon and Redmond 110:2
they had, in the hands of I. B., kept up a certain noise and excitement 145:4 *see also* 121:5
**Bycut:** have put B. to great cost 23:6

**Cabhair:** Is deise c. Dé 24:5
**Cabin:** Out from many a mud-wall c. 40:10
**Cabins:** our response to mud c. 63:10
**Caesar:** Proud C. fell down right before him 161:8
where Christ and C. are hand in glove 78:9
You've heard of Julius C. 62:4
**Cailín:** A little Irish c. 58:2
c. deas crúite na mbó 19:7
C. Domhnaigh 24:10
**Caillech:** Is mé C. Bérri Buí 13:12
Uaigní mé ioná an C. Béarra 134:12
**Caindel:** Colum Cille, c. 10:13
Ní báitter mo shecht c. 11:5
**Caiseal:** C. gan cliar, fiailteach ná macraí ar dtúis 128:5
**Caisleán:** 'sin c. óir a bhfuil na daoine beaga ina gcónaí' 99:12
**Caith:** Nuair c. tú an choinneal 25:2
**Cake:** having cut the grocer's c., . . . found it was the usual conglomerate of tallow, sawdust, bad eggs and gravel 146:1
Two women to be mixing a c. 68:11
**Calabar:** on board of the C. 19:11
**Calamity:** How often has public c. been arrested 34:17
**California:** So long as there's an 'if' in C. 111:1
**Call:** I would c. you to book 98:6
**Camera:** Keep the c. whirrin' 63:7
**Camps:** into two hostile c. 76:6
**Canary:** the soft flame of a c. 111:3
**Candle:** As a white c. in a holy place 38:1
burn / like a c. 58:6
*Colum Cille, c. of Ireland* 10:13
For every year of life we light / a c. on your cake 144:11
*Since you've burnt the c.* 25:2
**Candlelight:** I cut her throat by c. 64:4
washing her feet by c. 38:2
**Candles:** All clean collars and long white c. 84:5
*May my seven c. not be quenched* 11:5
**Cannon:** As the c. ball carries itself down the hill 86:2
shaking scythes at c. 72:7
to bring c. to such a place 25:16
**Capitalist:** to manage the affairs of the c. class 46:5
**Captain:** the c.'s Spanish tears 31:13
As for the C. o' Cutters 39:2
A successful c. of enterprise 83:9
**Captains:** the c. and the kings 30:3
**Capital:** the c. of the finest nation 20:2
**Car:** a low-backed c. she drove 90:1
the open sides of the c. 32:8
**Carageen:** the extension of the c. moss industry 48:8
**Carbery:** C.'s hundred isles 51:3
**Cards:** a table and a pack of c. 73:10
**Card-tables:** the c.-t. of Dublin 30:12
**Care:** He didn't c. a damn 81:6
**Carina:** Perge C. / Per mare longum 132:7
**Caritas:** Amavi Deum, amavi vos, et c. nunquam excidit 99:15
**Carleton, William:** C. was the man sent by God 56:3
**Carmelites:** the C. will do their best to get him 122:4
**Carrick:** the ladies from C. I ofttimes have seen 21:11
**Carry:** could c. all he knew 66:10
**Carson, Edward:** Sir E. [C.] is a stage Irishman 57:6
that sink of acidity — Lord C. 66:1
the Right Honourable Sir Edward Henry C. 57:5
**Casacht:** c. reilige 25:5
**Casement, Roger:** *see* 142:13
**Cash:** more c. circulated at the card-tables 30:12
**Cassidy:** C.'s hanging hill 81:1
with little Mary C. 58:1
**Castle:** The little boats beneath the Norman c. 97:9
the pleasant gardens of C. Hyde 19:8
the rich man in his c. 9:4
**Castles:** C. are sacked in war 69:4
roofless c. 30:15
*Those are the golden c.* 99:12
**Casualty:** Our first c. was some poor fool 77:10
**Cat:** Briseann an dúchas tré shúile a' c. 24:12
*c.'s place by the fire* 24:7
Níl áit a' c. sa luaith aige 24:7
pepper in the c.'s milk 28:8
you never were the stuff / To be the cottage c. 93:6
**Cathaír:** *Above the children of C. Mór* 129:12
**Cathedrals:** where two c. sit upon opposing hills 30:6
**Cathleen:** C. wept her thousand welcomes 77:7
On which the feet of C. have rested 91:5
**Catholic:** Are you C.? 60:7
going to be governed by C. ideas and by C. ideas alone, you will never get the North 165:5
he admired the C. religion 82:1
I, as a C., obey my Church authorities 47:6
nothing civilised about a mob, be it Protestant or C. 154:3
the C. church has behaved . . . in an identical way as

the Orange Order 34:1
the enemy is the Roman C. Church 131:5
the Roman C. Church is getting nearer to Communism every day 131:7
to go near the C. idolators 71:3
**Catholics:** All C. were under orders 71:4
C. are out to destroy Ulster 33:12
I began to think about C. 88:3
If you treat Roman C. with due consideration and kindness they will live like Protestants. 127:4
Of 31 porters at Stormont, 28 are R.C. 10:10
the C. have been interfering in Ulster affairs since 1641 131:6
the C. of Ireland still remember they have a country 118:15
the C. take their beliefs 83:15
the C. we'd scarcely loved 89:15
what is Ireland without C.? 36:2
**Cause:** I die in a good c. 25:19
**Cavan:** In C. of the little lakes 104:9
**Caveto:** C., filole / Feminarum species 44:14
**Ceann:** Is cuir do c. dílis 16:4
**Ceiltis:** Focal deas séimh é 'C.' 74:6
**Celibacy:** c., late marriage and emigration 103:14
**Celibate:** waiting for a c. churchman in Mother Rome 111:7
**Cell:** mice were squealing in my prison c. 30:1
There's not much room to walk in a c. twelve feet by seven 135:3
**Cells:** and the prison c. 72:17
**Celtic:** *'C.' was a nice respectable word* 74:6
**Centre:** things fall apart; the c. cannot hold 164:11
**Ceo:** c. draiochta i gcoim oíche do sheol mé 130:4
**Ceol:** A Chrínóc, cubaid do c. 117:3
c. ba binne ná do c. 15:8
**Cerberus:** may the dog C. make a meal of his rump 28:7
**Ceremony:** to be executed without c. 29:8
**Chain:** a link of the British c. 67:8
break in twain the galling c. 80:2
**Chance:** Now is your c. Now or never 42:2
**Change:** nor wished to c. his place 66:8
when we all c. places 68:13
**Changed:** Are c., c. utterly: / A terrible beauty is born 164:2
if he c. his countenance at all 71:1
**Character:** this demoralized c. persists 57:1
**Charity:** as long as men hold c. 35:2
**Charm:** what c. can soothe her melancholy 67:1
**Charming:** being so c. in spite of it 90:11
**Charms:** if all those endearing young c. 107:3
**Chaste:** be c. till you're tempted 49:9
Ireland green and c. 81:15
**Cheek:** Her soft c. was glowing against mine 87:14
**Cherry-trees:** would answer your c.-t. 49:12
**Chest:** Many a manly c. was throbbing 40:10
**Chesterfield:** the great and good Lord C. 29:8
**Chicken:** I swear she's no c. 150:11
**Chieftains:** C. are scattered far 69:4
these two C. whom we have lost 110:8
**Chignon:** Nor did she wear a c. 133:4
**Child:** A c. is normally completely immersed 84:2
A young healthy c. well nursed is at a year old almost delicious 150:6
And made me in these Christian days / A happy English c. 159:9
I dreamt I was a c. once more 83:1
walks the c. a man? 10:7
*Twenty years a c.* 25:4
**Childers, Erskine:** *See* 124:5
**Childhood:** coming out suddenly . . . among this blasphemy of c. 151:10
In my c. trees were green 97:2
like Dolmens round my childhood 106:1
some soft, almost physical appendage of c. seems to have fallen away 111:8
Trains came threading quietly through my dozing c. 98:3
**Children:** Being c. of a staunch Protestant quarter 71:3
by which c. are brought up 67:4
didn't rat on their c. 90:6
I have no c. by which I can propose to get a single penny 150:7
It was more lasting than all their c. 103:8
Our c. . . . brought up for export 52:8
shooting of mothers of English-speaking c. 66:4
take my c. to the altar and swear them to eternal hostility 135:5
Yet like Lir's c. 72:17
**Chimneys:** you'll have to put a goose down these c. some day soon 145:5
**Chinese:** like the ways of the heathen C. 77:5
**Chivalry:** the age of c. is gone 34:14
**Choices:** two c. lay at her disposal 35:7
**Chords:** Have c. of deep longing 31:1
**Christ:** *C. owns the seed* 18:8
*C. the Son of God the Father* 31:9
*C. with me, C. before me* 11:4
C. with me, C. before me 133:3
I am the gilly of C. 37:10
Jesus C. her little child 9:5
That reach the age of C. 84:8
*to become an exile for C.* 9:1
where C. and Caesar are hand in glove 78:9
with no C. in between 48:5
**Christening:** that was the c. 64:1
**Christian:** Ah, kind C., do not grudge / the sixpence promised on the brudge 166:5
freedom to pursue the un-C. path cf communal strife 127:2
you wouldn't meet a C. out of doors, unless it was a snipe or a dispensary doctor 145:6
**Christmas:** And Father C. mourn his revels lost 150:3
C. Day is come; let's all prepare 158:3

It was a sort of white C. 84:5
**Christo:** pro C. peregrinari volens 9:1
**Church:** an alien C. 54:2
anyone who ran round the church three times 43:1
beyond the bridge the c. lurked 96:4
for which Grandmother C. 78:10
High C., low steeple 151:3
Mother C. ranks at the very top 53:4
My mind was like Swift's c. 73:13
the C. has ever been the enemy of Irish Freedom 105:5
Rather to drive men out of the C. 101:1
Respect the decision of the Head of the C. 49:4
Scarlet C. of all uncleanness 127:12
ten thousand sages of the C. 39:9
there's a c. for service 19:8
they painted his toenails and turned him into a c. 112:9
**Churchill, Winston:** Mr. C. is proud 53:1
**Churchyard:** *By the c. of Creagan* 92:3
In Bodenstown C. 51:4
**Ciall:** Ní thagann c. roimh aois 130:1
**Ciaróg:** Aithníonn c. c. eile 25:14
**Cill:** Ag Úr-C. an Chreagáin chodail mé 92:3
Is mise Stoc na C. 117:9
Ní bhíonn súil le c. 25:3
Níl trácht ar C. Cais 16:5
**Cinn:** id luí thú ar chúl do chinn 94:1
**City:** Bates every c. upon the say 20:2
died with his face to the c. 22:1
Do you think them proud c. folk will listen to his ballads 102:1
Fly the c., brothers tried 69:7
Impossible to fathom why I like this c. 95:8
In Dublin's fair c. 17:7
In the c. of the flesh 27:7
like a foreigner in a great c. 64:10
like the flame-blackened ruin of some mighty c. 120:13
Once in Royal David's c. 9:5
Strumpet C. in the Sunset 78:2
the c. dweller who passes through 33:9
they brought her to the c. / And she faded slowly there 161:7
this arrogant c. 92:7
without a c. wall 9:6
**Civilisation:** A c. can be imprisoned 63:11
**Civilised:** any c. people so beggarly wretched 30:10
more worthy of a c. people 94:4
when we shall all be c. 82:10
**Clannaib:** fil for c. Cathaír Máir 129:12
**Clare:** the girl from the County C. 61:9
**Class:** it has not been confined to any one c. 114:4
that c. will always have it in their power to plunder 46:2
**Clay:** C. in his thoughts 37:9
C. is the word 81:4
screams the apocalypse of c. 81:7
sourness in the c. 84:11
Would I were stretched in my bed of c. 100:7
**Cleanliness:** the want of c. 23:4
**Cléir:** Ná bí mór nó beag leis a' c. 24:6
**Clergy:** All that the c. banish from the mind 42:7
All that the c. teach their young 42:11
*neither intimate nor distant with the c.* 24:6
**Climate:** the c. is temperate 88:13
This peculiar c. . . . has caused or increased a tendency to nervous depression 152:1
**Cloak:** a meet bed for a rebel, and an apt c. for a thief 146:4
**Chloch:** Chím mar chaith an c. gach fear 121:11
**Cloch:** Mórchuid c. is gannchuid cré 121:11
**Clogher:** three dioceses, Derry, Raphoe, C. 89:2
**Clongowes:** C. is my dwellingplace 79:1
**Cloonagh:** the little roads of C. 67:6
**Cloth:** poor man's smell in c. 48:9
**Clothes:** On a Saturday night I sell second-hand c. 82:4
**Clouds:** the c. are dark o'er Ardnalee 86:7
the c. were rent asunder 41:2
**Cloyne:** jumped from C. to Derry 72:13
**Cluiche:** c. n-aímin indel áig 11:6
**Cnámha:** Is do c. sínte 94:1
**Cnó:** Cride hé / daire c. 11:7
**Coach:** A great family c., . . . lumbers along a narrow Irish road 106:5
**Coaches:** nobles often do c. ride 19:8
**Coalisland:** Old miners at C. 111:3
**Coals:** burning anything that came from England except their people and their c. 150:9
**Cockles:** Crying 'C. and mussels, alive, alive, oh!' 17:7
**Cockroach:** the honeymoon of the c. 51:11
**Codail:** C. beagán beagán beag 14:3
**Codladh:** Tá mo mháthair 'na c. 15:10
**Coffin:** living idiots pressing round that new / Oak coffin 153:4
Must carry his own c. 42:11
Peel's smile was like the silver plate on a c. 120:4
suspended like Mahomet's c. 33:5
**Coinneal:** Nuair chaith tú an c. 25:2
**Cold:** A curse for the cold, a cup for the bold 110:10
*As c. as the first day of Spring!* 104:5
C. as your own wan smiles 87:8
*C. is the night in the Great Bog* 14:5
*'It's c.,' said the old man* 99:13
It's only a little c. I have 118:10
**Coleraine:** C. for lasses 30:8
**Collar:** He wore his c. the wrong way round 97:3
**Colleen:** She's called the C. Bawn 32:2
**College:** the C. is outwardly a rectangular plain building 116:3
**Collins, Michael:** *see* 110:8
**Colmcille:** *Brigid, Patrick and C.* 51:14
*C.'s advice* 25:9
*C. candle of Ireland* 10:13

Comhairle C. 25:9
**Colonel:** Said the King to the C. 54:12
**Colonels:** C. up from the Curragh 82:12
**Colour:** Any organization may adopt a special c. without infringing the law 123:2
the c. might all come away 62:3
**Colours:** It's c. they are fine 128:2
**Columba:** Brigida, Patricius at que C. 51:14
*St. C. passed from earth to heaven* 9:2
**Column:** no rising c. marks this spot 56:6
**Come:** And did we c. into our own 89:15
*C. back, c. back, my dear one!* 17:1
*C. back early or never c.* 97:2,3
C. back, Paddy Reilly 61:8
C. back to us sometime 34:5
C. in! for it is growing late 105:1
When you c. back to me 55:4
Will you c. to the bower 19:9
**Comhairle:** c. Cholmcille 25:9
**Commandments:** Home Rule and the Ten C. 83:8
How Adam and Eve Broke All the Commandments at Once. 157:1
**Commemorate:** O c. me where there is water 81:8
**Commonsense:** he wrote c. 69:10
**Communion:** C. breads I ate from the vestry but they were unblessed. 154:7
**Communism:** The Roman Catholic Church is getting nearer to C. every day 131:7
**Communists:** Socialists are a Protestant variety of C. 131:12
**Company:** God's choice, about the c. He keeps 93:13
You should always except the present c. 125:6
**Compassion:** judged . . . by our own c. 48:5
**Complaint:** this c. is no new thing 54:13
with less c. than a Sinn Féiner makes 57:7
**Complexions:** the best c. 30:13
**Compliment:** they have been paying you a handsome c. 90:11
**Compliments:** C. pass when the quality meet 29:15
**Condemnation:** except with profound and bitter c. 65:5
**Condemned:** the c. man gets the priest 30:2
**Condition:** the c. upon which God has given liberty 49:11
**Confectioners:** 'Tis there you'll see c. with sugar sticks and dainties 20:5
**Conflict:** *pleasant games in innocent c.* 11:6
the end of the c. of centuries 69:12
will not end the centuries of c. 52:4
**Congreve, William:** W. C. is the only sophisticated playwright England has produced 156:7
**Conn:** Is that C. the Shaughraun? 32:3
**Connacht:** Some C. garb around me clings 96:11
Tá adharca fada ar bhuaibh i gC. 25:10
the brown wind of C. 38:9
*the C. man has both accuracy and tunefulness* 17:4
**Connachtach:** Tá ceart agus blas ag an gC. 17:4
**Connollys:** To our horror we met the C. — a less appetising pair I have never seen out of the Zoo 161:15
**Conquerors:** *the hold she has won over her c.* 95:5
**Conquest:** the worst badge of c. 51:8
**Conscription:** defeated C. in spite of their threats 23:9
**Consonants:** literary awareness . . . as consonants 72:11
the iron / flash of c. 71:8
**Conspiracy:** a c. against the honour of Britain 41:13
**Constance:** Council of C. in 1415 55:5
**Constellations:** Amid the c. 71:2
**Constitution:** to meddle with the buttresses and walls of our ancient c. 138:5
who gave you the Free C.? 61:2
**Consumption:** c. has no pity / For blue eyes and golden hair 161:7
**Contemptible:** most c. of all the peoples of Europe 40:7
**Continent:** it is on the C . . . that we find anything like similarity of circumstances 104:7
**Contraception:** to leave c. on the long finger 90:9
To speak of a right to c. 103:11
**Convict:** she has been a c. in the dock 83:17
**Cooks:** with a legion of c. 36:3
**Coolnagar:** beyond in C. 38:10
**Coombe:** Off Blackpits near the C. / With my poor wife, Sally 166:1
the best shawls of the C. 73:5
**Co-op:** He found it hard to say c. 64:1
**Cootehill:** stop when half-way to C. 61:8
**Corde:** Manet in meo c. Dei amoris flamma 44:6
**Cork:** Dublin and Belfast and C. and Derry are . . . cosmopolitan 90:10
in the county of C. 48:12
the legs of the ladies of C. 95:2
To come from C. / On a summer's day 99:10
**Corkmen:** Most C. know a lot; but this one knew everything 114:1
**Corn:** they're cutting the c. down in Creeshlough 61:11
whoever could make two ears of c. to grow . . . where only one grew before 149:14
**Corpse:** a c. on the dissecting-table 83:17
As his corse to the ramparts we hurried 161:12
than for the c. 55;7
worse than Marid or Afrit, / Or c.-eating Ghool 100:8
**Corpses:** C. lying in fever sheds - / C. huddled on foundering decks, / And shroudless dead on their rocky beds 160:1
**Corr:** ná c. ar cairde 25:8
**Corrymeela:** Och, C. an' the blue sky over it! 126:12
**Couch:** If that c. could write a book 63:4
**Cough:** *A graveyard c.* 25:5
**Coulin:** I will fly with my C. 109:8
**Countenance:** If he changed his c. at all 71:1

**Country:** A c. rising from its knees 58:5
A thing called a c. cannot be formed 92:5
do more essential service to his c. than the whole race of politicians put together 149:14
father of his c. 35:13
for him who'd bleed in his c.'s need 110:10
for the good of his c. 67:10
he served his c. 51:2
I do not give up the c. 68:1
information on the material conditions of the c. 46:10
It is a strange c. 111:9
let me honour this c. 98:8
no c. so faithful 69:8
No man has the right to say to his c., 'Thus far shalt thou go and no further' 132:4
No other motive than the public good of my c. 150:7
Our c. is not a poetical abstraction 98:9
that is no c. for old men 164:9
this sinister c. 77:1
when my c. takes her place 56:8
'Will you give up your c.?' 35:9
your c. will need all your devotion 51:10
**Court:** *In many a c. and strong fortress* 92:2
sent the . . . Bill to the Supreme C. 54:5
**Courting:** courtin' in the kitchen 19:10
**Courts:** the c. are open to anyone 34:2
**Covenant:** pledge ourselves in solemn C. 24:1
**Coventry:** by putting him into moral C. 132:2
**Cow:** *I went to the fair and I sold my c.* 16:2
**Cowards:** though c. flinch and traitors sneer 45:16
**Cows:** *c. in Connacht have long horns* 25:10
Hearing the c. gadding in the heat 112:13
O woman of three c., agra! 100:10
woman with the three c. 16:1
Your absent-minded goats along the road, your black c. 98:7
**Crack:** hark away to the c. 66:17
**Crank:** A c. is a small instrument that makes revolutions 144:1
**Creagáin:** Ag Úr-Chill an C. 92:3
**Creature:** She was just the sort of c., boys, that nature did intend 133:4
**Creatures:** All c. great and small 9:3
Ma says you get used to the c. 61:7
to plunder and enslave the remainder of their fellow c. 46:2
**Creeshlough:** down in C. the day 61:11
**Crew:** vainly violent, lawless c. 68:7
**Cricket:** The officers in the barracks played proper c. 120:9
**Crime:** any c. as shameful as poverty 58:12
I'm guilty not of any c. 129:13
'Paradin' me c.,' sez she 62:7
pretended that c., like wine, improves by old age 119:2
the all but complete disappearance of c. 83:13
they have never committed a useless c. 134:4
you must show him your detestation of the c. he has committed 132:2
**Críost:** Ag C. an síol 18:8
C. limm, C. reum, C. im degaid 11:4
C. macc Dé Athar di nim 31:9
**Criticise:** let them c. on that point 69:14
**Criticized:** if she is c., they are publicly furious and privately amused 155:9
**Critics:** employ as drama c. journalists who are . . . hopelessly astray 138:4
**Crob:** Is scíth mo c. ón scríbainn 13:7
**Croí:** Cuireann sé gliondar ar mo c. a bheith annso iniu 113:2
Gile mo c. do c.-se. A Shlánaitheoir 130:5
Gloine ár gc. agus neart ár ngéag 124:2
**Cromwell, Oliver:** Far too briefly C. ruled 10:8
not forgetting Oliver C. 28:7
One of the many rooms in Ireland in which C. is said to have stabled his horse 145:8
**Croon:** the banshee's lonely c. 40:10
**Crop:** A plenteous c. of soldiers 40:13
**Croppies:** Down, down, C. lie down 127:7
**Crops:** gather in your agent's c. 23:5
Keep an eye on the state of the c. 89:3
**Cross:** clasping a black c. 76:5
let me carry your c. for Ireland 25:18
Out of her pocket she drew a c. 22:12
thief calling to thief from his c. 48:5
**Crosses:** No longer, the full hundred c. / Filling the sky 129:5
**Crossmaglen:** the dalin' men from C. 81:16
**Crow:** some black as the c. 61:7
**Crowd:** he was one of the real old c. anyway; sure there's only a few of us left. 159:14
swarmed with a gaily coloured c. 78:4
**Crown:** not loyal to the c. 74:4
**Crows:** like a flock of human c. 97:1
the tolerance of c. 54:8
**Crubeen:** a big c. for threepence 20:5
**Crucifixes:** there were c., big and small, of wood and metal 96:5
**Crúiscín:** is go nglaofad ar mo c. lán 15:9
with my charming little c. lawn 20:1
**Cruiskeen:** C. Lawn is 10 years old today 113:6
**Cry:** thy wrathful c. is still 59:15
To c. in public 126:4
**Cuach:** le seinm na gc. ar bhruach 92:1
**Cuckoo:** *When the c. intones its peaceful notes* 92:1
**Cudgel:** gain more renown in c.-playing 67:3
**Cúil:** ar chnámh a cúil's a súile iata 104:3
**Cuimhne:** Beidh c. orainn go fóill 121:12
**Cuirithir:** *I have loved C.* 12:1
**Cúirt:** Is iomaí c. agus caisleán láidir 92:2
**Culdrevny:** After the battle of C. 9:1
**Culmore:** C is for C., where crossing it we had our falls 127:9
**Cunning:** Silence, exile and c. 79:4
**Curam:** Habete c. mei 99:15
**Curate:** I can send him a c. who will break his heart

in six weeks! 143:11
**Cured:** *that cannot be c.* 24:4
**Curragh:** Colonels up from the C. 82:12
**Curse:** the c. of Swift is upon him 67:10
We often c. our material 112:5
**Curtain:** would bring his c. down 42:4
**Cushla:** c. ma chree! 49:6
**Custom:** *'It is the c.', said Jesus* 11:1
**Cynic:** What is a c.? A man who knows the price of everything and the value of nothing. 160:16

**Daedalus:** D., too busy hammering 76:4
**Dáil:** in defence of the D. 82:12
in order to get into the D. 52:9
**Dalkey:** along the D. tramline 32:10
**Damned:** d., d., d. Ireland! 62:11
**Dan:** I hope it's Michael D. 54:11
'I thank you Ma'am' says D. 21:1
**Dan Van Vought:** You put up your proclamation says the D.V.V. / To agitate Paddy's nation / Says the D.V.V. 166:3
**Dance:** How can we know the dancer from the d.? 163:7
it is not sweet with nimble feet / To d. upon the air! 160:5
owing to the welcome presence of the Redemptorist Fathers in the town there would be no d. on Sunday 155:7
The sea became a d. 112:1
**Danced:** d. the discreet waltz of their day 117:1
**Dances:** all sorts of nonsensical d. 21:5
But he d. there 37:9
**Dancing:** d. around the stage in an expletive manner 32:4
No such sight can be found as an Irish lass d.! 158:9
went d. back to the age of gold 130:6
**Dangerous:** in short, a very d. opponent 83:9
**Danny:** Dear D., I'm takin' the pen 61:11
**Danube:** where the waves of the blue D. roll 61:6
**Daoine:** Na d. is lú ciall i n-Éirinn 126:7
thugas iarracht ar mheon na nd. a bhí i mo thimpeall a chur síos 121:6
**Daoirse:** Is níl laistigh d'aon d. / Ach saoirse ó'n d. sin 129:2
**Dark:** All I know is a door into the d. 72:4
*O my d. Rosaleen* 17:3
peculiar and d. 77:5
when it's d. / the Fenians will get ye 105:1
**Darkness:** the d. in the air was beginning to lift 121:3
to set the d. echoing 72:6
**Darling:** 'D., d.,' she murmured. 'I live in you' 87:14
Oh, he's a d. man, a d. man 118:1
your d. black head 59:14
**Daughter:** *He had named the boat after his daughter* 118:14
**Daughters:** Make for her d. . . . good matches 35:10
**David:** Once in Royal D.'s city 9:5
(*See also* Lloyd George) to London to D. 23:10
**Davis, Thomas:** under God, to T. D. 59:16
without any disrespect to D. 56:5
**Davitt, Michael:** M. D. underneath the sod 70:2 *See also* 53:10
**Dawn:** *Carelessly sauntering in the d.'s first glint* 104:2
D., day, dark, frost, cloud 115:7
She's fairer than the d. 32:2
the blush of eternity's d. 82:11
the d. on the hills of Ireland 89:11
**Dawning:** I met a maid in the greenwood shade / At the d. of the day 159:1
**Days:** *Ancient / of days and unbegotten* 44:5
**Dé:** Is deise cabhair D. 24:5
**Dead:** And Brian be d.! / D., O Kinkora! 100:4
And your ignorant d. 98:7
are ever idolised when d. 46:1
As if his kin were d. 37:9
*D. with tea* 25:7
For they were young and eager who are d.! 147:13
I am going there alive or d. 86:10
it is d., but it has an affectation of life 105:6
It shrouded oft our martyred d. 45:15
*Many d. he do to death, this d. man under the headstone* 128:3
She was d. within a week 123:10
she will not / Have me alive or d. 97:10
that I should live, and Brian be d.! 100:4
the d.-bells chime! 50:8
the d. didn't brag 43:2
the slow, downstreaming d. 84:7
there are d. upon the roadside 87:9
upon all the living and the d. 78:3
Was it not a live fly that was in the d. man's mouth 120:3
where the living collogue with the d. 96:8
**Dean:** See, how the D. begins to break 150:14
**Dear:** to all the country d. 66:8
**Death:** Accidental d. 68:6
All life ends in d., but stone lives on 103:8
And when sergeant d. . . . shall embrace me 19:1
Arrest and d. come late and soon 117:6
d. is the most embarrassing universal 117:2
did not put him to some easy d. 49:12
early this morning I signed my d. warrant 43:12
Folks are kinder in d. than they are in life 154:8
hazard and d. 31:12
I am glad I am getting a soldier's d. 43:5
I'm bound for d. or glory 19:6
In balance with this life, this d. 164:3
in the presence of d. all outward show of indifference or patience is forgotten 151:7
I regret the accident of lord Cavendish's d. 135:4
I stand face to face with d. 40:9
Is there a life before d.? 72:10

may they walk in living d. 51:1
the angel of d. would be unlikely 77:6
the decent inn of d. 89:1
*there are three who await my d.* 15:7
they looked like anatomies of d.; they spoke like ghosts 146:3
*To the deed that I see / and the d. I shall die* 134:11
toil, sickness, ignominy, d. 105:4
We do not want sentence of d. 40:2
We'll watch till d. 51:6
When in d. I shall calm recline 109:11
**Decay:** All doomed to d. 22:11
**Deceive:** I tremble lest she may d. me 42:11
**December:** *Green D. fills the graveyard* 25:11
that bleak day in D. 10:1
the bleak D. day 22:2
**Decompose:** d. in a barrel of porter 54:7
**Defeat:** Never be got to accept d. 53:1
When our Boys you did d. 20:4
**Defendants:** the whole number of the d. 48:3
**Deirdre:** D. is dead, and Naisi is dead 151:11
**Delusion:** We have been too long a prey to that deep d. 135:12
**Demesne:** Purple-blue distances bound your d. 31:1
**Denial:** she gave a flat d. 19:10
**Deputies:** the policy of the Hungarian d. 69:11
**Dereliction:** few are the steps from d. to persecution 34:16
**Derg:** chena is álainn cech nd. 12:3
**Derry:** A'll walk frae here tae D. 141:4
D I'm sure you all know well, Our Maiden D.'s Walls 127:9
D. of the little hills 87:11
D.'s sons alike defy / Pope, traitor or pretender 155:5
Dublin and Belfast and Cork and D. are . . . cosmopolitan 90:10
Fair D. fixed her reign 155:6
*have my house in D.'s gentle centre* 14:8
jumped from Cloyne to D. 72:13
never comes near D. 93:13
the Donegal border comes so near to D. city 104:8
the high walls of D. look dismal and grey 21:6
the Prentice-Boys of D. 10:1
three dioceses, D., Raphoe, Clogher 89:2
**Description:** He answered the d. 59:1
**Desert:** 'Tis the rose of the d. 37:5
To the gloom of some d. 109:8
**Design:** the d. will be here merely reproduced 111:14
**Desmond:** in deep-valley'd Desmond 37:2
**Desolation:** the d. it was to be the mother of a fool 34:7
**Despair:** black d. succeeds brown study 45:5
For them that never knew d. 70:2
they shriek with pitiable d. before the horror of the fate to which they are doomed 151:7
was but the misnomer for the flight from d. 121:5
**Desperate:** Not sick so much as d. 62:8
**Destiny:** Hanging and marriage go by d. 59:2
we hug our little d. again 72:10
**Destroy:** in the end they always d. 33:8
Out to d. faith and fatherland 60:10
**de Valera, Éamon:** forced to come to close quarters with Mr. de V. 42:3
**Devil:** for he was the d. 87:15
Going where the d. drives 22:5
May the d. jump down his throat 28:7
Maybe the d. will give me time! 60:8
Now I've been a d. for most of my life 21:3
Said the d.'s work must cease 96:12
'Tell the truth and shame the d.' 123:11
that only the d. could invent 51:13
the D. in a Pigskin Swimsuit 131:3
the Pooka MacPhillimey, a member of the d. class 116:1
would meet the D. on the third time round 43:1
**Dew:** And sipped his mountain d. 80:3
*As d. from grass on summer day* 104:6
As the night d. that falls on the grass o'er his head 108:5
the d. on the forest green 22:13
the real old Mountain D. 22:7
**De Wet:** they called him D.W. 48:13
**Dialect:** never had any difficulty with the d. 59:12
**Dice:** An' the divil's in the d. 87:16
**Dictions:** I push back / through d. 71:8
**Did:** We all d. something, but none d. what he set out to do 106:11
**Die:** A man does not d. of love or his liver or even old age; he dies of being a man 157:2
And love me, it was sure to d. 109:13
Because of the distant past they would d. friendless 156:4
Clinch your teeth hard and never say d. 43:3
*even the English — maybe they might d.* 16:6
I d. a persecuted man for a persecuted country 129:11
I d. in a good cause 25:19
*I will not d. for you* 15:4
if the oaks and stars could d. for sorrow 151:11
If you don't d. you live through it 29:1
not d. here in a rage, like a poisoned rat in a hole 150:2
Rody McCorley goes to d. 38:11
that he had not to d. in a stuffy bed of a trumpery cough 143:1
*to d. this way, unbeknownst to anyone at all* 136:8
you would d. for me 87:14
**Died:** the dog it was that d. 66:12
**Diesel:** I journeyed by d. 31:2
**Difference:** the undying d. 81:3
**Dig:** I'll d. with it 71:9
**Dignity:** better to walk without shoes and barefooted than to walk without d. 135:9
carried himself with considerable d. 63:14
*Its bareness is its d.* 121:8
**Digressions:** D., incontestably, are . . . the life, the soul of reading! 148:6

**Dilemma:** the horns of a d. 30:6
**Dillon, John:** every popular leader, O'Connell, Butt, Parnell, D. and Redmond 110:2
**Dioceses:** the meeting of three d. 89:2
**Dip:** As a halfpenny d. is to an arc lamp 66:2
**Diseases:** those d.s which are the scourge of such crimes 23:4
**Disgrace:** he is a thundering d. 54:5
**Disposal:** the d. of these my body, mind and soul 29:8
**Dispositions:** the gaiety and levity of their d. 67:2
**Ditch:** she has died in the last d. repeatedly 83:17
**Division:** d. starts early 88:3
**Doctor:** wouldn't meet a Christian out of doors, unless it was a snipe or a dispensary d. 145:6
**Doctors:** the d. say I'm a very interesting case 153:9
**Doctos:** Doctos grammaticos presbiterosque pios 141:11
**Doctrines:** d. fashion'd to the varying hour 66:8
**Dog:** like Lanna Macree's d. 33:2
none but the d. calling after you 68:11
the d. it was that died 66:12
the Protestant was top d. always 34:6
**Doggerel:** In d. and stout 98:8
**Dogs:** D. and pigs were lapping up his blood 53:3
Lucian began to think of the ubiquity of d. in Ireland 158:6
**Doire:** a luin D. an Chairn! 15:8
Agam ar lar caomh Doire 14:8
**Dolmens:** like D. round my childhood 106:1
**Domhnaigh:** Bhí tú 'do shagart Dia D. 17:1
cailín D. 24:10
Go Glenn na gCuach Dé D. 91:1
**Dominicans:** the cardboard shields the D. used in Spain 116:12
**Dominion:** the great must submit to the d. 35:1
**Domuin:** Trí aithgin in d. 12:6
**Donaghadee:** six miles from Bangor to D. 23:2
**Donegal:** Back home to D. 133:6
I do not know what particular part of Southern Ireland D. is 47:4
the D. border comes so near to Derry city 104:8
the gray mountains of dark D. 55:6
the last bit of ould D. 61:11
**Doneraile:** Be still the food for D. 125:7
**Donn:** A dhroimeann d. dílis 16:9
Ar an droighneán d. 16:8
**Donnybrook:** Oh, D. capers, to sweet catgut-scrapers 18:3
success to the humours of D. fair! 18:2
**Door:** All I know is a d. into the dark 72:4
her face was like a gaol d. 101:5
Ireland has been knocking at the English d. long enough 132:5
Ireland's a d. 96:8
**Doras:** Is deise cabhair Dé nó an d. 24:5
**Doubloons:** falling like d. 31:13
**Dove:** d. of tenderness 68:4
**Dowager:** An ancient, weel-jointured, superannuated d. 95:1
**Down:** *In D. three saints one grave do fill* 51:14
**Dragon:** the d.'s teeth were sown 40:13
**Dream:** a d., born in a herdsman's shed 84:1
a d. without reason or rhyme 43:7
as love's young d. 108:6
*I saw in a d. a man called Victor* 133:2
last night I had a happy d. 20:6
that they may d. their dreamy d.s 78:10
**Dreamers:** city of savage d. 78:2
**Dreaming:** Oh the d.! the d.! the torturing, heartscalding, never satisfying d., d., d. 143:6
**Dreams:** d. of being Taoiseach 71:6
We are the dreamers of d. 129:14
**Dreolín:** Is fearr d. sa dorn 25:8
**Drink:** let's d. and be merry 23:1
only having seven hours to d. on a Sunday 125:1
*with plenty to d.* 27:1
**Drinking:** he after d. for weeks, rising up in the red dawn 152:6
**Drogheda:** bless our endeavours at D. 48:3
D. was as Jericho 91:3
**Droighneán:** atá ar an d. donn 16:8
**Droimeann:** A D. donn dílis 16:9
**Dromedary:** in addition to being a d. 57:4
**Drop:** not a d. she'll take on board her 58:3
**Drown:** preferred to d. than visit it again 74:2
**Drug:** Poetry's a mere d. 58:15
**Drum:** Not a d. was heard, not a funeral note 161:12
**Drumcondra:** And a white rose against a brick wall in D. 159:3
**Drumlister:** I'm livin' in D. 101:4
**Drunk:** disgraceful for a priest to be d. in Jerusalem 156:5
d. — that their councils might not want vigour 148:8
When a man is d., it is no matter upon what he has got d. 99:1
**Dubh:** ar mo Róisín D. 17:3
**Dublin:** All flock from D. to gape and to stare 18:2
Along D. Bay on a sunny July morning 32:10
An August Sunday afternoon in the north side of D. 145:11
As I walked down through D. city 38:2
Did you ever hear of the skulls they have in the city of D. 152:10
Down from the D. hills 83:3
D. and Belfast and Cork and Derry are . . . cosmopolitan 90:10
D. has reason to be proud of Easter Week 122:11
D. in the late nineteen forties 48:6
D. . . . is not as bad as Iceland 77:2
D. made me 92:6
D., that city of tedious and silly derision 142:9
for not supporting in D. 66:1
He came to D. for the rehearsals 59:11
In a little city like D. one meets every person whom one knows 147:18

In D. they call it the Coombe 82:4
In D. town he built a church, and upon't put a steeple 166:4
In D.'s fair city 17:7
Now we're in D. and still talking 162:1
Och D. city, there is no doubtin' 20:2
on the rocky road to D. 22:8
Owing to the action of the D. government 42:3
served in all the pubs in D. 54:7
the card-tables of D. 30:12
the D. of old statues 92:7
the D. worker is not a natural revolutionary 83:11
the highly developed aestheticism of D. 66:3
the story of the D. Parliament 46:10
the week of the D. Horse Show 36:1
twenty men from D. town 69:7
what was missing in wit and poetry in D. was more than made up for in mordant criticism 159:10
your first day in D. 30:14
**Dúchas:** Briseann an d. tré shúile a' chait 24:12
Is treise d. ná an oiliúint 24:11
**Ducks:** And ate his mutton and his d. 23:6
Four d. on a pond 10:9
**Dúiche:** I doineann na d. ró-dhoineanta; / 2 bréantas na d. ró-bhréan; 113:1
**Dungannon:** And D. sits on the hill 101:3
**Dunghill:** that d. isn't doing anyone any harm 87:6
**Dungloe:** I wished I was in sweet D. 21:8
take the train to D., where they can still be stalked 140:8
**Dunlop:** D. tyres are made by darkies 66:3
**Dunno:** Ach, I d.! 61:7
**Dusk:** *between d. and daybreak* 94:6
**Dust:** to be dealt with as d. by the wind 100:2
**Duties:** Property has its d. 55:1
**Dying:** My grandmother made d. her life's work 88:11
We are witnessing its d. convulsions 53:5

**Eagle:** e. of the empty eyrie 59:15
**Eagles:** they were e. in the morning sun 58:5
**Earrach:** glass úar e. aigide 13:10
Ní fuacht go he. 104:5
**Earraigh:** Anois teacht an E. 128:6
**Earth:** e. receive an honoured guest 26:2
I scoop at the e. 84:11
might claim that it sprang from e. 111:4
The e. is like a weary child 155:11
the e. was fruiting 46:14
**Easter:** Dublin has reason to be proud of E. Week 122:11
**Eat:** as oft as you've nothing to eat 49:9
**Eating:** By e., dear joy, when I can get it 59:3
**Echo:** How sweet the answer E. makes 107:10
**Echoes:** *Heave, lads, and let the e. ring* 45:1
**Economics:** A textbook of e. might well be condensed into the single word 135:2
*Screw the laws of e.* 136:9
**Economy:** Irish ideas as to social and agricultural e. 104:7
the principles of abstract political e. 65:4
**Eden:** the Garden of E. has vanished 61:8
**Education:** *A Board of E. was set up* 74:6
A female of repellent aspect, remotely connected with e. 160:13
Lectures on the following brands of E. 38:13
**Edwards, Hilton :** *see* 95:6, 96:1
**Egg:** I know that the e. is addled 46:9
You're an eyeless, noseless, chickenless e. 18:1
**Eggs:** Dear Lord, the day of e. is here 139:13
**Eileen:** E. Oge, and that the darlin's name is 61:10
**Éire:** Men of E. awake! 54:14
Mise É — Sine mé ná an Cailleach Béarra 134:12
**Éirinn:** pé in Éirinn í 124:3
**Elegance:** holds my mind with her seedy e. 97:10
**Elephant:** Swung right at Elvery's where the e. was 111:5
**Elizabeth:** E. canopies 71:8
E. frigidly stretched 76:5
**Elopement:** there was an e. down in Mullingar 21:10
**Elvery's:** before you swung right at E. 111:5
**Emancipation:** I will never get half credit enough for carrying E. 119:7
the first condition of their own e. 101:9
**Emerald:** an e. set in the ring of the sea 49:6
away from the E. Isle 61:11
I'll lay down my life for the E. Isle 99:4
**Emeralds:** E. big as half the county 86:6
shone the e. plain 31:2
**Emigration:** celibacy, late marriage and e. 103:14
**Emigré:** An inner e. 72:2
**Emma:** Oh E., who'd ever be wise 72:14
**Emmet, Robert:** Bold R. E., the darling of Erin 99:3,4
it was a play about R. E. 96:13
May we write your epitaph now, Mr. Emmet 63:5
the blood of Mr. E. 53:3
**Emperor:** than E. without her be 58:1
**Empire:** a great e. and little minds 34:12
Can trample an e. down 129:15
perilous to the unity of the E. 24:1
the course of e. takes its way 30:9
the E. that has grown from an island 40:5
**Empires:** Great E. have been overturned 42:1
**Employer:** A 'good e.' as it is called 83:9
**Employers:** I am not the leader of the e. 112:11
When the e. sacrifice wan victim 117:11
**End:** When will it all end? 43:10
without the courage to e. 29:2
**Endians:** Big-e. and Small-e. 149:12
**Enemies:** these people are regarded, not as alien e., not as planters 124:8
**Enemy:** the worst e. Ireland ever had 105:7
who surrenders the initiative to the e. 46:7

you cannot talk peace until the e. surrenders 131:5
**Energy:** the seasonable e. of one man 34:17
**Engage:** Will you e. yourself to me? 119:5
**Engine:** An e. ready-made 86:2
**England:** as free . . . as the people of E. 69:10
burning anything that came from E. except their people and their coals. 150:9
E. and Ireland may flourish together 35:4
E., the never-failing source of all our political evils 155:2
have been feeding those of E. 94:7
He is going to bonny E. 21:6
If E. drives us forth 85:2
Ireland gives E. her soldiers 104:1
King of E. applied for admission 55:5
let E. fight her own battles 73:9
let E. quake 51:6
little inferior to her realm of E. 31:11
O stranger from E., why stand so aghast? 47:11
Oh God bless E. is our prayer 82:9
Over here in E. I'm helpin' wi' the hay 126:12
Over to reap the harvest in E. 35:14
thanked God that E. was free at last 96:1
the conduct of E. towards Ireland 65:5
the king embarked for E. 88:1
the laws of E. is queer 69:1
the question that remains is whether E. will ever understand 145:10
What is E. without Ireland? 36:2
where we've E.'s power defied 69:7
which the generosity of E. was sending back 39:3
**English:** and better still are E. 30:3
And made me in these Christian days / A happy E. child 159:9
As long as there is E. spoken in the home 66:4
asked to sing the E. version 39:4
Awaken a consciousness in the E. workers 101:9
be spaking such beautiful E. 55:4
Bulgrudderies of the E. stage 39:2
By dreams of E. justice fooled 124:1
call all those opposed to us traitors, E. men and Freemasons 92:5
carried their talents to the E. market 39:3
continues to apparently hate the E. 74:7
either the E. Government 27:3
E. rule drove me and mine out of Ireland 143:8
*even the E. — maybe they might die* 16:6
finding E. a necessary sin 71:5
has paid the E. a very well-deserved compliment 134:4
He had no E. but only the Irish 48:13
It is E. circumstances and E. ideas that are peculiar 104:7
literary awareness nourished on E. 72:11
Many E. of the said land 14:7
no hope from E. justice 51:7
safely deposited on the E. woolsack 66:1
She says all the E. poets and great men was Irish 143:3
*Shoneens:* Apers of E. manners 110:3
the battlefield of E. parties 88:2
the E. seem to bid adieu to common feeling 145:3
the E., transplanted there 67:2
their cursed E. spleen 22:2
the superior utility of the E. tongue 120:2
thinkest thou that it standeth with Oneile his honor to writhe his mouthe in clattering E.? 146:9
this unemployment scheme is purely an E. scheme 103:5
what secretly enrages the E. man 76:2
*Whose E. is broken and whose Irish is faulty* 126:7
**Englishmen:** only doing what E. would do if it were their misfortune to be invaded 142:12
What I especially like about E. 90:11
**Enthusiasm:** hard to muster up e. 48:8
**Enthusiasts:** the help of its e. 64:8
**Éolas:** co festar cech n-é. 12:3
**Epitaph:** Be my e. writ on my country's mind 51:2
let no man write my e. 56:8
may we write your e. now 63:5
**Eric:** Call me E. 59:6
**Erin:** Are not all the people in E. Hibernians? 103:10
Beyond the limits of green E. 51:10
Bold Robert Emmet, the darling of E. 99:4
converts the wild harp of E. 71:7
Dear E., how sweetly 49:6
E., the tear and the smile in thine eyes 107:6
for E.'s sake 51:6
In E. old there dwelt a mighty race 103:3
No son of E. will offer me harm 108:10
O what matter, when for E. dear we fall! 149:4
Oh! E! in thine hour of need 50:5
the hatred of tyrants and E.'s applause 128:9
the language of E. is brilliant as gold 100:3
the warriors of E. in their famous generations 139:8
to lov'd E. the Green 19:9
to make E. a nation yet 59:16
**Erne:** the winding banks of E. 10:3
**Erotic:** Unless you make every act of your life an e. one, you are not fully alive 157:2
**Essentials:** the e. of freedom 52:3
**Etan:** Ní fetar / cía lassa fífea E. 12:10
**Eternity:** And gather me / Into the artifice of e. 164:10
e. is not long enough nor hell hot enough 110:6
spiderless e. of the fly 51:11
the clock of e. rung out its awful chime 101:10
**Europe:** All E. is dying for national ends 40:7
buildings of all E. don their sackcloth 50:4
his sole allies in E. 57:2
I have wandered about E. from Lapland to the Aegean Sea 136:11
most . . . charming people of E. 74:8
proudest people in all E. 14:9
the glory of E. is extinguished 34:14
The whole map of E. has been changed 42:1
**European:** she must become E. 83:8

**Eve:** in the lonely hush of e. 87:11
**Evening:** As I roved out one e. fair 22:13
pain of loss in the e. 79:8
**Evil:** Brimstone on e. 59:8
E. is our only means of self-preservation 78:1
*No one ever sank to the depths of e. all at once* 99:9
withered by an e. chance 83:5
**Exact:** not to be e. 34:9
**Excess:** Nothing succeeds like e. 161:1
**Executed:** Fifteen of the rebel leaders were e., most of the other prisoners were released 157:3
not murderers who are being e. 54:1
**Execution:** stay of e. for six years 40:2
**Executive:** weakest e. in the world 54:2
**Exercises:** health-giving e. in their own way 48:2
**Exile:** An e. in my circumstances 105:6
Silence, e. and cunning 79:4
*to become an e. for Christ* 9:1
**Existence:** to a more healthy state of existence 85:3
**Expect:** It is folly to e. men to do all that they may reasonably be expected to do 159:7
**Export:** our children . . . brought up for e. 52:8
**Exquisite:** I think it e. to stand 58:8
**Externals:** takes little account of e. 76:2
**Eye:** A grey e. weeping 59:8
by the rolling of her e. 92:8
Christ in every e. that sees me 133:3
*Grey e. there is that backward looks* 13:6
I never saw a man who looked / With such a wistful e. 160:3
To say black was the white of my e. 82:5
**Eyeless:** an e., noseless, chickenless egg 18:1
**Eyes:** And dream of the soft look / Your e. had once, and of their shadows deep 165:1
come with vengeance in their e. 38:11
E., beaming with welcome, shall throng round 109:7
His e. were blacker than the sloe 38:10
fixed like all Irish e. on futurity 65:10
*I blinded my e. / For fear I should fail* 134:10
*I opened my e. as I writhed in pain* 104:4
In faded e. that long have wept 109:12
lifted my e. beyond the little houses 96:7
My e. are filmed, my beard is grey 100:7
*Nature breaks through the e. of a cat* 24:12
No wonder those e. of his got sore in the end 122:8
sitting by the fire with those grave e. / Full of good counsel as it were with wine 164:7
the e. that shone / Now dimmed and gone 109:15
the tear and the smile in thine e. 107:6
thought through my e. 79:11
to cloud your bright e. 62:10
'twas the truth in her e. ever beaming 110:11
where no more those e. can harm me 19:6

**Face:** *Fireflush and whiteness compete in her f. boldly* 128:4
her f. was like a gaol dure 101:5
*I have turned my f. / To this road before me* 134:11
I stand f. to f. with death 40:9
*whose f. has been / My endless bane* 124:3
wondering at my f. I have at last perfected the mask 148:15
**Faces:** I see the loving f. round me 105:11
Only the f. and the names remain 93:1
**Factory:** the sake of my f. girl 20:3
**Facts:** An obtuseness to the logic of f. 83:17
**Fade:** the summer bloom will f. away 83:7
**Fáinne:** le fáinne geal an lae 17:2
**Fair:** *I went to the f. and I sold my cow* 16:2
she moved through the f. 44:13
the Irish are a f. people 77:3
Trottin' to the f. 68:5
**Fairs:** All the f. of Ireland 30:12
Offered for sale in twenty f. 81:9
**Fairy:** But the f. was laughing too 80:3
*The Hairy F.*: AE 110:3
**Faith:** I finally abandoned the f. of my fathers 123:6
least instructed in the rudiments of the F. 37:6
My lack of f. in human nature 27:6
out to destroy f. and fatherland 60:10
people . . . of the devoutest f. 60:3
**Faithful:** f. to her freedom 68:2
so f. to the marriage bond 69:8
**Fall:** they f., they pass 70:2
We shall not f. alone 85:2
**Fame:** His f. was rescued by a single plank 10:4
**Famine:** scoop at the earth, and sense f. 84:11
the dark privations of literary f. 39:3
the years of Irish f. 39:3
there's f. in the land 87:9
**Fanatics:** high councils of f. and schemers 34:4
work of a few f. 49:5
**Farm:** I come from scraggy f. 72:5
When a man takes a f. from which another has been evicted 132:2
**Farmer:** let the f. praise his grounds 20:1
**Farraige:** Mo bhrón ar an bhf. 16:10
**Fasting:** humble your bodies with f. 49:9
**Fat:** A certain f. gentleman conceived himself in the greatest danger 158:4
F., fair and forty 125:5
**Fate:** It is a strange, strange f. 40:9
Oh think o' my f. when ye dance at a fair 127:1
our folly or our f. 52:1
so tragic-comic in its f. 46:10
the strong rope of f. 37:1
this is our f.: eight hundred years' disaster 72:17
**Father:** At the Siege of Ross did my f. fall 102:4
F. Pat he banged the pulpit 96:12
*I killed my poor f., Tuesday was a week* 152:5
I . . . saw my f. kissing Bridget at the end of one summer holiday 156:3
My f. made the walls resound 97:3
my f. who keeps stumbling 72:3

Old f., old artificer 79:5
*Our F. who reigns* 51:15
the epithet of f. of his country 35:13
**Fatherland:** out to destroy faith and f. 60:10
**Fathers:** here my f. built their house 73:1
My dark f. lived the intolerable day 83:4
the dear land of our f. 19:9
**Fatty:** When F. walks the street, the paviors cry, / 'God bless you, Sir!' And lay their hammers by 161:9
**Faulkner, Brian:** Mr. F. has sat down with the greatest IRA man of them all 131:9
**Faults:** Irish f. are not so very new 68:7
**Fawn:** Unpractis'd he to f. 66:8
**Fear:** for f. of having one of our members cut off 71:3
less for the pain than the show of f. 71:1
the f. of the Workhouse will never come again 60:5
Why should we f. to join our friends 65:8
**Fears:** Who f. to speak of Ninety-Eight? 76:1
**Feast:** a f. laid out for consumption 63:2
**Feet:** And little bare f. that were blue with cold 130:6
Herbert's f. . . . had died of cold 32:9
I am broken by their passing f. 163:12
on which the f. of Cathleen have rested 91:5
Washing her f. by candlelight 38:2
**Fellow:** A tawny, thick-set f. 59:11
**Fellows:** these f. ought to be shot 57:1
**Female:** A f. of repellent aspect, remotely connected with education 160:13
the f. worker is the slave of that slave 46:8
**Feminine:** And she's of the f. gender 125:3
**Fenian:** Out and make way for the Bold F. Men! 141:9
the fathomless depths of the F. conspiracy 110:6
they have left us our F. dead 134:5
**Fenianism:** As to what is called F. 49:5
**Fenians:** The F. will get ye 105:1
**Fermanagh:** To Crichton of F. 23:5
we see the dreary steeples of F. and Tyrone 42:1
**Fern:** the f. uncurled to look at her 41:6
**Fianna:** *gave the F. their confidence and pride* 124:2
the object of Na F. Éireann 134:8
**Fiche:** F. bliain 'do leinbh 25:4
**Fiction:** held together with the plaster of f. 52:2
**Fiddle:** an' from his f. coaxes 69:3
every string of his f. was keyed 102:1
I bought a wee f. for ninepence 37:11
I'd rather hear the f. strings 96:11
twiddle on the f., O 62:6
**Fidelity:** Anchored here with f. 68:2
**Field:** broken out again in the heather f. 101:7
in the corner of a f. 81:3
o'er the green f. she flew 18:10
who made a f. for his bride 81:5
**Fields:** In far foreign f. 50:11
in these green f. I pray 74:5
O men from the f! / Come gently within 44:9
She was islanded by f. 87:5
walking the hushed f. 73:4
**Fiend:** If the F. takes to watery games 89:3
**Fight:** My F. for Irish Freedom 33:7
Ulster will f., and Ulster will be right 41:12
will f. and be fought for 40:5
**Fights:** religion that expressed itself in faction f. 76:6
**File:** D'aithle na bhf. n uasal 117:5
Mise Raifteirí an f. / lan dóchas is grá 128:7
**Files:** *We will leave a heap of f.* 121:12
**Film:** a f. you'll run over and over 63:7
f.-making will be good for me 95:6
**Filthy:** A f. people, wallowing in vice 37:6
**Finality:** It has no more f. 69:13
**Find:** *you will not f. Him* 13:3
**Finger:** Between my f. and my thumb 71:9
**Finn:** in search of F. 39:8
**Fios:** Dá mbeadh f. agam go mbeadh a leath, ná a thrian 141:6
**Fire:** I can sit at the f. and do my knitting 60:5
I had f. enough, when young and bold 100:9
*massively tall pillar of f.* 9:2
Not with the f. in me now 29:5
O sages standing in God's holy f. 164:10
Oh, the old turf f. / And the hearth swept clean 133:7
*the cat's place by the f.* 24:7
*the f. of God's love stays in my heart* 44:6
*where there is smoke there is f.* 24:8
**Fires:** Some gentle f. of passion 34:8
**Fírithir:** is f. ad fíadar 12:1
**First:** I got there f. 43:8
Your f. day in Dublin 30:14
**Fish:** *Sure there were often f. to be had at the roadside* 113:4
*the f. of Ireland are in motion* 13:5
When she's loaded down with f. 58:3
**Fishmonger:** I got from an old f. 22:14
**Fist:** *Better a wren in your f.* 25:8
hand in hand with the mailed f. 33:4
**Flag:** At Stormont we're nailing the f. to the mast 47:12
Died not for the f. 84:1
the people's f. is deepest red 45:15
'Well, here's to the f!' 43:2
**Flaitheas:** má théim go f. 92:2
**Flames:** Tyrella, Rostrevor, are flickering f. 73:2
**Flash:** the iron / f. of consonants 71:8
**Fleas:** the f.s they made a strong attack 20:9
**Fleet:** the Poet launched a stately f. 10:4
**Flesh:** and clay is the f. 81:4
For fifty generations of our f. 44:8
grew temptingly fat on human f. 77:11
he's gone the way of all f. 45:12
Holy Moses! Take a look! / F. decayed in every nook 139:14
she had been mistress of her f. 50:6
**Flints:** would walk the f. with you 38:12
**Flood:** fellows that the f. could not wash away 45:8
**Floods:** Preserve us from deluge and f. 89:3

**Floor:** Fashioned a hieroglyph upon the f. 122:2
from a chink in the f. of the old Wicklow house where I was staying 152:3
wasn't a day . . . you wouldn't get feeding for a hen and chickens on the f. 145:9
**Flower:** Father O'Flynn as the f. of them all 68:3
There's not a f. in Erin's bower 127:10
**Flowers:** these f., that look so fresh and gay 83:7
**Flute:** Because she loved f. music 83:6
Dropped from a blackbird's f. 87:13
with a toot of the f. 62:6
**Fly:** spiderless eternity of the f. 51:11
that would wash a f. away 58:3
**Fog:** As easy as November f. 64:3
the f. lifts, and you get a glimpse 62:9
**Fogamar:** Ráite fó foiss f. 13:8
**Fola:** 'Níl braon de mo chuid f. ionat' 123:8
**Folk:** Wee f. good f., / trooping all together 10:6
**Folklore:** the f. collector . . . has to spend months, even years, with one mind 111:13
**Folly:** A compound of f. and wickedness 49:5
Such is our pride, our f. 52:1
things we in our f. do 53:11
When lovely woman stoops to f. 67:1
*Women will not cease from f.* 10:11
**Food:** Be still the f. for Doneraile 125:7
their own f. became gradually deteriorated 94:7
When f. is scarce and you see the hearse 22:14
**Fool:** I am not so great a f. as you take me for 41:5
I speak that am only a f. 134:1
outwardly pleased while inwardly condemning the writer as a f. 155:9
the seeming needs of my f.-driven land 163:6
to be the mother of a f. 34:7
**Foolish:** Ireland green and chaste and f. 81:15
**Fools:** a shoal of f. for tenders 45:13
f. who came to scoff 66:9
To build a house for f. and mad 151:2
we f., now with the foolish dead 84:1
**Football:** clerical f.-kickers 39:5
**Force:** Ireland could rely only on f. 91:4
your act of f. will be resisted by f. 39:10
**Foreign:** in far f. fields 50:11
She has no f. friends 51:10
**Foreigner:** like a f. in a great city 64:10
**Forgive:** F. us that we have not lived 48:5
**Fortress:** An old f. of crumbled masonry 52:2
**Fortune:** How hard is my f. 37:1
*My f. in my hand* 15:10
never spent aught o' your f. 21:7
since Da made his f. in land 61:7
**Forty:** Fat, fair and f. 125:5
looking at least f. 59:11
over the f. mark, that you're passified 63:4
passing rich with f. pounds a year 66:8
**Fountain:** Almost every f. in this country 67:3
**Fountains:** a thousand wild f. 37:2
Weep no more, sad f. 54:9
**Fowlpest:** I have reason to believe that the f. outbreaks are the work of the IRA 131:10
**Fox:** We rode from Kilruddery in search of a f. 110:7
**Foyle:** As long as the silver F. runs deep 101:3
**France:** My Jamie's safe and well away in F. 87:9
since I saw the Queen of F. 34:13
they order, said I, this matter better in F. 148:3
**Free:** a right to be as f. a people 69:10
could rely only on force . . . to f. herself 91:4
gave me a F. State 23:10
old Ireland f. once more 20:6
who gave you the F. Trade? 61:2
**Freedom:** a beacon at which the world shall light the torch of F.! 144:4
*And only the unfree / Can know what f. is* 129:2
Apostles of F. are ever idolised when dead 46:1
energy enough completely to achieve her f. 85:3
faithful to her f. 68:2
For Ireland and F. were here to a man 23:9
F. is a thing you cannot cut in two 52:3
My Fight for Irish F. 33:7
of the same order as my fight for other sorts of f. 120:8
offers f. to achieve f. 44:1
strikes for her f. 24:2
the Church has ever been the enemy of Irish F. 105:5
the only pleasure in f. is fighting for it 123:1
the struggle for Irish f. 53:12
the struggle for Irish f. has two aspects 46:2
to accept as true f. what in reality is only a new form of slavery 136:2
to sail to f. 94:10
We have been given our f. 39:7
With their traditional love of f., the people of England encouraged and applauded revolution in France 159:11
**Freemasons:** Call all those opposed to us traitors, Englishmen, F. 92:5
**French:** if we once permitted the villainous F. masons to meddle 138:5
'Oh! the F. are in the bay' 22:10
to be killed by the F. 89:5
**French, Percy:** When P. F. sends me a new manuscript 44:4
**Friar:** I am a f. of orders grey 125:4
**Friend:** He was a decent skin all the same, always the good word for an old f. 159:14
or rather the most fatal f. 105:7
To any f. I have left 31:6
**Friends:** As to their old f., the transition is easy 34:16
Kind f. and companions 23:1
Our f. go with us as we go 65:8
She has no foreign f. 51:10
the best of f. must part 70:1
the poor make no new f. 55:3
trying to please sitters and make f. 87:3
**Front:** stop him in the rear, while he was catching him at the front 138:7

**Fruit:** when all f. fails 58:7
**Fuar:** 'Tá sé f.' arsa an seanduine 99:13
**Fuiniud:** F. i mmedón laa 11:2
**Fun:** A hell of a lot more f. 63:1
in the spirit of Irish f. 78:8
No one will understand the f. there was 63:6
**Furey, Michael:** where M. F. lay buried 78:3
**Future:** It's to hell with the f. and live on the past 47:13
the f. and the past 31:12

**Gab:** An áit a mbíonn mná bíonn g. 24:8
blessed wae gift o'g. 64:11
**Gael:** in the territory of the G. life seemed to hold possibilities 104:8
the heart-cry of the Gael! 34:5
the last splendour of the G. 140:7
**Gaeilge:** ag caint G. libh-se ar an fheis Ghaelaí seo i lár na Gaeltachta 113:2
Dá gcaillfí an G. chaillfí Éire 133:8
**Gaelach:** Is dócha ná beidh seana-bhean comh G. liom 141:7
tháinig an gnáthghalar G., scoilteadh 117:10
**Gaelachas:** g. na dúiche ró-ghaelach 113:1
**Gaelic:** insufferable G. snobs 39:7
Nothing less than a miracle could give us at once G. readers 139:10
our G. satirist 42:6
*to be here today talking G. to you at this G. feis in the most G. part of the Gaeltacht* 113:2
with a G. tag in your mouth 39:9
**Gaelic Athletic Association:** run motor-cars and the G.A.A. 39:7
**Gaelic League:** met in O'Connell Street to found the G.L. 133:9
**Gaels:** the Great G. of Ireland 41:7
**Gaeluinn:** Dá mba ná béadh agam acht an G. anois 125:10
**Gáeth:** G. ard úar 12:8
Is aicher in g. in-nocht 12:7
**Gaffer:** you've turned me into a likely g. in the end of all 153:2
**Gaiety:** the g. and levity of their dispositions 67:2
**Gaim:** G. dub dorcha dethaite 13:9
**Gallda:** ná thrácht ar an mhinistéir G. 15:3
**Gallows:** high upon the g. tree 23:11
**Gall-stones:** attack of mental g-s. 66:1
**Galway:** G. is Irish in a sense 90:10
O the crossbones of G. 97:11
quilt of silk on G. City 50:4
that's made near G. Bay 22:7
the laughter of the G. sea 98:4
tinker folk at G. Fair 96:11
**Games:** *pleasant g. in innocent conflict* 11:6
*still be on fire for the wildest of* g. 104:3
**Gaoith:** Ní bhfuair sé ó'n g. é 25:13
tagann an fhearthainn de ghualainn na g. 104:5
**Gaol:** her face wos like a gaol dure 101:5
**Garden:** And I met her in the g. where the praties grow 133:4
Dark upon the cloister-g. / dreams the shadow of the ancient yew 139:9
Grafton Street becomes a g. of girls 36:1
the G. of Eden has vanished 61:8
The sunlight on the g. 98:1
**Gardens:** the pleasant g.s of Castle Hyde 19:8
the public g. along the Dalkey tramline 32:10
**Garlic:** I should continue to wear a clove of g. round my neck 115:3
**Garments:** the free fold of her g., damask grain 122:2
**Garrick, David** *see* 66:13
**Garrynapeaka:** In the townland of G. 48:12
**Garryowen** she lives in G. 32:2
**Garvagh:** G. for asses 30:8
**Gas:** Swinging, for fear of the g. 111:3
**Gate:** Sitting on a wooden g. 81:6
the poor man at his g. 9:4
**Gates:** rose up and shut the g. 10:1
**Gazelle:** I never nursed a dear g. 109:13
**Geese:** the wild g. are flighting 85:1
**Gemma:** ut in Argenti vase auri ponitur g. 44:6
**Gems:** Rich and rare were the g. she wore 108:9
**Gena:** Trí g. ata messa brón 12:4
**Generation:** a blood sacrifice in every g. 73:8
than we are the final g. 69:13
the historic task of this g. 88:6
**Generations:** and of the dead g. 24:2
these are the salt of the g. 134:6
**Generosity:** which the g. of England was sending back 39:3
**Generous:** So g. as an Irishman? 129:10
**Genius:** A people so individual in its g. 145:2
All that the g. of man hath achieved 100:2
I have nothing to declare except my g. 161:3
Ireland is a fruitful mother of g. 129:1
Our men and women of g. 39:3
*there is a g. to be found in this country* 95:5
to have possessed a g. 67:10
What a g. I had when I wrote that book 151:5
**Genteel:** You must use me g. 22:3
**Gentle:** She is of a g. nature 64:6
**Gentleman:** an officer and a g. 77:12
what g. . . . will be induced to remain 60:4
What is a g. 86:5
**Gentlemen:** All Graduats and G. shall have access to the said Library 101:2
Forty Foot G. Only 158:8
g. every inch of them 28:5
G. to the backbone 28:5
half-mounted g. 28:5
**Gently:** Come g. within 44:9
**Gentry:** separated the g. of the country 28:5
**Georgian:** Balls to you and your G.! 84:4
**Germany:** the ancient Goths of G. . . . had all of

them a wise custom 148:8
**Ghool:** worse than Marid or Afrit / Or corpse-eating G. 100:8
**Ghost:** I was growing impatient at being lectured at by a g. 135:6
May she marry a g. and bear him a kitten 147:8
that my shadow and your g. 69:2
to banish g. and goblin 22:8
who was not afraid of a g. 49:8
with London's g. 64:3
**Ghostly:** *My speech, my face are g.* 11:8
**Ghosts:** *The ghosts took flight – I was wide awake!* 104:4
they spoke like g. crying out of their graves 146:3
**Giant:** I wished to see Ireland's G. 137:1
Is not the G.'s Causeway worth seeing? 77:4
**Gifted:** In the middle classes the g. son of the family is always the poorest 151:14
**Gile:** G. na g. do chonnarc ar slí in uaigneas 128:4
**Gilly:** I am the g. of Christ 37:10
**Girl:** an agricultural Irish g. 18:9
Exit the nice g. 115:4
for the sake of my factory g. 20:3
steps like a laughing g. 83:3
*Sunday* g. 24:10
the g. from the County Clare 61:9
the kind of g. who had a special dispensation 88:9
**Girleen:** an ownshock of a lebidjeh of a g. that's working above in the bank 112:6
**Girls:** All the g. liked him 87:15
He loved virtuous g. 82:1
reduce the two g. to shillings and pence 62:2
that let me hear what was being said by the servant g. in the kitchen 152:3
the g. that we love true 20:10
where the g. are so pretty 17:7
young g. hanging from the sky 81:13
**Gladstone, W.E.:** G. starved me till my flesh was rotten for want of nourishment 122:8
**Glances:** from unexchanged g. it was plain 112:7
**Glas:** Maidid g. for cach lus 13:4
Nollag g., reilig mhéith 25:11
**Glasnevin:** She says . . . that Lazarus was buried in G. 143:3
**Glass:** If you take a g. along with a lass 20:8
the g. is falling hour by hour, the g. will fall for ever 97:7
will fill your g. with us 76:1
**Gleann:** Ins an ng. nar tógadh mé 75:2
**Glen:** Down the rushy g. 10:6
in the G. of the Hazels 106:2
In the g. where I was reared 75:2
made good ale in the g. 37:3
one eve in the g. 38:10
Silent now is the wild and lonely g. 105:10
*To the Cuckoos' G. I'd often stroll* 91:1
**Glencolumbkille:** forced upon us in G. 102:10
**Glendalough:** At G. lived a young saint 90:3
**Glimpse:** You get a g., an intuition 62:9
**Globe:** to convey us to any part of the g. 54:3
**Glories:** Remember the g. of Brian the brave 108:8
**Glory:** a page of g. that as yet remains uncut 62:4
a sad exception to the g. of our country 65:5
and say my g. was I had such friends 164:6
But we left him alone in his g. 161:14
I'm bound for death or g. 19:6
Our g. is in your happiness 74:3
the g. of Europe is extinguished 34:14
**Gloves:** long enough with kid g. 132:5
**Glutton:** Feast for no foul g. be 50:8
**Go:** It's no g. my honey love 97:7
let's g. 29:10
You must g. on 29:9
Why should I want to g. back 97:6
**Góa:** Téora seithir g. 12:5
**God:** An Irish Atheist is one who wishes to G. he could believe in G. 99:8
and thanked him with G. d-s 23:6
and the breaking of G.'s peace 96:12
Bless thou our banners, G. of the brave! 100:11
deep longing for Ireland and G. 31:1
G. bless England is our prayer 82:9
G. has been our help in 1641, 1688, 1690, 1798, 1912 and 1920 131:8
G. hungers for situations 51:13
G. made the world, right? And fair play to him 112:9
G. made them, high or lowly 9:4
G. Save — as you prefer — the King or Ireland 97:5
G.'s choice about the company He keeps 93:13
hatin' each other for the love of G. 20:2
if G. grant this, then, under G. 59:16
if it isn't time from G. I'll get 60:8
In the name of G. and of the dead generations 24:2
in the presence of Almighty G. 23:7
It has pleased G. to bless our endeavours 48:3
may G. wither up their hearts 51:1
more fitting for a false g. 82:13
Nobody was alive but myself and G. Almighty 96:7
O'G.'s Almighty plan 54:11
praise G. that we are white 30:3
prays to G. to give him strength 50:2
put your trust in G., my boys 31:8
the GAA for the greater glory of G. 39:7
the G. of nature never intended 67:5
the great G. never planned 51:5
*the help of G. is nearer* 24:5
the life G. desires that man should live 52:10
the men that G. made mad 41:7
the minister of G.'s retribution 65:1
the people of G. have long passed out of earshot 111:7
thought on the Lamb of G. 73:7
upon which G. has given liberty 49:11
**Godot:** We're waiting for G. 29:10
**Gods:** G. made their own importance 81:2
**Gogarty, Oliver St. J.:** I mistook G.'s white-robed maid 81:14

**Going:** I know where I'm g. 20:11
**Gold:** All the g. in Ballytearim is what's stickin' to the whin 126:11
never place your mind on g. 21:12
what is left is going to be precious, precious g. 63:6
**Golden:** G. stockings you had on 65:7
*Those are the g. castles* 99:12
**Gombeen Man:** the g.m. and the higgler, the only surviving contemporaries of the cave tiger 140:8
the small-town merchant . . . is called a g.-m. 135:2
**Good:** Anybody can be g. in the country 160:6
G. is not worth while 78:1
things seem and are not g. 84:10
**Goose:** you'll have to put a g. down these chimneys some day soon 145:5
**Gossip:** full of song and g. 48:7
*where the women are there is g.* 24:8
**Gothic:** menace of a G. mountain 74:5
**Gougane Barra:** in lone G.B. 37:2
**Governed:** g. like every other free country 65:3
**Government:** driven out of one g. 40:4
**Governments:** G. in a capitalist society 46:5
**Gown:** the g. she wore was stained with gore 20:7
**Grace:**fold my towel with what g. I can 84:9
Naturally, we fall from g. 105:14
**Grafton Street:** G.S. becomes a garden of girls 36:1
**Grandmother:** 'I had it all arranged to kill my g.' 120:11
My g. made dying her life's work 88:11
**Granny:** where G. Godkin exploded 27:5
**Granuaile:** deep distress of poor old G. 20:7
**Grass:** a smooth skinn of tender g. 64:5
**Grave:** barley grew up out of the g. 72:7
For her heart in his g. is lying! 108:11
going to my cold and silent g. 56:8
*none from the g.* 25:3
round her g. I wander drear 80:4
subsides like a new g. 30:5
there is a green g. 51:4
There's a g. where the waves of the blue Danube roll 61:6
they give birth astride of a g. 29:13
*three saints one g. do fill* 51:14
when we sunk her bones at noonday in her narrow g. 153:1
*will soon be laid in the g.* 27:1
*with one foot in the g. and the other on its brink* 141:5
**Graves:** Up on the hill are the arguing g. of the kings 139:1
while Ireland holds these g. Ireland unfree shall never be at peace 134:5
**Gravestone:** kissing your g. 63:15
**Gravestones:** mouldered among its g. 30:4
**Graveyard:** *A g. cough* 25:5
*Green December fills the g.* 25:11
*I am the G. Trumpet!* 117:9
Kilbarrack the healthiest g. in Ireland 29:16
to the peace of the g. 94:3
**Graveyards:** I have no bone to pick with g. 29:3
**Great:** the g. must submit to the dominion of prudence 35:1
**Greatness:** I have had g. thrust upon me 112:11
it is the nature of all g. 34:9
**Green:** a g. island in lone Gougane Barra 37:2
a wreath that will be g. for ever 86:4
and they wore the jackets g. 141:10
Behold how g. the gallant stem 61:4
cease the G. to flourish 61:4
cruel law agin the wearin' o' the G. 18:6
*Far away hills are g.* 25:10
*G. December fills the graveyard* 25:11
g. jacket, red cap 10:6
how sweetly thy g. bosom rises 49:6
In my childhood trees were g. 97:2
Ireland g. and chaste 81:15
my lovely g. Ireland 62:11
Now and in time to be, / Wherever g. is worn 164:2
ripped the g. velvet back off the brush 79:2
soon the bright O put down the G. Rag 127:7
Supposin' ye got all the Orange sashes and all the G. sashes 103:7
*The crops are g. and fields are all in flower* 142:2
the dew on the forest g. 22:13
the grass it is g. around Ballyjamesduff 61:8
the g. leaves all turn yellow 83:7
the g. plant withered 83:5
the valleys of G. Inishowen 55:6
their g. banners kissing the pure mountain air 141:8
there is a g. hill far away 9:6
**Gregory, Lady:** Lady G. asked me 73:11
**Grey:** A g. eye weeping 59:8
*g. eye there is that backward looks* 13:6
O stony g. soil of Monaghan 81:12
**Grief:** *My g. on the sea* 16:10
my g. that Parnell should be lying 70:2
the act of violence a g. 51:12
the tears of g. fell from her eyes 20:7
*three smiles that are worse than g.* 12:4
thus g. still treads upon the heels of pleasure 45:11
**Griefs:** My g. are over 49:7
**Grieve:** do not let this parting g. thee 70:1
I g. not eagle 59:15
**Griffith, Arthur:** *see* 110:8
**Ground:** bid goodbye to the Holy G. 20:10
**Groves:** the g. of Blarney / they look so charming 105:2
**Grudge:** Belfast owes us a mighty g. 66:1
**Gruel:** like g. spooned up off a dirty floor 28:3
**Guard:** Nor g. the land that gave them birth 50:5
**Guest:** Earth receive an honoured g. 26:2
**Guilt:** can wash her g. away? 67:1
draw the equal guilt / Over our naked g. 139:4
**Guinea:** clean linen and a g. 90:12
**Gulls:** *You* — the other G. — would go for the sashes every time! 103:7
**Gun:** A giddy son of a g. 149:7

instead of the g. and the bearna baoil 94:4
shure as a g.'s iron 76:7
**Gunne:** Old Cathal Bwee MacGilla G. 59:7

**Hades:** three old ladies from H. 93:2
**Hag:** being carried away by the H. 60:6
Remember '98, says the gay old h. 20:4
**Hail:** H. fellow, well met, / All dirty and wet 150:8
**Hair:** All her bright golden h. / Tarnished with rust 160:18
*Once I was yellow-h.ed 14:1*
With her h. as bright as seaweed 41:6
**Half:** I knew h. of her: the lower h. 116:9
**Hall:** Eyetalian marbles in the City H. 47:11
this is Liberty H. 66:14
**Hammers:** Where h. clang murderously on the girders 97:8
**Hand:** A metallic giggle, a fumbling h. 98:6
Christ and Caesar are h. in glove 78:9
*Forbid your h. to rove* 41:1
h. in glove 51:12
he felt like raising his h. towards them 46:15
joined happily h. in h. 34:8
*My h. is tired from writing* 13:7
She would put her lily h. down into sewerages 115:6
**Hands:** my h. are so free from blood 40:9
the h. from shivering and the sinewes from shrinking 146:6
**Handsome:** than any of our h. young men 38:10
**Hang:** cannot comprehend that anyone wants to h. me 40:9
I'll h. my harp on on a weeping-willow tree 70:1
it's yourself you must h. 87:16
**Hanging:** h. and marriage . . . go by destiny 59:2
**Happiness:** do little towards the h. of people 35:5
H. is no laughing matter 159:6
She gave me thirty-four years of the purest h. 119:5
**Happy:** you think you'll be h. for life 62:10
**Harbour:** the dredger grumbling / All night in the h. 97:11
Where the bottle-neck h. collects the mud 97:9
**Hare:** the h. she led on 18:10
**Harp:** Dear H. of my Country! 107:5
My gentle H! once more I waken 108:2
the h. he loved ne'er spoke again 109:2
the h. that once, thro' Tara's halls 108:16
the wild h. of Erin 71:7
**Harvest:** and then the h.'s done 37:10
give a hand in a corn h. field 111:12
to reap the h. in England 35:14
Weary of the warm h. we lay together 154:7
**Hat:** a big h. and no morals, a bankrupt's baggage! 148:2
all around my h. I wear 82:8
**Hate:** apparently h. the English 74:7
I h. thee, Djaun Bool 100:8
must have h. at the bottom of it 76:6
take away this murdherin' h. 118:5
**Hatred:** Out of Ireland have we come / Great hatred, little room 164:8
**Hatreds:** I have tried to break the chains of ancient h. 127:3
**Haughey, C. J.:** If I saw Mr. H. buried at midnight at a cross-roads 115:3
**Haws:** we welcome h. 58:7
**Hawthorn:** Set my back to a h. tree 22:13
**Headstones:** on the crooked crosses and h. 78:3
**Hearse:** and you see the h. 22:14
the h. stopped at the foot of the lane 121:1
**Heart:** A h. that leaps to a fife band 98:6
An Irishman's h. is nothing but his imagination 143:5
bear my h. to my mistress dear 109:11
Consume my h. away; sick with desire 164:10
every road in Ulster veined my h. 103:1
For her h. in his grave is lying! 108:11
go rambling through my h. 67:6
have drenched my h. in spray 67:7
his h. was going like mad and yes 80:1
I had only to examine my own h. 52:6
I looked into the h. of this life 81:15
if a country can heave from its h.'s core 71:7
keyed to the crying of your own h. 102:1
Many a h. shall quail 102:9
my h. always so compassionate and pitiful 40:9
*My h. was lively in my breast* 75:2
never blunders of the h. 56:2
Oh the h.-cry of the Gael! 34:5
pent-up love of my h. 89:11
rests my h. ever 40:11
*the fire of God's love stays in my h.* 44:6
the foul rag-and-bone shop of the h. 163:10
the h. that has truly loved, never forgets 107:4
*the light in my h., O Saviour, is Thy h.* 130:5
there is a lake in every man's h. 106:9
We had fed the h. on fantasies, / the h.'s grown brutal from the fare 164:5
We hold the Ireland in the h. 140:6
Well, the h.'s a wonder 152:12
*Where fierce indignation can no longer tear his h.* 151:6
With breaking h. whene'er I hear 80:4
'You gave me the key of your h., my love' 128:8
You must have a very narrow h. that wouldn't go down to the town and stand your friends a few drinks 163:2
You thought you had my poor h. broke 21:7
**Hearts:** h. that once beat high for praise 108:16
May God wither up their h. 51:1
O she melted the h. 89:6
One by one the merry h. are fled 105:10
Our h. are devoted to you 74:3
take away our h. o' stone . . . an' give us h. of flesh! 118:5
the cheerful h. now broken! 109:15

Too long our Irish h. we schooled 124:1
**Heath:** On Carrigdhoun the h. is brown 86:7
**Heather:** A rebel hand set the h. blazing 102:7
has broken out again in the h. field 101:7
**Heaven:** and h. my expectation 79:1
blotting h. as it towered 84:7
Hath deprived me of h. 121:7
He fell asleep and woke in h. 126:1
I shall not go to h. when I die 158:1
If the anger of h. be against her 64:6
*passed from earth to h.* 9:2
to h. for justice cries 56:6
Would you think H. could be so small a thing / As a lit window on the hills at night? 158:2
**Head:** I am lying with my h. 89:13
it . . . preserueth the h. from whirling, the eies from dazeling, the toong from lisping 146:6
lightning in his head 37:9
no right to be in the h. of Michael Clancy 60:9
one small h. could carry all he knew 66:10
pillow my h. on his lily-white breast 23:13
your darling black h. 59:14, 16:4
**Heads:** throw our bleeding h. upon that table, to stare us in the face 138:5
**Hebrew:** A small taste of H. upon the Masoretic text 39:1
**Heifer:** the Mullingar h. was beef to the heels 21:10
**Height:** such a terrible h. of a wall 68:10
**Heights:** that we would know from what h. it fell 111:4
**Hell:** eternity is not long enough nor h. hot enough 110:6
I ne'er was in h. till I met with your wife 21:3
there is wishful thinking in H. 89:7
this country's going to h. at a hundred mile an hour 144:9
to H. with the Pope 97:5
with a clean carcass to h. 28:7
written on the gates of h. 15:2
**Help:** I want h. 40:6
*the h. of God* 24:5
with the h. of its enthusiasts 64:8
**Henry:** *the ballocks of H. the Eighth* 15:3
**Hens:** I've a shelter for the h. 62:1
**Herd:** to h. alone, / and be accepted 129:6
**Hero:** and the starry h. 57:5
every hill has its h. 30:7
He got no h.s inch 68:6
the land where her young h. sleeps 108:11
**Heroes:** all the great h. dead 39:8
**Heron:** *than a h. on loan* 25:8
**Herring:** various parts of the h.'s anatomy 48:8
**Hibernians:** are not all the people in Erinn H.? 103:10
**Hibernicis:** H. ipsis Hibernior 10:12
**Hidden:** *nature cannot be h.* 24:12
**Hill:** And Dungannon sits on the h. 101:3
Cassidy's hanging h. 81:1
*I would I were on yonder h.* 18:4
On the hem of the Royal Hill 93:11
'Tatter Jack Welsh' upon Bellewstown H. 19:2
the H. can hould tight enough! 148:14
the lonely churchyard on the h. 78:3
the moon behind the h. 83:1
there is a green h. far away 9:6
where every h. has its hero 30:7
Yet dearer still that Irish h. 10:3
**Hills:** behind it the blue line of wandering h. 106:12
Down from the Dublin h. 83:3
*Far away h. are green* 25:10
good-bye the chequered and the quiet h. 98:7
in Derry of the little h. 87:11
My black h. have never seen the sun 81:10
Over the dim blue h. 40:11
Sit upon opposing h. 30:6
the dawn on the h. of Ireland 89:11
*the great h. of evil have been cut down with spear-points* 123:3
The vivid chequer of the Antrim h. 98:5
**Hillside:** the h. blushed 72:7
**Hire:** 'What made me h. with this man' 20:9
**Hiring:** you're sure to miss your h. time 20:8
**Historian:** When the h. . . . turns to Ireland 91:2
**Histories:** to upset all the h. 58:5
**History:** be justified in h. at all 40:4
blot upon the pages of its h. 65:5
H. of Ireland — lawlessness and turbulency 10:5
Man watches his h. on the screen with apathy 115:2
the 'facts' of h. 63:12
the pitch and toss / of h. 72:5
*the secret of her tragic h.* 95:5
What's Irish h.? 10:7
**Histrionic:** H. ability is not lacking 59:10
**Hives:** we have rather chosen to fill our h. with honey and wax 149:6
**Hollies:** *Twisted h. hurt the stag* 13:4
**holy:** Ant of the h. lande of irlande 14:6
As a white candle in a h. place 38:1
Ireland still remains the H. Isle 57:2
We must bid good-bye to the H. Ground 20:10
**Home:** A h. so grand 51:5
As long as there is English spoken in the h. 66:4
I hope this finds all well at h. 126:13
in every land a h. 31:4
is here at h. 58:8
It's h., sweet h., where'er I roam 10:3
It was to him the symbol of h., of a real h. 154:9
lost, / Unhappy and at h. 72:9
My Last Night At H. 63:7
**Home Rule:** H.R. and the Ten Commandments 83:8
H.R. morally is a great betrayal 10:2
H.R. will work wonders under English guidance 143:7
H.R. would be disastrous 24:1
if the GOM went for H.R. the Orange Card would be the one to play 41:11

the most extreme form of H.R. 142:10
We must be prepared . . . the morning H.R. passes 47:8
you are going to pass H.R. 39:10
**Homesteads:** bright with cozy h. 52:10
**Honest:** Honesty is the best policy; but he who is governed by that maxim is not an h. man 159:8
**Honey:** Oh mouth of h. 59:14
**Honeymoon:** this is the h. of the cockroach 51:11
**Honour:** a conspiracy against the h. of Britain 41:13
nature did me that h. 32:5
they love h. and virtue more! 108:10
**Hoor:** The Long H. 44:3
**Hope:** H., the great divinity, is domiciled in America 163:3
*I have lost all h. of going* 92:1
no h. from English justice 51:7
no more h. for the Irish cause 55:7
Our h. and strength, we find at last 124:1
*Spanish ale shall give you h.* 17:3
the bedposts fall. No h. 81:7
there is h. for all of us 29:1
*there is h. from the sea* 25:3
these days our h.'s mechanical 129:5
**Hopes:** Cold as the h. of our youth 87:8
'Tis on you my h. are set 59:16
**Horns:** like the h. of a dilemma 30:6
the great h. of the moon 32:11
**Horror:** an occasional passing flicker of h. or indignation 115:2
**Horse:** it was your h. shtole me! 32:3
My soul was an old h. 81:9
One of the many rooms in Ireland in which Cromwell is said to have stabled his h. 145:8
the equable gallop of a h. in the Bayeux Tapestry 145:7
the week of the Dublin H. Show 36:1
white h. on the wall 47:11
**Hospitality;** the h. of an Irishman is not the running account of posted and ledgered courtesies 119:1
**Hostel:** lived in a sort of h. 48:7
**Hounds:** tearin' like mad afther the h. 32:3
the Irish seem . . . like a pack of h. 65:6
**Hour:** doctrines fashion'd to the varying h. 66:8
**Hours:** the stillness of the small h. began to creep into the revel 46:12
**House:** A handsome h. to lodge a friend; / A river at my garden's end 149:16
As long as I'm in this h. 87:6
At the great h. 28:4
I thought I was in a bad h. 64:2
permission to build himself a mansion h. 77:8
Since her people died, she will not go into the H. or into the enormous yard 146:2
stands in the doorway of his h. 81:7
the h. of the planter 42:9
the youngest or newest in the H. 71:6
We ask Deputies in this H. 88:5
what Lord Chesterfield calls the necessary h. 29:8
**Houses:** accounting for the reduction in rents of the lower h. 121:2
American eating h. 82:13
**Howth:** back to H. Castle and Environs 78:5
H. was a seal floating darkly in the sun 111:10
the outlines of H. began to melt 106:13
**Human:** grew temptingly fat on h. flesh 77:11
Ireland is in the main stream of h. existence and h. feeling 104:7
'Priests are h., Willy' 33:10
**Humane:** more h. that buckshot be used 61:3
**Humble:** A h. Jesuit would be like a dog without a tail 116:11
h. your bodies with fasting 49:9
**Humbugs:** unnecessary state-paid h. 39:7
**Humour:** select my most tragic moments for your irresistible strokes of h. 143:7
the lovely sinse of h. he has 94:9
**Hunger:** Fainting forms, h.-stricken, what see ye in the offing? / Stately ships to bear our food away 160:2
*H. is good sauce* 25:6
You'll know you died of h. 22:14
**Hungry:** A h. feeling came o'er me stealing 30:1
**Hunter:** The horn of the h. is heard on the hill 47:14
**Hunting:** we daren't go a-h. 10:6
**Hurry:** an old man in a h. 41:13
**Hurt:** h. us as much as you are able, and we shall h. you to the best of our ability 126:8
**Husband:** Oh you're my h. right enough 93:6
worn to a shadow from striving to preserve her h. from designing and persistent females 147:17
**Hussy:** Heeding that h. of a clotty of a plótha of a streeleen 112:6
**Hut:** *I desire a hidden h.* 13:1
**Hy-Brasil:** they called it H.-B. 69:5
**Hyde, Douglas:** *see* 106:8
**Hypocrisy:** and being really good all the time. That would be h. 160:19
**Hypocrite:** that murdering h. 53:7

**I:** *'I' wasn't born until 'I' died* 129:4
**Iasc:** is minic go raibh i. le fáil ar thaobh an bhealaigh 113:4
**Icarus:** chancer I. 76:4
**Ice:** Obedience is i. to the wine 43:7
**Iceland:** not as bad as I. 77:2
**Ideas:** It is with i. as with umbrellas 83:12
**Idioms:** I extend the sea, its i. 89:12
**Idle:** it is an i. boast 51:7
we alone stand by idle 40:7
'You are i.' is the cry 35:14
**Idly:** stand i. by 90:7
**Ignorant:** as i. of the Irish people 39:2
proud and i. people 60:10

**Iliad:** I made the I. from such 81:2
**Illegal:** of course it was i. 40:3
**Illegitimate:** there are no i. children 53:6
**Ills:** What is the reason of all our i.? 27:3
**Illusions:** the sooner I pay for my i. the better 40:6
**Image:** A man will touch his i. 58:6
**Images:** those i. that yet / Fresh i. beget 163:8
**Imagination:** Its people . . . excite their i. 90:10
**Imitate:** continues to i. them 74:7
**Impatient:** you are i. for the sacrifice 56:7
**Impediment:** I have enjoyed an attractive i. in my speech 38:4
**Impossible:** attempting i. things, deeming them alone worth the toil 134:2
**Impropriety:** I'd advance ye widout i. 68:3
**In:** Put Him I. To Get Him Out! 24:3
**Incense:** blest unfabled I. Tree 50:7
They're very good at raising clouds of i. to cloak their real purpose 158:7
**Inch:** *burn the i.* 25:2
**Inchigeela:** in the district of I. 48:12
**Independence:** a people marching to i. 51:9
the economic foundation of i. 88:6
**Indignatio:** Ubi saeva i ulterius cor lacerare nequit 151:6
**Indignation:** *where fierce i. can no longer tear his heart* 151:6
**Industry:** we lost that i. here 66:3
**Inevitable:** In Ireland the i. never happens 99:6
It seems perfectly simple and i. 41:9
**Infant:** the i. is plunged . . . in cold water 67:4
**Informer:** destroying . . . the spy and the i. 43:9
neither internee nor i. 72:2
**Inishowen:** the valleys of Green I. 55:6
**Injustice:** but half-atoned i. 65:1
**Ink:** an i. whose lustre will keep fresh 44:8
**Innisfallen:** Sweet I., fare thee well 108:15
**Innocent:** revenge on persons quite i. 28:10
**Inquisition:** too nice an i. ought not to be made 35:3
**Inse Fáil:** Siúbhladh ar iasc I.F. 13:5
**Insolence:** i. of British politicians 53:11
**Instinct:** along the fingertips of i. 106:3
**Insurrection:** opposed to any proposal . . . involving i. 98:10
**Intellectuals:** stand up to the i. 60:10
**Interfere:** they dared not i. 40:3
**International:** the task of the 'I.' is everywhere . . . to side openly with Ireland 101:9
**Internee:** neither i. nor informer 72:2
**Invention:** I. flags, his brain grows muddy 45:5
**Inwit:** Agenbite of i. 79:13
**Íosa:** A Í., a Spioraid Naofa 93:14
**IRA:** A tailor an' an IRA 50:3
I have reason to believe that the fowlpest outbreaks are the work of the IRA 131:10
the greatest IRA man of them all—Jack Lynch 131:9
**Ireland:** A country cannot be formed in I. 92:5
a small, narrow and even romantic view of I. 96:9
all matters except our relations with I. 65:5
all the fairs of I. 30:12
and I., long a province, be 50:10
an' I wisht I was in I. the livelong day 126:12
any friend I have left in I. 31:6
At the creeke of Bagganbun / I. was lost and wun! 146:8
Dear Old I.! / I., boys, hurrah! 149:3
deep longing for I. and God 31:1
design for the separation of I. from Britain 41:13
encouraged revolution in France, Hungary and Italy, while hastening to suppress it in I. 159:11
England and I. may flourish together 35:4
For I. and Freedom we're here to a man 23:9
For I.'s freedom we fight or die 102:7
full of his high discourse in praise of I. 134:13
go back / To you, I., my I. 97:6
God save — as you prefer — the King or I. 97:5
Good night, then, I. and Irish tumults 105:3
he called it the dear little shamrock of I. 41:4
He left I. 55:7
He was to God and I. true 126:1
History of I. — lawlessness and turbulency 10:5
Histrionic ability is not lacking in I. 59:10
How could Southern I. keep a bridal North in the manner to which she is accustomed? 127:5
'How's poor ould I., and how does she stand?' 18:6
I am also King of I. 55:5
I am the hired servant of I. 120:1
*I am I.: I am lonelier than the Old Woman of Beare* 134:12
I come from an island, I. 97:12
I found I. on her knees 67:9
I offer my pain for I. 98:11
I see good for I. 35:13
I shall have been three years in I. 74:1
I would have liked to go to I. but my grandmother would not let me 161:5
Icham of I. 14:6
If I. was a nation, tell me when? 10:7
if it had not been for the loyalty and friendship of Northern I. 42:3
In I. a policeman's lot is a supremely happy one 123:5
In I. that crime may almost invariably be traced to a wild feeling of revenge 156:1
In I. the inevitable never happens 99:6
I. can cease to be the battlefield 88:2
I. could rely only on force 91:4
I. gives England her soldiers 104:1
I. green and chaste and foolish 81:15
I. has been . . . conquered at least three times 83:17
I. has been knocking at the English door long enough 132:5
I. has controlled its population growth 103:14
I., I.! that cloud in the west 65:1
I. is a fruitful mother of genius, but a barren nurse 129:1
I. is a little Russia 106:7

I. is a small but insuppressible island 83:16
*I. is a small country* 28:9
I. . . . is like a young wench 64:5
I. is my nation 79:1
I. . . . is one of the goodliest provinces of the world 31:11
I. is the old sow 79:3
I. is to be dealt with . . . like every other free country 65:3
I. never was contented 86:6
I.'s a door 96:8
I. stands at your bar expectant 65:5
I. still remains the Holy Isle 57:2
I. . . . summons her children 24:2
I., the most western part 67:2
is fit to rule all I. 72:12
let me carry your Cross for I. 25:18
like Shaw, Sheridan and Wilde, his nearest rivals, he was brought up in I. 156:7
mad I. hurt you into poetry 26:1
May I. always continue to give witness before the modern world 136:6
My mission is to pacify I. 65:2
My only programme for I. 83:8
My sentimental regard for I. does not include the capital 142:8
my small town of I. 31:3
Nerve and muscle, and heart and brain, / lost to I.—lost in vain 160:1
never intended that I. should be a province 67:5
Northern I. cannot remain static 33:5
not done anything to promote the well-being of I. 57:5
O I. isn't it grand you look 89:11
O I. my first and only love 78:9
Oh, I.! thou emerald of the ocean 144:4
old I. that Romantic lady 129:7
Old I.'s surrounded with sadness and gloom 99:3
one affection . . . is my love for I. 40:1
Out of I. have we come, / Great hatred, little room 164:8
peculiar in the nature and condition of I. 85:3
Puritan I.'s dead and gone 106:4
Romantic I.'s dead and gone, / It's with O'Leary in the grave 164:12
Swift wrote to the whole people of I. 69:10
that I. was not able of herself to throw off the yoke, I knew 155:3
That island, I believe, will be I. 40:5
that it is impossible to free I. from English Rule 122:7
the best traitors I. has ever had 53:4
the biggest rascal in the whole of I. 33:3
the Brother / the Plain People of I. 113:7
the coast of I. will be defended from foreign invasion by her armed sons 138:2
the entire ownership of I., moral and material 86:3
*the fish of I. are in motion* 13:5
the Great Gaels of I. 41:7
the healthiest graveyard in I. 29:16
the impossibility of writing about I. in such a way as to win approval from Irishmen 155:9
the inhabitants of I. are not likely . . . to consider themselves as one people 145:1
the land of I. belongs to the people of I. 53:9
the meanest cottager in I. 67:8
the moment the very name of I. is mentioned, the English seem to bid adieu to common feeling 145:3
the most important week in I. 36:1
the national emancipation of I. is no question of abstract justice 101:9
the people and circumstances of I. 65:4
the people of I. have been feeding those of England 94:7
the pillar towers of I. 91:6
the prop of I. become its battering-ram 40:12
the road was in I. 32:8
the worst enemy I. ever had 105:7
Think what I have got for I. 43:12
through the midlands of I. 31:2
Till I., a nation 51:4
'Tis the fashion of I. 59:3
to help in promoting I.'s interests 69:11
to train the boys of I. to fight I.'s battle 134:8
to try to help national I. 40:6
understand by I. not merely a country 35:11
used the enemies of I. as a springboard 66:1
We hold the I. in the heart 140:6
What is England without I.? 36:2
what Lord Beaverbrook thought about I. 38:3
What more do you demand of me, damned I.? 62:11
When I. lay broken and bleeding 139:12
When the historian . . . turns to I. 91:2
While I. holds these graves, I. unfree shall never be at peace 134:5
Who strikes the first blow for I. 86:4
whose lives are pledged to I. 82:6
Would to God this was shed for I. 141:3
Young people of I., I love you 136:5
**Irene:** even without I. 68:8
**Irish:** a little I. cailín 58:2
all the I. political songs 51:9
*All us I., inhabitants of the world's edge* 45:2
along with I. radically 39:1
An I. atheist is one who wishes to God he could believe in God 99:8
An I. bull is always pregnant 99:7
An I. state governed by Irishmen for the benefit of the I. people 139:11
an I. Walter Scott 56:3
And now the I. are ashamed 101:8
*Another old woman on this island as devoted to I. as I was* 141:7
as ignorant of the I. people 39:2
being a woman is like being I. 111:11
can do three things in I. politics 59:9
cannot except the I. Melodies from censure 71:7

dearer still that I. hill 10:3
de-Davisisation of I. national literature 56:5
destitute as the common I. 30:10
Ere long there shall be an I. army on the I. hillsides 126:6
Even if I did speak I. 63:8
Everywhere in I. prose there twinkles and peers 140:5
fixed like all I. eyes on futurity 65:10
free at last from 700 years of I. domination 96:1
Galway is I. in a sense 90:10
had been compelled to write in I. 99:5
He had no English, but only the I. 48:13
help the I. race to develop 74:8
how any Irishman can be considered an I. patriot 122:7
*I can only speak Ulster I.* 113:3
I had changed my Munster I. into Connacht 95:3
I have heard of an I. traitor 71:1
I was always an I. separatist 40:8
*If I could speak only in I.* 125:10
*If I. were to be lost Ireland would perish* 133:8
If the I. theatre ceases to reflect I. life 69:9
in the spirit of I. fun 78:8
interrupted by Edward calling on him to speak in I. 106:8
I. ideas as to social and agricultural economy 104:7
I. Republic tonight at midnight 96:1
I. sentiment sticks in this half-way house 74:7
I. women are the most virtuous 69:8
Irishness . . . is the condition of being involved in the I. situation 115:1
It is a symbol of I. art 79:10
It is not the perfection of I. thought 139:10
it was the world's failure to recognise the I. Edmunds that made for the disparagement of the I. Williams 159:10
let the I. vessel lie 26:2
like the howling of I. wolves 142:4
*More I. than the I.* 10:12
My father and mother were I. 37:11
My Fight for I. Freedom 33:7
my grasp of the I. language became so firm 38:5
My I. is gone with my Algebra 93:4
no more hope for the I. cause 55:7
Now for our I. wars 142:7
of the I. Brigade 50:11
or the I. Board of Works 27:3
Our I. blunders 56:2
*professional feelings of I. servants* 32:6
rather . . . a Scotch interest than an I. interest 48:4
She says all the English poets and great men was I. 143:3
so long as he expresses it in I. 79:7
some of them aren't even I. 47:2
struggle for I. freedom 53:12
that is the I. Question 54:2
The Belfast Quasimodo to the I. Esmeralda 121:4
the British officer seldom likes I. soldiers 143:2
the Church has ever been the enemy of I. Freedom 105:5
the I. are a fair people 77:3
the I. breed like rabbits 77:9
the I. faults are not so very new 68:7
the I. government can no longer stand by 90:7
the I. have not the heart 84:2
the I. have the thickest ankles 30:13
the I. peasant must not . . . know 57:2
the I. people would sink into a lethargy 147:4
the I. police barrack is invariably clean 31:5
the I. poor are singing 48:10
*the I. Question has so many sides* 32:7
the I. Republic! 74:3
the I. seem to me like a pack of hounds 65:6
the I. Treaty is in the air 76:2
The I. writer of English . . . has no such gloomy problem 95:4
*the lively I.* 60:2
the lower orders of the I. 23:4
the Man who spoke I. at a Time when it was neither Profitable nor Popular 113:7
*the opening words 'The voice of the I.'* 133:2
the property and respect of the I. nation 60:4
the struggle for I. freedom has two aspects 46:2
the time has long since gone when I. men and I. women could be kept from thinking 46:4
the years of the I. famine 39:3
then I. instinctive manhood can be relied on 43:4
they threw over I. civilisation 110:2
To marry the I. 54:6
traditional I. mercy 53:5
upon which all I. men could meet 75:1
We would no I. sign efface 140:7
West-Britons: Anglo-I. 110:3
What I mean by an I. school 134:7
what the I. people wanted 52:6
where there are I. there's loving and fighting 85:1
who has lived in real intimacy with the I. peasantry 152:2
witness without a sigh the gradual disuse of I. 120:2
Ye brave I. lads 66:17
you I. give more trouble 54:12
You're an I. schoolmaster! 39:6
**Irish Times:** In spite of the *I.T.* or anything else 47:6
**Irishman:** An I., a very valiant gentleman 142:5
An I.'s first duty is to his country 155:1
An I.'s heart is nothing but his imagination 143:5
clowning character, known as 'the stage I.' 32:4
No true I. sees a distinction between the battlefield and the scaffold 143:10
not merely that of being an I. but of being a nationalist I. 142:13
Sir Edward is a stage I. 57:6
So generous as an I.? 129:10
tempted to suppose I was an I. 84:2
the common name of I. in place of the denominations of Protestant, Catholic and Dissenter 155:2

The emancipated and liberal I. . . . may go to Mass 154:10
the hospitality of an I. is not the running account of postered and ledgered courtesies 119:1
the I. displays the most ferocious cruelty 28:10
To every I. on earth 31:7
What is an I. but a mere machine 83:2
**Irishmen:** are I. today 50:9
Oh I. forget the past 82:10
the divine right of I., and I. alone, to rule Ireland 138:1
To all true I. on earth 117:6
**Irlandais:** La difficulté irlandaise' 32:7
l'amour propre professionel des domestiques i. 32:6
Les gais i. 60:2
**Irlande:** L'I. est une petite contrée 28:9
**Iron:** an i. closet and an i. blind 122:6
**Island:** a green i. in lone Gougane Barra 37:2
a small but insuppressible i. 83:16
*another old woman on this i. as devoted to Irish as I was* 141:7
Deep in Canadian woods we've met, / From one bright i. flown 149:3
*Each of the living has found an i.* 129:3
has used this i. on the edge of Europe 136:3
I come from an i., Ireland 97:12
must go naked to an i. 58:4
*Signature of the rugged i.* 121:10
that i., I believe, will be Ireland 40:5
this i. of dark green 123:7
to breathe, in this our i. 67:8
We tend to overlook your i. 63:9
**Islands:** very useful in the Andaman I. 68:14
**Isle:** away from the Emerald I. 61:11
Carbery's hundred i. 51:3
cold i. of our love! 87:8
Ireland still remains the Holy I. 57:2
the i. of the blest 69:5
When first I saw thy fairy i.! 108:15
**Ísu:** oc Í. úasail aidid 31:10
**Ísucán:** cin beth im ucht Í. 13:2
Is bréc uile acht I. 11:10
**Iveleary:** in the parish of I. 48:12
**Iveragh:** In I. of the singing birds 43:6

**Jail:** I have had enough of j. 43:5
In Mountjoy j. 23:11
into cold Kilmainham j. 23:3
**James, Henry:** I have just read a long novel by H.J. 163:4
**Jar:** *May I call for my j. to be full* 15:9
**Jeans:** no money and tight blue j. 50:6
**Jerry-builders:** created largely by j.-b. 25:17
**Jerusalem:** a new J. 25:17
**Jesuit:** A humble J. would be like a dog without a tail 116:11
He comes, the J. sly 31:8
**Jesus:** *At the death of noble J.* 31:10
**Jesuseen:** *J., who is in his home above* 13:2
**Jew:** J., Turk or Atheist 15:1
**Jewel:** j. of joy arise 68:4
**Jo:** Auld J. he is a bo 50:2
**Job:** the very man for the j. 83:10
**Johneen:** an' he's two foot long — Baby J. 126:14
**Johnny:** J., I haredly knew ye! 18:1
lovely J., he is now goin' away 21:6
to go with my love J. 20:11
**Jokes:** All womankind . . . from the highest to the lowest . . . love j. 148:11
**Joseph:** St. J., St. Peter, St. Paul 89:3
**Journeys:** *a fine season for long j.* 13:11
**Jovial:** you'd find none so j. 19:4
**Joxer:** so long as he goes with that shoulder-shruggin' J. 117:12
**Joy:** And yet I have my j. 134:3
**Joyce, James:** Eat and drink all you can and leave J. J. to blow his own trumpet 115:8
enemies of J. and Swift 30:15
I could not write the words Mr. J. uses 143:4
**Judgement Day:** *the lord be good to me on J. D.* 12:9
**Jug:** the song he sang was a j. of punch 21:2
**Julia:** But J. soon scattered their fancies 21:5
**July:** stood on a headland of J. 81:13
**Jump:** I will j. no more 72:13
**June:** early in the month of J. 21:2
mem'ries came like flowers of J. 83:1
redden the hills when J. is nigh 53:2
**Jungle:** it is watchful as the j. 33:9
**Junta:** in the charge of a j. of colonels 82:12
**Jury:** when they . . . look upon the j., . . . they see twelve of their brethren in massacre 144:3
**Justice:** as long as men hold charity and j. 35:2
No hope from English j. 51:7
to heaven for j. cries 56:6
Violence only delays the day of j. 136:4

**Kathleen:** come back to me, K. 55:4
K. Mavourneen! the grey dawn is breaking 47:14
**Kavanagh, Matthew:** Mr. M. K. Philomath and Professor 38:13
**Kearney, Kate:** Must die by the breath of K. K. 110:4
**Keen:** the grief of the k. is no personal complaint 151:7
**Kells:** crazily tangled like the Book of K. 72:17
**Kerns:** We must supplant these rough rug-headed k. 142:7
**Kerry:** upon the sandy K. shore 83:6
**Kevin:** the crooning of old K.'s pipes 38:10
**Kick:** we will k. it into the ground 53:5
**Kidneys:** he liked grilled mutton k. 79:12
**Kids:** To bash the k. on Monday 50:2

**Kieran:** Stands St. K.'s city fair 139:8
**Kilbarrack:** K. the healthiest graveyard in Ireland 29:16
**Kilcash:** *No one speaks of Kilcash* 16:5
**Kill:** going to k. a boy 40:9
I went out to k. French 33:6
**Killarney:** Laune, west of K. 48:13
**Killed:** I k. my poor father, Tuesday was a week 152:5
**Killen:** On sweet K. Hill 94:8
**Kills:** Yet each man k. the thing he loves 160:4
**Kilmainham:** into cold K. Jail 23:3
**Kilrea:** K. for drinking tay 30:8
**Kilruddery:** We rode from K. in search of a fox 110:7
**Kind:** A k. Irish landlord reigned despotic 28:4
*and loved his k.* 51:2
**Kindness:** I distrust such acts of k. 27:6
**Kindred:** My k. 93:9
**King:** a bloody summer, and no k. 17:5
God Save — as you prefer — the K. or Ireland 97:5
I am also K. of Ireland 55:5
said the K. to the Colonel 54:12
the k. embarked for England 88:1
We are K.'s men 47:10
who is the k. of your castle 97:6
**Kings:** Change k. and we will fight it over again 141:2
the captains and the k. 30:3
**Kingstown:** under its new name, 'K.' 88:1
**Kinkora:** Dead, O K.! 100:4
He returns to K. no more! 108:8
**Kinvara:** Not far from old K. 58:2
**Kip:** when you get up close, it's a k. 89:1
**Kiss:** you must not k. and tell 45:7
**Kissed:** he k. me under the Moorish wall 80:1
**Kisses:** With their k. under a hedge 42:5
**Kitchen:** Courtin' in the kitchen 19:10
**Knack:** k. of doing everything the wrong way 90:4
**Knee:** In clabber to the k. 101:4
**Knees:** a country rising from its k. 58:5
And your little k. together 65:7
Down on your k. now 60:7
His k. drawn up, his head dropped deep 139:2
I found Ireland on her k. 67:9
thickest part of her legs below the k. 88:9
**Knife:** A k. thrower / hurling himself 89:14
*there was an old k. beside him* 118:13
With my little red k. 64:4
**Knives:** five gross of scalping k. . . . intended to be given to the American Indians that they might scalp the French 165:4
**Knock:** now she will k. with a mailed hand 132:5
**Know:** many a thing a man might k. 68:12
Whenever I wanted to k. 52:6
**Knowe:** at the foot of the Sweet Brown K. 21:7
**Knowledge:** Heat is in proportion to the want of true k. 148:7
*until all k. is known* 12:3
**Labour:** between l. spent / And joy at random 98:4
the insupportable l. of doing nothing 147:1
**Lace:** Limavady for Irish l. 30:8
**Lad:** *I was a pure-hearted, quiet, uncomplicated l.* 117:4
I wouldn't give a thraneen for a l. that hadn't a mighty spirit in him 152:8
*tender lad / a darling this* 11:7
**Ladder:** the last step of this glorious l. 36:4
**Ladies:** Old l. with stern faces 30:3
three old l. from Hades 93:2
When the l. are calling 66:17
**Lady:** My L. Bountiful 58:10
who should I spy but a Spanish l. 38:2
**Lae:** le fáinne geal an l. 17:2
**Laighneach:** Níl ceart ná blas ag an L. 17:4
**Lake:** settles on the l. for evermore 87:1
the summerhouse by the l. 27:5
there is a l. in every man's heart 106:9
**Lakes:** In Cavan of the little l. 104:9
**Lamb:** *Holy Spirit and L.* 93:14
thought on the L. of God 73:7
**Lámh:** coingibh uaim do l. 41:1
**Lamp:** as a halfpenny dip is to an arc l. 66:2
I looked for the l. which she told me / Should shine 109:5
Turn down the candid l. 139:4
**Lamps:** like illumined pearls the l. shone 78:4
**Land:** Always returned with fresh appreciation of my own l. 136:11
and free our native l. 80:2
And leave me in this l. 42:11
I disclaim . . . all tilled l. 92:7
Is the terrors of the l.! 82:7
One law, one l., one throne 85:2
sodden and friendly l. 72:16
solution of the l. question 53:9
the l. and instruments of labour from which mankind derive their substance 46:2
the l. question contains . . . the materials 86:1
the l. that reigns all l.s above 82:9
the l. where her young hero sleeps 108:11
this lovely l. that always sent 78:8
this soft l. quietly / Engulfed them 93:1
what had been . . . his own land 77:8
What's right in a country when the l. goes sour? 112:8
**Landlord:** A kind Irish l. reigned despotic 28:4
A l. in Ireland can scarcely invent an order which a servant . . . dares refuse to execute 165:7
Shoot a l. — be of use 161:6
the l. and the sheriff came 22:2
*Whether you're a l., duke or king* 27:1
**Landlordism:** abolition of l. 53:9
**Landlords:** You must show the l. that you intend to keep a firm grip 132:1
**Landscape:** no longer matches the l. . . . of fact 63:11
**Language:** forsaking the English l. 14:7

images of the past embodied in l. 63:12
it is a rich l. 63:10
It seemed to me a l. suitable for the celebration of an antique Celtic rite 106:8
lost entirely the national l. 51:8
my grasp of the Irish l. became so firm 38:5
obsolete l. which he cannot speak 57:7
perfect l. to sell pigs in 71:5
*perhaps the l. of the stranger will be the one to go under* 130:3
the l. of Erin is brilliant as gold 100:3
the l. of the tribe will always elude me 63:8
this neglected l. 33:11
use the l. as a neutral field 75:1
**Languages:** Professor of the Learned L. 38:13
**Lanigan:** learning a step for L.'s ball 21:5
**Lark:** as I hear the sweet l. sing 60:1
sounds the l.'s merry song 82:3
the little red l. 68:4
**Lass:** Amo, amas, I love a l. 125:3
Drink to the l., / I'll warrant she'll prove an excuse for the glass 144:8
**Lasses:** Coleraine for l. 30:8
**Last:** My L. Night at Home 63:7
to be my l. and latest words 39:11
**Late:** Come in! for it is growing l. 105:1
Finds too l. that men betray 67:1
too l., too l. are they 38:11
**Latin:** the ivied L. of churchmen 71:8
**Laugh:** the loud l. that spoke the vacant mind 66:7
**Laughter:** I have to sit down and rock with l. 44:4
**Law:** denying and defying all British l. 105:5
It is nature's l. 78:7
One l., one land, one throne 85:2
People . . . must order their lives either by l. or by the strong hand 124:9
**Laws:** brutal l. may kill the Irish 23:12
Refused to write certain l. on paper 39:9
right back to . . . the Penal L. 76:3
the l. of England is queer 69:1
the most favourable l. can do little 35:5
to make l. to bind Ireland 67:8
**Lawyers:** ways of l. are like the ways of the Heathen Chinese 77:5
**Lazy:** l., trifling, inattentive, negligent, slobbering, profligate 165:8
**Leader:** every popular l. . . . has perpetuated this primary contradiction 110:2
I am not the l. of the employers 112:11
**Leaders:** Betrayed her own l. one by one 78:8
some mad political l. have stirred up 110:9
We have lost two people who were the l. 110:8
**Learning:** together with various branches of l. 39:1
**Leave:** for I must l. thee 70:1
**Leaves:** his face was pressed into the wet l. 87:7
the green l. all turn yellow 83:7
**Lecky, W. E.:** *see* 46:10
**Lecturer:** is sending round a l. 68:9
**Lectures:** he l. on the following branches of Education 38:13
**Ledwidge:** L. renames you 59:7
**Lee, River:** the lovely waters of the L. 23:8
**Left:** you l. off before you began 45:10
**Lego:** Aut l. vel scribo 142:1
**Léim:** is phreabas de l. ón bpéin im dhúiseacht! 104:4
**Leinbh:** Fiche bliain 'do l. 25:4
**Leinster:** *the L.man's speech has neither flavour nor accuracy* 17:4
**Leisured:** important that we should keep in this country a certain l. class 165:2
**Leithéidí:** mar ná beidh ár leithéidí arís ann 121:6
**Lent:** Beat against the hard stones of L. 139:3
**Lethargy:** would sink into a l. from which it would be impossible . . . to arouse them 147:4
**Letter:** If I send this l. it is war 89:10
**Letters:** I am a man of l. 29:17
in a breach of promise l. are a great help 101:12
'not writin' l.' sez she 62:7
**Leviathan:** a goodly L. roll'd from the waves 36:3
**Liadán:** *I am L.* 12:1
**Liar:** After they have called you a thief and a l. 90:11
Man is a born l. 123:11
thou l. of the first magnitude 45:6
**Liberal:** the emancipated and l. Irishman . . . may go to Mass 154:10
**Liberties:** For others' l. they bleed 50:5
Our l. were not lost in any disastrous battle 119:4
**Liberty:** A voice from America shouted to l. 61:1
bold Robert Emmet the darling of Erin and Kevin Barry gave his young life for the cause of l. 159:13
Fair L. was all his cry 151:1
For the cause of l. 23:11
from arms to l. 67:9
God has given l. to man 49:11
in the assertion of a people's l. 103:13
no tones to awaken L. 71:7
this is L.-Hall 66:14
to breathe . . . the air of l. 67:8
**Library:** a circulating l. in a town is an ever-green tree of diabolical knowledge! 144:5
shall have free access to the said L. 101:2
Walking in a l. door is like / Being raped by an army 114:3
**Lie:** *never decline to l. unclothed* 104:3
reluctant to thieve or l. 60:3
**Lies:** so many l. I never heard in praise of anything 134:13
**Life:** a faint, far-away amusement at l. 95:7
and take my l. 58:13
blather about the l. to come 29:4
*But hadn't life let him down?* 118:13
have still a l., and a view of l., that are rich and genial and humorous 153:8
He lived the good l. 90:5
I looked into the heart of this l. 81:15
Is there a l. before death? 72:10

L. has long ago taken on a new . . . rhythm 68:8
L. is a cheap *table d'hôte* 83:14
L. repeating itself and surviving 63:13
more familiar ways of falling out of l. 103:2
my lamp of l. is nearly extinguished 56:8
My l. is my own 91:7
planned a new heroic l. for herself 115:6
the l. that God desires that man should live 52:10
there is an unchanging, silent l. within every man 106:12
*There is yet a world of living and of l. in this back of beyond* 136:9
This was indeed a deadly moment in our l. 42:3
two ways of looking at l. 76:2
when l. shone warm in thine eye 107:1
Who leads a good l. is sure to live well 125:4
**Liffey, River:** I give you the L. and the vast gulls 98:4
*in triumph on L.'s cheek to the strand of the sea* 129:12
the L. is to the Shannon 66:2
**Light:** brings the l. / Of other days around me 109:15
dazzles their eyes with a l. all its own 100:3
Goes answering l. 107:10
in the headstrong l. 31:13
like an unexpected l. surprises! 107:15
Oft may l. around thee smile 108:15
the blessed warning l. 40:10
the l. gleams an instant 29:13
the port l. always fascinated him 154:9
'Twas Eden's l. on Earth a while 100:1
We forget what l. / led us, lonely, to this place 105:14
**Lightning:** l. in his head 37:9
**Lights:** Whose l. are fled 110:1
**Lilli Burlero:** Ho, Brother Teague, dost hear de Decree? / L. B. Bullena-la 159:4
**Lily:** then heigho the l.-o, / the royal, loyal l.-o 127:10
till then the Orange l. be 61:5
**Limavady:** L. for Irish lace 30:8
**Limerick:** L. is beautiful, as everyone knows 32:2
**Line:** he cast a lovely l. 90:5
**Linen:** clean l. and a guinea 90:12
yer Ma was a piece ov fine l. 76:8
**Lion:** with the head of a l. 59:11
**Lips:** her l. so sweet that monarchs kissed 20:7
my poor l. freeze 63:15
on her l. a spirit of life 68:1
**Liquor:** I'd call for l. of the best 21:8
**Lir:** Yet like L.'s children 72:17
**Lisconnell:** L. has never been skilled 28:1
**List:** it's only us I say could l. to him 102:1
**Literary:** A l. movement: five or six people who live in the same town 140:9
**Literature:** and they call his writing l. 105:9
de-Davisisation of Irish national l. 56:5
not much given to l. 54:10
So it was with l. 39:3
the Anglo-Irish l., which certainly mirrors the life of Ireland 139:10
we're not familiar with your l. 63:9
**Little:** Says l., thinks less 58:11
wants but l. here below 66:11
**Live:** some people l. through adapting 33:8
Was it not a l. fly that was in the dead man's mouth 120:3
**Lives:** If it is necessary to take the l. of many individuals then the l. of many individuals will be taken 124:7
**Living:** No man at all can be l. for ever and we must be satisfied 153:7
too busy picking up half a l. 122:10
Vertuus l. dyd I long relinquish 146:7
**Lloyd George:** going to defeat old L.G. 23:9 *See also* 23:10
**Loan:** *than a heron on l.* 25:8
**Loathe:** put under another which they l. 40:4
**Loch Dearg:** Truagh mo thuras go L.D. 15:6
**Loch Léin:** *On the shores of L. L.* 17:2
**Lock:** and last night — I changed the l.! 128:8
**Locks:** until his l. grew grey 38:12
**Loime:** Is é a dhighnit a l. 121:8
**Loins:** A shudder in the l. engenders there / the broken wall, the burning roof and tower 164:4
**Lon:**Binn sin, a l. Doire an Chairn! 15:8
l. do chraíb / charnbuidi 11:9
**London:** a place much worse than L. 77:2
came to be a nurse in L. 115:4
I didn't go to L. 52:5
We have this L. word in our name since 1613 102:3
with L.'s ghost 64:3
**Loneliness:** filled the air with light cries of l. 103:9
**Lonely:** I'm very l. now, Mary 55:3
**Long:** leave contraception on the l. finger too l. 90:9
nor wants that little l. 66:11
The L. Hoor 44:3
**Looked:** I have l. him round and l. him through 147:10
**Lord:** and if the L. allows me 10:3
knocking down any man that now calls me 'My L.' 119:9
prayed that the L. would on him call 22:9
'Twas the L. who gave the word 10:1
where the dear L. was crucified 9:6
**Lore:** that louith goddis lore 104:6
**Lose:** to l. one parent, Mr. Worthing, may be regarded as a misfortune 160:12
**Lothlind:** Laechraid lainn ó L. 12:7
**Loud:** the l. laugh that spoke the vacant mind 66:7
**Lough:** at the end of the melancholy l. 97:8
**Lough Neagh:** On L. N.'s bank, as the fisherman strays 108:1
**Louser:** But still that l.'s gone 93:5
**Lout:** Was l., son of l., by old l., and was da to a l.! 147:6
**Love:** a l. that was unrealized 87:4
a noise to go with l. 144:13
All for my true l. 82:8

*and the l. of my soul* 16:10
as l.'s young dream 108:6
Belfast, dear object of my l. 40:12
But L. has pitched his mansion in / the place of excrement 164:1
by l. I am betrayed 17:8
*hurry my l., hasten* 18:5
I could not l. you half so well / without my practice shots 144:12
I know who I l. 20:11
I l. my l. in the morning 69:6
*I may not seal our l.* 41:1
I met the L.-Talker one eve 38:10
Ireland my first and only l. 78:9
it's that kind of poacher's l. you'd make, Christy Mahon 152:11
kill your belief that l. is all 62:10
Little thought I that night / that our love ties would loosen! 135:1
L. is the discovery of an unsuspected . . . value 64:9
l. / like a tinsmith's scoop 72:8
L. serve the feast with his own willing hand 109:7
l. since you'll have me 22:3
*lovely are decisions about l.* 14:4
More substance in our enmities / Than in our l. 164:5
Oh shadows of l., inebriations of l., foretastes of l., trickles of l., but never yet the one true l. 115:9
one affection . . . is my l. for Ireland 40:1
one far kind glance from my l. 37:3
our bitterness and love 51:12
Over the years the l. turned to something else 115:4
That L. lacks surveillance 94:8
*the fire of God's l. stays in my heart* 44:6
the girl I l. is beautiful 32:2
the laugh from my l. you thieved 81:12
the ship that my true l. sails in 23:13
the words of l. then spoken 109:15
there my true l. sits him down 70:1
this worldis l. is gone awai 104:6
to l. and be wise 34:11
to l. her was a liberal education 146:10
To l. oneself is the beginning of a lifelong romance 160:10
to tramp it barefoot and be in l. again 93:5
we must always treat them with the spirit of meekness and l. 101:1
where all we l. foregathers 65:8
who . . . could deny you l.? 59:14
**Loved:** *I have l. Cuirithir* 12:1
*I l. God, I have l. you* 99:15
*the three things I l. best* 14:2
**Lover:** where my dark l. lies 79:6
**Lovers:** as l. sometimes do 21:12
I'm simply surrounded by l. 61:7
L. will find / A hedge-school for themselves 42:7
poor l. who may not do what they please 42:5
through the grove the young l. by moonlight are roving 158:10
**Loves:** Yet each man kills the thing he l. 160:4
**Loyal:** not l. to the crown 74:4
**Lying:** *three sisters of l.* 12:5
**Lynch, Jack:** the greatest IRA man of them all — J.L. 131:9

**MacBride, Maud Gonne:** Tea with Madam Gonne MacB. 95:7
**MacDonagh, Thomas:** keening for T. MacD. 59:7
MacD. and MacBride / And Connolly and Pearse / Now and in time to be 164:2
**MacEntee, Seán:** Mr. MacE. asked me what Lord Beaverbrook thought about Ireland 38:3
**Mac-Liag:** I am M.-L., and my home is on the Lake 100:4
**MacMahon:** A M. had tipped his hat 77:8
**Maccán:** M. mall secht mblíadan mbinn 117:4
**Machine:** but a mere m. 83:2
Dick met, and meeting, smote the light m. 45:3
**Machines:** If m. could be so constructed 54:3
**Mackerel:** She viced a m. by the gills 96:3
**Madness:** if m. be loving of thee? 72:14
now Ireland has her m. 26:1
**Magairle:** ach m. Annraoi, Rí 15:3
**Mahomet:** like M.'s coffin 33:5
**Maiden:** Here's to the m. of bashful fifteen 144:8
**Maidin:** M. mhoch do ghabhas amach 17:2
Vowed the M. on her throne, boys, / Would be a M. still 155:6
**Maire:** Rot rath, a M., mórbúaid 31:9
**Majority:** A minority who happen to be a m. 90:8
according to the sentiments of its m. 65:3
the Protestant ruling m. 88:4
you had the m. on your side 54:1
**Mallow:** live the rakes of M. 22:4,5,
**Malone, Mollie:** on sweet M. M. 17:7
**Maloney, Moll:** Me an' M. M. 68:5
**Man:** by the seasonable energy of one m. 34:17
**Manger:** in a m. for His bed 9:5
**Manhood:** Irish instinctive m. can be relied on 43:4
Mourn the way that m. ought 54:15
**Mankind:** All m. was pleased with her / And she with all m. 105:13
**Manners:** if after being admonished He does not amend His m. 101:2
**Manuscript:** the whole landscape a m. 106:3
**Maps:** I travel without m. 27:7
**Marbh:** Is iomaí m. do mharaigh an m. so fútsa, a líog! 128:3
M. le tae 25:7
**March:** the bright shillings of M. 81:11
the m. of the human mind is slow 34:10
**Marching:** Bad luck to this m. 89:5
**Marines:** greeted my fellow-m. with a fluent *Céad Míle Fáilte* 38:5

**Mark:** claimed to m. the meeting of three dioceses 89:2
**Market:** If we enter the Common M. 88:8
'Twas on a m. day 90:1
**Marriage:** believe in the sacredness of property, in the sacredness of m. 149:1
celibacy, late m. and emigration 103:14
Hanging and m. . . . go by Destiny 59:2
Since m. is a holy thing, / That there are none in heaven?' 161:11
so faithful to the m. bond 69:8
the sanctity and the indissolubility of the m. bond 136:6
**Marry:** *If you m. the cistern maker* 16:7
*m. a mountain woman* 24:9
M.'d in haste, we may repent at leisure 45:11
May she m. a ghost and bear him a kitten 147:8
Resign — m. — return 138:3
the dear knows who I'll m. 20:11
to m. the Irish 54:6
**Martyn, Edward:** *see* 106:8
**Martyr:** Another m. for old Ireland 23:12
slaughter a man in this position without making him a m. 142:11
**Martyrs:** By corners where the m. fell 117:7
**Marvell:** hear sung M., by a wiser Muse 74:2
**Mary:** I'd roll my M. in my arms 21:8
*M., a great gift was given to you* 31:9
M. Magdalene, that easy woman 139:3
M. was the Mother mild 9:5
Sittin' on the stile, M. 55:2
That made me love M., the Rose of Tralee 110:11
**Mask:** I have at last perfected the m. 148:15
wearing a m. of patriotism 49:5
**Mass:** Going to M. last Sunday 92:8
move between the fields to M. 30:16
Walking to the parish church for Midnight M. 84:5
**Massacre:** Escaped from the m. 72:2
**Master:** believed that the Young M. had come for her at last 38:6
'three cheers for old Ireland,' says M. mcGrath 18:10
**Masters:** We were m. of reserve 58:7
**Matches:** what she called good m. 35:10
**Material:** if we know our m. and respect it 112:5
**Máthair:** 'Le do mh. a chuaigh tú' 123:8
**May:** As I went a-walking one morning in M. 22:11
in the merry month of M. 58:2
**Mayflowers:** the erotic m. / of Provence 71:8
**Mayo:** He marched to the County M. 98:12
there won't be our like in M., for gallant lovers 152:12
*Till I set my foot down in the middle of County M.* 128:6
underneath the sod in far M. 70:2
**McCann, Tom:** What made me hire with this man called T. McC.? 20:9
**McCorley, Rody:** R. McC. goes to die 38:11
**McGrath, Mrs.:** 'Oh Mrs. McG.' the sergeant said 21:9
**McCracken, Henry Joy:** the duty fell on H. J. McC. 73:14
**Mé:** Níor saolaíodh mé gur cailleadh é 129:4
**Meadow:** In the m. where you ran 65:7
**Meal-bin:** sunk past its gleam in the m.-b. 72:8
**Means:** by peaceful, persuasive m. 88:7
**Measure:** I strip this formidable m. 35:9
**Meath:** of our most lovely M. 73:4
**Mediterranean:** We feel closer to the warm M. 63:9
**Meet:** Compliments pass when the quality m. 29:15
might never all m. here again 23:1
**Meeting-house:** Ravara m.-h. mouldered 30:4
**Melancholy:** lose their serious m. air 67:2
What charm can soothe her m. 67:1
**Melodies:** cannot except the Irish M. from . . . censure 71:7
those little ponies, the *M.*, will beat the mare, *Lalla* 109:14
**Melody:** three syllables of m. 87:13
**Melts:** *the Irish m. into the tune* 39:4
**Memorial:** *so that some m. of them might remain* 121:6
**Memories:** so rich with m. 78:2
**Memory:** a geographical expression, a misty m. 83:17
abolishing the m. of past dissensions 88:5
Besides, his m. decays, / He recollects not what he says 150:14
Fond M. brings the light 109:15
let my m. be left in oblivion 56:8
My m. ever glides 100:7
red-lettered in m. 64:10
that's all you have now — just the m. 63:6
the glorious, pious and immortal m. 28:7
the m. came faint and cold 29:2
the m. closes over 30:5
this town is eaten through with m. 126:10
**Mental:** attack of m. gall-stones 66:1
**Mercy:** to whom the praise of this m. belongs 48:3
traditional Irish m. 53:5
**Mermen:** M. keep the tone and time! 50:8
**Merry:** let's drink and be m. 23:1
Let us be m. before we go 49:7
living short but m. lives 22:5
the m. eye of a people who had little to laugh about in real life 140:5
**Messiah:** the M. of royalty comes! 36:3
**Method:** yield to perseverance and m. 35:6
**Mice:** the m. were squealing in my prison cell 30:1
**Mickeys:** territory held by the M. 71:3
**Midday:** *Sunset at m.* 11:2
**Middle-class:** than we of the m.-c. suffer 63:1
**Midlands:** through the m. of Ireland 31:2
**Midnight:** M. had come and gone 46:12
**Mildew:** the m. has spotted *Clarissa's* spine 112:4
**Miles:** Oh! It's six m. from Bangor 23:2

**Militia:** the South Down M. 82:7
**Mill:** a faint, almost inaudible hum from the now empty M. 121:3
every tear would turn a m. 18:4
**Milton:** M. makes it plain 74:2
**Mind:** Dear thoughts are in my m. 60:1
fits perhaps the m. not less than the body 67:4
Health of body, peace of m. 90:12
I knew her m. was altered 92:8
loud laugh that spoke the vacant m. 66:7
march of the human m. is slow 34:10
Murphy's m. pictured itself 29:7
My m. was like Swift's church 73:13
Reading is to the m. what exercise is to the body 147:2
She holds my m. with her seedy elegance 97:10
Short Trots with a Cultured M. 38:8
**Minds:** a great empire and little m. 34:12
All was lit up in their m. 120:13
until we purge our m. of childishness 92:5
**Minister:** *By Monday morning were a m.* 17:1
*Don't speak of the alien m.* 15:3
the m. of God's retribution 65:1
**Minority:** I am proud to consider myself a typical man of that m. 165:5
**Minstrel:** how the heart of the M. is breaking! 108:12
the M. fell! — but the foeman's chain 109:2
**Minute:** We cannot cage the m. 98:1
**Mirror:** plainly in the m. of my soul 84:8
**Miseries:** Coherent m., a bite and sup 72:10
**Mission:** My m. is to pacify Ireland 65:2
**Mist:** Och! but I'm weary of mist and dark 44:12
*through the deep night a magic m. led me* 130:4
watching the green waves tossing in the m. 106:13
**Mistress:** She had been m. of her flesh 50:6
sprinkle his m. with Holy Water 154:10
**Mists:** thro' the m. of the ages 47:7
**Mná:** A mhacaoimh m. 59:13
An áit a mbíonn m. bíonn gab 24:8
de ní scarat m. re báis 10:11
**Mob:** there's nothing civilised about a m. 154:3
**Mock:** When cowards m. the patriot's fate 76:1
**Moderation:** m. must go hand in hand with the mailed fist 33:4
**Móin Móir:** Úar ind adaig i M. M. 14:5
**Molly:** lovely M., the Rose of Mooncoin 82:3
**Molly Bawn:** Come listen to my story, M.B. 19:6
**Monaghan:** O stony grey soil of M. 81:12
**Monday:** In Mountjoy jail one M. morning 23:11
think of sin all day M. 102:6
To bash the kids on M. 50:2
**Money:** *many ways of gathering money* 27:1
my m. is all my own 21:7
We want some of your m. / For Manet and Monet 129:8
When m.'s tight and is hard to get 116:5
**Monstrosity:** I do not know of any greater m. 66:5
**Monument:** any greater monstrosity than the Wellington M. 66:5
**Monuments:** the sombre m. / That bear their names 84:6
**Moon:** at the rising of the m. 40:10
great horns of the m. 32:11
By the m. that shines above us 30:3
change places at the Rising of the M. 68:13
I had an affair with the m., in which there was neither sin nor shame 148:4
Inundher the bright new m. 69:3
the howling of Irish wolves against the m. 142:4
the m. behind the hill 83:1
the m. is very thin and cold 100:5
**Mooncoin:** the Rose of M. 82:3
**Moonlight:** Captain M. will take my place 132:3
**Moor:** Brennan on the M. 19:5
**Moore, George:** that old yahoo G. M. 28:3
**Moore, Thomas:** and M. from Ely Place 105:8
before I go, T. M. 36:5
Mr. M. converts the wild harp 71:7
Tommy M.'s roguish finger 79:15 *See also* 122:7
**Moral:** m. development of the rural classes 68:9
**More:** 'Twas Eden's light on earth a while, and then no m. 100:1
**Morgan, Lady:** An' L. M. makin' tay 20:2
**Morning:** As I went a-walking one m. in May 22:11
*Early one morning I went out* 17:2
I bid you the top of the m. 89:11
I love my love in the m. 69:6
m. steps like a laughing girl 83:3
Stink in the m. 79:8
the m. of St. Patrick's Day 27:2
*the m. screech on you* 25:12
the wild freshness of M. 107:12
**Mortality:** the m. rate is consistent with the national average 88:13
**Moss-cheeper:** A m.-c., swaying on a reed like a mouse 103:9
**Mot:** ont inventé un nouveau m. 60:2
**Mother:** a m. surrounded by her spinster children 30:4
he should have his m. around 38:7
however picturesque his m. may be 56:4
I am not your m. 55:8
if his m. was right 81:5
It is not that I half knew my m. 116:9
Mary was that m. mild 9:5
not wishing to annoy his m. 82:2
over the sea you will be carried from me, your m. 123:9
to be the m. of a fool 34:7
*'You took after your m., you useless, lazy little good-for-nothing'* 123:8
**Mothers:** the first and heaviest crop of m. 35:8
the shooting of m. of English-speaking children 66:4
**Motor-cars:** run m.-c. and the GAA 39:7
**Mountain:** and climb an Irish m. 111:12
And sipped his m. dew 80:3

Join us on the m. side 69:7
*marry a m. woman* 24:9
menace of a Gothic m. 74:5
the grand road from the m. 67:6
The m. was inaccessible 71:3
the real old M. Dew 22:7
Up the airy m. 10:6
**Mountains:** from their home in the m. 37:2
God bless the gray m. 55:6
I think the m. ought to be / Taught a little modesty 147:15
long ranges of blue m., the streak of bog, the rotting cabin 106:5
look how the snowy m. 54:9
the M. of Mourne 62:3
The m. were thrown higgledy-piggledy into the distance 96:4
When you can see the M. of Mourne 88:10
**Mountjoy:** In M. jail one Monday morning 23:11
**Mourn:** M. the way that manhood ought 54:15
**Mourne:** great lads, the tinkers o' M. 140:4
the mountains of M. 62:3
**Mourning:** keyed the m. to another note 59:7
So tear up your m. and hang up your brightest colors 143:1
**Moustache:** and a terrifying m. 59:11
His m. was golden 65:10
**Moustaches:** they all wear enormous m. 57:1
**Mouth:** a Gaelic tag in your m. 39:9
*A silent m. is melodious* 24:14
Better keep your m. shut 76:3
Oh, m. of honey 59:14
The m. . . . was fixed and rather cruel-looking, with peculiarly sharp white teeth 148:12
the rotted leaves were sucked into his m. 87:7
With a honeyed m. 89:4
**Moyle:** Silent, O M. be the roar of thy water 108:13
**Muigheo:** Go seasfaidh mé síos i lár Chontae M. 128:6
**Muimhneach:** Tá blas gan ceart ag an M. 17:4
**Muir:** Bíonn súil le m. 25:3
**Muirnín:** A m. dílis is a fhaoileann óg 16:7
Is go dtéidh tú, a m. slán 18:4
**Mulier:** Ergo modo miro m., si uiderit illud 132:6
**Mulligan, Buck:** Stately, plump B. M. 79:9
**Mullingar:** like waiting for a train in M. 94:11
the M. heifer 21:10
**Mundi:** ultimi habitatores m. 45:2
**Munster:** in the province of M. 48:12
*The M. man's speech is tuneful but inaccurate* 17:4
**Murder:** Another m. for the crown 23:12
'Commit a m. and die a happy death' 30:2
which have led to . . . m. in Ireland, are usually very different from those which have led to m. elsewhere 156:1
**Murdered:** Here our m. brother lies 54:15
Someone m. / We know, we guess 87:2
**Murderer:** never yet heard of a m. 49:8
**Murderers:** not m. who are being executed 54:1
Strike on your blood-cemented thrones the m. of your friends 154:1
**Murphy:** M.'s mind pictured itself 29:7
**Murphy, Father:** Then F. M., from old Kilcormack 102:7
**Murphy, William:** W. M. is a humane man 83:9
**Music:** *a lovelier m. than yours* 15:8
Because she loved flute m. 83:6
before I dare think of setting it to m. 44:4
her beauty / Was m. in mouth 42:8
M. hath charms to soothe a savage breast 45:9
The better would the m. be 62:5
the cultivation of instrumental m. 37:7
the m. of the laughter and tears of her people 129:7
the soul of Music shed 108:16
To m. at night 107:10
We are the m. makers 129:14
**Muskerry:** in the barony of West M. 48:12
the M. sportsman 19:4
**Mutton:** ate his m. and his ducks 23:6
**Muttonburn:** great cleansing power, the M. Stream 21:11
**Myth:** Against the sceptred m. to hold / The golden heresy of truth 140:7

**Naked:** A man must go n. to an island 58:4
**Name:** has left but the n. 109:10
Like the asylum's name 89:13
They needn't chaff him any more about his n. dying 103:8
thinking it was his n. 48:13
**Names:** Only the faces and the n. remain 93:1
sombre monuments / That bear their n. 84:6
take my stand by the Ulster n. 73:2
**Napoleon:** N. hopes to build his own 36:2
**Nation:** a n. / Built upon violence 97:12
a n. has no right to surrender its declared and established Independence 41:8
A N. once again! 50:10
'A Nation Once Again'. Am very ready to meet you 42:2
a small n. that stood alone 53:1
And show'd by one satiric touch, / No n. wanted it so much 151:2
his career of striking at the heart of this n. 124:5
If Ireland was a n., tell me when? 10:7
No offer will be accepted by the n. 52:3
Politically we are a young n. 92:4
the life of this n. and the honour of this n. is worth the lives of many individuals 124:7
the n. still moves on 70:2
These people are part and parcel of the n. 124:8
things a man must not do to save a n. 126:4
Till Ireland, a n. 51:4

to fix the boundary of the march of a n. 132:4
to make Erin a n. yet 59:16
to opt out of a n. 90:8
What ish my n.? Who talks of my n.? 142:6
Who made you a n.? 61:2
**National:** All Europe is dying for n. ends 40:7
consistent with the n. average 88:13
lost entirely the n. language 51:8
the N. Guard being a non-military or civil organization 123:2
time the Republic replaced the N. Anthem 94:4
to soothe n. sensibilities 99:5
to try to help n. Ireland 40:6
**Nationalism:** n. imposes its dominion on man today 136:2
**Nationality:** interpreting the n. of his country 56:5
to promote the cause and acquire the reality of n. 122:9
**Nationhood:** her old tradition of n. 24:2
**Nations:** her place among the n. of the earth 56:8
**Native:** The savage loves his n. shore 129:9
**Natives:** the bulk of your n. to be the most pernicious race of odious little vermin 149:13
**Natural:** not a n. revolutionary 83:11
On the stage he was n. 66:13
**Nature:** Did I sound the alarm within, or N.? 148:9
It is the n. of all greatness 34:9
My lack of faith in human n. 27:6
*N. cannot be hidden* 24:12
N. did me that honour 32:5
*N. is stronger than rearing* 24:11
She is of a gentle n. 64:6
The God of n. never intended 67:5
**Neat:** How n. one must be 89:5
**Negative:** attitude uncompromisingly n. 56:4
**Neighbours:** Shake hands with all of the n. / And kiss the colleens all 133:6
**Néill:** ro mósam túaid i tír N. 117:3
**Nest:** I'd there build my n. 23:13
This is a real n. of singing birds 43:11
**Neutral:** *an impossible task to stay n.* 32:7
**Neutrality:** N. had left a wound 48:6
**New:** *Everything n. is neat* 14:4
on the nothing n. 29:6
**News:** What's the n.? What's the n.? 102:8
**Ní Houlihan:** oh Kathaleen Ní H. your road's a thorny way 38:12
**Ní Uallachain, Caitlín:** There is no such person as C. Ní U. 98:9
**Nickname:** the n. the neighbours stuck upon him 90:4
**Night:** Committed always to the n. of wrong 83:4
every n. . . . we write our new creation 95:4
N. spreads her spangled quilt 50:4
Oft in the stilly n. 109:15
*She wouldn't whine after a n.'s hard labour* 104:3
The n. before Larry was stretched 21:13
to steal a few hours from the n. 109:6
**Nile:** as headstrong as an allegory on the banks of the N. 144:6
**Ninety-Eight:** Who fears to speak of N.E.? 76:1
**Noblest:** the two n. of things, which are sweetness and light 149:6
**Noise:** a noise to go with love 144:13
by the n. of the acclamation 34:15
the n. they made was a continual caw of calumny 97:1
**Nollag:** N. ghlas, reilig mhéith 25:11
**Nora:** My N.'s lid that seldom rises 107:15
**Norman:** I give you the smell on N. stone 98:5
N. devices 71:8
**North:** He came from the N. and his words were few 103:4
How could Southern Ireland keep a bridal N. in the manner to which she is accustomed? 127:5
our N.-East countrymen will need no persuasion 44:2
The organisation of the n. being the deranged 73:14
What answer from the N.? 85:2
**Norway:** *the wild warriors from N.* 12:7
**Nothing:** We see n. We think of n. 78:7
**Novelist:** and the n. groans 123:5
**November:** As easy as N. fog 64:3
now thinned by N. 73:4
**Nua:** Gel cech n. 14:4
**Nubbling chit:** When he came to the n. c. 22:1
**Numerals:** meditating on the nature of the n. 116:1
**Nun:** *I am the N. of Bearra Baoi* 13:12
that kind of n. who will never have to trouble about the vow of poverty 116:14
**Nurse:** N. of murders, treason's factor 154:5
**O'Brien, Flann:** *see* 42:6
**O'Casey, Seán:** Last year it was all S. O'C. 73:12
**Ó Conaill:** 'Sé Dónall binn Ó C. caoin 18:7
**Ó Conaire, Pádraic:** into the company of P. Ó C. 95:3
**O'Connell, Daniel:** every popular leader, O'C., Butt, Parnell, Dillon and Redmond 110:2
*It was noble Daniel O'C.* 18:7
O'C. was . . . the worst enemy Ireland ever had 105:7
you'll see O'C. spoutin' 20:2 *See also* 105:5, 137:1, 154:5, 166:3
**O'Connell Street:** I am going to O'C. Street on Sunday 86:10
**O'Connor, Frank:** A myth of O'C. and Ó Faoláin 106:4
**O'Conor, Don:** *'And in Celtic' said the O'C. D.* 74:6
**O'Cutter:** As for the Captain O'C.s 39:2
**Ó Dálaigh, Cearbhall:** *See* 54:5
**O'Donnell:** dread war-cry, 'O'D. Aboo!' 102:9
**Ó Faoláin, Seán:** A myth of O'Connor and Ó F. 106:4
**O'Flynn, Father:** Father O'F. as the flower of them all 68:3
**O'Leary:** Romantic Ireland's dead and gone, / It's with O'L. in the grave 164:12

**O'Lynn, Brian:** B. O'L. and his last hour was due 93:8
B. O'L. and his wife and wife's mother 17:6
**O'More, Rory:** 'there's luck in odd numbers', says R. O'M. 90:2
**O'Neill:** thinkest thou that it standeth with O. his honor to writhe his mouthe in clattering English? 146:9
**O'Neill, Eoghan Ruadh:** dare to slay E. R. O'N. 51:1
**O'Rourke:** O'R.'s noble fare / Will ne'er be forgot 150:12
**O'Ryan:** You'll see O'R. any night 71:2
**Oars:** *Pull on your sturdy o.* 121:9
**Oath:** I am not prepared to take an o. 52:9
**Obedience:** I will yield implicit o. 23:7
*O. is ice to the wine* 43:7
who will have to wrestle with o. 116:14
**Obedient:** I am always an o. subject 49:4
**Obscene:** And not at all o. 96:10
**Obscure:** Because I never am o. 96:10
**Occupation:** an army of no o. 83:13
**Ocean:** o'er the free boundless o. 19:9
Rise — Arch of the O. 54:14
**Och:** O. hone! O. hone! O. hone! O. hone! 18:11
**Ocras:** Is maith an t-anlann an t-o. 25:6
**Odour:** In o. of sanctity dwelling 90:3
**Office:** to perform an o. which nobody else on earth could perform 125:9
**Officer:** an o. and a gentleman 77:12
**Officers:** commands of my superior o. 23:7
**Offspring:** Time's noble o. is the last 30:9
**Óg:** Is ó. i mo shaol a chonaic mé 94:5
**Oíche:** Ceo draíochta i gcoim o. do sheol mé 130:4
Ní labharfadh focal dá mb'obair an o. 104:3
**Oifig:** Inár ndiaidh in O. Stáit 121:12
**Óige:** Níl aon bhaol ná gur brea í an ó. 130:1
**Oileán:** comh Gaelach liom ar an O. so go deo arís 141:7
Níl éinne beo nach bhfuair o. 129:3
Sin é teist an scéird-o. 121:10
**Oiliúint:** Is treise dúchas ná an o. 24:11
**Oireachtas:** The O. has laid the foundation of the State 47:5
**Oisín** *See* 14:1
**Ól:** Ag cur preab san ó. 27:1
**Old:** Both o. men had the air of those who had been unexpectedly let loose 125:9
Never get o., child 33:1
That wrong-headed o. man 64:7
the ambition of an o. man in a hurry 41:13
This o. man was feeble 22:9
You'll be getting o. and I'll be getting o. 151:13
**Oleographs:** gaudy o. of martyrs and mystics 96:5
**Once:** I saw her o., one little while 100:1
**Opera:** An o. company . . . must pay its way 46:11
**Opinion:** judge of the generality of the o. 34:15
**Opinions:** o. that are dying away 35:3
**Opposed:** I am definitely o. to any proposal 98:10
**Oppression:** By consistent o. 57:1
**Orange:** And the O. will decay 22:10
Bring O. Ulster down 23:5
Can match the O. lily-o 127:10
cannot give the O. growth 61:4
in an identical way as the O. Order 34:1
may there be strife between O. and Green as long as Alexander McCracken has a bad farm of land to sell 159:2
soon the bright O. put down the Green Rag 127:7
Supposin' ye got all the O. sashes 103:7
the O. Card would be the one to play 41:11
the O. Maid of Sligo 127:11
the President would be O. Peel 119:3
the voodoo of the O. bands 97:4
**Orangeman:** I am an O. 47:9
**Orangemen:** A body of armed O. fall upon and put to death a defenceless Catholic 144:3
then O. remember King William 127:8
your Ulstermen and O. men 50:9
**Orator:** An o. shall yet arise 35:13
**Ordeal:** I am ready for my fourteen years' o. 105:4
the day of your o. is at hand 39:11
**Others:** the sort of woman who lives for o. 89:8
**Out:** Put him in to get him o.! 24:3
**Outsider:** I'd always be an o. here 63:8
**Ovid:** Burn O. with the rest 42:7
**Ownabwee:** To swell the angry O. 86:7

**Pacify:** My mission is to p. Ireland 65:2
**Padric:** P. sits in the garden 69:3
**Page:** the blots on the p. are so black 97:6
**Paid:** I have p. them back in their own coin 43:9
**Pain:** 'And such p.' 87:4
became a vague p. in his own and everybody else's arse 112:9
give up all I have without a p. 93:5
I offer my p. for Ireland 98:11
**Pair:** No age could furnish out a p. / Of nymphs so graceful, wise and fair 150:13
**Pangur Bán:** *Meisse ocus P. B.* 12:2
**Pants:** what concentration it takes / to be caught with my p. down 144:14
**Papacy:** May hail thee, blood-stained P. 127:12
**Papers:** many many examination p. 74:1
**Papish:** to save a single P. sowl 54:11
**Papist:** but not a p. 15:1
**Papists:** had the P. gain'd the day there would have been open murder 127:6
**Parachute:** Trailed like some fine, silk p. 111:4
**Paradise:** *earth be one with P.* 51:15
**Pardon:** We cannot beg for pardon 98:1
**Parents:** only illegitimate p. 53:6
**Parishes:** in the old man-killing p. 72:9
**Parliament:** a Home Rule p. in Ireland 24:1

anything except injustice from an English P. 119:11
the story of the Dublin P. 46:10
**Parnell, Charles Stewart:** every popular leader, O'Connell, Butt, P., Dillon and Redmond 110:2
From 1877 it was P. who carried the horn, a grim disdainful master 145:4
P. may be the Uncrowned King of Ireland 126:2
that P. should be lying cold and low 70:2
till P. is on the shelf 23:3
told him that P. was a bad man 79:2
**Parnellism:** P. is a simple love of adultery 131:13
**Parody:** A poet writing . . . a p. 31:7
**Parrthais:** Mar déantar i gcrích P. 51:15
**Part:** this day we must p. 48:1
**Parties:** I stood well with all p. 28:6
Like other p. of the kind 36:4
**Party:** has this p. stood between the people of this country and anarchy 47:2
the P. that was to end Partition 125:2
**Passage:** The town of P. / Is both large and spacious 99:10
**Passion:** some gentle fires of p. 34:8
The p. of bigotry 50:1
**Password:** I may learn the p. 63:8
**Passwords:** carefully-enunciated p. 72:1
**Past:** A part of our p. disinherited 106:3
a people with a p. 88:3
Because of the distant p. they would die friendless. 156:4
back to the P., though thought brings woe 100:7
it is not the literal p. 63:12
It's to hell with the future and live on the p. 47:13
Oh Irishmen forget the p. 82:10
She asks a blessed oblivion of the p. 65:5
the future and the p. 31:12
The p. did have meaning 63:13
The shadows of the p. draw near 105:11
**Patchworks:** Old p. that the pitch and toss 72:5
**Path:** Men are standing in the p. today, armed men 124:6
the long p. where Beauty wends 65:8
stay on the straight and narrow p. between good and evil 155:10
**Patricius:** Brigida, P., atque Columba 51:14
Ego P. peccator rusticissimus 133:1
viri in Christo beati, Patricii, episcopi 142:3
**Patrick, St.:** *Brigid, P. and Colmcille* 51:14
*I am P., a sinner, the least learned of men* 133:1
No more St. P.'s Day we'll keep 18:6
On P.'s day in the morning 22:3
St. P., he lifted his finger, / But Fin-ma-Cool lifted his toe. 161:8
St. P. was a gintleman, he came of decent people 166:4
Since St. P. has filled it with vermin 98:13
*the merits / of a man blessed in Christ, P. the Bishop* 142:3
the morning of St. P.'s Day 27:2
the wealth that's in St. P.'s Isle 21:12
'Twas St. P. himself sure that set it 41:3
Wearing by St. P.'s bounty 86:6
**Patrick's Cathedral:** Hordes of wild children used to play round the cathedral of St. P. 151:10
the bells of St. P.'s . . . began to play a little tune 135:7
**Patrick Street:** At P. S. corner 82:5
**Patriot:** Thy badge my p. brother 61:5
When cowards mock the p.'s fate 76:1
**Patriotism:** If these prettinesses pass for p. 71:7
wearing a mask of p. 49:5
**Pattern:** Banned the gathering and the P. 96:12
**Pay:** An opera company . . . must p. its way 46:11
**Peace:** a man of p. 52:4
leads to the p. of the graveyard 94:3
Our imaginary P. Line 89:15
the period in which we have enjoyed the consciousness of p. 47:5
Was it to be p. or the sword 35:7
When can a man get down to a book in p.? 43:10
You cannot talk p. until the enemy surrenders 131:5
**Peacock:** he sthruttin' about from mornin' till night like a p.! 117:12
**Pearl:** brooding under a sky that is one vast p. 123:7
**Peasant:** I see a p. from Connaught going over 35:14
**Peel, Robert:** P.'s smile was like the silver plate on a coffin 120:4
**Peelers:** into the hands of the p. 28:1
**Peerage:** You should study the P., Gerald 161:2
**Peggy:** When first I saw sweet P. 90:1
**Pen:** All could use the sword and p. 86:6
I'm takin' the p. in me hand 61:11
The squat p. rests 71:9
with a schoolboy's p. 39:9
**Penal:** right back to . . . the P. Laws 76:3
**People:** a p. so individual in its genius 145:2
a savage and barbarous p. 60:4
Amidst a barbarous p. harsh of speech 140:1
Dolmens Round My Childhood, the Old P. 106:1
*I have tried to describe the mind and character of the p. I knew* 121:6
One of the most original, artistic, literary, and charming people 74:8
that the local p. were the meanest and most rapacious . . . in the whole of the country 155:8
the p. of God have long passed out of earshot 111:7
the p. who were / And the p. who are 93:9
We are one of the great stocks of Europe. We are the p. of Burke; we are the p. of Grattan; we are the p. of Swift, the p. of Emmet, the p. of Parnell 165:5
**Pepper:** did put p. in the cat's milk 28:8
**Peregrinari:** pro Christo p. volens 9:1
**Perfect:** Nothing is p. There are lumps in it 148:1
**Perfection:** The intellect of man is forced to choose / P. of the life, or of the work. 163:9
the very pink of p. 66:16
**Persecution:** few are the steps from dereliction to p. 34:16

**Perseverance:** yield to p. and method 35:6
**Personalities:** their p. mixed up with the p. of their bicycles 116:13
**Perspiration:** I remember a light beading of p. even appeared upon my forehead 38:3
**Peter St.:** Repent or St. P. will not let you through 93:8
**Petravore:** the Pride of P. 61:10
**Phantoms:** the p. of the overhanging sky 84:7
**Phil:** Have you heard of P. the Fluther 62:5
**Philadelphia:** their songs of P. 48:10
**Philosopher:** there was a p. once who lived in a little room 122:10
**Philosophy:** *I read and write and teach, p. peruse* 142:1
our p. will prove indestructible 76:2
this is their sorry p. 46:13
**Phósfainn:** P. thú gan bha 16:3
**Phrase:** whose p. was always right 64:7
**Picturesque:** P., eloquent, prophetic 83:10
**Pier:** that used to glad the old stone p. 105:11
the grass-grown pier 97:11
**Piety:** they say p. has a smell 116:10
**Pigs:** perfect language to sell p. in 71:5
p. and popery are prohibited 101:11
the P. that Got the Permanent Waves 131:4
the p. that remained alive 77:11
this land of Popes and P. and Booze 74:2
**Pill:** P., p., a rúin ó 17:1
**Pills:** never forget to take my p. 74:5
**Pink:** the legs of the ladies of Cork were bright p. 95:2
the very p. of perfection 66:16
**Pint:** A P. of Plain is Your Only Man 116:5
**Pipe:** tobacco you stuff in your p. 93:3
**Pipers:** In the tents play the p. 19:2
**Pipes:** the crooning of old Kevin's p. 38:10
**Pippins:** Bobbed like p. in the weather 65:7
**Pity:** Have p. at least on the spuds 89:3
**Place:** *It was like this in the p.: 1. the foulness of the weather was too foul* 113:1
Searching the darkness for a landing p. 84:7
**Plain:** loveliest village of the p. 66:6
shone the emerald p. 31:2
**Plank:** rescued by a single p. 10:4
**Plant:**the green p. withered 83:5
there's a dear little p. that grows in our isle 41:3
**Planter:** the house of the p. 42:9
**Play:** a p. about Robert Emmet 96:13
In a good p. every speech should be as full flavoured as a nut or apple 152:4
seeing a real p. by living writers 44:7
the wildest sayings and ideas in this p. are tame indeed 152:2
**Playboy:** I've lost the only P. of the Western World 153:3
**Please:** To tax and to p. 34:11
**Pleasure:** more fond of p. 67:2
the pursuit of p. was but the misnomer for the flight from despair 121:5
through p.'s flow'ry maze 108:3
where P. lies carelessly smiling at Fame 108:4
**Plovers:** coming in clouds like the p. 61:7
**Pluto:** P. [make] a snuff-box of his skull 28:7
**Poacher:** It's little you'll think if my love's a p.'s, or an earl's itself 152:11
**Pocket:** well he wasn't slow to put his hand in his p. 159:14
**Poems:** P. are different 144:14
**Poet:** A p., writing . . . a parody 31:7
before the rising he may have been only a minor p. 142:11
every p. to have a spare wife 81:14
has never yet produced a great p. 126:3
*I am Raftery the p., / Full of hope and love* 128:7
I began as a p. 72:11
No p. will ever sing for them 88:4
the p. launched a stately fleet 10:4
**Poetry:** emptied of its p. 26:2
Ireland hurt you into p. 26:1
P.'s a mere drug 58:15
**Poets:** *more beautiful than any of the p. have sung* 94:5
*the high p. are gone* 117:5
**Póg:** tháinig ainnir fá mo dhéin le p. 92:3
**Poison:** they slew with p. him 51:1
when p. from the air 92:9
**Police:** believe . . . in the security of society, in the p. force 149:1
the Irish p. barrack is invariably clean 31:5
the P. as P., in this city, is null and void 118:9
**Policeman:** In Ireland a p.'s lot is a supremely happy one 123:5
smiling derisively at a p. 28:8
**Policemen:** Mrs. Makebelieve did not admire p. 147:17
**Policy:** a useless, degrading and demoralising p. 69:11
**Political:** all the Irish p. songs 51:9
so long as we remained non-p. 75:1
the principles of abstract p. economy 65:4
**Politics:** do three things in Irish p. 59:9
Magnanimity in p. 34:12
that was called p. 79:2
the people no longer interested themselves in p. 149:2
to every one whatever his p. 74:8
**Polling:** when they get inside a p. booth 60:3
**Pony:** on a single p. 68:5
**Pool:** *I often went to the edge of the p.* 104:2
**Poor:** the p. make no new friends 55:3
the secret Scripture of the p. 84:1
**Pope:** bless the P. this time 48:11
Here's to the P. in Killybuck 159:2
the old P. too. He is not righteous either. 131:2
to Hell with the P. 97:5

**Popes:** this land of P. and Pigs and Booze 74:2
**Population:** Ireland has controlled its p. growth by three measures 103:14
you have a starving p. 54:2
**Pork:** ordered not to eat p. 77:11
**Port:** in every p. he finds a wife 31:4
**Portadown:** A saint but born in P.! 163:5
P., a town politically reliable 136:7
**Porter:** decompose in a barrel of p. 54:7
**Pós:** Má p. tú an sistealóir 16:7
p. bean sléibhe 24:9
**Pose:** not above a bit of p. 105:9
**Posterity:** What has p. done for us? 138:8
**Potato:** exclusively thrown on the p. 94:7
**Potatoes:** and a diet of p. 63:10
mere machine for converting p. 83:2
**Poteen:** O long life to the man who invinted p. 166:2
P. — p. — p. 63:8
**Poverty:** any crime as shameful as p. 58:12
I'd rather live in p. 58:1
people with a culture of p. 63:1
to look for p. 54:6
**Powder:** keep your p. dry 31:8
**Power:** the ruling p. is adverse to them 35:5
**Praise:** let the greater p. belong! 59:16
**Prátaí:** Má sciobadh uainn a raibh de p. ins an ghort againn 113:4
**Pray:** came to scoff, remained to p. 66:9
I p. against barbed wire 74:5
**Prayers:** But I will say my p. 42:12
**Preach:** P. not because you have to say something, but because you have something to say 159:5
**Preacher:** every accusation possible has already been hurled at the p. 131:1
**Pregnant:** An Irish Bull is always p. 99:7
**'Prentice:** Peal to heaven their 'p. cry / Their patriot — 'No Surrender!' 155:5
**Prentice-boys:** the p.-b. of Derry 10:1
**Presbytery:** withered away in the dilapidated P. 84:3
**President:** amazing when the P. sent the . . . Bill 54:5
**Pressure:** politically conservative p. group 34:1
**Pretend:** I've had to p. I'm some money-grabbing gombeen man 112:10
**Pride:** Of p. and thick red Spanish wine and gold 126:10
Such is our p., our folly 52:1
Wasn't she the P. of Petravore 61:10
**Priest:** A parish p. and his sexton 96:2
condemned man gets the p. 30:2
the p. condemned for a long space to confess nuns 163:4
thinking it disgraceful for a p. to be drunk in Jerusalem 156:5
What can a bishop do with a parish p.? 143:11
'Women there are, but I'm afraid / they cannot find a p.' 161:11
*you a p. on Sunday* 17:1
*You still behave like a parish p.* 123:13
**Priesthood:** young p. who run motorcars 39:7
**Priests:** *Golden p. and wooden chalices* 136:1
Of p. we can offer a charmin' variety 68:3
'P. are human, Willy' 33:10
p. often put themselves at the head 67:3
the land swarming with p. 39:8
**Principle:** such bitter disregard of every p. of morality 47:3
the p. I state, and mean to stand upon 86:3
**Principles:** acted invariably from the highest p. 59:5
To apply . . . the p. of abstract political economy 65:4
**Prison:** My p. chamber now is iron-lined 122:6
**Prisoner:** *Rules of Life for a Long Sentence P.* 43:3
**Prisoners:** Upon that little tent of blue / which p. call the sky 160:3
**Procrastinator:** I always knew you were a prognosticator an' a p. 118:6
**Professor:** Philomath and P. of the Learned Languages 38:13
**Progenitor:** *Great p.* 44:5
**Programme:** a negative p., a purely destructive p. 124:5
**Promises:** P. and pie-crust are made to be broken 150:10
**Promotion:** to write in Irish for the sake of official p. 99:5
**Proof:** A'm p. the-night 'gen win' an' snaw 141:4
**Prop:** Shall the p. of Ireland become its battering-ram? 40:12
**Property:** P. has its duties 55:1
**Prosator:** Altus p. 44:5
**Prosperity:** if nothing . . . arises to retard its p. 88:2
**Prostitutes:** Supplying England, America, Australia etc. with p. 57:1
**Protectors:** his p. have put Bycut to great cost 23:6
**Protestant:** A P. Parliament for a P. people 33:13
An angular people, brusque and P. 139:6
and the P.s theirs *à la carte* 83:15
children of a staunch P. quarter 71:3
for the sake of P. schooling, land or soup 90:6
I have found that there are 30 P.s. 10:10
nothing civilised about a mob, be it P. or Catholic 154:3
only too glad to join arms with the armed P. in the North 138:2
P., awake to a sense of your condition 144:2
responsible for the government of the P. province of Ulster 47:8
So praise God, all true P. 127:6
Socialists are a P. variety of Communists 131:12
*sour-faces*; P. 110:3
the P. boys are loyal and true 128:1
the P. ruling majority 88:4
the P. was top-dog always 34:6
they want to nullify the P. vote 33:12
they will live like P., in spite of the authoritative

nature of their Church 127:4
**Proud:** I speak with the p. tongue of the people 93:9
not half so p. as you 100:10
sufficient p. and ignorant people 60:10
**Province:** never intended that Ireland should be a p. 67:5
the integrity of this p. 33:4
**Prudence:** submit to the dominion of p. 35:1
**Prudish:** my p. hands would refuse to form the letters 143:4
**Psalms:** I hope he'll give you the penitential p. 120:10
**Public:** of their p. polity 51:7
**Publishers:** I don't believe in p. 139:15
**Pubs:** remembered him only in p. 76:4
served in all the p. in Dublin 54:7
**Puint:** Ní mé ar Áit an P. 117:8
**Pulls:** the world p. itself up 64:8
**Pulse:** Two people with the one p. 97:13
**Punch:** the song he sang was a jug of p. 21:2
**Purgatory:** I'd sooner be delayed in P. 69:2
**Puritan:** P. Ireland's dead and gone 106:4
**Purpose:** moves on with p. set 70:2
**Push:** I p. back / through dictions 71:8

**Quality:** Compliments pass when the q. meet 29:15
**Quarrel:** to put a private q. 28:1
**Quarrelling:** like a q. man and wife 39:4
**Queen:** Hurrah for the darling little q. 119:6
Q. of the West! 54:14
since I saw the Queen of France 34:13
sits evermore like a q. on her throne 55:6
thou q. of the west 49:6
**Queries:** Some q. proposed 30:10
**Question:** Curled like a q. mark asleep 139:2
I have a right . . . to ask a q. 53:7
I see nothing in it but one q. 35:9
Q. not the silence 87:1
solution of the land q. 53:9
Such a q. there is in the land 86:2
that is the Irish Q. 54:2
*the Irish q. has so many sides* 32:7
the land q. contains . . . the materials 86:1
The one great principle of any settlement of the Irish q. 138:1
**Quill, Thady:** the Muskerry sportsman, the bould T. Q. 19:4
**Quilt:** her spangled q. of silk 50:4
**Rabbits:** the I. breed like r. 77:9
**Race:** I alone am left of my name and r. 102:4
In Erin old there dwelt a mighty r. 103:3
May no weak r. be wronged 128:9
the rebellion of the aboriginal r. 91:3
the uncreated conscience of my r. 79:5
**Rachray:** In R. there's no Christianity there 127:1
**Radio:** inch of r. breath 68:6
**Raftery:** *I am R. the poet, / Full of hope and love* 128:7
**Rag:** you're a r. on every bush 33:3
**Rags:** no scandal like r. 58:12
**Rahoon:** Rain on R. falls softly 79:6
**Raiders:** prepare for r., all lamps hidden 50:4
**Raifteirí:** Mise R., an file / lán dóchas is grá 128:7
**Rain:** Above the wailing of the r. 87:12
Encounter the r. that it stops 89:3
R. on Rahoon falls softly 79:6
that's a sure sign it'll rain 88:10
**Rainbow:** a r. / fractured 89:14
**Raindrop:** before a r. / unhouses it 42:5
**Rainstorm:** *A terrible r. beats down* 14:5
**Rakes:** Live the r. of Mallow 22:4,5,6
**Ram:** Doesn't the world know you reared a black r. at your own breast 152:7
**Rambling:** For r., for rovin' 19:4
**Ramparts:** What you call R. 25:16
**Raped:** like / Being raped by an army 114:3
**Raphoe:** three dioceses, Derry, R., Clogher 89:2
**Rascal:** the biggest r. in the whole of Ireland 33:3
**Rasher:** *Quality of r. in use in household* 116:2
**Rat:** I smelt a r.; I see him forming in the air 138:9
**Ratschilds:** the R. were the richest people 49:3
**Read:** Patsy Devlin did not r. much poetry 31:7
**Reading:** my roots were crossed with my r. 72:11
R. is to the mind what exercise is to the body 147:2
they are the life, the soul of r.! 148:6
**Reality:** Our country is a concrete and visible r. 98:9
the r. of experience 79:5
**Rearing:** *Nature is stronger than r.* 24:11
**Reasoning:** less addicted to r. 67:2
**Rebel:** He comes, the open r. fierce 31:8
**Rebellion:** first r. that ever took place 54:1
the r. of the aboriginal race 91:3
**Rebels:** Up the R., to Hell with the Pope 97:5
**Red:** *everything r. is beautiful* 12:3
green jacket, r. cap 10:6
little Black Rose shall be r. at last 53:2
R. brick in the suburbs 47:11
the little r. lark 68:4
the people's flag is deepest r. 45:15
with my little r. knife 64:4
with r. scent chalicing the air 50:7
**Redemptorist:** Owing to the welcome presence of the R. Fathers in the town there would be no dance on Sunday 155:7
**Redmond, John:** every popular leader, O'Connell, Butt, Parnell, Dillon and R. 110:2
**Refusal:** its bleak, bowler-hatted refusal of the inevitable 95:8
**Region:** a r. of sunshine and rest 69:5
**Regret:** the only r. of your unworthy representative 49:12
**Regula:** Benchuir bona r. 11:3
**Rehearsals:** He came to Dublin for the r. 59:11
**Reilig:** Casacht r. 25:5

Nollag ghlas, r. mhéith 25:11
**Reilly, Paddy:** Come back, P. R. 61:8
**Religion:** essential, integral parts of r. 35:2
he admired the Catholic r. 82:1
R. . . . had arrayed the inhabitants into two hostile camps 76:6
she could choose r. and be his tyrant 35:7
that's their r. 102:5
they take their r. very seriously 30:2
We have just enough r. to make us hate 150:5
**Religious:** obedient subject in r. matters 49:4
R. meetings are never known to pass 67:3
**Remember:** Do you r. that night 135:1
Oh, then r. me 107:8
R. '98, says the gay old hag 20:4
To r. for years / To r. with tears 10:9
**Remembered:** *We will be r. yet* 121:12
**Remembering:** To be sure, he said, r. brightly 79:14
**Renewals:** *three r. of the world* 12:6
**Rent:** A fair r. is a r. the tenant can reasonably pay 132:1
**Repeal:** R. had always to be dragged 86:2
**Repent:** we may r. at leisure 45:11
**Repression:** suffer much less r. 63:1
**Repressive:** angry and r. old crone 34:3
**Reptile:** R. it ran, and skimmed along the green 45:3
**Republic:** I stand as a symbol for the R. 52:5
Irish R. tonight at midnight 96:1
Soldiers of the R. 52:7
the Irish R.! 74:3
The Irish R. now virtually established 23:7
those who have destroyed the R. 52:7
time the R. replaced the National Anthem 94:4
**Republicans:** God's good, and the R. won't always be down 118:4
**Reserve:** We were masters of r. 58:7
**Resign:** R. — marry — return 138:3
**Resist:** I can r. everything except temptation 160:15
I will r. it to the last gasp of my existence 135:5
**Resistance:** how r. can ever be justified 40:4
**Resolve:** will be fought with the same r. 89:9
**Respect:** give place and pay due r. to their Betters 101:2
**Respectability:** I damn r., and call it a disgrace 105:8
**Respects:** paid the last r. in sad tobacco 73:6
**Response:** our r. to mud cabins 63:10
**Responsibilities:** the r. of that freedom 39:7
**Restlessness:** a man with a r. is a savage bugger 62:8
**Retribution:** the minister of God's r. 65:1
**Revenge:** takes r. on persons quite innocent 28:10
to r. themselves on fortune 46:13
**Reveries:** bathing in her sexual r. without breath or comma 140:10
**Revolution:** applauded r. in France, Hungary and Italy, while hastening to suppress it in Ireland 159:11
not a revolt but a r. 133:9
**Revolutions:** Successful r. are not the product of our brains 46:3
**Rheumatic:** 'twould a r. — he'd jump up ecstatic 19:2
**Rhyme:** come join me in r. 23:1
I r. / To see myself 72:6
list to me till I say my rhyme 116:6
whatever most can bless / the mind of man or elevate a r. 163:11
**Rhyming:** 'the curse-o'-God r.' 82:2
**Rhythm:** a new and satisfying r. 68:8
**Ribbon:** I wear a three-coloured r. 82:8
**Ribbonman:** I am no Rogue, no R. 129:13
**Rich:** are but committees of the r. 46:5
passing r. with forty pounds a year 66:8
R. and rare were the gems she wore 108:9
**Riding:** r. alone, my lord! 49:10
**Right:** Are ye r. there, Michael? 61:8
to speak of a r. that cannot even exist 103:11
**Rights:** individuals who brood too much over their r. 92:4
its duties as well as its r. 55:1
Unbowed I claim my r. 129:6
**Ring:** there was a time when I wore the r. 93:4
**Ríoghain:** ag amharc ar an R. Óig 92:3
**Riots:** When the r. stopped business came back 84:3
**Riposte:** a fine fashioner of r. 50:1
**Rising:** Change places at the R. of the Moon 68:13
the day before the r. he may have been only a minor poet 142:11
**Ritz:** open to anyone — like the R. 34:2
**River:** Flow on lovely r. 82:3
like the rushing r. / that sweeps along to the mighty sea 100:6
respond to the movement of the r. 96:6
strays a wild r. 40:11
**Riverrun:** R., past Eve and Adam's 78:5
**Rivers:** *Great r. washed by our door* 113:4
**Road:** A piece of the r. with everybody 33:2
every r. in Ulster veined my heart 103:1
*I first saw the r. that matched my desire* 94:5
I think I'll take the r. I used to know / that goes by Shere-na-garagh and the sea 158:1
on the rocky r. to Dublin 22:8
the grand r. from the mountain 67:6
the r. was in Ireland 32:8
your road's a thorny way 38:12
**Roads:** Now I was finished with walking the r. 135:3
R. where there's never a house or bush 44:12
the eternal bogs and bleak mountain r. 96:9
the little r. of Cloonagh 67:6
then the wet, winding r. 44:10
**Robbed:** She swore I r. the house 19:10
**Robber:** A brave undaunted r. 19:5
**Rock:** *I see how the r. has worn each man down* 121:11
**Ród:** Do thugas mo ghnúis / Ar an r. so romham 134:11

**Roisín:** ar mo R. Dubh 17:3
**Roll:** R. me from the wall 22:9
**Roman:** Taller than R. spears 103:3
**Romance:** R. and alcohol were difficult commodities to mix, especially in a dignified ballroom 156:2
To love oneself is the beginning of a lifelong r. 160:10
**Romantic:** R. Ireland's dead and gone, / It's with O'Leary in the grave 164:12
**Romantics:** We were the last r. 163:11
**Rome:** a virgin in R. 50:6
any body of cardinals in R. 53:12
*to go to R. is much labour* 13:3
turned his back on R. 77:8
waiting for a celibate churchman in Mother R. 111:7
who had a special dispensation from R. 88:9
**Room:** myself in a little r. under the roof 112:13
**Roots:** my r. were crossed with my reading 72:11
**Rope:** the strong r. of fate 37:1
**Ros Dhá Loch:** dá mbeifeá ar chéibh R. D. L. 118:14
**Rosaleen:** *O my dark R.* 17:3
**Rosalinde:** Here lies fair R. 105:13
**Rose:** A white r. against a brick wall in Drumcondra 159:3
I see His blood upon the r. 135:11
little Black R. shall be red at last 53:2
the R. of Mooncoin 82:3
the wild r. that's waiting for me 62:3
tho' lovely and fair as the r. of the summer 110:11
'Tis the last r. of summer 109:9
'Tis the r. of the desert 37:5
*Viva la,* the r. shall fade 50:12
**Roses:** an orchard wall where r. 81:13
if at those r. you ventured to sip 62:3
the breath of young r. 37:4
the scent of the r. will hang round it still! 107:7
**Ross:** At the siege of R. did my father fall 102:4
**Roved:** As I r. out one evening fair 22:13
**Rover:** No more a r. 49:7
**Row:** from such / a local r. 81:2
**Royal Canal:** along the banks of the R. C. 30:1
**Royalties:** my r. are lean 96:10
**Ruin:** they suit him — the r. and the gloom 51:4
**Rule:** *the little r. of Bangor* 11:3
**Rules:** *R. of Life for a Long Sentence Prisoner* 43:3
**Russell, George (AE):** the Hairy Fairy: AE 110:3
**Russia:** Ireland is a little R. 106:7
she died in R. 55:8
**Rustics:** the gazing r. rang'd around 66:10

**Sabbath:** they love to keep the S. and anything else they can lay their hands on 139:15
**Sack:** wor pirta s. people 76:8
**Sackcloth:** buildings of all Europe don their s. 50:4
**Sacrifice:** a blood s. in every generation 73:8
Further s. of life would now be vain 52:7
the pangs and the pains of the s. 25:18
those who shrink from the ultimate s. 134:6
you are impatient for the s. 56:7
**Sad:** All their songs are s. 41:7
the beauty of the world hath made me s. 134:9
**Sadness:** every degree of s., from that of the man who is merely mournful 152:1
**Safety:** The s. of women consists in one circumstance 99:1
**Sagart:** Bhí tú 'do s. 17:1
S. óir is cailís chrainn 136:1
Tá nós an ts. paróiste agat fós 123:13
**Sages:** Ten thousand s. of the Church 39:9
Where s. drone and drowse 47:7
**Sail:** Here she comes i' faith full s. 45:13
**Sailor:** How happy is the s.' life 31:4
**Sailors:** Come all ye dry-land s. bold 19:11
**Saint:** At Glendalough lived a young s. 90:3
under the patronage of some s. 67:3
**Saints:** discredited s. 30:15
face always stuck in the lives a the s. 94:9
It is much frequented by s. and cattle-dealers 101:11
*three s. one grave do fill* 51:14
**Saíthó:** mór s., becc torbai 13:3
**Sand:** In the wormless s. shall he 50:8
**Sang:** He hammered and s. with tiny voice 80:3
**Saol:** Ach nár loic an saol? 118:13
comh misniúil is do bhí i dtosach mo s. 141:6
**Sarsfield, Patrick:** down the glen rode S.'s men 141:10
S. and the siege-train, he thought, the Island of Saints and Scholars 159:13
S. is the watchword — S. is the man 141:1
**Sashes:** you — the other Gulls — would go for the s. every time! 103:7
**Satan:** Where thy father S.'s eye 127:12
**Satire:** S. is a sort of glass wherein beholders do generally discover everybody's face but their own 149:5
**Satirist:** our Gaelic satirist 42:6
**Sauce:** *Hunger is good s.* 25:6
**Savage:** a man with a restlessness is a s. bugger 62:8
a s. and barbarous people 60:4
The s. loves his native shore 129:9
**Saxon:** I don't believe the S. will ever relax his grip 122:9
**Scaffold:** blood of Mr. Emmet on the s. 53:3
No true Irishman sees a distinction between the battlefield and the s. 143:10
Whether on the s. high, or in battlefield we die 149:4
**Scaldcrows:** I'll not be fed to s. 102:5
**Scandal:** no s. like rags 58:12
**Scapegoat:** the s. for the people 73:8
**Scéal:** 'Gonadh é sin mo s.-sa go nuige sin' 125:11
**Scent:** with red s. chalicing the air 50:7
**Scholar:** *Sweet is the s.'s life* 15:5
the boy ought to be a s. 122:4
**School:** From the Rough Field I went to s. 106:2
Instead o' s., I wove my wab 64:11

*We were most reluctant to attend s.* 130:2
What I mean by an Irish s. is a s. that takes Irish for granted 134:7
**Schoolboy:** with a s.'s pen 39:9
**Schoolmaster:** the s. said with a great deal of sense 62:2
you're an Irish s.! 39:6
**Scian:** Bhí sean s. lena thaobh 118:13
**Scoff:** fools who came to s. 66:9
**Scoil:** ba mhór é ár ndochma roimh an s. 130:2
**Scoláire:** Aoibhinn beatha an s. 15:5
**Scotch:** overrun by a S. interest than an Irish interest 48:4
**Scotia:** de S. ad Brittaniam 9:1
**Scotland:** *If I owned the whole of S.* 14:8
**Scott, Walter:** An Irish W. S. 56:3
**Scoundrel:** a most unscrupulous s. 86:9
one only s. 39:5
**Screaming:** s., steadily, into one another's faces 38:6
**Screech:** *the morning s. on you* 25:12
**Scríbaimm:** Caín s. fo roída ross 12:9
**Scríbainn:** Is scíth mo chrob ón s. 13:7
**Scripture:** the secret S. of the poor 84:1
to burn any s. they found 71:4
**Sea:** A man who is not afraid of the s. will soon be drowned 151:8
far over the s. you will be carried from me 123:9
goes shining to the s. 67:6
I extend the s., its idioms 89:12
into the same old s. 87:10
It's the life of a young man to be going to the s. 153:6
like a rock in the s. 87:5
*My grief on the s.* 16:10
Set in the ring of the s. 49:6
that dolphin-torn, that gong-tormented s. 163:8
the s. became a dance 112:1
*there is hope from the s.* 25:3
**Seal:** Howth was a s. floating darkly in the sun 111:10
**Seanad:** going to be no meeting of the S. 37:8
**Seas:** the slow, sad murmur of far distant s. 147:12
**Secession:** Any attempt at s. will be fought 89:9
**Seditious:** The *United Irishman* is wildly s. 28:2
**See:** not worth going to s. 77:4
**Seed:** *Christ owns the s.* 18:8
**Seen:** should have s. me last Tuesday 95:4
**Segetes:** Nunc viridant s., nunc florent germine campi 142:2
**Sell:** perfect language to s. pigs in 71:5
**Seminary:** in his S. at the above-recited place 38:13
**Senators:** brainless s. 30:15
**Sensual:** Caught in that s. music all neglect / Monuments of unageing intellect 164:9
**Sentiment:** Irish s. sticks in this half-way house 74:7
**Sentiments:** express s. of peace, justice and brotherhood 94:4
**Separate:** s. schools, s. jobs, s. dances, s. pubs 88:3
**Separatist:** I was always an Irish s. 40:8
**Sepulchre:** I'm a whited s. 57:4
**Sepulcrum:** Continet hec hominis cuiusdam terra s. 132:6
**Sergeant:** 'Oh Mrs. McGrath', the S. said 21:9
the S. turned and waddled towards the building 63:14
**Sermon:** What kind of s. was it? 79:8
**Servant:** cracked looking glass of a s. 79:10
I am the hired s. of Ireland 120:1
**Servants:** *the professional feelings of Irish s.* 32:6
**Serve:** will not s. that in which I no longer believe 79:4
**Servitude:** exchange for s. to Westminster 53:12
s. is at once the consequence 49:11
**Seventeen:** the knowledge of thirty-five and the blood of s. 99:2
**Sewer:** the s. of their clique 78:10
**Sex:** She could choose s. and meet him unarmed 35:7
Surely we won't for the sake of easy s. 90:6
**Sexton:** a parish priest and his s. 96:2
**Sgread:** S. mhaidne ort 25:12
**Shabbiness:** moved by the tragic s. 77:1
**Shadow:** to know that my s. and your ghost 69:2
**Shakespeare:** S? he said. I seem to know the name 79:14
**Shame:** under it she can hide both her burden and her s. 146:5
**Shameless:** it was as if what they did was s. 117:1
**Shamrock:** he called it the dear little S. of Ireland 41:4
the s. is by law forbid 18:6
the S. shine for ever new! 50:12
**Shan Van Vocht:** Says the S.V.V. 22:10
**Shandon:** I often think of / those S. Bells 99:11
the Bells of S. 23:8
**Shannon, River:** the dark mutinous S. waves 78:3
the Liffey is to the S. 66:2
the River S.'s full of fish 32:2
**Shawl:** in an ould plaid s. 58:2
**Shawls:** the best s. of the Coombe 73:5
**Sheaf:** some garnered s. of tragedy 87:2
**Sheep:** I saw the s. with their lambs 73:7
**Shelmalier:** O my bold S. 102:8
**Shelter:** there is no s. on it for a sparrow 66:5
**Shepherds:** While s. watched their flocks by night 154:2
**Sheridan:** where were S. and Colman 36:4
**Shift:** *I used to wear a s. that was always new* 13:12
**Shillings:** reduce the two girls to s. and pence 62:2
the bright s. of March 81:11
**Ship:** the s. that my true love sails in 23:13
**Ships:** And my thoughts on white s. 44:10
the builders of s., / Tramp thro' the winter eve 140:3
**Shit:** in cow s. and horse s. and sheep s. 58:8
**Shooting:** S. is a popular sport in the countryside 114:4
**Shore:** leaves us, at eve, on the bleak s. alone 107:11
My boat is on the s. 36:5
**Short:** S. Trots with a Cultured Mind 38:8
**Shot:** I am to be s. at dawn 43:5

**Shout:** Such is your s. 74:3
**Shower:** A coming s. your shooting corns presage 149:8
**Shroud:** buried us without s. or coffin 72:7
**Síabra:** S. mo chobra mo gné 11:8
**Sigh:** long sort of s. seemed to rise from us all 61:11
**Sign:** like a s. from the Almighty 84:3
**Signboard:** he paused at the door, and looked up at the s. 111:14
**Signed:** What I have s. I will stand by 69:12
**Significance:** it has no other s. 52:9
**Silence:** filled by the long s. of reply 87:2
Question not the s. 87:1
S., exile and cunning 79:4
that promise of s., exile and cunning 116:8
the cold chain of s. had hung o'er thee long 107:5
to face the s. that would sourly thicken as their own two deaths came closer 156:4
**Silent:** *A s. mouth is melodious* 24:14
s. is this wakehouse 73:6
S., Oh Moyle! be the roar of thy water 108:13
they sat s., without a move 34:8
**Siller:** Anything that had the s. 95:1
**Silver:** Mine were not born with s. spoon in gob 139:7
**Silvis:** En s. caesa fluctu meat acta carina 45:1
**Simple-mindedness:** he mocked at my s.-m. 120:7
**Simplicity:** beautiful and affecting s. 33:11
**Sin:** English a necessary s. 71:5
s. abounded in the dusty places of the office 135:8
there is no s. except stupidity 160:8
**Sing:** Asked to s. the English version 39:4
*Crionog, it is proper to s. of you* 117:3
I hear the sweet lark s. 60:1
**Singing:** Swelled with the mournful s. / of a sad century 135:10
**Sinister:** this s. country 77:1
**Sinn Feiner:** less complaint than a S.F. makes 57:7
**Sins:** Our s. are tawdry, our virtues childlike 123:5
Two s. I remember 154:7
**Síol:** Ag Críost an s. 18:8
**Sister:** Lord, confound this surly s. 153:5
**Sisters:** I would have the two s. embrace like one brother 138:6
**Situations:** God hungers for s. 51:13
**Siúl:** ag s. le ciumhais na habhann 104:2
S., s., s., a rúin 18:5
**Sixpence:** Ah, kind Christian, do not grudge / the s. promised on the brudge 166:5
I meant to have got s. apiece all round 35:12
**Skibbereen:** another reason why I left old S. 22:2
**Skidar:** Ivan Potschjinski S. 61:6
**Skill:** their s. is . . . beyond that of any nation 37:7
**Skin:** let the weather lend a s. 58:4
**Skinn:** a smooth s. of tender grasse 64:5
**Skirts:** S. were shorter than ever 95:2
**Skreen:** the verdant banks of S. 22:13
**Skull:** a snuff-box of his s. 28:7
take this stick and smash this s. 60:9
**skulls:** Did you ever hear of the s. they have in the city of Dublin 152:10
**Slack:** you seldom are s. 66:17
**Slat:** Nuair a críonas an ts. ní bhÍonn uirri trácht 25:15
**Slattery:** S.'s Mounted Fut 62:4
**Slaughter:** there was great s. then 72:15
**Slave:** all a knave or half a s. 76:1
the female worker is the s. of that s. 46:8
**Slaves:** and an army of s. 36:3
as if they had never been s. 51:9
crawling s. like them . . . prevent our being a nation 119:7
for slumbering s. 51:5
instead of angry s. make us contented citizens 144:2
To oppressors more hateful to s. more endeared 128:9
**Sleep:** *Etan will not s. alone* 12:10
I start in my s. 82:11
*s. a little, a little, little* 14:3
When you are old and grey and full of s. 165:1
**Sléibhe:** Na mórsh. andaig ro tesctha co rinnib 123:3
Pós bean s. 24:9
**Sliabh Gallion:** bonny, bonny S. G. braes 22:11
**Slides:** illustrated by magic lantern s. 68:9
**Sligo:** the Orange Maid of S. 127:11
**Sloe:** blacker than the s. 38:10
If I go by many a s. bush 73:3
*My beloved is like s.-blossom* 16:8
**Small:** when the s. rise up 68:13
**Smell:** a sweet, rich, poor man's s. 48:9
Dublin, which objected to the s. 66:3
only the absence of the s. of women 116:10
**Smile:** sporting an eye-glass, a lisp and a s. 86:5
**Smiles:** Cold as your own wan s. 87:8
Tell her it lived upon s. and wine 109:11
*three s. that are worse than grief* 12:4
**Smiling:** s. derisively at a policeman 28:8
**Smoke:** the s. from that man's pipe 68:14
'there's no use asking you to s.' 122:5
Turf s. is talked upon 48:9
*Where there is s. there is fire* 24:8
**Snail:** not a s. on our walls 88:8
**Snakes:** the s., in a manner most antic 98:12
**Sneer:** Where men can do nothing but s., they no longer s. at other nations 142:9
**Sniper:** the s. turned over the dead body 123:12
**Snobs:** insufferable Gaelic s. 39:7
**Snow:** s. was general all over Ireland 78:3
**Snuff-box:** a s.-b of his skull 28:7
into a musical s.-b. 71:7
**Sober:** s. — that they might not want discretion 148:8
while s., be grave and discreet 49:9
**Social:** to say nothing of his s. standing 53:10
**Socialism:** cannot wait until the people are ready for s. 102:10

**Socialist:** the S. workers are his sole allies 57:2
**Socialists:** S. are a Protestant variety of Communists 131:12
**Socks:** to arrive with s. to darn 77:6
**Soft:** A s. day, thank God! 89:4
**Softly:** Tread s., s., / O' men coming in 44:9
**Soggarth:** S. Aroon 27:4
**Soil:** O stony grey s. of Monaghan 81:12
**Soils:** We took the kindlier s. 72:16
**Soilse:** gan mhairg, gan mhoill, ar s. an lae 104:2
**Soldier:** he is a natural s. 83:11
I am glad I am getting a s.'s death 43:5
the s. is proof against an argument 103:12
Would you like to make a s. out of your son Ted? 21:9
**Soldiers:** a plenteous crop of s. 40:13
And S., Red S., you've seen many lands 44:11
if your s. were able to put as good a fight 54:1
Ireland gives England her s. 104:1
Irish s. give impetus to those military operations which require . . . more devilment than prudence 143:2
S. are we 82:6
the brave stupidity of s. 94:2
**Sole:** a maid so neat about the s. 38:2
**Solitude:** the sense of s. was immense 151:9
**Solomon:** S.! Where is thy throne? 100:2
**Someris:** So dew on grasse in s. dai 104:6
**Song:** Bird S. had shrivelled and died 96:4
full of s. and gossip 48:7
I sing you a s. of peace and love 82:9
Joxer's s., Joxer's s. 118:3
of s. to his sunburst flies 68:4
Roll forth my s., like the rushing river 100:6
there came a s. into my mind 104:9
three with a new s.'s measure 129:15
*Wouldn't a s. be better than a scowling face?* 92:2
**Songs:** All the Irish political s. 51:9
All their s. are sad 41:7
crooning s. of hatred 56:4
marching down with s. of joy 40:7
She sings the wild s. of her dear native plains 108:12
the s. that were sung in the days we were young 133:5
their s. of Philadelphia 48:10
thy s. were made for the pure and free 109:3
**Sons:** her trust is in her s. 51:10
My s. were faithful and they fought 134:3
**Sorrow:** Has s. thy young days shaded 107:9
Of his fault and his s. behind 109:10
they leaped from their pit of s. 46:13
**Sorry:** s. I did not go for his throat 53:8
**Soul:** a faithful s. would walk 38:12
As if that s. were fled 108:16
Could not bring that proud s. under 109:2
forge in the smithy of my s. 79:5
has never surrendered her s. 53:1
He did not feel he was a free s. 106:13
His s. might have burned with a holier flame 108:4
His s. swooned slowly 78:3
in heaven your s. find rest 22:12
My immortal s.? 62:11
my s. soars enchanted 60:1
My s. was an old horse 81:9
plainly in the mirror of my s. 84:8
remember to pray for the s. 61:6
'Room for the s. of the Wanderer!' 101:10
save a single Papish s. 54:11
that can tell how beloved was the s. that's fled 107:13
the chain on the s. 51:8
the release of the s. from hateful and hated bodies 96:5
thou s. of love and bravery! 109:3
while I deliver / My s. of thee! 100:6
**Southern:** a reference made here to S. Ireland 47:4
**Sow:** the old s. that eats her farrow 79:3
**Spain:** And the King o' S.'s daughter 44:10
**Spancelled:** as the s. will until time be over 46:13
**Spanish:** Riding on two S. asses 60:6
*S. ale shall give you hope* 17:3
the captain's S. tears 31:13
who should I spy but a S. lady 38:2
**Spare:** S. all I have 58:13
**Spark:** like a rosy s. 68:4
**Sparrow:** no shelter on it for a s. 66:5
**Speaking:** not qualified for public s. 73:13
**Speech:** manned every s. with checkpoints 72:1
that child's grandchild's / s. stumbles 105:15
*the Munsterman's s. is tuneful* 17:4
**Sphere:** pictured itself as a large hollow s. 29:7
**Spires:** the green s. of Ardoyne 103:6
the sharp s. of St. Peter's 103:6
**Spirits:** the quantity of ardent s. 23:4
**Spoilers:** the crafty s. prey 50:9
**Sport:** Shooting is a popular s. in the countryside 114:4
**Sports:** foreign and fantastic field s. 48:2
**Spot:** those fellows we put on the s. were going to put a lot of us on the s. 43:8
**Spring:** A wet winter, a dry s. 17:5
*as cold as the first day of s.!* 104:5
Be green upon their graves, O happy S.! 147:13
*Bitter cold is icy S.* 13:10
First withered in despair the growth of S. 92:9
Now, with the coming in of the S., the days will stretch a bit 147:7
*Now with the coming of S., the day is beginning to stretch* 128:6
On a s. day surprised us 76:5
S. brought to Rome the first of the wild asparagus 35:8
**Spy:** how the body of a s. 49:12
**Square:** in an open s. 84:6
**Stag:** dragging down some noble s. 65:6
**Stage:** Bulgrudderies of the English s. 39:2
known as 'the s. Irishman' 32:4

Merely to have stood there in the very middle of the s. 96:13
On the s. he was natural 66:13
Sir Edward is a s. Irishman 57:6
'the s!' came from me pat 73:11
**Stammer:** I have never permitted the use of the word 'stammer' 38:4
**Stand:** the Irish government can no longer s. by 90:7
**Star:** But s.-chaser 76:4
by the light of the true lover's s. 61:6
that, sir, was the north s. of my affections 95:1
Truth is a fixed s. 69:4
went her way homeward with one s. awake 44:13
**Starling:** a s. taught to halloo in his ear 61:2
**Stars:** And in the s. the glory of His eyes 135:11
didn't ever remember the sky to have been so full of s. 46:15
I have seen the s. 100:12
shying clods against the visage of the s. 152:6
The s. will wither in the skies before I forgive you 112:12
what is the s., what is the s.? 118:2
When s. are weeping I fly 107:1
**Starved:** Me father was s. dead, and I was s. out to America 143:8
**Starving:** the lads do be tired of s. 27:8
you have a s. population 54:2
**State:** The Corporate S. must come in the end, in Ireland as elsewhere 154:4
**Statesmanship:** s. should avoid an ambiguity 92:4
**Stay:** I can no longer s. with you 70:1
**Steed:** the Arab's Farewell to his S. 114:5
**Steel:** they feared to meet with s. 51:1
**Steeple:** High church, low s. 151:3
**Steeples:** the dreary s. of Fermanagh and Tyrone 42:1
**Stem:** how green the gallant s. 61:4
**Stephen:** S. Dedalus is my name 79:1
**Stick:** the time a little s. would seem as big as your arm 151:12
**Sticks:** the s. and stones of an old grudge 89:15
**Stiff:** *left you s. on the broad of your back* 94:1
**Stile:** I'm sittin' on the s., Mary 55:2
**Stitch:** that they s. on the sheets 89:13
**Stockings:** Golden s. you had on 65:7
**Stóir:** ag déanamh s. 27:1
**Stole:** it was your horse s. me! 32:3
**Stone:** All life ends in death, but s. lives on 103:8
build in s. for ever after 72:15
On the s. outside Dan Murphy's door! 133:5
*Wealth of s. and dearth of clay* 121:10
**Stones:** Erupting on our hands in s. 51:12
the little s. on which the feet of Cathleen have rested 91:5
**Stoneybatter:** in a tumbledown house in a back lane off S. 122:10
**Storm:** Head to the s. as they faced it before! 85:1
she will not bluster or s. 64:6
**Stormont:** at S. we're nailing the flag to the mast 47:12
Of 31 porters at S., 28 are Roman Catholic 10:10
the S. government is no longer in control 90:7
**Story:** All you need to make a s. 96:2
the s. begins where I say it begins 63:3
the s. I might have told 29:2
**Storyteller:** listen to a s. at a fireside 111:12
**Storytelling:** 'Such is the extent of my s.' 125:11
**Stranger:** gain by the feuds of the s. 51:10
**Stream:** many a s. comes rushing down 86:7
**Streams:** I carry off their filthy s. 78:10
**Streets:** Stalls are laid out on the s. 82:4
**Stretched:** the night before Larry was s. 21:13
**Strike:** this is not a s., it is a lock-out 86:9
**Struggle:** the s. for Irish freedom 53:12
**Struggles:** mixed with the profane class-s. 57:2
**Strumpet:** S. City in the Sunset 78:2
**Students:** heating the steps for the comfort of the s. 116:3
University s. are rarely able to cope with universals 117:2
**Study:** if he could have borne the drudgery of that s. 56:1
**Stutter:** that I should s. all through the part 82:14
**Suicide:** Yeh never killed that wan. It's a clear case of s. 122:3
**Súil:** ar chnámh a cúil's a s. iata 104:3
Bíonn s. le muir 25:3
Fil s. nglais 13:6
Scaras lem néall, do réidheas mo s. 104:4
**Suit:** a s. of dress clothes so much too big for him as to make his trousers twin concertinas 145:12
Dressed in a s. of immaculate style 86:5
Far better they s. him 51:4
**Summer:** a bloody s., and no king 17:5
*S. has come, winter gone* 13:4
*S. is a fine season for long journeys* 13:11
the s. bloom will fade away 83:7
**Summerhouse:** the s. by the lake 27:5
**Summons:** taking out a s. against you 69:1
**Sun:** have never seen the s. rising 81:10
heaven's s. doth gently waste 54:9
Seeing the s. but seldom, eating strange meats 140:1
the brass / Belt of serene s. 98:5
the summer s. is falling soft 51:3
the s. shone, having no alternative 29:6
they were eagles in the morning s. 59:5
up to the s., and down to the centre 86:3
**Sunbeams:** a project for extracting s. out of cucumbers 149:15
**Sunday:** goes to Church each S. 50:2
Going to Mass last S. 92:8
she was the S. / In every week 42:10
*S. girl* 24:10
the hardship involved in only having seven hours to drink on a S. 125:1
*you a priest on S.* 17:1

**Sunlight:** The s. on the garden 98:1
**Sunrise:** S. will find us 94:8
**Sunset:** half an hour nearer the s. 83:16
*S. at midday* 11:2
**Surrender:** peal to heaven their 'prentice cry / Their patriot — 'No S.!' 155:5
**Swain:** cheered the labouring s. 66:6
**Swan:** As the s. in the evening moves over the lake 44:13
O s. of slenderness 68:4
When shall the s., her death-note singing 108:14
When the s. drifts upon a darkening flood 163:11
**Swear:** I . . . do solemnly s. allegiance 23:7
**Sweet:** there's nothing half so s. in life 108:6
**Sweethearts:** Having s. but no wives 22:5
**Swift, Jonathan:** enemies of Joyce and S. 30:15
If Berkeley and S. . . . had been compelled to write in Irish 99:5
My mind was like S.'s church 73:13
the curse of S. is upon him 67:10
when S. wrote to the whole people of Ireland 69:10
**Swimsuit:** the Devil in a Pigskin S. 131:3
**Swoon:** in a s., but she is not dead 68:1
**Sword:** All could use the s. and pen 86:6
fall the bright s. of Erin 107:2
I hail the s. as a sacred weapon 103:13
in after life he can grasp a s. 84:2
lay his s. by his side 107:14
put to the s. the whole number 48:3
Was it to be peace or the s. 35:7
**Swords:** Your s. they may glitter 87:16
**Symbol:** I stand as a s. for the Republic 52:5
It is a s. of Irish art 79:10
**Symbols:** No s. where none intended 29:14
**Sympathy:** never had any s. with the fight 76:6
**Synge, J. M.:** enemies of S. 30:15
the chap that writes like S. 79:14
who had drowned himself in the Liffey . . . had in his pocket a copy of S.'s play 'Riders to the Sea' 165:3

**Table:** even a word across the t. 52:5
*the width of a t.* 57:3
**Tabula:** T. tantum! 57:3
**Tae:** Marbh le t. 25:7
**Tailor:** A tinker an' a t. 50:3
**Talam:** t. for-rabai rochrith 31:10
**Talents:** feeble and ostentatious t. 60:4
used his t. for the good of his country 67:10
**Talk:** quackery, puffery and endless t. 105:3
**Talked:** I expected to be t. about at the end of a thousand years 139:16
There is only one thing in the world worse than being t. about, and that is not being t. about 160:17
**Talker:** I met the love-t. one eve 38:10
**Talking:** It is a lovely country, but very melancholy, except that the people never stop t. 162:1
We never stop t. The Irish are the most gifted people in that line 161:15
**Tall:** I noticed a t. man seated 65:10
**Tallow:** our necessity of eating the composition of t. and starch did not only nourish and support us 158:4
**Tandy, Napper:** I met wid N. T. 18:6
**Tangerine:** I peel and portion / A t. 98:2
**Tanyard:** Down by the t. side 17:8
**Taoiseach:** dreams of being T. 71:6
**Tar:** a bold young Irish t. 19:11
**Tara:** And when T. rose so high 86:6
*T. is grass* 16:6
the harp that once, thro' T.s halls 108:16
**Task:** the historic t. of this generation 88:6
**Taste:** and a small t. of Hebrew 39:1
postage stamps and coinage . . . as the silent ambassadors on national t. 165:6
**Tavern:** there is a t. in the town 70:1
**Tax:** to t. and to please 34:11
**Tea:** *Dead with t.* 25:7
Kilrea for drinking t. 30:8
Put whiskey in me t. 81:16
t. and toast and muffin rings 30:3
T. with Madam Gonne MacBride 95:7
**Teachers:** *we learned t., yes, and pious priests* 141:11
**Teaches:** *any anvil . . . t. the one who strikes it* 11:1
**Teamair:** Tá an T. 'na féar 16:6
**Teanga:** Nach fearr ná san an dá t. bheith aige? 130:3
**Tear:** each t. was large as hail 20:7
*every t. would turn a mill* 18:4
It is not the t. at this moment shed 107:13
the t. and the smile in thine eyes 107:6
**Tears:** Her cold t. splattered 77:7
In t. our last farewell was taken 108:2
let its t. of blood evaporate 71:7
Sad, silent and dark, be the t. that we shed 108:5
the captain's Spanish t. 31:13
**Teeth:** The dragon's t. were sown 40:13
**Telescope:** I wish I had brought my t. 68:14
**Temperament:** his impetuous t. 53:10
**Temples:** brassy t. of American eating houses 82:13
**Tempt:** All things can t. me from this craft of verse 163:6
**Temptation:** I can resist everything except t. 160:15
**Ten:** Before that I was t. 64:11
sooner than t. pound in my hand 69:2
**Tenant:** the evicted t. takes terrible reprisals 28:10
**Tenants:** All disputes between the t. were then settled 28:4
**Tender:** you know I'm but t. 22:3
**Terrier:** keen as a t. in those days 63:4
**Territory:** to cross t. held by the Mickeys 71:3
**Terror:** that t. dogs us 72:15
**Thady:** T., foe to sober thinking 73:10
**Theatre:** If the Irish t. ceases to reflect Irish life 69:9
**Theory:** had evolved a strange t. 73:8

**Thief:** a black-an'-tan / a t. 50:3
After they have called you a t. and a liar 90:11
T. calling to t. 48:5
**Thieve:** reluctant to t. or lie 60:3
**Thieves:** One of the t. was saved 29:12
**Thing:** many a t. a man might know 68:12
we were sent to get one t. 69:14
**Things:** All t. bright and beautiful 9:3
One day these t. must and will be achieved 127:3
The drunkenness of t. being various 98:2
these calm and lovely t. 65:9
t. seem and are not good 84:10
**Thinking:** could be kept from t. by hurling priestly thunderbolts 46:4
there is wishful t. in Hell 89:7
**Thirty:** not . . . t. of the whole number escaped 48:3
**Thought:** Sit in silent trance of t. 54:15
Tony-we-have-the-good-t.-for-you-still 163:1
**Thoughtful:** grown long-haired and t. 72:2
**Thoughts:** Dear t. are in my mind 60:1
Holding men's t. 93:7
Keep your t. off yourself all you can 43:3
T. have tripped my words 42:12
Wak'ning t. that long have slept 109:12
**Three:** O woman of T. Cows, agra! 100:10
*the t. things I loved best* 14:2
*There are t. who await my death* 15:7
t. hard wearying years 74:1
*T. renewals of the world* 12:6
*t. saints one grave do fill* 51:14
*T. sisters of lying* 12:5
*T. smiles that are worse than grief* 12:4
T. things one should do every year 111:12
*T. things that cannot be cured* 24:4
you can do t. things in Irish politics 59:9
**Throat:** And cut her t. And serve her right! 147:11
I can catch you by the t. 59:4
I cut her t. by candlelight 64:4
sorry I did not go for his t. 53:8
**Throne:** One law, one land, one t. 85:2
**Thrush:** I heard a t. sing in a bush 21:2
**Thumb:** ran it through the O of the t. and forefinger 96:3
**Thunder:** Loud roared the dreadful t. 41:2
**Thunderstorm:** lent me his top-coat in the t. 32:1
**Tide:** the t. of lawlessness and the t. of lust and loot 110:9
**Tiger:** Oh, we hate the cruel t. 45:14
**Timber:** *What will we do for t.* 16:5
**Time:** And there t. goes slow 126:9
Dug from the tomb of taste-refining time 143:9
For T., the churl, hath beckoned 108:7
it isn't this t. of year at all 65:10
maybe the devil will give me t.! 60:8
that passed the t. 29:11
The t. of the Barmecides 100:7
these conquerors of t.! 91:6
T.'s noble offspring is the last 30:9
T. was away and somewhere else 97:13
with t. changing the plates 83:14
**Times:** that the good t. were all gone 111:6
**Tine:** An áit a mbíonn toit bíonn t. 24:8
**Tinker:** A t. an' a tailor 50:3
Of t. folk at Galway Fair 96:11
**Tinkers:** Great lads, the T. o' Mourne 140:4
**Tinsmith:** like a t.'s scoop 72:8
**Tipperary:** head of them lived in T. 49:3
**Tír:** Tá genius ag baint leis an t. seo 95:5
**Tir Connell:** T. C.'s dread war-cry 102:9
**Tirconail:** T.! On the hem of the Royal Hill 93:11
**Tithe:** 'goidé an cinéal tithe iad sin?' 99:12
**Tobacco:** may be growing unlicensed t. 68:14
smoking a pipe of Irish-grown t. 125:2
the last respects in sad t. 73:6
who'd choose t. in place of a wife? 93:3
**Tobar:** go triomaítear an t. 25:1
**Toit:** An áit a mbíonn t. bíonn tine 24:8
**Tolerance:** the t. of crows 54:8
**Tolerates:** surprised that God t. them so long 14:9
**Tomb:** can build him a t. 51:4
my t. remain uninscribed 56:8
*this land holds also the t. of a man* 132:6
though in her t. she lies 68:1
**Tongs:** I'll send this red-hot t. fizzling 60:7
**Tongue:** I can look at my own t. for less money 144:10
they still / speak the old t. 105:15
to lose your native t. 51:8
**Took:** We t. it from them 72:16
**Toome:** On the Bridge of Toome today 38:11
**Top-coat:** he lent me his t.-c. 32:1
**Tourist:** a worried t. 27:7
**Towel:** I fold my t. with what grace I can 84:9
**Towers:** He sees the round t. of other days 108:1
the pillar t. of Ireland 91:6
**Town:** At half-past one the t. was silent 73:10
Dublin made me and no little t. 92:6
five or six people who live in the same t. and hate each other 140:9
I know a t. tormented by the sea 126:9
If I had not heard similar claims made for every little Irish t. I had ever known 155:8
O my small t. of Ireland 31:3
The t. of Passage / Is both large and spacious 99:10
this was never my t. 97:10
who passes through a country t. 33:9
**Townland:** But the best is my own t. 93:10
**Towns:** One of the most flourishing t. in Ireland 88:1
**Trace:** I cannot t. the line of my own future life 65:1
**Trade:** *each at his own t.* 12:2
who gave you the Free T.? 61:2
With equitable taxation and flourishing t. 44:2
**Trades Unions:** the T.U . go one betther be sacrificin' a hundred 117:11
**Traditions:** the t. to which we are heirs 65:5
**Tragedy:** some garnered sheaf of t. 87:2

**Train:** like waiting for a t. in Mullingar 94:11
the Traveller complained to the guard of the t. 163:2
**Trains:** T. came threading quietly through my dozing childhood 98:3
**Trait:** one t. of Mrs. Jephson's character 35:10
**Traitor:** I am no t.; I die a persecuted man 129:11
I have heard of an Irish t. 71:1
**Traitors:** Among the best t. 53:4
call all those opposed to us t. 92:5
though cowards flinch and t. sneer 45:16
**Tralee:** That made me love Mary, the Rose of T. 110:11
**Tram:** from dangling so long in the t. 32:9
**Tramline:** along the Dalkey t. 32:10
**Tramp:** the gifted son sinks also, and soon is a t. on the roadside 151:14
**Trance:** Sit in silent t. of thought 54:15
**Translate:** Such as cannot write, t. 52:1
**Translation:** scarcely possible for any t. fully to convey 33:11
**Transom:** a boot up the t. 54:4
**Trap:** a t. waiting to spring 63:2
**Travel:** In her t. it is her cloak and safeguard 146:5
**Traveller:** let it once grip a t. 111:9
**Treachery:** His t. had made two parts of him 120:12
**Treaty:** a solemn t. which stipulated for Ireland liberty of conscience 119:4
I am against this t. 52:4
I was bound . . . to oppose the T. 41:8
the Irish T. is in the air 76:2
We have first and foremost to implement the T. 110:8
**Tree:** a branch cut from its t. 105:6
A t., a hill, a wind, a sky 147:9
A woman is a branchy t. / And man a singing wind 147:14
I set my back to a hawthorn t. 22:13
I shall be like that t., I shall die at the top 151:4
Or crab t. from Renvyle 73:3
*sloe blossom on the dark thorn t.* 16:8
unfabled Incense T. 50:7
**Trees:** In my childhood t. were green 97:2
Is known by the t. 42:9
the t. are growing tall, my love 19:3
**Treíde:** T. as dile lem for-ácbas 14:2
**Trí:** Go réidh, a bhean na dt. mbó! 16:1
T. aithgin in domuin 12:6
T. gena atá messa brón 12:4
T. ní nach dtig a leigheas 24:4
T. seithir góa 12:5
'T. tréithe do dhaingnigh sinn' 124:2
**Trial:** I was sent for t. 19:10
the hour of her t. draws near 25:18
**Triangle:** that old t. / Went jingle jangle 30:1
**Trinity College Dublin:** It takes forty years to become a Senior Fellow of T.C.D. 99:9
**Triúr:** T. atá ag brath ar mo bhás 15:7
**Troopers:** the t. of her Majesty 23:6
**Troth:** 'Here is back your plighted t.' 22:12
**Trouble:** there's t., black and bitter 87:9
**Trousers:** *'I wonder . . . would Mici's t. fit you?'* 99:14
**Trowel:** She lays it on with a t. 45:4
**True:** But a t. man like you, man 76:1
He was to God and Ireland t. 126:1
**Trust:** her t. is in her sons 51:10
put your t. in God, my boys 31:8
**Trusts:** not one t. the other 43:11
**Truth:** instead of telling the t. and making enemies 87:3
the golden heresy of t. 140:7
the t. is rarely pure and never simple 160:11
T. from his lips prevailed 66:9
T. is a fixed star 69:4
**Tuesday:** 'Ah but you should have seen me last T.' 95:4
**Tune:** a lovely dreamy t. 69:3
Irish melts into the t. 39:4
**Tunes:** the t. to the elegant measures you trod 31:1
**Turf:** t.-scented air 31:3
T. smoke is talked upon the darker blue 48:9
**Turk:** Jew, T. or Atheist 15:1
**Turnips:** his eyes were the size of t. 60:6
**Turpissimus:** Nemo repente fuit t. 99:9
**Twenty:** T. golden years ago 100:9
T. men from Dublin town 69:7
*T. years a child* 25:4
**Two:** There were t. glasses and t. chairs 97:13
**Typist:** reduced him to pawing the hot and willing t. 135:8
**Tyranny:** on the basis of your t. Napoleon hopes to build 36:2
To subvert the t. of our execrable government 155:2
**Tyres:** Dunlop t. are made by darkies 66:3
**Tyrone:** In T., Fermanagh, Down and Antrim 111:2
we see the dreary steeples of Fermanagh and T. 42:1

**Uball:** Mé tuc in n-u. an-úas 10:11
**Ugly:** An u. race 88:4
**Uisce:** Níl meas ar an u. 25:1
**Uladh:** níl Gaeilg ar bith agam ach Gaeilg Chúige U. 113:3
**Úll:** Nuair a bhéas an t-u. apaigh 24:13
**Ulster:** A typical 'U.' conversation 76:3
an iron net through darkest U. 97:4
as she, U., cannot have the *status quo* 142:10
bring Orange U. down 23:5
Catholics are out to destroy U. 33:12
every road in U. veined my heart 103:1
foul U. Tories who have always ruined our party 41:10
I am U., my people an abrupt people 139:5
*I can only speak U. Irish* 113:3
Nobody but an U. man can understand the U. mind 76:9
take my stand by the U. names 73:2

the Catholics have been interfering in U. affairs since 1641 131:6
the country folk of U. 54:10
the material well-being of U. 24:1
*the U. man is accurate but tuneless* 17:4
to become responsible for the government of the Protestant province of U. 47:8
U. Unionists are not loyal to the Crown 74:4
U.: where every hill has its hero 30:7
U. will fight and U. will be right 41:12
*We grew up in the north, in U.* 117:3 *See also* 40:3, 40:4
**Ulstermen:** but your U. 50:9
**Ultach:** Tá ceart gan blas ag an U. 17:4
**Ultramontane:** Am I an U. 49:4
**Umbrellas:** It is with ideas as with u. 83:12
**Unemployment:** It is bad that u. money should be paid at all 103:5
the u. in our bones 51:12
**Unexpected:** In Ireland . . . the u. constantly occurs 99:6
**Unhappiness:** U. like mine, there's no annihilating that 29:4
**Union:** the U. was therefore a manifest injustice 119:2
**United:** both are now, and by God's blessing will, I hope, remain, u. and inseparable 155:1
Make both u. flourish 61:4
**United Irishman:** the U.I. is wildly seditious 28:2
**United Kingdom:** equal citizenship in the U.K. 24:1
We cannot be part of the U.K. merely when it suits us 127:2
**Unity:** U. has got to be thought of 88:7
**Unpleasant:** capacity for making himself u., remarkable even in a native of his province 159:12
**Urinal:** did right to put him over a u. 79:15
**Usna:** who the brave sons of U. betrayed 107:2

**Vacant:** loud laugh that spoke the v. mind 66:7
**Valley:** I'll wander through v. and dell 20:3
Murmurs passed along the v. 40:10
not in this wide world a v. so sweet 109:1
the v. of eternal night 40:7
**Valleys:** the v. of Green Inishowen 55:6
through the v. of our land 91:6
To view yon fair v. 22:11
**Valour:** My v. is certainly going! 144:7
**Value:** A man who knows the price of everything, and the v. of nothing 160:16
an unsuspected and exceptional v. 64:9
**Vampire:** like the V., Dracula, he has bitten me 78:1
**Vase:** You may ruin the v. if you will 107:7
**Venetian:** a black-eyed V. girl before me 36:5
**Vengeance:** come with v. in their eyes 38:11
**Venice:** Ottolie was a very V. 27:7
**Vessel:** let the Irish v. lie 26:2
While a plank of the v. sticks together 68:2
**Vetustus:** v. / dierum et ingenitus 44:5
**Victoricus:** vide in visu noctis virum . . . cui nomen v. 133:2
**Victory:** the materials from which v. is manufactured 86:1
V. must be allowed to rest 52:7
**Vigil:** a Muscovite maiden her v. doth keep 61:6
**Vigilance:** condition . . . is eternal v. 49:11
**Village:** a ghastly midland v. inhabited entirely by a savage peasantry 158:5
loveliest v. of the plain 66:6
**Villages:** *glimmering v. glimpsed* 94:6
**Vinegar Hill:** On V.H., the fatal conclave 72:7
**Violence:** Built upon v. and morose vendettas 97:12
I beg you to turn away from the paths of v. 136:4
the act of v. a grief 51:12
V. inevitably leads to the . . . graveyard 94:3
**Virgin:** and a v. in Rome 50:6
Your drums and your dolled-up v.s 98:7
**Virginal:** a kind of v. beehive 48:7
**Virtuous:** He loved v. girls 82:1
Irish women are the most v. 69:8
through a v. day 48:5
**Visage:**She is very fayre of v. 64:5
**Visible:** Ineluctable modality of the v. 79:11
**Vision:** *Cherish the living coal of your v.* 121:9
**Visions:** He had v. of himself 73:8
**Vitality:** showed astonishing v. in a man of his years 148:12
**Vitam:** perfectamque propter v. aequatur apostolis 142:3
**Voice:** A v. from America shouted to liberty 61:1
find, if you can, a single v. 65:5
He hammered and sang with tiny v. 80:3
Her v. it was chanting melodious 19:7
His v. is of the deep 32:11
his v. sweeter far 38:10
his v. was kind and his heart was true 103:4
I've said everything I can . . . with my v. 91:7
kept her v. up to the very last 79:15
repeatedly raised my v. against it 49:5
Sad is his v. that calls me 79:6
some v. like thunder spake 51:6
*the opening words, 'the v. of the Irish'* 133:2
**Voices:** with the music of our two v. 116:4
**Volunteers:** cannot bear to hear of V. 61:2
So were the V. 40:3
**Voodoo:** the v. of the Orange bands 97:4
**Vowels:** Irish pieties as v. 72:11
**Vox:** legi principium epistolae continentem 'V. Hiberionacum' 133:2

**Wait:** I sit and w. and write 77:12
**Waiting:** I think I know what they're w. for 111:2
We're w. for Godot 29:10

**Wake:** Wasn't it a shame I didn't bear you along with me to Kate Cassidy's w. 153:1
**Wakehouse:** Silent is this w. 73:6
**Walk:** better to w. without shoes and barefooted than to w. without dignity 135:9
*My w. was fine from place to place* 75:2
**Walked:** Oh, she w. unaware 93:7
**Wall:** If there was a w. of brass 30:11
Such a terrible height of a w. 68:10
**Walls:** the high w. of Derry 21:6
**Wanderer:** 'Room for the soul of the w.!' 101:10
**Want:** what can a man w. more? 62:1
**Wants:** w. but little here below 66:11
**War:** action, when it came to the disastrous point, in w. 41:8
As long as w. is regarded as wicked, it will always have its fascination 160:7
created in this country after the Civil W. 88:5
If I send this letter it is w. 89:10
if they want w. they can have it 86:9
no crime in detecting and destroying in w.-time, the spy 43:9
On those who resisted he had made w. 91:3
the w. came down on us here 97:11
w. made upon its vital interests 47:3
**Warrant:** make the w. out in haste 23:3
**Warrior:** He lay like a w. taking his rest, / With his martial cloak around him. 161:13
**Warriors:** *the wild w. from Norway* 12:7
thy w. wander o'er the earth 50:5
**Wars:** all their w. are merry 41:7
**Washing:** bringing down their wee w. to the Muttonburn Stream 21:11
She held that w. was very unhealthy and took the natural gloss off the face 147:16
**Water:** Against the lurid sky over the stained w. 97:8
fight and be fought for on w. 40:5
float them on your clearest w. 65:9
Golden w. for the cart-horses 98:5
hewers of wood and drawers of w. 91:3
Not to use w. for drink 98:13
plunged every day in cold w. 67:4
Sweet w. and space 94:10
*the w. is not thought much of* 25:1
till the w. lips the gunwale 58:3
where there is w. 81:8
**Waters:** As the w. fall short, we see the dreary steeples of Fermanagh 42:1
in whose bosom the bright w. meet 109:1
over a urinal: meeting of the w. 79:15
the lovely w. of the Lee 23:8
your murmuring w. and turf-scented air 31:3
**Wave:** Each w. that we danced on 107:11
W. follows w. into the same old sea 87:10
**Waves:** single / Streak of decency in these w. now 114:2
The burning w. boomed over his sinning head 101:10
the little w. of Breffny 67:7
**Way:** like Dolan's ass, I went a bit of the w. with everybody 120:8
**Weakness:** *they succumbed to the chronic w. of the Irish, and split* 117:10
**Weapons:** *lay your w. down, young lady* 59:13
**Weary:** I w., w. / Of the long sorrow 134:3
**Weather:** has her madness and her w. still 26:1
let the w. lend a skin 58:4
you won't hold up the w. 97:7
**Web:** Instead o' school, I wove my w. 64:11
**Wed:** *I'd wed you without herds* 16:3
**Wedding:** celebrate the w. of Madame Blavatsky and Finn Mac Cumhail 122:1
**Weep:** I w. when I'm waking 82:11
W. no more, sad fountains 54:9
Will w. many days together 64:6
**Welcome:** 'Dan me dear, you're w. here' 21:1
**Well:** I hope this finds all w. at home 126:13
*till the w. goes dry* 25:1
**Wellington:** any greater monstrosity than the W. Monument 66:5
**Wench:** like a young w. that hath a greensickness 64:5
**Wept:** Cathleen w. her thousand welcomes 77:7
**West:** Hurrah for the men of the W.! 139:12
queen of the west! 49:6
Queen of the W.! 54:14
that cloud in the W. 65:1
the W.'s awake 51:6
**Westward:** W. the course of empire 30:9
**Wexford:** I will go to W. and take their place 102:4
We are the boys of W. 80:2
**Wheel:** Ere the w. and the reel stopping their ringing and moving 158:10
when he lay pining on the w. 71:1
**When:** W. he who adores thee 109:10
**Whiskey:** I'd drink nothing but w. and wather 166:2
Put w. in me tay 81:16
**Whisky:** W., drink divine! 126:5
**Whispering:** the Wood of the W. they do call this wood 105:12
**White:** and w. owl's feather 10:6
*Myself and W. Pangur* 12:2
pillow my head on his lily-w. breast 23:13
praise God that we are w. 30:3
**Whores:** do not think of helpful w. / as abberrational blots 144:12
**Why:** 'that's the w.' 'Ah w.?' 58:7
**Wicked:** I hope that you have not been leading a double life, pretending to be w. 160:19
**Widow:** a consumptive, toothless, phthisicky, wealthy w. 95:1
Did you hear of the W. Malone 89:6
I'm a buxom fine w. 82:4
**Wife:** every poet to have a spare w. 81:14
hurried home to my waiting w. 64:4
I ne'er was in hell till I met with your w. 21:3
In every port he finds a w. 31:4

like a quarrelling man and w. 39:4
They get sober, take a w. 22:6
who'd choose tobacco in place of a w.? 93:3
**Wigs:** Forget their feuds, and join to save their w. 149:9
**Wild:** grant me some w. expressions 58:14
**Wilderness:** *a hidden hut in the w.* 13:1
O my child, this w. 39:5
**William:** great and good King W. 28:7
then Orangemen remember King W. 127:8
where they were shown the spot on which King W. landed 110:5
**Willow-tree:** hang my harp on a weeping w.-t. 70:1
**Wind:** A ragged sculpture of the w. 81:7
A w. from the south 89:4
and think the rough w. / less rude 109:8
*Bitter is the w. tonight* 12:7
*breaks in like a stone from a sling* 12:11
*did not get it from the w.* 25:13
It is gone in the w. 100:2
the brown w. of Connacht 38:9
*the rain is carried in on the back of the w.* 104:5
the w. began to play, like country fiddlers 112:1
*the w. is high and cold* 12:8
the w. rose, the sea rose 135:10
'the w. that shakes the barley.' 80:4
**Window:** Would you think Heaven could be so small a thing / As a lit w. on the hills at night? 158:2
**Winds:** let winter w. rave 51:4
**Wine:** Obedience is ice to the w. 43:7
**Winter:** A wet w., a dry spring 17:5
*Summer has come, w. gone* 13:4
the plate glass of w. 89:14
this w. eve how soft! how mild! 155:11
*W.: black, dark and smoky* 13:9
**Wire:** I pray against barbed w. 74:5
**Wisdom:** the w. of serene old age 52:10
*W. comes only with age* 130:1
**Wise:** Since the w. men have not spoken 134:1
to love and be w. 34:11
Who'd ever be w. 72:14
**Wishes:** Ye gods! my w. are confined 90:12
**Witness:** the only representative who was a w. 53:7
**Wits:** Your w. can't thicken in that soft moist air 143:6
**Wives:** proud stupidity of soldiers' w. 94:2
**Woman:** A w. can be proud and stiff/ When on love intent 164:1
A w. is a branchy tree / And man a singing wind 147:14
A w. that's healthy and loving 93:3
an intense passion for a w. 78:7
*any w. that sees this tomb / Breaks wind or laughs* 132:6
being a w. is like being Irish 111:11
*Beware, my son, / W. kind* 44:14
*but a beautiful w.* 17:2
For tho' they love w. and golden store 108:10
*I am an old w. now* 141:5
I heard the Poor Old W. say 87:11
Last week I saw a w. flayed 149:11
[like] a w. without knickers on her 116:11
*Marry a mountain w.* 24:9
My only books / Were W.'s looks 109:4
No w. should ever be quite accurate about her age 160:14
*O w. full of wile* 41:1
O W. of three Cows, agra! 100:10
Oh, God, who does not exist, you hate w. 115:5
the sort of w. who lives for others 89:8
the w. once had danced 83:6
What is a w. with children when nature lets her down? 112:8
What's a w. for? 102:6
When lovely w. stoops to folly 67:1
where every w.'s son 42:11
who would listen to an old w. with one thing and she saying it over 153:6
**Womankind:** All womankind . . . from the highest to the lowest . . . love jokes 148:11
**Women:** And w. with petticoats coloured like flame 130:6
Irish w. are the most virtuous 69:8
It's true that the w. are worse than the men 21:4
some fine fish-w. 73:5
The safety of w. consists in one circumstance 99:2
the w. had hardly a stitch on them 64:2
Two w. to be mixing a cake 68:11
Wake him not with w.'s cries 54:15
Wantin' w. an' drink 140:2
When w. gets wicked they're tarra 101:6
*where the w. are there is gossip* 24:8
'W. there are, but I'm afraid / they cannot find a priest.' 161:11
*w. will not cease from folly* 10:11
**Wonder:** still the w. grew 66:10
**Wood:** the W. of the Whispering they do call this w. 105:12
*When the w. hardens there is no give in it* 25:15
**Wood-kerne:** A w.-k. escaped 72:2
**Wooing:** *A man who comes a-w.* 14:4
**Woolsack:** safely deposited on the English w. 66:1
**Word:** Clay is the w. 81:4
even a w. across the table 52:5
For whom the w. is still a fighting w. 139:6
*have invented a new w.* 60:2
**Words:** but a few more w. to say 56:8
*Few there be, alas / that love the w. of God* 104:6
He came from the North and his w. were few 103:4
hearing w. would put you thinking on the holy Brigid 152:9
Her w. are the w. of truth and soberness 65:5
I could not write the w. Mr. Joyce uses 143:4
I only speak with borrowed w. 43:6
If w. were banknotes, he would filch a wad 112:2
moved only to w. 40:7

so soft that it smudges the w. 98:8
to be my last and latest w. 39:11
W., w., or I shall burst 58:14
**Work:** like lying down after a long day's w. 41:9
My grandmother made dying her life's w. 88:11
My w. is undistinguished 96:10
Perfection of the life, or of the w. 163:9
the terrible w. we all fear this week 102:2
washing out our whole life w. 54:1
W. is the curse of the drinking classes 161:4
w. of such a nature as permanently satisfies the human spirit 47:1
W. your hands from day to day 97:7
**Worker:** the Dublin w. is not a natural revolutionary 83:11
the w. is the slave of the capitalist society 46:8
**Workers:** th' sort o' thing that w. are fed on 118:11
**Workhouse:** begins with me stuck in the gawddam w.! 63:3
the fear of the W. will never come again 60:5
**Working:** the Gift of God is a W. Man 116:6
**World:** a more real w. 64:10
Ah ye w. that I hold dear 115:7
call my spirit from this stormy w. 108:14
God made the w., right? And fair play to him. 112:9
it is time for me to have done with the w. 150:2
'It's not a fair w., love,' said my father 111:6
may the w. go well with thee 70:1
Mere anarchy is loosed upon the w. 164:11
one of the goodliest provinces of the w. 31:11
Over the edge of the w. 89:13
Search the w. all around, from the sky to the ground 158:9
Take the w. fine and aisy 49:1
the end of the w. would put a stop to that 96:3
*the whole w. became dark* 31:10
th' whole w.'s in a terrible state o' chassis 118:8
the w. is large enough for us both 35:4
the w. is only a blue bag 49:2
the w. pulls itself up 64:8
the w. seemed at a standstill 96:7
the w. will wag its head away 69:9
*this w.'s love is gone away* 104:6
*three renewals of the w.* 12:6
We must take some things in this w. by instalments 125:8
w. is crazier 98:2
**Worm:** Have fed the same w. as Blackstone and Gibbon 112:4
**Worth:** not w. going to see 77:4
**Wounds:** prevents her w. from ever healing 85:3
**Wren:** *Better a w. in your fist* 25:8
**Wrens:** if w. he'd make them king 112:2
**Wretch:** Some skull-faced w. 92:9
**Wrists:** cut his w. before we even landed 77:10
**Write:** *I w. well under the woodland trees* 12:9
let no man w. my epitaph 56:8
such as cannot w., translate 52:1
**Writer:** A w., a word that doesn't mean anything 29:17
A w. is to think first 56:5
the Irish w. of English — has no such gloomy problem 95:4
the w. should never forget that he is also a reader 120:6
Unless a w. sink himself into the heart of his own people 47:1
**Writers:** Her w. and artists to banishment 78:8
**Writes:** the chap that w. like Synge 79:14
**Writing:** I've no intention of w. anything 91:7
*My hand is tired from w.* 13:7
**Wrong:** better to do the w. thing 59:9
For sure I don't w. you 66:17
that w.-headed old man 64:7

**Yard:** to stand in the y., my feet on the ground 58:8
**Year:** It isn't this time of y. at all 65:10
*the y. now has its hour* 142:2
To see themselves in one y. tamed 101:8
you're asked to blow each light, each y., / out with your breath 144:11
**Years:** It may be for y. 48:1
My best y. are gone 29:5
Of twice a thousand y. 103:3
the y. like great black oxen tread the world 163:12
the y. to come seemed waste of breath, / A waste of breath the y. behind 164:3
Twenty golden y. ago 100:9
**Yeats, W. B.:** But W. B. was the boy for me 105:9
'Off Willie Y.', sez she 62:7
Referred to by my elders as 'old Parson Y.'s grandson' 44:7
W. Y. is laid to rest 26:2
Y. founded a realistic theatre 106:11
Y. had not dreamed an unstubbed butt 42:4
Y.'s occult mission . . . was to celebrate the wedding 122:1
Y.'s *Terrible Beauty* has become a. . . repressive old crone 34:3
Y. was one of the most devious men 120:7
**Yellow:** *once I was y.-haired* 14:1
the green leaves all turn y. 83:7
**Yes:** and y. I said y. I will y. 80:1
**Yield:** nothing which will not y. to perseverance 35:6
**Young:** *As high-spirited and cheerful as they were when I was y.* 141:6
Not y. and not renewable 84:9
Oh the bonny boy was y. 19:3
Politically, we are a y. nation 92:4
She that was y. and fair / Fallen to dust 160:18
the y. / In one another's arms, birds in the trees 164:9
*there's no doubt it's great to be y.* 130:1
Too fast have those y. days faded 107:9
Y. people of Ireland, I love you 136:5

**Young Ireland:** the ardour of Y. I. had evaporated 147:3
**Youngster:** To be a swaggering y. for an hour 93:5
**Youth:** Cold as the hopes of our y. 87:8
I'd have for mine a y. so fine 22:9
I have looked my last on y. 84:8
squandered the splendid years that the Lord God gave my y. 134:2
with my long-lost y.'s compeers 100:7
y. must with time decay 69:4

# *Bibliography*


Carney, James, *Medieval Irish Lyrics,* Dolmen Press, 1967

Carroll, Joseph, *Ireland in the War Years 1939-1945,* David & Charles, 1975

Dudley Edwards, Owen, & Pyle, Fergus, *1916: The Easter Rising,* MacGibbon Kee, 1968

Greene, David, & O'Connor, Frank, *A Golden Treasury of Irish Poetry (A.D. 600-1200),* Macmillan, 1956/67

Kee, Robert, *The Green Flag,* Weidenfeld & Nicolson, 1972

Lyons, F. S. L., *Ireland since the Famine,* Weidenfeld & Nicolson, 1973

Mansergh, N., *The Irish Question 1840-1921,* Allen & Unwin, 1975

Maxwell, Constantia, *The Stranger in Ireland,* Jonathan Cape, 1954

Murphy, Gerard, *Early Irish Lyrics,* Oxford University Press, 1956

O'Brien, Conor Cruise, *States of Ireland,* Hutchinson, 1972

Ó Tuama, Seán, & Kinsella, Thomas, *An Duanaire: 1600-1900,* Dolmen Press, 1981

Quinn, D. B., *The Elizabethans and the Irish,* Cornell University Press, 1966

Rose, R., *Governing Without Consensus,* Faber & Faber, 1971

Taylor, Rex, *Michael Collins,* Hutchinson, 1958

# *Acknowledgements*

The author and the publisher wish to thank the following for permission to reproduce copyright material:

**Auden, W. H.** Faber & Faber, London, and Random House, New York;
**Banville, J.** and Secker & Warburg;
**Beckett, M.** Poolbeg Press, Dublin;
**Beckett, S.** John Calder, London;
**Behan, B.** Beatrice Behan and Hutchinson, London;
**Bell, S. H.** Blackstaff Press, Belfast;
**Berryman, J.** Faber & Faber, London, and Farrar Straus & Giroux, New York;
**Betjeman, J.** from *Collected Poems,* John Murray (Publishers) Ltd., London;
**Birmingham, G. A.** A. P. Watt Ltd., London;
**Boland, E.** Arlen House, Dublin;
**Bowen, E.** from *The Collected Stories of Elizabeth Bowen,* reproduced by permission of Curtis Brown Ltd., London (literary executors of the estate of Elizabeth Bowen), Jonathan Cape Ltd., and Alfred A. Knopf, Inc., New York;
**Broderick, J.** John Johnston, Literary Agent, London;
**Bullock, S.** from *The Loughsiders,* Ward Lock Ltd., London, and Harrap Ltd., London;
**Burke, H. L.** Poolbeg Press, Dublin;
**Campbell, J.** Simon Campbell and Allen Figgis, Dublin;
**Campbell, P.** Mrs. Campbell and Blond & Briggs, London;
**Carroll, P. V.** Macmillan, London;
**Clarke, A.** Dolmen Press, Portlaoise;
**Coghill, R.** Allen Figgis, Dublin;
**Colum, M.** Dolmen Press, Portlaoise;
**Colum, P.** Dolmen Press, Portlaoise;
**Corkery, D.** Mercier Press, Cork and Gill & Macmillan Ltd., Dublin;
**Craig, M.**;
**Cronin, A.** Poolbeg Press, Dublin;
**Cross, E.** Mercier Press, Cork;
**Daiken, L.** Dolmen Press, Portlaoise;
**Daly, I.** Poolbeg Press, Dublin;
**Deane, S;**
**Doyle, L.** Gerald Duckworth & Co. Ltd., London;

**Dunleavy, J. P.** J. P. Dunleavy and Olympia, London;
**Durcan, P.** Gallery Press, Dublin;
**Eglinton, J.** The Educational Company of Ireland, Dublin;
**Ervine, St. John** The Society of Authors as the literary representative of the estate of St. John Ervine;
**Fallon, Padraic** Dolmen Press, Portlaoise;
**Fallon, Peter** Gallery Press, Dublin;
**Farrell, M.** from *Thy Tears Might Cease,* Kevin Farrell and Hutchinson Ltd., London;
**Farren, R.**;
**Fitzmaurice, G.** Dolmen Press, Portlaoise;
**Friel, B.** and Faber & Faber, London;
**Gallagher, P.** Templecrone Co-operative Society, Donegal;
**Galvin, P.**;
**Gibbon, M.**;
**Gogarty, Oliver St. John** Oliver Gogarty and Doubleday & Co. Inc. New York;
**Gregory, P.** P. & B. Gregory, Belfast;
**Gwynn, S.** Dundalgan Press (W. Tempest);
**Harbinson, R.**;
**Hartnett, M.** Gallery Press, Dublin;
**Heaney, S.** from (a) *North* (b) *Death of a Naturalist* (c) *Door into the Dark* (d) *Wintering Out,* reprinted by permission of Faber and Faber Ltd. and Farrar Straus & Giroux, New York;
**Hewitt, J.** Blackstaff Press, Belfast;
**Higgins, F. R.** Maurice Fridberg, Dublin;
**Hobson, B.** Anvil Books, Dublin;
**Howard Jones, S.** Oxford University Press;
**Hutchinson, P.** Gallery Press, Dublin;
**Ireland, D.** Blackstaff Press, Belfast;
**Iremonger, V.** Dolmen Press, Portlaoise;
**Irvine, A.** Appletree Press, Belfast;
**Johnston, J.** Jennifer Johnston and Hamish Hamilton;
**Johnston, D.** Denis Johnston and Colin Smythe;
**Joyce, J.** The Society of Authors, London; Random House, Inc., New York, and The Bodley Head, London, for *Ulysses*; Jonathan Cape Ltd., London and the executors of the James Joyce Estate for *A Portrait of the Artist as a Young Man, Dubliners, Stephen Hero;* Viking Penguin Inc., New York, for: (1) From *Dubliners* by James Joyce. Copyright 1916 by B. W. Huebsch. Definitive text Copyright © 1967 by the Estate of James Joyce. (2) From *Finnegans Wake* by James Joyce. Copyright 1939 by James Joyce. Copyright renewed 1967 by George Joyce and Lucia Joyce. (3) From *A Portrait of the Artist as a Young Man* by James Joyce. Copyright 1916 by B. W. Huebsch. Copyright renewed 1944 by Nora Joyce. Definitive text Copyright © 1964 by the Estate of James Joyce. (4) 'Pomes Penyeach' from *Collected Poems* by James Joyce. Copyright 1918 by B. W. Huebsch. Copyright renewed 1946 by Nora Joyce;
**Kavanagh, P.** Katherine B. Kavanagh, Dublin;
**Kelly, M.** Poolbeg Press, Dublin;
**Kearney, P.** P. J. Burke, Dublin;

**Kennelly, B.** Gallery Press, Dublin;
**Kilroy, T.** Thomas Kilroy and Faber & Faber, London;
**Kinsella, T.** Thomas Kinsella and Dolmen Press, Portlaoise;
**Kipling, R.** A. P. Watt Ltd., London and Doubleday & Co. Inc., New York, for excerpt from 'Ulster', copyright 1912 by Rudyard Kipling from the book *Rudyard Kipling's Verse: Definitive Edition.* Reprinted by permission of the National Trust and Doubleday & Company, Inc.;
**Lavin, M.**;
**Leitch, M.** Deborah Rogers Ltd., London, for *The Liberty Lad and Poor Lazarus*;
**Leonard, H.**;
**Leslie, Sir Shane** Lady Iris C. Leslie;
**Lewis, C. S.** William Collins Sons & Co. Ltd., London and Macmillan Publishing Co. Inc., New York, for *The Screwtape Letters* ;
**Longley, M.** Arts Council of Northern Ireland, Belfast;
**Luce, A. A.** from 'Fishing & Thinking', reprinted by permission of Hodder & Stoughton Ltd., Kent;
**Lynd, R. W.** J. M. Dent & Sons Ltd., London;
**MacBride, M. G.** Sean MacBride;
**MacDonagh, D.** Faber and Faber Ltd., London, from *The Hungry Grass*; and Maurice Fridberg, Dublin
**MacGill, F.** Caliban Books, London;
**MacGrianna, S.** An Gúm, Baile Átha Cliath;
**Macken, W.** Macmillan, London and Basingstoke and Harold Matson Company Ltd., New York;
**MacLiammóir, M.** Dublin Gate Theatre;
**MacMahon, B.** B. MacMahon and A. P. Watt Ltd., London;
**MacManus, F.** Mercier Press, Cork, Jonathan Cape, London and the estate of Francis MacManus;
**MacNeice, L.** from *The Collected Poems of Louis MacNeice,* Faber & Faber, London;
**McCabe, E.**;
**McFaddan, R.** Blackstaff Press, Belfast;
**McLaverty, M.** Poolbeg Press, Dublin;
**MacNamara, B.** Anvil Books, Dublin;
**MacNamara, G.** The Educational Company of Ireland Ltd., Dublin;
**Mhac An Tsaoi, M.**;
**Milligan, A.** Gill & Macmillan Ltd., Dublin;
**Molloy, M.**;
**Montague, J.** Dolmen Press, Portlaoise;
**Muldoon, P.**
**Mulkerns, LV.**;
**Murdoch, I.** Chatto and Windus Ltd., London;
**Murphy, M. J.** Blackstaff Press, Belfast, and Dolmen Press, Portlaoise;
**Murphy, R.** from *Sailing to an Island* and *High Island,* Faber & Faber Ltd., London;
**Murphy, S.** Routledge & Kegan Paul Ltd., London;
**Murphy, T.**;
**na gCopaleen, M.** Granada Publishing, Hertfordshire and Seaver Books, New York;
**Ní Chuilleanáin, E.** Gallery Press, Dublin;
**O'Brien, E.**;

**O'Brien, F.** Granada Publishing Ltd., Hertfordshire, A. M. Heath & Co., London; the Estate of the late Flann O'Brien; quotes from *At Swim Two Birds* and *The Third Policeman* by Flann O'Brien, used by permission of Walker & Co., New York;
**O'Brien, K.** Arlen House, Dublin and David Higham Associates, London;
**O'Brien, K. C.** Poolbeg Press, Dublin;
**O'Byrne, D.** estate of the late Sir Arnold Bax;
**O'Casey, S.** from *Juno and the Paycock* and *The Plough and the Stars,* Macmillan, London and Basingstoke and St. Martin's Press Inc., New York;
**O'Connor, F.** reprinted by permission of A. D. Peters & Co. Ltd.;
**Ó Criomhthain, T.** Oxford University Press;
**O'Direáin, M.** Stiofán B. Ó Hannracháin;
**O'Faolain, S.**;
**O'Duffy, E.** Macmillan, London and Basingstoke;
**O'Flaherty, L.** Wolfhound Press, Dublin; Jonathan Cape Ltd., London, for *The Short Stories of Liam O'Flaherty*;
**O'Floinn, C.** C. Ó Marcaigh, Baile Átha Cliath;
**O'Ríordáin, S.** Sáirséal Ó Marcaigh, Baile Átha Cliath;
**Ormsby, F.** Oxford University Press;
**Ó Súileabháin, M.** The Educational Company of Ireland, Dublin;
**Phelan, J. L.** Sidgwick & Jackson, London;
**Plunkett, J.** reprinted by permission of A. D. Peters & Co. Ltd.;
**Powell, A.** William Heinemann, London;
**Power, R.** Poolbeg Press, Dublin;
**Praeger, R. L.** Allen Figgis & Co., Dublin;
**Robinson, L.** The National Theatre Society, Dublin;
**Rodgers, W. R.** from *Europa and the Bull,* Secker & Warburg, London;
**Rowley, R.** Blackstaff Press, Belfast;
**Russell, G.** Colin Smythe, Buckinghamshire;
**Sayers, P.** Oxford University Press;
**Shaw, G. B.** The Society of Authors on behalf of the Bernard Shaw Estate;
**Shiels, G.** Macmillan, London and Basingstoke;
**Simmons, J. S. A.** Blackstaff Press, Belfast;
**Somerville & Ross** John Farquharson, London;
**Stephens, J.** The Society of Authors on behalf of the copyright owner Mrs. Iris Wise, Macmillan Publishing Co. Inc. New York, *The Crock of Gold* (Copyright 1912 by Macmillan Publishing Co. Inc. renewed 1940 by James Stephens) and *Collected Poems* of James Stephens. Copyright 1912, 1915, 1916, 1918 by Macmillan Publishing Co., Inc., renewed 1940, 1943, 1944, 1946, by James Stephens;
**Strong, E.**;
**Stuart, F.**;
**Tracy, H.**;
**Trevor, W.**;
**Ussher, A.** from *The Mind and Face of Ireland,* Dolmen Press, Portlaoise; Anthony Sheil Associates Ltd.;
**Wall, M.**;
**Watters, E. R.** Allen Figgis & Co., Dublin;
**White, T. de V.** Richard Scott Simon, London;
**Woolf, V.** the author's literary estate and the Hogarth Press Ltd. for the short extracts

from Virginia Woolf's letter to Vanessa Bell, dated 3 May 1934, and from her letter to Katherine Arnold-Forster, dated 8 May 1934, from *The Sickle Side of the Moon,* Volume 5 of *The Letters of Virginia Woolf,* edited by Nigel Nicolson. Excerpts from *The Letters of Virginia Woolf,* Volume V, edited by Nigel Nicolson and Joanne Trautmann, copyright © 1979 by Quentin Bell and Angelica Garnett. Reprinted by permission of Harcourt Brace Jovanovich, Inc., New York;

**White, J.** Harvey Unna, London;

**Yeats, J. B.** Dolmen Press, Portlaoise;

**Yeats, W. B.** A. P. Watt Ltd., London and Macmillan Publishing Co. Inc., New York, for excerpts from *Collected Poems* by W. B. Yeats (Copyright 1912, 1916, 1919, 1924, 1928, 1933, 1934 by Macmillan Publishing Co. Inc.), renewed 1940, 1944, 1947, 1952, 1956, 1961, 1962 by Bertha Georgie Yeats. Copyright 1940 by Georgie Yeats, Michael Butler Yeats and Anne Yeats.). Excerpt from *Letters of W. B. Yeats,* edited by Allan Wade, (copyright 1953, 1954 by Anne Butler Yeats). Excerpts from William Butler Yeats *Autobiography* (copyright 1916, 1936 by Macmillan Publishing Co. Inc., renewed 1944, 1964 by Bertha Georgie Yeats), *Collected Plays* (selections from *The Countess Cathleen* and *On Baile's Strand* — copyright 1934, 1952 by Macmillan Publishing Co., Inc.), and *Explorations* (excerpt from *Samhain,* Oct. 1903 — copyright © Mrs. W. B. Yeats 1962).

Every effort has been made to contact copyright holders. If, however, any oversight has occurred we ask the holders of such copyright to contact the publisher immediately.

# *List of Translators*

*(unlisted translations by Sean McMahon)*

**Brendan Behan:** 15:3.

**James Carney:** 11:7, 141:11, 142:1, 142:2.

**David Green and Frank O'Connor:** 10:11, 10:13, 11:1, 11:2, 11:4, 11:5, 11:6, 11:8, 12:1, 12:2, 12:3, 12:4, 12:5, 12:6, 12:7, 12:8, 12:9, 12:10, 12:11, 13:1, 13:2, 13:3, 13:4, 13:5, 13:7, 13:8, 13:9, 13:10, 13:11, 13:12, 14:2, 14:3, 14:4, 14:5, 31:9, 31:10, 117:4, 123:3.

**Aubrey Gwynn:** 132:6, 132:7.

**Douglas Hyde:** 16:10.

**Thomas Kinsella:** 15:4, 15:5, 15:6, 15:7, 15:8, 16:8, 16:9, 59:13, 92:3, 117:5, 130:4, 130:5.

**James Clarence Mangan:** 17:3

**Kuno Meyer:** 133:3.

**Gerard Murphy:** 11:9, 11:10.

**Eugene O'Curry:** 15:10.

**P. H. Pearse:** 133:8, 134:10, 134:11, 134:12.

**Victor Power:** 136:8, 136:9.

**Douglas Sealy:** 27:1, 41:1, 44:5, 44:6, 74:6, 91:1, 92:1, 92:2, 93:14, 94:1, 94:5, 94:6, 104:2, 104:3, 104:4, 104:5, 113:1, 113:2, 113:3, 113:4, 113:5, 117:8, 117:9, 117:10, 118:13, 118:14, 121:6, 121:8, 121:9, 121:10, 121:11, 121:12, 123:8, 123:9, 123:10, 123:11, 123:12, 123:13, 124:2, 124:3, 125:10, 125:11, 126:7, 128:3, 128:4, 128:5, 128:6, 128:7, 129:2, 129:3, 129:4, 130:1, 130:2, 130:3, 136:1, 141:5, 141:6, 141:7.